Oberammergau
in the Nazi Era

Oberammergau in the Nazi Era

*The Fate of a Catholic Village
in Hitler's Germany*

HELENA WADDY

2010

OXFORD
UNIVERSITY PRESS

Oxford University Press, Inc., publishes works that further
Oxford University's objective of excellence
in research, scholarship, and education.

Oxford   New York
Auckland   Cape Town   Dar es Salaam   Hong Kong   Karachi
Kuala Lumpur   Madrid   Melbourne   Mexico City   Nairobi
New Delhi   Shanghai   Taipei   Toronto

With offices in
Argentina   Austria   Brazil   Chile   Czech Republic   France   Greece
Guatemala   Hungary   Italy   Japan   Poland   Portugal   Singapore
South Korea   Switzerland   Thailand   Turkey   Ukraine   Vietnam

Published by Oxford University Press, Inc.
198 Madison Avenue, New York, New York 10016

www.oup.com

Oxford is a registered trademark of Oxford University Press.

Library of Congress Cataloging-in-Publication Data
Waddy, Helena, 1945–
Oberammergau in the Nazi era : the fate of a Catholic village in Hitler's
Germany / Helena Waddy.
    p.   cm.
Includes bibliographical references and index.
ISBN 978-0-19-537127-7
1. Oberammergau (Germany)—History—20th century. 2. Oberammergau
(Germany)—Social conditions—20th century. 3. Oberammergau (Germany)—
Biography. 4. Catholics—Germany—Oberammergau—History—20th century.
5. Community life—Germany—Oberammergau—History—20th century.
6. Political culture—Germany—Oberammergau—History—20th century.
7. Oberammergau (Germany)—Politics and government—20th century.
8. Nazis—Germany—Oberammergau—History. I. Title.
DD901.O2W33 2010
943'.36—dc22   2009043484

9 8 7 6 5 4 3 2 1

Printed in the United States of America
on acid-free paper

To my father, Lawrence Heber Waddy,
and
to my son and fellow historian, Nicholas Lawrence Waddy

Preface

In August 1934 German chancellor Adolf Hitler attended a performance of the world-famous Oberammergau Passion Play. Three hundred years earlier villagers had committed themselves and their descendants to dramatizing the Passion story once every ten years. By the Nazi era they were attracting a vast international audience of Christians who came to watch the Crucifixion unfold before their eyes as a means of "salvation, reconciliation and peace." Hitler, however, was witnessing a drama that, as he saw it, preserved Germany's folk traditions and revealed "the whole muck and mire of Jewry." His visit has mistakenly branded Oberammergau as a Nazi stronghold.[1]

Like other German communities, the Passion Play village was split between party supporters and their opponents. Third Reich activists took charge of local politics and worked to impose a new culture that would control individual thought and behavior. However, these efforts to establish a totalitarian society fared poorly in Oberammergau, where centuries of communal experience had shaped citizens into both Catholics and Passion players with a deeply held belief in their unique identity. Decades of feedback from distinguished visitors had reinforced these citizens' positive self-image as bearers of the Gospel's message. Even the village's Nazi leaders operated out of the same bedrock conviction, which led them to confront their superiors when local interests and values were at stake. Consequently, all of Oberammergau's inhabitants made fateful choices throughout the Nazi era. I explore their motivations in this collective biography set at a time, as Thomas Mann writes, "when every day hurled the wildest demands at the heart and the brain."[2]

In *Oberammergau in the Nazi Era* I use the community's special history to explain the reasons and the degree to which some villagers became Nazis whereas others fought to retain their Catholic lifestyle. The two sides clashed frequently, drawing on the rich democratic culture that Germans had developed before 1933. Since traces of that democracy survived in Oberammergau even during the challenging times of Hitler's ascendancy, local political activities revived quickly after the end of World War II.[3]

Oberammergau's history as the Passion Play village also leads me to challenge Daniel Goldhagen's famous condemnation of virtually all Germans in the Nazi era as "Hitler's willing executioners." Rather than echo Goldhagen's discovery of "exterminationist anti-Semitism," as James Shapiro did when writing in 2000 about Oberammergau's Nazi past, I emphasize the diverse relationships with Jews developed by local inhabitants. Nevertheless, I also explore how the play mirrored a Gospel-based antipathy to Jews in the heart of Western culture. Because elite Europeans and Americans repeatedly validated Oberammergau's interpretation of the Crucifixion story, their commentaries illustrate the shared perception of Jews that linked Germans with the rest of the Western world.[4]

Oberammergau in the Nazi Era reflects my lifelong fascination with Hitler's Germany. As a British child born within weeks of Victory in Europe Day, I grew up in the shadow of the war he had caused. My childhood memories include London's bombed-out houses and the shelters I played in under Kentish skies that had seen dogfights during the Battle of Britain. My father told war stories about his exploits as chaplain of the cruiser *Jamaica* guarding northern convoys headed for Arctic Russia.

We baby-boomers were born too late to experience Nazism firsthand, but we devoured the stories and chased the mysteries behind the Germans' fall from grace. Why would seemingly decent people embrace so vile and murderous a regime? Studying history at Cambridge University in the 1960s I found myself frustrated by my professors' hesitation to confront these recent events in their own lives; the requisite distance for sober analysis was lacking. Yet, as I became a professional historian, I was sidetracked by curiosity about Alpine Bavaria's religious folk culture, inspired by Blue Rider artists like Wassily Kandinsky. My research took me to Germany and to the Nazi heartland at that, but I wrote about an earlier period ending in 1914.

Nevertheless, I still had an eye on the Third Reich. My chance came once I discovered Oberammergau as the Passion Play community with an intriguing Nazi past. When I first arrived in the Ammer valley, riding the train through the mountainous countryside that had enchanted innumerable Passion guests, I recalled the English village carved from an ancient moorland where I had spent childhood holidays with my grandparents. There, heather turned rocky stretches to shades of mauve and purple, whortleberries grew low amid scattered boulders and blackberries high above hedge-lined lanes, trout lurked in mountain streams and fuel in the rich peat soil. Farming families welcomed us throughout the village and beyond, their sheepdogs, chickens, and in one case fierce geese running proud and free. Livestock grazing moory grasses provided wool for my grandmother's spinning wheel and the best cream in the world to spoon over berry pies.

I loved these holidays, and the smells, sights, and sounds of the rural life remain precious to me as an adult. Not surprisingly, therefore, my first visit to Oberammergau felt like a return to old haunts. I caught an evocative whiff of manure and glimpsed cows grazing on sundrenched slopes as the music of their bells rang out over the clear mountain air.

In Oberammergau, woods and meadows clothe the surrounding hills almost to their stony peaks, and the wide Ammer valley is only partially given over to moory wasteland; there are also hay-producing fields to supply stall-fed animals. Just to the south, soaring Alpine ranges come into view, including the majestic Zugspitze. This landscape soon challenged my sense of familiarity, as did the village's complex social structure. Local farmers had for centuries lived cheek to jowl with cottagers dependent on income from manufacturing. Situated near the Brenner pass, they traded products on a ready European market. Their specialty was carved crucifixes and Catholic devotionalia.

These Alpine villagers were as Catholic as their consumers, and so their religious beliefs and practices also distinguished them from my Protestant moorland farmers. Whereas English authorities had abolished medieval devotions centered on the saints and especially Mary, Bavarians had retained and developed these customs into the modern and still vibrant form that I encountered during my visits. I found Oberammergau's mixture of the familiar and the foreign irresistible as an object of study.

This special village's history was certainly unique. However, as I soon discovered, the community had also evolved in a way surprisingly illustrative of the changes taking place elsewhere in Germany once industrial and service sectors developed within rapidly expanding urban centers. Oberammergau did not experience a factory-based transformation; rather, locals offered the new city-dwellers a seemingly traditional tourism center, a romantically bucolic retreat tucked away in the Bavarian highlands. Nevertheless, in creating this idyll, villagers came to share with their fellow Germans a series of disruptive social forces and crises that prepared the way for a Nazi victory.

Studying Oberammergau as a typical German community would allow me to move beyond the voluminous literature about national, regional, and even local patterns of belief and behavior during the Third Reich. Because the village was so small, I anticipated gaining a deep and intimate understanding of its individual residents. Crucial was an extraordinarily rich cache of records generated during Passion seasons, which included scores of firsthand accounts detailing the colorful experiences of playgoers. Plentiful archival documents, a local newspaper, and eyewitness accounts added much penetrating information about the generations of villagers whose life stories intersected with the Nazi era. These biographical details would make it possible to reconstitute both Nazis and their Catholic opponents as complicated human beings embedded in a myriad of social and cultural networks.[5]

My first opportunity to explore the village's Nazi history came in 1990. I was also there to attend the Passion Play. Almost half a million visitors converged on Oberammergau that summer, as they do once every ten years, in the final year of each decade, when the play is performed, and I observed the crowds swirling around the large theater. Crammed in with the expectant audience, I watched spellbound as hundreds of performers filled a vast open-air stage redesigned in spare fashion for the 1930 season.

In 1990 the Passion players were using a controversial script that has drawn repeated criticism since the Holocaust, despite a series of modifications. A decade later, Shapiro was to record further efforts by leading villagers to reform the content of their play, but he also drew from inadequately researched and therefore flawed indictments of Oberammergau's history during the Third Reich. Titling his account "the troubling story of the world's most famous Passion Play," Shapiro demonstrated that what he calls "Hitler's shadow" still hangs over the community. However, his book also reveals the shadowy nature of literature about their Nazi past and the relationship of Aryan ideology to the play's text and staging.[6]

Now the upcoming season in 2010 once again puts a spotlight on the Passion Play village's relationship to Hitler's regime. My hope is that *Oberammergau in the Nazi Era* will finally give shape to the shadows of their encounter with Nazism. It is high time that criticism be fairly grounded in the historical record when it is deserved and that the critique encompass the good, as well as the bad. Oberammergau was a community of human beings who responded in complex ways to extraordinary challenges. Capturing that complexity is the aim of the narrative that follows.[7]

Acknowledgments

When I began research for *Oberammergau in the Nazi Era* in 1990, I was fortunate to discover an extensive archive in the village. Twenty years later I can look back on many productive hours spent poring over the documents accumulated there. I am thankful to the community of Oberammergau for giving me such ready access to this wonderful collection.

Central to my successful work in Oberammergau has been the support and assistance of archivist Helmut Klinner. His insightful and meticulous organization of Oberammergau's historical records has made it possible for me to conceive of and bring to completion the manuscript that has become *Oberammergau in the Nazi Era*. I owe him a deep debt of gratitude.

Repeated visits to Oberammergau over the last thirty years have brought me into contact with many helpful people. In particular, I would like to thank Michael Schötz for taking all of the photographs that appear in *Oberammergau in the Nazi Era*. The Zwink family have offered me not only their friendship but also their generous hospitality; Oberammergau has become a second home for me as a result. While staying in Bavaria, I have also benefitted from thoughtful discussions with Nicole and Georg Altherr.

Many other people have contributed to the completion of this book. I am grateful to the members of SUNY Geneseo's History Department, especially our encouraging and sympathetic chair, Tze-ki Hon, and secretary, Barb Rex-McKinney. Friends and colleagues have supported my research and writing along the way, including Randy Bailey, Marilynn Board, Ganie DeHart, John

Delaney, Thomas Finkenstaedt, Robert Goeckel, Todd Goehle, Aline Hornaday, Marita Krauss, and Bob and Nerys Levy. I am particularly thankful for the feedback provided by participants in the 1997 National Endowment for the Humanities Seminar led by John Komlos, director of the University of Munich's Institute of Economic History. I also want to thank John and his family for allowing me to use their wonderful home in Gräfelfing during two research visits to Munich.

Much helpful financing along the way has supported my research for *Oberammergau in the Nazi Era*, for which I am extremely appreciative. The German Academic Exchange Service provided me with grants in 1993 and 2001, and the National Endowment for the Humanities supported my attendance at the Summer Seminar in 1997. In addition, SUNY Geneseo gave me two summer fellowships and three sabbaticals, including the entire academic year of 2008–2009.

The book draws on and reproduces material from my articles "Beyond Statistics to Microhistory: The Role of Migration and Kinship in the Making of the Nazi Constituency," *German History* 19(3) (2001) (World Copyright: The German History Society); "Saint Anthony's Bread: The Modernized Religious Culture of German Catholics in the Early Twentieth Century," *Journal of Social History* 31(2) (1997); and "The Religious Context of Crisis Resolution in the Votive Paintings of Catholic Europe," *Journal of Social History* 23(4) (1990). I am indebted to the editors of these journals for their permission to incorporate this material into *Oberammergau in the Nazi Era*. The book also benefitted from the constructive comments provided by anonymous readers for Oxford University Press.

Finally, I would like to thank my editor at Oxford University Press, Cynthia Read, for her faith in this project. She has guided my efforts to complete the writing in time for the 2010 Passion Play season, and her wise insight has helped me to shape the manuscript into its final form as *Oberammergau in the Nazi Era*.

Contents

Oberammergau
in the Nazi Era

I

Catholics

When Hitler attended Oberammergau's Passion Play in 1934, one reluctant witness was the prologue, Catholic loyalist Anton Lang. In memoirs published a few years later, Lang emphasized the Führer's support for the play's continued existence. Hitler, he said, had argued that "Oberammergau, an exponent of German culture, must preserve its Passion Play unchanged in spirit and production." Out of concern for the future of the communal vow, this prominent anti-Nazi was prepared to accept Hitler's patronage, for, as he so rightly says, "just to be in the Play is a longing that stirs everybody's heart and soul."[1]

If any single person embodied Oberammergau's traditions as a Catholic village filled with humble craftsmen who doubled as Passion players, it was Lang. Anton and his wife, Mathilde, were typical supporters of Bavaria's Catholic party, the Bavarian People's Party (BVP). They were immersed in a religious way of life that inspired their political loyalties and later sustained their opposition to the victorious Nazis.

Although not the typical crucifix carver, Lang was a simple master potter who also made decorative tiles for ceramic stoves. In 1900 he first played Christ just when the Passion Play was becoming a mass phenomenon, and he reprised the role twice—in 1910 and 1922. The (London) *Times'* correspondent observing his debut wrote admiringly of Lang's simple piety, which infused his acting. When the Angelus rang out during dinner, he "at once excused himself and, rising from his place, stood in the middle of the room facing eastwards, his hands folded and his head bent in silent prayer. . . . It was a simple, entirely natural, and beautiful scene in the low-roofed room at twilight." However, he also looked the part, according to P. W. Browne. "Tall and graceful with long flowing locks; large, fair eyes; an open, manly countenance; delicately moulded features, a kindly yet earnest look; majestic, as he sat upon the colt led by John." He became one of the most famous men in the world.[2] (Figure 1.1 reproduces this scene as photographed in 1910.)

The Langs married shortly after Anton's first successful season as Christ, taking charge of a large pension that author Toni Schumacher describes as "new, elegant," and up to date. Its attractive dining tables were set with Lang's own decorated pottery. In this way, the couple also contributed to the transformation of their simple community into a tourism center. The vast audience that periodically descended on Oberammergau demanded ever more sophisticated lodgings and services, requiring local officials to find ways of exploiting these facilities in the many off-season years to make them pay. The result was growth and diversification of the village population as hundreds of migrants responded to new economic opportunities. Later they contributed to the growth of the local Nazi party.[3]

Newcomers coexisted uneasily with long-time residents, who jealously guarded their exclusive right to control and take part in the Passion Play. A powerful sense of local identity created by the fulfillment of Oberammergau's

FIGURE 1.1. Anton Lang as Christ and Alfred Bierling as Saint John take part in the 1910 Passion Play's "Entry in Jerusalem."

vow only gradually emerged in these incoming workers, who had to learn the special cultural values instilled during the upbringing of local men like Anton Lang. His grandfather had played King Herod before Anton's birth in 1875, and his father became Ezekiel, a Jewish priest, before taking up the Herod part in his turn. According to Anton's daughter Martha, as a child born into this family of actors he "liked nothing better than to listen to his father and grandfather practice the Passion text. Later he practiced the whole . . . text with his father as they worked at the potter's wheel." No outsider could truly make up for the lifelong grounding in Passion service that a local boy like Anton received as his birthright.[4]

Lang was a child of the Alpine highlands. His village sits on the banks of the Ammer river, where tantalizing shreds of evidence hint at an ancient cultic presence. Moreover, the Roman outpost, ad Coveliacas, a link on the road between Verona and Augsburg, may have lain beneath the beloved local landmark, a rocky outcropping called the Kofel. However, it was not until medieval times that continual settlement took place in the valley; later its population was subject to Bavaria's ruling family, the Wittelsbachs.[5]

Oberammergau's villagers soon became underlings of powerful local monasteries. In particular, a royal foundation, the Benedictine monastery in Ettal, received local farms among its land grants. The monks' control was limited, however, by inheritance rights that encouraged their tenants to think like independent freemen. They were strongly positioned to exploit economic opportunities put within their reach by Europe's capitalistic development. Families came to depend on these outside sources of income as splintering of the original holdings left them searching for a livelihood beyond farming.[6]

Nevertheless, an elite group of villagers with substantial agricultural interests developed in Oberammergau. The key to their success was the right granted in 1332 to haul goods along the trade route that followed the Brenner pass from Venice to southern Germany. These men became wealthy by local standards. Farming still provided a living for a number of privileged landowners in the Nazi era. Close to thirty families lived primarily from agriculture, although only a handful were "true" farmers; others, like Anton Schiestl in 1910, provided "comfortable, elegant" transportation services. The leading commercial family also owned a wide stretch of farming land.[7]

This well-heeled elite contrasts with the many impoverished villagers who were lucky to keep an animal or two and a cottage garden and to have some access to common lands. In the Nazi period local families still owned the odd animal; cows left daily at the sound of an Alpine horn to graze in nearby meadows. Some of these householders became artisans like the potter Anton Lang, serving as smiths, weavers, carpenters, tailors, shoemakers, and the like; others worked as day laborers. However, Oberammergau's geography offered a variety of occupations beyond these standard poor-man's outlets.[8]

Ammer valley communities had been carved out of the forests covering highland Bavaria, which left much opportunity to harvest both wood and animals. Forestry officials managed the surrounding woodlands from an imposing building near the church and became an important fixture in village life. Their personnel were, according to Oberammergau's priest in the 1850s, "hardened, robust, true mountaineers." More than twenty were still living in the village in 1930. Louise Parks-Richards observed them at work when she stayed in the village one winter: "The principal street scene . . . is the hauling of great logs, eighty feet long, through the one long street to the saw mill."[9]

Other smallholders took up Oberammergau's distinctive trade of wood-carving. Like innumerable European villagers who were not agriculturally self-sufficient, these families mass-produced goods for foreign markets out of their own homes. A renewed emphasis on pilgrimage after the Catholic Reformation supported this trend, as did the hard times that wars and plagues often brought to Catholic customers. While famous for their crucifixes, these carvers also produced images of Mary and the saints, many-figured Nativity scenes, as well as secular products like toys. Eduard Devrient describes the range of goods that he saw in 1850. Unfinished crucifixes and statues of saints lay in family workshops, while "old women and children sat outdoors working to paint elephants and moorish kings, donkeys and oxen, farmer dolls in the national costume, in bright colors." Visiting the leading workshop he observed unpainted artistic carvings of such quality that they could be copies of medieval sculpture.[10]

Successful adaptation to competitive forces meant that around two hundred of Oberammergau's craftspeople were active in woodcarving and the more monumental sculpting during the early twentieth century. The whole family produced small wares and, especially in winter, worked long hours together. Households where the living area doubled as the family's woodcarving workshop were still quite typical when the Nazis seized power in 1933.[11]

This proliferation of artistic crafts in Oberammergau came to depend on the marketing skills of local merchants. Soon a firm founded by Georg Lang, a distant relative of Anton's, became the key player in exporting village goods. In the late 1840s Georg's son Johann Evangelist claimed that he enjoyed trading connections with firms in "Prussia, Saxony, Frankfurt, Hamburg, Switzerland, France, Belgium, Holland, England, North and South America, and East India." Lang and his immediate descendants subsequently joined the village elite as landowners, shopkeepers, and merchants.[12]

Lang's firm served as a major source of work for local carvers, although most remained technically self-employed. Other merchants also exported local wares, including entire altars and church furniture in some cases. Dominikus Schilcher, for example, advertised his "religious art establishment for wood carvings of all kinds—altars, pews and confessionals, religious statues, pilgrim stations, reliefs, and Nativity groups. Figures of Christ in every kind of wood, as well as crucifixes of every style." Retailing directly to tourists eventually allowed the woodcarvers the choice to preserve their independence. A cooperative named Heimatkunst also offered members a sales outlet during the hard times following World War I.[13]

Craft-oriented communities like Oberammergau faced industrial competition during the nineteenth century. Many declined as cheap versions of their once-successful products poured out of the new urban factories. Others developed into centers of commercial agriculture to supply metropolitan centers. Tourism offered an alternative transformation when communities were able to provide visitors with natural and cultural attractions, a development that for Oberammergau alleviated the crisis of industrial competition. Nevertheless, the villagers faced hard times during the early decades of the twentieth century, a period of crisis that leaders like Anton Lang worked to resolve by drawing on the community's Catholic traditions.[14]

Oberammergau's Christian history reaches back to an ancient chapel known simply as Kappl. The village sat in the "Priests' Corner," a vibrant region full of monasteries like those with local connections. Rottenbuch provided a series of parish priests to inspire Catholic family life and regular church attendance; Ettal became both Oberammergau's secular overlord and a pilgrimage site where locals experienced the practices associated with worship of the saints. In this context the crucifix carvers both reflected and reaffirmed their Catholic beliefs.[15]

Medieval Bavarians had developed a religious culture in which saints, especially Mary, helped to ensure for them both access to heaven and practical assistance on earth. Thus, shrines where pilgrims could visit relics or images of saints proliferated. They chose Ettal in particular because it housed a beloved Italian statue of the Madonna and sat on a major route to Rome.[16]

The Reformation threatened these traditional practices, but Catholics managed to preserve their old culture. Gradually they developed a modern lifestyle that still centered on pilgrimages to shrines like Bavaria's official Marian center at Altötting. Removed from the arena of everyday living, these sacred spots gave pilgrims access to the saints' supernatural powers, often bolstered by the curative properties of natural phenomena like springs, trees, and rocks. As an eighteenth-century memento from Altötting puts it, the shrine "is the place where one finds true luck."[17]

Pilgrims flocked to these shrines in enormous numbers; for example, sixty to seventy thousand visited Ettal each year in the mid-eighteenth century. These seekers of saintly assistance would often heighten the drama of their visit by making the journey (or at least the final approach) physically challenging; they hoped in this way to improve their chances of benefiting from a saint's supernatural powers. For this reason they often chose to travel on foot and added bodily mortifications like carrying a heavy cross. The lucky recipient of a saint's miraculous intervention would also go on pilgrimage to deliver a votive gift or descriptive painting at the helper's shrine. Oberammergau's villagers took a painting of this sort to Saint Anthony after the rectory was hit by lightning in 1731. In it, the saint appears as fire rises menacingly from the village center; a scroll in one corner reads as follows: "Ammergau, the grateful community and parish, offers you this painting." Churches filled up with such gifts, covering walls and ceilings, as is still the case in Altötting today.[18]

These pilgrimage customs faced attacks from "enlightened" church and state officials, but believers fought successfully to preserve their traditions. The famous Wieskirche, a perennial favorite of Oberammergau's faithful, faced closure in Bavaria's great secularizing year, 1803, but was later saved. Visits resumed to the church's Baroque statue depicting a lugubrious Christ at the column, bloody from his beating by Roman soldiers. Later, however, an annual festival honoring the prototypically modern protector, the Guardian Angel, drew carloads of urbanites to the shrine. By contrast, Oberammergau's pilgrims rode the train part of the way and then took an old country route to enjoy the ancient communal approach on foot.[19]

Oberammergau's overlords in Ettal were not so lucky since the monastery was shut down until 1900. By then, the church hierarchy had shaped a revival of Catholic piety that inspired an increase in the number of pilgrimages to large Marian centers like Altötting. Modern transportation improvements supported this concentration on big, famous shrines where large groups could arrive by train or bus. One such shrine was the wildly popular Lourdes, in southern France, with its cult figure located in a grotto. A copy was added near Oberammergau, where a shady piece of rock face beneath the Kofel created a grottolike effect.[20]

Once reestablished, Ettal soon joined these modern Marian centers as a thriving destination for pilgrims. Already in 1907 the local newspaper noted the pilgrims coming "from near and far . . . to worship Mary and plead for her advocacy." A favorite route was by train to nearby Oberau and then on foot up the steep Kienberg hill to the monastery. In 1930, for example, members of the venerable Augsburg Pilgrim Association left the train and "climbed singing and praying up to Ettal." At that point, its monks were fulfilling a vow, made in thanks for surviving a Communist-led attack after the war, to complete a Stations of the Cross, which would enhance this lovely pathway through "Promise Valley."[21]

Ettal came into its own during the first three decades of its revived existence as a thriving example of the modernized cult scene. A new hotel even offered up-to-date accommodations in which to enjoy a mixture of "spiritual and physical recreation." This important shrine so close to Oberammergau again influenced local piety. It became a place where locals offered masses to the saints; Passion Play actors would visit Ettal after each successful season, while three of the village's annual rogation processions ended there, as they had in the Baroque era.[22]

Individuals from Oberammergau also became pilgrims. Anton Lang visited Saint Anthony in Padua, "at whose tomb I venerated my patron." He and his wife visited Jerusalem, as her father had done before her. Anton also visited Rome in 1925, the high points of which were a meeting with the pope and Thérese of Lisieux's declaration of sainthood.[23]

Oberammergau's most remarkable pilgrim, however, was Katharina Kopp, or "Rom Kathl." This laboring woman continually saved her earnings to make the eleven pilgrimages on foot to Rome that she achieved before she died in 1934. One story records her eight-week winter walk to Rome when she was past the age of seventy. A priest found her in Saint Peter's Square, wearing "a dusty pilgrim cloak, a simple kerchief over the white hair," and clutching postcards of Oberammergau to give to the pope.[24]

Villagers also dealt with the saints close to home. Their yearly round included communal services dedicated to saints Leonhard, Gregor, Sebastian, and Agatha, protectors who specialized in cattle, floods, infectious diseases, and fire. Rogation processions set off to nearby shrines, while the Corpus Christi procession marked an annual highpoint in village life. Four altars awaited the lines of costumed participants as they wound through the local streets, and at each altar a Gospel reading invoked the protective powers of Christ himself.[25]

Individual villagers also frequently called on saintly assistance, sponsoring masses at Oberammergau or Ettal to honor them. Increasingly popular became a cluster of saints identified with an ever-greater demand for charitable assistance in the early twentieth century. The best-loved helper in need was still the Madonna, but her husband, Saint Joseph, was also popular in his protective role as father of the Child Jesus. Because Joseph was considered a virile "head of household," the saint's patronage of local workers and craftsmen recommended him just when a solid family life seemed the best protection in a crisis-ridden world.[26]

Added to the Holy Couple were two saints whose universal appeal began with the exigencies of modern life. The Apostle Jude specialized in desperate causes, and therefore his popularity and the general sense of crisis that typified the whole era went hand in hand. This was the same unsettled context in which Saint Anthony's cult became quite popular because it emphasized meeting the needs of Jude's poorest clients. The two were sometimes invoked together for extra effect.[27]

Anthony was a saint about whom, a local guidebook claims, the people "felt instinctively that he is their Helper. They know that his heart opens wide even for the smallest concerns and needs." He had grown beyond his specialties as a patron of soldiers, as a finder of lost possessions, and as a protector of children, reflected by his depiction carrying the Child Jesus. Monetary donations known as Saint Anthony's bread became popular after a French woman started the practice in the 1890s. Catholic churches set up images of Saint Anthony at which the recipients of his help would deliver offerings to assist the poor. This development stressed Anthony's role as a model for charitable care for the poor, so many of whom were children.[28]

The same link between child and charity appears clearly in images of a new Bavarian saint whose popularity mushroomed in the early 1930s—Brother Conrad. After this longtime porter at Altötting's Saint Anne monastery died in 1894, his cult developed in the pilgrimage center itself, joining its beloved Marian patron. After beatification in 1930 he was declared a saint in 1934. Images of this homegrown saint soon appeared in Bavarian churches because he was meeting a heartfelt need in the local Catholic population during the Depression. One typical painting still hangs in Munich's Saint Peter's Church; the porter hands out bread to a crowd of poor, especially children. In this way, a brand-new saint, Brother Conrad, joined Anthony and the Holy Couple in protecting the children symbolized by the Child Jesus.[29]

When Oberammergau's residents invoked the assistance of charitable saints, they were trying to bolster their own efforts to resolve the contemporary problems that worried them. Miracle paintings reveal how human and supernatural agents had traditionally cooperated in fighting crises. One example from 1783 illustrates this process well. As a fire consumes the shingled roof of an Alpine-style farmhouse, several male figures work with buckets to quench the blaze, climbing a ladder propped up against the roof. Meanwhile, Saint Florian, the popular protector against fire in these parts, pours water from his essential attribute—a bucket—to augment the human efforts.[30]

On the parish level, the founding of charitable clubs allowed twentieth-century villagers to pursue this traditional approach to crisis resolution by new means, crafting them to meet the challenges of a rapidly urbanizing community. Central to this vision were the Lang couple, Anton and Mathilde. During World War I Anton helped to set up a local war orphans' home while Mathilde became involved with the new village kindergarten. In the terrible postwar years, the two continued to raise funds for needy locals, particularly children, as well as to house the elderly infirm. It is no wonder that the local newspaper marked their silver wedding anniversary by calling attention to "the great charitable works . . . that in the most abundant amount Mr. and Mrs. Anton Lang have taken upon themselves for the community."[31]

The young couple had embarked on their charitable path just when club activities were beginning for Ammer valley Catholics. In 1907 Anton helped to found a journeyman's club, which combined practicing craftsmen with youthful trainees and nurtured the many wanderers passing through their village, especially in the Depression years. Its members enjoyed close connections with the other male Catholic club in Oberammergau, a workers' club launched in 1922, when the number of blue-collar workers, both temporary and permanent, was growing apace. Oberammergau's Catholic community also managed to establish a boys' club in 1927. These groups shared a relationship with Saint Joseph, honoring him each March on his feast day, one of the few legal holy days left in Bavaria. Anton Lang took the inspiration and protection he provided so much to heart that he chose the Holy Family as his personal cult.[32]

For the local women, Joseph's wife, Mary, provided both protection and an active model for their own lives as wives and mothers, as well as public actors. Mathilde Lang in particular helped with an imaginative rethinking of traditional Catholic customs as head of the local branch of the Bavarian Women's Union. In the climactic revolutionary atmosphere of 1919, Lang led a group of women on pilgrimage to Ettal, where they founded the club. Like their male counterparts, these club members aimed to "reelevate family life" along Christian lines, but they also worked to ensure that modern women attained "their proper place in public life." These aims left them more independent and forward-thinking than members of the local Mothers' Club, which flourished from 1922 under the aegis of the local priest.[33]

The Women's Union played a lively role in interwar Oberammergau by providing many practical services to the villagers. Their particular emphasis was on the needs of local children, for whom Lang organized many recreational activities, including participation in plays. The club also encouraged the Christian training of these young people, especially supporting first communion ceremonies. Soon a local branch of the Marian Congregation for female adolescents augmented their efforts. Loyalty to Mary inspired a beautiful "sky-blue" banner displaying Murillo's portrayal of her as the "most pure . . . ringed with delicate roses and lilies." The suffering mother holding her son's corpse on the reverse side was to "guard Ammergau and its Passion."[34]

The Women's Union built on their village's protective arsenal by providing a new schedule of pilgrimage opportunities, alternating between the area's two modern shrines, Ettal and the Wieskirche, where hundreds of members would converge. However, its leaders watched for opportunities to add further trips and were also sensitive to the concern that Catholics must "earn Heaven through our life in the present." Thus, they stressed the availability of indulgences like a "Jubilee indulgence" to be won with a September 1926 pilgrimage to Ettal, to which "all women and girls are invited."[35]

While keeping alive the traditional outreach to Bavaria's saints, however, club activists adapted the pilgrimage experience to female needs in modern society. Converging at regional shrines, they combined traditional customs with the novel feature of leadership conferences and general conventions with lectures. In this spirit, more than five hundred met at Ettal in 1932, some on foot, "praying loudly." After taking communion, miracle seekers visited the Madonna statue. Later a general assembly featured a talk titled "Strong Women in the Time of Crisis."[36]

As a fitting symbol of Oberammergau's modernized religious culture, a small ceremony took place in the parish church in May 1933. "Friends and admirers" of Altötting's Brother Conrad, who was already "much revered" in this area, dedicated a large gilded statue of the saint commissioned from a local sculptor. This depiction of Conrad cradles in his left arm a large basket of the region's bread rolls; his right hand reaches out with a single brown roll in a gesture of compassion. Through their dedication ceremony, villagers declared their support for this new saint so symbolically linked to their updated religious life with its charitable core. Secure in his new spot, Conrad could look out across the church's nave at the eighteenth-century altar of his fellow saint, Anthony. From these complementary vantage points both popular saints would continue to protect the interests and inspire the charity of Oberammergau's Catholic faithful.[37]

Out of this bedrock of Catholic culture had emerged the vow to perform a Passion Play every ten years, which turned Oberammergau itself into an object of pilgrimage. During the Thirty Years War, the village hosted perhaps its most important visitor ever when an epidemic arrived with Swedish troops. As the death toll mounted, communal leaders mobilized the votive practices so readily illustrated in the shrines of Catholic Bavaria; they committed themselves and their descendants to performing the Passion once a decade. After their dramatic vow, the visitation ended, and survivors first staged a play in 1634. After 1674 they moved the performances to the beginning of each decade and soon drew a sizeable audience. No wonder that the villagers fought back— successfully—when Bavaria's "enlightened" leadership threatened to quash their Passion Play along with many other popular rituals.

Oberammergau attracted both secular adventurers and traditional pilgrims because the play offered a dramatic journey ending in an exciting day of sacred performance. Travelers were inspired by a stunning mountainous setting where they encountered exotic peasants and intriguing ethnic customs. Pilgrims faced a difficult approach that offered the bodily mortifications they desired when approaching a holy spot. One observer reported "countless processions on foot—from time to time the men barefoot . . . with joyful voices praying and singing holy songs from the Lord's sufferings and death." The play itself reproduced the Passion story in a way that provided pilgrims with a moving devotional experience.[38]

All of the travelers, whatever their class, faced a daunting journey to see the Passion Play until modern improvements reduced the time and effort involved. After George Doane left his Catholic parish in Newark, New Jersey, in 1871, he spent a miserable ten days crossing the Atlantic in a "paddle-wheel steamer," then traveled by train to cross the English Channel and on through Belgian and German cities. Reaching Munich, he proceeded by train and "carriage" to Oberammergau. From the north, visitors approached through the Loisach or Ammer valleys. Those arriving from the south made their way through Alpine passes.[39]

Whatever the weather, most of the travelers would clamber out and walk up the steep Kienberg hill to Ettal, taking the load off straining horses and sometimes "dilapidated" conveyances. Observers were struck by the mix of classes, as secular and religious notables joined the humble peasantry. Ethel Tweedie found "represented . . . all nationalities and costumes. Peasants clad in their picturesque holiday dresses, and most devoutly telling their beads, mingled with English clergymen, foreign priests, and American tourists. Within a dozen yards, you might have counted as many languages and dialects." Alexander Sellar mentions in particular the "Englishmen . . . contrasting grimly in their business-like grey cloth suits."[40]

The countryside that made the trip to Oberammergau so challenging also made it inspiring and full of natural and cultural interest. Before setting out to see the play, Beatrix Cresswell imagined the village "in those mountainous regions of romance where castles, Miracle Plays, nay perhaps knights and dames abounded in a [medieval] realm." Alpine views were for a priestly visitor so spiritual a force that they embodied "the secret of eternity." To the eye of artist Anna Mary Howitt, these stretches were quite inspiring. "What wonderful gradations of color! What sharp, bold, stern lines of composition! . . . Even Turner's wonderful tints and magical power over atmosphere seemed cold and feeble in recollection as we gazed at this lovely vision painted for us by God's own hand!" An American comparison was to the Hudson valley, while the Kienberg heights reminded a British visitor of Perthshire. The way was full of flowers: "meadow-sweet with long white tassels, a yellow daisy, large blue centaureas, hare-bells, lovely sweet butterfly orchids, and yellow monkshood." However, Parks-Richards hit a somber note as "bordering the route there stood, like posted sentinels, many a beautiful mountain ash tree, upon whose branches hung thick clusters of scarlet berries. Like great globules of blood they hung, as though Nature herself were joining in the remembrance of Calvary."[41]

Observers found ethnic interest in the clothing of the pilgrims with whom they traveled. One found "groups of pure Tyroleans, with their green sugar-loaf hats adorned with golden cord and tassels, tufts of feathers or artificial flowers; there were many semi-Tyrolean dresses, and vast numbers of women wearing the queer, heavy, Tartar-looking cap of badger-skin, peculiar, I believe, to the Ober-Ammergau district." Another was intrigued by men dressed in "the well-known costume of long coats with many bright buttons, the green hat and feather, and the stockings, or rather half hose, tied with a bunch of ribbon at the knee."[42]

Eventually, all of the travelers reached the village at their journey's end. Archdeacon of Westminster F. W. Farrar loved its setting: "[T]he hills . . . are soft slopes, clothed to the summit with the exquisitely intermingled light green of the larches and dark green of the pines." Doane exclaims that "nothing can be more picturesque than the sight it presents as it is gradually approached, a cluster of little cottages, with the parish church in the middle, set in a plain of green fields, and that again surrounded by mountains, the highest peak of which is surmounted by a cross. . . . It presents the appearance of a town of religious houses."[43]

Arriving ahead of the audience, Henry Blackburn marveled that so small a place would soon welcome several thousand people. Somehow, visitors as well as conveyances, including "carriages, carts, traps of all kinds and shapes," found their place in streets so crowded that livestock struggled to make their way home. Street vendors sold a wide variety of goods, not only photographs and carvings but also food, further complicating the chaotic scene. Particular points of concentration were the Lang establishment, filled with local wood-carvings, and the nearby Post Inn. Many found their way into the inn, disgusting Howitt with their noises and smells. A fellow sufferer shared her distaste for the atmosphere in guesthouses filled with obnoxious locals imbibing the region's brew.[44]

Beyond this raucous village life, Oberammergau's "dear old homesteads" soon caught the visitor's eye. Gables decorated with carved wooden slats rose above images of Ettal's Madonna. Shingled roofs weighted down with heavy rocks hung over whitewashed or frescoed walls. Flowers greeted visitors in window boxes, notably "the carnations loved in the mountains." Fenced gardens, often including fruit trees, completed this charming picture.[45]

Nineteenth-century commentators agreed that visitors to Oberammergau found generous and obliging hosts. Nevertheless, finding room in the village's quaint houses was quite a challenge. Apart from the Post Inn, houses where elite guests could find suitable accommodation were few and far between. Alterations at the Langs' home had made that residence more spacious. All possible rooms were furnished with beds, and a dining room was set up in the main sitting area. The vicarage was also available to well-connected travelers. However, conversion of homes into sleeping quarters was the norm in Oberammergau. When all of the beds were filled, a host might permit an unfortunate to curl up on a chair or bench or even on straw in the living area, stretch out in a hall or stairway, or sleep in the attic; beyond these alternatives were sheds and the hard ground. Country visitors used their own covered wagons, which they parked around the village.[46]

Inside most of Oberammergau's homes were simple accommodations enhanced by ethnic touches; visitors accepted inconveniences in these early days because of their curiosity about highland life. Schumacher describes the humble house where she first stayed in 1880. The immaculate bedroom was a typical room with a small window and spare furniture made of painted fir; a carved crucifix and saints' images hung on the wall, and a corner altar bore a blue-clad Madonna. Wild grapevines outside the window framed views of the parish church and distant Kofel. Steep stairs led down to the living room with its typical bench-lined ceramic stove and crucifix-blessed corner, where the guests' table awaited in a special dining area. Nearby, the family, servants, and journeymen ate together. The effect was like a painting by the famous artist of Bavarian ethnic scenes, Franz von Defregger.[47]

In 1830 the villagers moved their theater to a spacious meadow where a large audience could comfortably be seated. Performances took place on Sundays before several thousand people. Soon the crowds of visitors arriving every

FIGURE 1.2. A diverse audience watches a scene from the Passion Play in 1871 (including the musicians in the orchestra pit).

weekend came to insist on repeat performances on Mondays for those prepared to wait their turn. The impatient were not above deploying ruses to gain entrance. One author hints at the offer of a bribe after his frantic efforts to buy a ticket proved fruitless; the women traveling with him resorted to tears.[48] (Figure 1.2 shows a typical audience of all classes attending the Passion Play in 1871.)

The play lasted for the entire day, an extended performance that tested the audience's endurance. Seating was simple for the ordinary pilgrims, whose benches stood out in the open. Rain fell on playgoers and players alike, but some mountaineers were well prepared, as one envious observer wryly reported: "The Tyrolese hunter wears a loose covering with a hole in the middle for the head to pass through, somewhat like the Moorish burnous." Wealthy visitors were soon provided with chairs in covered "boxes" that protected them from inclement weather.[49]

However minimal the seating, the action was gripping, and the stage's physical location, beyond which one saw—or heard—the village's cows as they grazed on Alpine stretches, spiritually uplifting. A self-styled "country Parson" compared it to ancient Greek theater. Isabel Burton loved being surrounded by "swallows and other birds and butterflies." She also enthused about "the open air, the magnificent background, and the side view of Nature in one of her most stupendous forms." When they took a break from this intense experience, the playgoers would either picnic in their places, lunch in the village, or mill around outside the theater, where they could purchase souvenirs and refreshments. There Eliza Greatorex observed "holy toys from the Tyrol, the Madonna and Child most numerous, wax saints in glass cases, and photographs. There are pilgrims from Jerusalem, selling beads of holy wood, and crosses of mother-of-pearl." Crowds mobbed all but the most costly food stands, warned one guidebook. Not surprisingly, then, "a notice was nailed up, warning one, in crooked letters, to 'Beware of Pik-pokets.' "[50]

Oberammergau's audiences viewed a play comprehensively revised by two clerics, Othmar Weis and Joseph Alois Daisenberger. Weis, a secularized Ettal monk, responded to the "enlightened" critics of traditional rituals, while Daisenberger, the village's beloved priest since 1845, reformed Weis's text in his turn. As a result, allegorical representations of the struggle between Jesus and devilish forces gave way to a human drama pitting him and his followers against the Jewish leadership and Roman authorities. Weis aimed at a historical and naturalistic text that would be true to the biblical record and purged of popular legends. Daisenberger revised the Weis text as a teacher of the faithful, connecting the audience to Jesus through surrogates in the action, including popular legendary figures like Veronica, who created the famous imprint of his face. Daisenberger worked during the midcentury revival, when priests struggled to control the devotional life of ordinary Catholics, but this process required compromises between the aims of the clergy and their flock's desire to preserve traditional customs. Daisenberger's text became a didactic yet dramatic expression of the Crucifixion story.[51]

The Passion Play that emerged from the Weis and Daisenberger reforms was a lengthy drama carried forward on several levels. In it, the story evolves through scenes that capture the hostile interaction of the protagonists and the role played by Jerusalem's ordinary population. Starting with popular jubilation at Jesus's entry into the city, the dismay of Jewish leaders mounts until their manipulation of that same crowd leads Pilate to condemn Jesus. His Crucifixion and eventual victory in the Resurrection provide the play's triumphal conclusion. This narrative flow is punctuated by a series of appearances by the prologue and the chorus. Together they provide commentary on tableaux drawn from the Old Testament that foreshadow the Gospel events unfolding on stage. In this way the action of crowd scenes and dramatic confrontations gives way to declarative and musical interludes that explain the static representations and encourage audience reflection.

The play's complex structure complicates its relationship with the New Testament texts, as does its use of legends beloved by traditionally minded Catholics, but all of the elements work together to emphasize the central dichotomy that gives the play its dramatic effect. On the one side, Jesus and his disciples offer a sympathetic picture of Christian piety and suffering. Major players in this camp include Jesus himself, his mother, Mary, disciples Peter and John, as well as Mary Magdalene. On the other side are ranged the Jews who cause Jesus's death, Caiaphas, Annas, and their fellow council members, as well as Judas, the betrayer from within the tight group of disciples. Also central to establishing Jewish guilt is the massive crowd, which accepts its murderous role. The Roman Pontius Pilate is caught between these two hostile camps and appeases Jesus's enemies by agreeing to his Crucifixion.

Weis's and Daisenberger's efforts to humanize and biblicize the play had the effect of blaming the Jewish protagonists for its ultimate outcome. Messages of reconciliation and forgiveness were balanced with this depiction of Jewish greed and betrayal. However, this was the biblically sanctioned drama that both players and audiences accepted as true to the Passion story.

Oberammergau's reformed playscript was complemented by a musical score and well-designed staging, all of which made the performances attractive to an elite audience that included royal and ecclesiastical leaders of society, while retaining the interest of lower-class pilgrims. News about the Passion Play spread throughout Catholic Europe, and then, during the "clash of cultures," when the united German state threatened their traditional lifestyle, Catholics could think of visiting Oberammergau as striking a blow for their political rights. The Passion Play also appealed to romantic German patriots who chose to claim it as a piece of national folk culture rather than a specifically Catholic relic. Moreover, the play built a reputation with Protestants. Pivotal in attracting German Evangelicals was the positive reporting in 1850 of the Protestant actor Devrient, whose opinion carried enormous weight with readers of premier newspapers. Further reports followed by Protestants who liked the play's ecumenical interpretation of the Gospels, including growing numbers of British and American guests.[52]

Their acceptance of Daisenberger's Passion Play is remarkable given the common suspicion of Catholic culture in northern Europe and the United States. As Blackburn points out, his fellow citizens were "educated in a severe, undemonstrative, undramatic religious school, where colour, imagination, and passion have little influence." German Evangelicals had concerns about the very playing of biblical scenes on the stage. Performances could be kitschy—"Judas hanging himself under a red umbrella!"—since Catholics seemed to like cheap theatrics, as when, "after the scene representing the last act of Judas in this world, they saw canvas rocks fall asunder and a company of strange devils, vomiting fire, exulting over the fallen traitor." Oberammergau's players and visitors, Protestants feared, might also indulge in the sort of irreverent and tasteless rituals that they had observed in Catholic areas. However, they were pleasantly surprised to find that the villagers and their audience took the play quite seriously.[53]

Gerald Molloy was moved to quote William Shakespeare's *Midsummer Night's Dream* after his visit in 1871: "I will hear that play; For never anything can be amiss When simpleness and duty tender it." This was a general response to the villagers' "reverential" demeanor. Observers found the acting to be generally quite good; one, in fact, thought that trained actors could not approach the evangelical purity of Oberammergau's performers. Doane carried away fond memories of the music and admired the accuracy of the costumes. Parks-Richards was mightily impressed by Ludwig Lang's designing of hundreds of new costumes for the 1910 season with fabrics from as far away as the Middle East. He had produced "the rarest, the most artistic creations I had ever beheld."[54]

Protestant commentators approved of the way in which the Passion Play interpreted biblical texts. A German opined that the play appealed to all of his country's Christian denominational groups because it lacked a specific confessional bias. He clearly agreed with the idea that this antimaterialistic and elevated play was "a biblical performance and could certainly as well be viewed by Protestants and Jews as by Roman Catholic Christians." Another observer found the excessive abstraction of evangelical teaching to be positively mediated by the play's pictorial nature, which animated the story of Jesus; this didactic effect was clearly free of papal restraints, which would have prevented such open access to the Bible's details.[55]

Non-Catholic observers accepted the play's script because it showed a "close and delicate appreciation of the Bible's simple tale, such as no Protestant villager that I ever heard of could approach, and none but the most educated and refined Protestants surpass." Even the reintroduction of the legends that Daisenberger found so instructive did not deter playgoers who were well aware of their nonbiblical foundations. All of this meant that the play "clung to the human side of our Lord's ministry, and enforced it with all the grand plainness of S. Matthew, with the mystic flavour of S. John."[56]

Critics found the script true to the biblical wording. Dialogue given Jesus was impressive because it was so completely drawn from the Gospel texts. However, the story had needed developing to bring out certain dramatic details glossed over in the original. Molloy argued along these lines:

> [T]he Gospel narrative is expanded, and . . . interpreted, by means of
> dialogue and dramatic action. This was, no doubt, a difficult and
> delicate task to undertake; but it has been accomplished with judg-
> ment and skill. The several narratives of the four Evangelists have

been blended together into one complete history; the apparent contradictions or inconsistencies, with which every one is familiar who has made a special study of the Passion, have been admirably adjusted; and, in the dramatic additions which have been made, every word, every movement, is in beautiful harmony with the tone and spirit of the Sacred Text.[57]

A crucial test for Evangelicals was the play's treatment of figures and scenes central to the Catholic faith. Peter was appropriately castigated for his failure to support Jesus during his trial. Moreover, Mary was never allowed to get too involved in the action, which would distort the biblical record to the distress of the non-Catholic public. Happily, she was "not the Queen of Heaven but the grieving mother of the Lord." Where the action did still betray its Catholic origins, at least in Howitt's opinion, was in the climactic Crucifixion scenes: "There was no sparing of agony, and blood, and horror; it was our Lord's passion stripped of all its spiritual suffering—it was the anguish of the flesh,—it was the material side of Catholicism." But in the end even she is positive.[58]

Bolstering this receptive attitude toward the play's biblical foundations was the audience's recognition that its staging reflected well-known paintings. The artistic sensitivity of Oberammergau's many woodcarvers made them perfectly suited to designing the action with famous paintings in mind. To the artist's eye it seemed "as though the figures of Cimabue's, Giotto's, and Perugino's pictures had become animated, and were moving before us." Knowledge of British collections led one observer to compare Josef Mayr's appearance as Christ with "a curious picture of the Agony in the garden, by Gian Bellini, in the National Gallery."[59]

For all of these reasons, Oberammergau's Passion Play clearly moved the members of its audience profoundly. Their behavior was generally devout. One observer wrote about the Anglo-American groups keeping track in the Bible, "father, mother, and daughters suffused in tears." Some peasants, however, seem to have behaved as if at a secular event, drinking and moving around, bringing children into the theater, and explaining the dialogue to elderly playgoers who could not follow it on their own. Judas elicited a variety of open responses; a critic deplored an interpretation of the traitorous disciple that made the audience laugh, whereas at least one person fainted when he committed suicide. Greatorex heard the story of a peasant whose fury at Judas's perfidy overcame him. Jumping to his feet, he screamed: "If I could but get hold of thee, thou rascal, I would teach thee something!" However, other reactions were more favorable, at least when the skillful actor Gregor Lechner won over his audience by making explicit Judas's all-too-human propensity to sin.

The overall attitude is nicely summarized by a "noble Protestant Miss, very pious," who declared that "she had never seen anything more moving."[60]

Players who took on major roles found themselves the object of curiosity because of the play's intense impact. In fact, visitors and villagers alike came to identify them by their parts. For example, instructions to write for lodgings and tickets suggested addressing one's letter to "our Lord and Savior Jesus Christ or His Majesty King Herod."[61]

Naturally, most of the audience's attention was directed at the player of Christ. Joseph Mayr was the first actor to become a star with an international following, particularly with English women. As one pointed out in 1890, "I suppose at that time he was one of the most talked-of men on the Continent." Royal visitors even paid him court; the Prince of Wales gave him a ring when they met in 1871. Mayr was once observed entering a local inn amid "a sort of hush, and we rose as the Christ walked in and took his seat amidst warm greetings and much shaking of hands. Nothing could be better, more dignified than his bearing. . . . All you saw was that his part had entered into his life, that he had not cast it off with his robes."[62]

Mayr's successor, Anton Lang, inherited this adulatory response, which his own interpretation of the Christ role made still more intense. He was the very image of Jesus in the Western imagination. Marianne Dale waxed enthusiastically about his beauty. His was "the most poetical face I have ever seen, and the best. Goodness is written large all over it." Lang's fame spread around the world, bringing the rich and famous to his door, as well as eager ladies in search of personal souvenirs. Americans supposedly begged him for autographs "because I came four thousand miles across the ocean to see you." Like Mayr, he received the recognition of Pope Leo XIII.[63]

Apart from Christ, Judas was the most likely to attract notice. Some visitors were not eager to lodge with this villain, as the story of one lady desperate to stay with a "good" player illustrates. She rejected lodgings with leading Jewish figures and perked up only when offered a disciple's home. However, the one disciple available was none other than—Judas, so she soon left in disgust. Lechner told the story that, when playing Judas, he had run into some drunken Tyroleans and was glad to escape with mere insults because he felt so threatened. Furthermore, a 1910 cartoon suggests that international visitors might also respond emotionally to Christ's betrayer; the drawing shows a British man boxing him on the nose while his female companion menaces him with her umbrella.[64] (Figure 1.3 reproduces this *Simplicissimus* cartoon.)

Reactions to the Passion Play, whether positive or negative, confirmed the general perception that it faithfully interpreted the Gospel texts. Decade

FIGURE 1.3. *Simplicissimus* takes a satirical look at the hostility toward Judas aroused in British visitors by the 1910 Passion Play.

after decade visitors expressed their approval of Daisenberger's playscript pitting Christians against Jews. Even the most anti-Jewish sections seldom elicited criticism and sometimes received open admiration, like the "tremendous scene" in which "the rage of the Priests is echoed and re-echoed by the wild frenzy of the mob. Priest and people, they stand each side of the balcony of Pilate, like mad dogs in the leash, howling for blood." For Burton these scenes were "just as in the East, where the Shaykh-el-Islam can so easily preach a *Jehád* or Holy War." She singled out Caiaphas, "a young man, violent, bigoted, and malicious. He forgets all dignity in his hot pursuit of vengeance." One account of the crowd accepting their guilt for the Crucifixion commented simply: "The Jews also pronounced sentence on themselves and on their people." Another liked the final triumph, when the risen Christ stands over his enemies, "the heathens and Jews, priests."[65]

Many prominent visitors validated the Passion Play. Bavarian and Austrian royalty soon caught on to this treasure in their region, including the fascinating Bavarian princess and later empress of Austria, Elisabeth. Her cousin King Ludwig II adopted Oberammergau after attending a special performance in 1871. Other Catholic royals and nobles followed. Moreover, Catholic intellectuals soon helped to publicize the play, and the well-known writer Guido Görres praised it already in 1840. Then came prominent ecclesiastics; in 1860, the papal nuncio in Munich, Count Chigi, attended, and a series of nuncios followed, including the future popes Pius XI and XII. Protestant notables arrived in their wake, notably the Prince and Princess of Wales and their relatives.[66]

A substantial English-speaking contingent attended each decade. In 1880 the London-based travel agent Henry Gaze even took over a local guesthouse, soon dubbed the "home of Old England." Observers were clearly intrigued by the modes of speech and behavior exhibited by these children "of Albion." Author Wilhelm Wyl overheard them greeting each other: "How do you do"— "Oh, how fine, how lovely." Henry Winkler was able to pick them out instantly, so obvious were the unique features of "John Bull in facial type and costume."[67]

American playgoers also stood out in the mix of visitors. There was a story about one with "golden hair and blue eyes, a husband, three little children, and a black nurse." The ever-perceptive Winkler was able to pick out a "Yankee-face" quite readily since it was imprinted with the look bred by a "long hunt after the almighty dollar." Conversations in many non-Anglo-Saxon languages were noted as well. In fact, the cry "To Oberammergau!" was to be heard "on the Mississippi as on the Spree, on the Danube as on the Thames, on the Seine as on the Rhine."[68]

By the late nineteenth century, the number of playgoers was topping the hundred thousand mark, and Oberammergau's leading citizens saw the need to organize their visitors' stay in the village. An approach suited to this task was suggested during the 1880 season, when British travel agents organized group trips to the Passion Play. The pioneer tour operator, Thomas Cook, was in Oberammergau that year, affiliated with Sebastian Zwink, whose new villa had housed the Prince and Princess of Wales. Cook and other skilled travel agents understood the package deal, in which each customer would be provided with travel, board, and lodging, as well as a ticket for the play. Such prearranged tours would avoid the problems that an uncontrolled arrival of guests could create. Thus, in 1890 local officials started making what they called the "arrangements," a process that eventually tied together the issuing of lodging and tickets.[69]

Fortunately, these arrangements were in place for the 1900 season, a watershed moment in which Oberammergau became a star attraction for close to 175,000 visitors. Before 1900 a railroad had been cut through the Ammer valley to the village, making the journey affordable to visitors of modest means. A lodgings committee office handled the bookings, and there a correspondent for the *Springfield Republican* encountered "four or five level-headed business men, who, in less than a minute, had given me two slips of paper, stating that ten of our party would stop at the house of 'Mary,' Anna Flunger, and six at the house of 'James the less,' Herr Klenker. The dispatch with which these villagers receive 4,000 visitors, feed and sleep them, would do credit to Chicago."[70] (Figure 1.4 reproduces a Michael Zeno Diemer painting of Oberammergau's panorama from the perspective of the new train station in 1900.)

Not all of the visitors were this impressed, however. Each train spewed out a crowd that made so determined a beeline for the office that local police had to fling themselves into the fray to contain them. One official even faced a possible shooting when a customer did not get the seat he craved. Newspapers published warnings about the deceptive notifications of bookings sent to prospective visitors that failed to materialize on site.[71]

Preparing for the 1910 season, the villagers worked to promote their Passion Play on an international basis. To that end, they made agreements with a group of official representatives who would also handle the "arrangements" and advertise the play. This included Cook's, "the biggest travel bureau in the world with 150 big Agencies in all important cities of the earth and many

FIGURE 1.4. A Zeno Diemer postcard depicts a panoramic view of Oberammergau from the new train station around 1900.

thousand employees," as well as North German Lloyd in Bremen, "probably the second biggest shipping company in the world. In 1905 the company possessed 128 liners and 48 coastal vessels. They employed 18,400 . . . and carried 353,686 passengers."[72]

Oberammergau now boasted several sizeable hotels, as well as the usual rooms, and visitors were coming to expect modern comforts. Additional eating establishments complemented the established inns and temporary bars and cafés set up in private homes. Shops full of fancy goods and Passion-related paraphernalia also multiplied during the seasons. Travel facilities improved; in 1910, there was even a huge parking garage for around two hundred automobiles. As Parks-Richards puts it, "There have come the honk! honk! the gasoline, and the rubber tires of the twentieth century." By then, direct trains to and from Munich were making the trip in a little more than two hours.[73]

The villagers also had to upgrade their play and theater to satisfy the audience's expectations. Starting in 1880, they redesigned costumes in an attempt to make them more realistic. In 1890 they improved the layout of the stage, while in 1900 a complete renovation of the auditorium provided fully covered seating for more than four thousand people. Overall, the villagers were prepared to invest much of their income in these needed improvements.[74]

World War I and its crisis-ridden aftermath made a 1920 Passion season impossible. Only in 1922 could the villagers take on the challenges associated with hosting several hundred thousand guests. The local economy was shaky, and diverting money from overburdened communal coffers into preparations for a play season was quite risky. Nonetheless, the visitor total was the highest ever, more than 300,000, around a third of them foreigners.[75]

The 1930 season came as the Depression was under way, yet once again Oberammergau's villagers needed to promote a successful season because of burdensome investments in updating their theater. A group of locals worked with outside experts to give the stage a sleek, modern look, but this reconstruction was very expensive. So was the usual renovation done to hotels and homes. Ultimately, these efforts succeeded since more than 400,000 people attended the play.[76]

The 1922 and 1930 seasons drew many foreigners, including leading social figures. In 1922 occupation soldiers from the United States and their commander attended. By 1930 the Americans were the largest contingent with more than fifty thousand, while the United Kingdom trailed with around thirty thousand. Ecclesiastical leaders included the future pope Pius XII in 1922, while among the prominent guests were politicians of the stature of

Herbert Hoover and British prime minister Ramsey MacDonald, as well as two U.S. senators. An occasional financier and industrialist also attended, most prominently Henry Ford.[77]

Close to three quarters of a million visitors, including elite leaders of Western society, attended the Passion Play in the period before the Nazi takeover. Their presence confirmed a general agreement about the play's accurate interpretation of the Gospel story. Yet, despite many changes in presentation by 1930, its text still highlighted the dynamic clash between Christian and Jewish camps. Hermine Diemer praised the play in 1922 for bringing out "the passionateness of the Jewish character which it expresses in the words 'An eye for an eye, a tooth for a tooth.'" High priests showed their fanatical Jewish character in leading the crowd's hostile reaction to Jesus, which represented a "blinded humanity driven by whipped up passion." Nevertheless, audiences found the play to be "a devout and religious service." A British cardinal mused in 1930 that attending a performance worked as well as visiting Jerusalem in reawakening Christian faith. Browne, writing for the Sisters of Mercy's publication, *The Magnificat*, agreed, arguing that the play "brings an ultimate personal knowledge of Christ on earth as the Man-God, such as one can never acquire by sermon or meditation."[78]

When Passion players and their audiences embraced Father Daisenberger's text as an accurate representation of the Gospel-based story of the Crucifixion, both groups made manifest the hostility toward its demonized Jewish protagonists that for centuries had poisoned Christian-Jewish relationships. Persistent religious anti-Semitism certainly contributed to the "polite Judeophobia" so widespread in the Western world and on which Nazi ideologues were able to build after 1933. This antipathy may well have depended on the outright racial distinctions suggested in Hermine Diemer's negative characterization of Jewish traits.[79]

The Bavarian side of this equation lived in a kingdom where, just when Daisenberger was starting to revise the Passion Play before 1850, thousands of citizens had sent petitions to protest the official Jewish emancipation; they commonly expressed a view of Jews as ineradicably different in their racial essence. However, for whatever reason, the people of Oberammergau did not take part in this petition drive. Decades later many politically active villagers had come to fear Jews as communist or capitalistic adversaries. By contrast, as Alpine Bavaria's tourism economy burgeoned, the citizenry got to know Jewish visitors staying in local hotels and pensions. Testimony about relationships forged between these guests and their hosts reveals the emergence of a positive bond that was able to survive the radicalized anti-Semitism fostered by Nazi activists. For some locals, their play's powerful villains, who might have validated the regime's intense propaganda, were counterpoised by vulnerable real-life people whose humanity became preeminent. Nevertheless, like most Germans, villagers did not show any general interest in assisting the Third Reich's Jewish victims. The historically determined social boundaries that dictated communal obligations were drawn too narrowly for this type of outreach.[80]

Based on the consensus about their play's value as Christian theater, a series of successful seasons encouraged villagers to develop an increasingly sophisticated tourism industry. Playgoers sought the tranquility and ethnic color of an Alpine hamlet, but pleasing them required a careful balancing act between a simple country lifestyle and novel urban standards of comfort.

Father Daisenberger lived to see the beginnings of this economic transformation supported by his revisions of the Passion Play. As they responded to the playgoers' demands, his villagers also updated the facilities available to tourists who remained after attending a performance. They could also visit nearby royal castles like Ludwig II's medieval fantasy at Neuschwanstein, and fashionable urban centers awaited in Garmisch and Partenkirchen. Some of the guests enjoyed local life so much that they stayed on for weeks or months; others arrived in the off-season years. Cresswell knew one such visitor; she and a friend had returned for three months in 1874, "so much did they fall in love with the village."[81]

In particular, artists and writers numbered among these guests. Greatorex spent the whole summer of 1871 in Oberammergau, enduring "many little discomforts" to "rest and live a better and happier life." This working artist sketched village scenes and captured ethnically rich data for her book. Her family enjoyed watching their hosts at work and play; they even went on haymaking trips to watch the girls expertly wielding their scythes. Evening entertainments delighted them, including traditional zither music and songs, as well as local dances.[82]

Greatorex's fellow writer John Jackson lingered in Oberammergau before the 1871 Passion season to take notes for his book, one chapter of which dealt with local mores, including the church's crucial influence and the villagers' "dramatic culture." Similarly, American writer Wyl stayed during 1879 and 1880 while writing about both place and players. In addition, Schumacher described her visits with Jakob Rutz's family for the seasons from 1880 to 1900. Charmed in her turn by ethnic scenes, she liked the old grandmother with her headscarf and bodice cradling the "small Dirndl" who would grow up to be Mathilde Lang. Schumacher enjoyed her host's singing, which was so "truly musical, the voice so fresh" that she was enchanted.[83]

Modest numbers of guests continued to choose Oberammergau in the early twentieth century. May Turner describes her "many happy holidays there," starting in 1909, when she and several relatives arrived for a walking vacation. They were also among the guests who came to love winter sports in the Ammer valley. A fellow British aficionado was Edith Milner, who "lived among the people in close and intimate relations" between the 1900 and 1910 seasons.[84]

Guests who stayed on were but a fraction of the great flood of Germans and foreigners who traveled to see the Passion Play. Yet the villagers needed to invest in ever more elaborate and expensive infrastructures each decade, suggesting the urgency of making Oberammergau into a permanent tourism center. Competition was fierce, however, in an area where established venues enjoyed natural advantages like Murnau's Lake Staffel or Partenkirchen's mountain backdrop. Not all of the guests would agree with Greatorex, who was "satisfied that our village was the best place in summer, and that if the scenery was not so fine as that around Partenkirchen, the people more than compensate for the difference." Much ingenuity was needed to transform Oberammergau into a desirable resort, a slow process that was still under way during the Nazi years.[85]

After Father Daisenberger's death, his pupil Guido Lang provided the needed leadership during a period of rapid social change before 1914. He launched a Beautification Club whose work complemented the improved lodgings and restaurants that tourists were demanding, personally adding a series of upscale establishments into the mix, as well as an elegant new museum. Guido's parents had inherited the Lang establishment; his mother, a child of the Post Inn, took over her husband's business after he died young, contributing her ability to entertain elite guests. Transferring the inn's postal business to their firm, in addition to the marketing of village crafts and substantial property management, she also ran a large general store. When Guido succeeded her, his varied business interests combined with Oberammergau's rising tourist trade just as German unification was expanding opportunities for the new empire's citizens.[86]

Members of Guido's Beautification Club, later dubbed the Tourism Club, created an attractive and accessible countryside that might compete with other Alpine retreats. They planted trees and created cool places for hillside walks, with inviting benches to provide needed rest stops. Before the 1900 season Guido contributed to this process by building a guesthouse and bathing facility near the remote chapel dedicated to Saint Gregor. Tourists could reach this new facility by following a stream that flowed down from Laber Mountain.[87]

To market their village, the community council reconceived Oberammergau as a "health resort" where visitors would benefit from the curative "mountain air" and "summer refreshment" of this spot in the "Bavarian High-lands, 840 meters above sea level." Moreover, the modernizing effects of electricity had arrived with the village's new railroad. As a summer retreat, therefore, Oberammergau had much to offer regular tourists. Then, interest in winter sports gave villagers the chance to develop a second season, for which local skiers were carving out Alpine trails. In 1912 the Tourism Club added a winter sports section to support this great new opportunity.[88]

Club members also worked to provide their guests with cultural attractions. Beyond regular musical and dramatic performances that trained young actors for Passion Play service, two folk costume clubs organized entertainment. Just before 1914 the cinema arrived when a local innkeeper added a large hall to show movies and host concerts and dances. Locals also learned new skills like gourmet cooking and foreign languages to serve sophisticated visitors. Math-ilde Lang, for one, spent time in England, where she learned how to run her guesthouse in a style popular with foreigners.[89]

These efforts complemented the enlargement and modernization of local inns. Moreover, new residences joined remodeled homes that could now house visitors in reasonable comfort. Fancy turrets and spires began to compete with the fresco-covered plaster walls of traditional village structures. Guido Lang added an extra story, allowing him to advertise his "comfortable and well appointed home" and its "39 rooms with 57 beds" in 1910. In addition, he touted "an extensive terrace, spacious balconies, an enclosed sun-parlor, and modern drawing-rooms." Despite all of these efforts, however, the visitor totals in normal years remained quite modest.[90]

Migration into Oberammergau was the inevitable result of the village's expand-ing economy and sophisticated building projects. Between 1878 and 1914 the population rose steadily, reaching around nineteen hundred before local men left for the front. In addition, many temporary residents worked on particular construction projects. Lodging houses filled up with this mobile workforce, which soon moved on to new assignments elsewhere.[91]

A very different but no less temporary workforce arrived in Oberammer-gau during play seasons. Humble men and women staffed the hotels, pen-sions, and restaurants, and railroad and postal workers expanded their services, while police forces swelled as well. Temporary stalls had long been part of the scene; in 1900 they lined the street from the station to the village center. At that point, Schumacher found to her chagrin "jewelers, art dealers, antique shops, people who have nothing to do with the Play in town to display their wares." Meanwhile, skilled outsiders ran the big permanent hotels during the season until owners with sufficient expertise were in place. Other outsiders ran new facilities like the Herrgottsschnitzer restaurant built for the 1890 season and another in 1910, sporting a "Central-Garage for 200 motor cars with Repair Shop, Garage Restaurant, Lodging House with 100 beds."[92]

Oberammergau's migrant population also came to include hundreds of permanent settlers drawn to the village by this economic upswing. Regular tourism seasons induced families to settle there and turn the leading inns into competitive resort hotels. Construction and transportation firms flourished, while the range of businesses expanded to include multiple bakeries, butcher shops, and grocery stores, as well as clothing and shoe outlets. Specialized shops began selling jewelry, taking photographs, feeding the discerning hungry with delicatessen and fancy baked goods, and supplying gardening items. The numbers of blue- and white-collar workers mushroomed as a result. Traditional professionals were joined by railroad and government officials. Migrant crafts-men swelled the ranks of woodcarvers, sometimes working for the Langs before establishing an independent household economy. Outsider Heinrich Uhls-chmid set up the Ammergau newspaper at the end of 1906.[93]

Members of the fine arts and professional communities also began to set-tle down or retire in Oberammergau. Writer Hermine von Hillern's decision to build a spectacular home in 1884 was a early example of this trend. Famous author Josef Ruderer settled after the 1900 season; a well-known artist, Maxi-milian Dasio, followed suit after visiting him for several years. Munich teacher Leo Marxer moved into his new home before the 1910 season; a plant specialist drawn by the Ammer valley's flora lodged in Oberammergau for years as well.[94]

Housing so many new families required a substantial expansion of the vil-lage's residential areas out from the core settlements. One district developed around the new station, spearheaded in 1890 by a substantial villa sporting a "turret with colored windows, woodcarving on the doors etc." This area soon grew to become the "Station Quarter." In 1900 a few homes and the station facilities, as well as the new Station Hotel, appeared, followed by extensive con-struction for the 1910 season. Businessmen also began to move into this quarter, notably the son of recently arrived station workers, Jakob Burger. Another favored area lay abreast the stream leading to Guido Lang's Saint Gregor complex, where a new carving school and hospital appeared, as well as another Lang construc-tion known as the Waldhaus. The area around von Hillern's villa on the road to Ettal filled up with houses. Eastern stretches of the village beyond the Osterbichl hotel also saw development, including a "castlelike villa" and a new guesthouse, the Friedenshöhe.[95]

(Figure 1.4 presents a view of Oberammergau from the new railroad sta-tion and Station Quarter. Behind the Passion Theater appears the Laber heights above Saint Gregor. The road to Ettal leads southward from the parish church. Beyond the right edge of the painting lies the Osterbichl.)

Migrants began a process of both social and religious diversification in the local population as they arrived from all over the new empire, including evangelical areas. By then, of course, the playgoers included Protestants, some of whom, like Greatorex, stayed on in the village. In 1900 those living in Oberammergau included 1,542 Catholics and 17 Protestants, and by 1921 the number of non-Catholics had risen to 100. After Guido Lang married a Protestant, the couple played a leading role in promoting the interests of these newcomers.[96]

Oberammergau's established population was reluctant to integrate so many new citizens into the village's social life, particularly into the special rights and obligations of Passion service. The traditional waiting period for a migrant was twenty years (or ten when married to a local woman). This exclusion from the activities that most clearly shaped the identity of local citizens spelled out the newcomers' tentative relationship with their chosen community's central values. In addition, it did not help that locals blamed outsiders for the charges of "shameless" and "piratelike" price gouging that were leveled against the villagers. Hermine Diemer captured this attitude in 1900 when she condemned the new owners of her uncle's Osterbichl hotel for replacing the "old Ammergau spirit" with their "coldblooded speculation!" The adulation of key players by prominent visitors over the decades only reinforced this division, once men like Anton Lang became world famous. Their self-perception as noble carriers of the Christian message led them to set a high bar that migrant residents were required to reach before they could suitably contribute to Oberammergau's important mission.[97]

This rite of passage into full citizenship was at once greatly desired and an introduction to extremely hard work. Over the decades, the play placed increasing demands for training on the participating section of the population. Between seasons they acted in a variety of community-sponsored plays; after 1900 a centrally located "Little Theater" replaced rudimentary facilities for these performances. Actors also signed on to serious rehearsing. Similarly, musicians and singers trained from childhood and worked regularly in addition to preparing for and performing in the play. Parks-Richards describes how, in 1900, director Johann Lang, who was terminally ill, "would rise from his bed of illness, and go out into the rain and storm to attend the rehearsals. Thus, night after night for months did this brave man . . . train his performers." A decade later, Musical Director Ferdinand Feldigl noted the backbreaking "250 musical rehearsals and 42 performances" that he had conducted. In the same vein Passion Committee members took on the extensive work that ensured a smoothly functioning and well-attended season.[98]

Ever bigger audiences also required a growing number of performances; the forty-seven in 1900 had risen to eighty-one by 1930. Moreover, the hundreds of participating villagers were frequently the same people doing household work and serving guests. Dale was struck by the fact that the girl who was serving her family's lodgers also turned up on stage: "Ottilie cooked my breakfast, washed the floor, etc, and an hour afterwards, looked like a princess in her lovely violet cloak and white robe." Another reporter was amazed at "Anna, . . . a beautiful girl, known the world over, about to appear in a great drama before 4,000 people, and yet calmly helping us to honey and eggs!" Jakob Rutz told Schumacher that he had to work twice as hard on the days when he was not performing because his role was so time consuming. Guests also disrupted the actors' private lives, as the 1850 Christ, Tobias Flunger, pointed out; he was worn out by playing and then having to "return to an unquiet house, irregular meals, and beds in the hay-loft."[99]

Exposure to the elements and the physical challenges of acting could be debilitating; the Christ in particular had to hang for an extended period on the cross. Illness could also be a problem, as Pastor Eichbaum discovered when Mayr contracted influenza. "The Saturday we were there he was very poorly, and there were rumours that he could not act the next day. Happily, however, he was able to be present, and bravely performed his part, though suffering from neuralgia." Johann Lang's herculean efforts to direct rehearsals despite his terminal illness also exemplify the depth of these physical challenges. Feldigl complained about wracked nerves after his directing marathon a decade later. Anton Lang even faced death threats in 1922.[100]

Players also suffered from hurtful criticisms. One reporter observed "Anton Lang smoking and drinking beer. I didn't like it. Never mind. The Son of Man came eating and drinking. Save me from bigotry and phariseeism!" *Simplicissimus* lampooned Lang in his new role dressed in high-heeled boots, coat, and leggings and carrying his beer mug and pipe; Lang's rather precious face is framed by his curly locks and beard. He addresses the costumed actor playing Pilate. "Get changed again, Pilate. We won't be playing today since the actors' hairdresser hasn't got here from Munich." Exploiting the fame that came with acting in a major role was also a potential minefield. For example, when the Mary of 1930 appeared in a brochure advertising Continental Typewriters, a critic was quick to mail in his official complaint.[101] (In Figure 1.3 Lang appears in similar vein as the British visitors bop Judas.)

The closely guarded right to perform grew out of an intense commitment to the village's ancient vow, whatever demands they had to meet. As

Hermine Diemer argued in 1922, local soldiers had taken part in the Great War with "this ideal in their hearts." Children loved Oberammergau's special mission, and "there is no worse threat for an Ammergau child than—'If you're not good, you can't be in the Passion.'" Games often centered on playing key scenes; local photographer Korbinian Christa captured one such staging in which three children hung on crosses, Christ adopting the classic pose, while their friends sat around as Romans. Boys might first appear on stage as toddlers, like Jakob Rutz, who was Adam's child in 1850. A decade later the teenager was both the Mount of Olives angel and a choir member. Rutz later served as a soloist, as choir director, and as prologue, ending up as an elderly man beneath the cross, the oldest player in 1934. For males this was a typical lifetime career. Females could act until they married or turned thirty-five.[102]

Acting in the Passion Play meant so much to natives that it drew migrants home, and old-timers sometimes clung to life in order to perform once again. Yet losing a beloved part to age was devastating. Parks-Richards reports that Mayr "wept like a child" when he became too old to play Christ. Like others with a "broken heart," he died soon after, apparently having lost any will to live. Similarly, when denied the chance to reprise Judas in his eighties, Gregor Lechner, according to his namesake, Gregor Ziemer, "fell on his knees, prayed, wept, besought the Committee to allow him to play his beloved role only once more." Repulsed, "he crept away, and was never seen to smile again."[103]

Conversely, an Oberammergau male's most intense joy was to have "realized the dream of a life time in *getting* his Caiaphas or his Herod, his Pontius Pilate or his Judas Iscariot, above all else his Christ." Young women longed to play Mary or the Magdalene, even delaying marriage to remain eligible. Ottilie Zwink told Parks-Richards that "'ten years I had thought of this hour. . . . Here was a happiness so deep, so immeasurable, that in all the wide world there was nothing more to wish for.'" Not surprisingly, prominent families soon turned choice roles into an inheritance. Moreover, play seasons became such important milestones in local life that even the measurement of time revolved around them. A child might be born two years before the 1910 season, for example.[104]

Players earned honoraria, as well as the satisfaction of upholding Oberammergau's sacred tradition. Mayr received 2,000 marks in 1890, and other leading figures more than 1,000, while the pay of hundreds more ranged from 400 to only 40 marks. The top figure in 1900 was 1,500 marks. Key actors could also profit from the audience's adulation since they might buy their wares. Mathilde Lang, according to her daughter, soon decided to turn "looking" into buying. An observer saw her husband preparing stock for the 1910 season, noting the risk he took should he not reprise as Christ. "I could definitely see the business advantage connected with his part," he remarked, although Anton himself did not seem aware of this benefit.[105]

Four years after the 1910 Passion season, World War I disrupted normal life in Oberammergau. The call to arms ultimately drew 365 of the community's men into the armed forces and five women into the Red Cross. Naturally, the village's craft, business, and tourism interests suffered with these lost workers; needed labor for a big village project had to come from Russian POWs. This economic decline made feeding the local population a mounting struggle. Eventually, a food committee distributed the basic necessities, while homeowners were asked to grow crops like potatoes and raise small livestock.[106]

The armistice of November 1918 rescued Oberammergau's tired and lean population from active warfare, but uncertain times persisted well into the 1920s. Gradually, all but the seventy or so soldiers who had died in the war returned home, but females exceeded males, perpetuating the crying need for labor in Oberammergau. Meanwhile, provisioning remained a challenge; the resulting desperation caused a notable rise in poaching. The year 1919 was one of crisis, leading Mathilde Lang to found the local branch of the Bavarian Women's Union that fall.[107]

Consequently, the villagers put off their 1920 Passion season. Only the following year did economic improvements make a 1922 season seem possible. Fears surfaced, however, that the consequent need for extra provisions would drive up prices in the entire region. A nearby city council even charged that in Oberammergau "religion was being misused to support speculation," an accusation given an anti-Semitic twist in yet another attack. These worries were so intense that the acquisition of a donkey for Jesus's entry into Jerusalem cast suspicion on the people involved. Eventually local officials arranged to bring in food from abroad to bolster supplies, so guesthouses and homeowners prepared to feed and house several hundred thousand visitors. In particular, the Wittelsbach Hotel's new owner upgraded his facility and added an "American Bar." Hundreds of villagers got set to take part in their play, prominent among them Anton Lang, repeating as Christ for a third time.[108]

This season generated complaints that food was scarce and prices exorbitant. A Breslau doctor reported that his host made him feel like Oliver Twist when he innocently exceeded the single portion of meat allotted to each guest. He had to buy food to stave off hunger and was not alone in enduring scanty meals in Oberammergau's lodging houses. A Munich man threatened to display his outrageous bill in the city's railroad station as a warning to travelers. The inflation that eroded the seasonal profits must have contributed to these negative experiences. Nevertheless, more visitors attended than ever, more than 300,000, roughly a third of them foreigners.[109]

Looking back in his 1930 guidebook, parish priest Franz Bogenrieder described the season as a "big financial disaster." At that time, housing had been in great demand, and fears about unemployment fueled a rumor early in 1923 that the Lang carving business was closing down. Guido Lang's widow responded vigorously that the firm was committed to its "standing" workforce. Tourism remained surprisingly good that summer, although the influx of guests tested the provisioning of basic foods. During the fall, inflation built relentlessly to unimaginable heights. Readers of the physically shrunken local newspaper could plot its track—until a dollar cost 4.2 trillion marks. Even before that point the community was clearly facing a "calamity," with food supplies either scarce or priced out of reach of the needy, as well as the pending demands of a cold Alpine winter. One response was another rise in poaching.[110]

Desperate to escape this catastrophe, a group of Oberammergau craftsmen organized the Heimatkunst cooperative to exploit American interest in their products. Sponsors in the United States organized a tour of ten cities for the group's representatives, who would reproduce an Alpine village and provide working demonstrations. So, as the inflation moved inexorably toward its climax, 130 Heimatkunst members prepared their goods. However, they faced acrimonious criticism from village merchants unhappy with their independent efforts to find markets for local crafts. Inclusion of important Passion players like Anton Lang also raised hackles, but he defended their plan, asking what the artisans were supposed to do in order to survive. On board ship and arrived in America, Lang found the sumptuous living hard to square with his fellow villagers' deprivations. He could "only compare" the situation at home with horrors caused by the Thirty Years War. Eventually this tour brought in thousands of welcome dollars and many needed orders for future work. The clear advantage of so many commissions from the United States soon quieted oppositional attacks.[111]

The inflationary crisis resolved, Oberammergau's economic fortunes revived. The Heimatkunst's "little people" acquired space to display their wares, and commissions kept them busy. Merchants also found success, particularly in supplying church furnishings. By late 1927 the newspaper was even talking of a "business and industrial upswing"; the carving industry was doing well and had enjoyed a particularly good Christmas season. As a story claimed in 1929, "there are always new businesses starting up in Oberammergau."[112]

The evolving tourism industry had helped with this recovery. Some local accommodations were now quite fancy, like the "most modern" rooms with balconies and usually a private bath provided by the Wittelsbach Hotel after a

1924 renovation. Visitors enjoyed a widening variety of restaurants, cafés, and specialty shops, while country cabins beckoned hikers as they explored carefully prepared local trails. The folk costume clubs, combined in 1927, provided dancing evenings and even "woodland festivals" as additions to the usual musical and theatrical entertainment. By 1924 the expanding Winter Sports Club had also developed a skiing venue good enough to attract a major competitive event, excellent publicity for Oberammergau's winter season; the sport became quite popular locally.[113]

Oberammergau's expanding economy attracted several hundred more migrants during the postwar period. Because they were both lower and middle class, these new citizens reinforced the village's social complexity. Laborers multiplied, together with white-collar workers employed in the tourism industry. Families also arrived to take advantage of numerous small-business opportunities. Dentists, doctors, veterinarians, and pharmacists opened their doors to clients. Oberammergau's elite came to include several distinguished artists, including professors Richard König and Otto Ackermann, as well as Hermine Diemer's husband, Zeno, a famous painter who returned to his native village after a distinguished career. The growing number of retirees included a handful of senior army officers like the major who came to live on the Osterbichl hill.[114]

This expanding population moved into the various neighborhoods that sprawled out from Oberammergau's original village holdings. The most extreme example was number 27, which reached toward Guido Lang's Saint Gregor complex. Whereas in 1873 there was a 27a and in 1890 a 27a, b, c, and d, by 1930 there were lots numbered 27b, c, d, e, f, f1/2, g, g1/2, g1/3, g1/4, g1/5, g1/6, g1/7, h, i, i1/2, i1/3, i1/4, k, k1/2, l, m, n, o, p, and q. Some of these contained the "beautiful country homes" mentioned in the 1930 guidebook. Altogether, several dozen new houses had appeared in Oberammergau since 1910.[115]

The Station Quarter's commercial facilities multiplied, and construction took place behind a post office built there. Like the Saint Gregor neighborhood, the Rainenbichl area beyond von Hillern's villa began a growth period that would mushroom in the Nazi period. Homes also kept popping up on the Osterbichl.[116]

A new round of construction and renovation started up before the 1930 Passion season. Most dramatic was the theater's new streamlined design and an associated extension of its auditorium. Beneath the stage a cellar housed the necessary machinery, while updated facilities for the players included new dressing rooms and a heated retreat. Meanwhile, brand-new homes appeared, like Professor Ackermann's villa painted with views of his old and new homelands. Alterations to existing homes and businesses were also common, including improvements in the now "Alte" Post Inn, as well as Lang's. One villager invested in an electric bakery, and another in a steam laundry; modernizing a dairy to provide milk for the season also involved steam machinery. The Weisses Rössl's owners upgraded their cinema, which competed with a fancy new one built by another business couple.[117]

While Oberammergau's economic picture was mostly positive as a result of these preparations, there were certainly signs of trouble. The Wittelsbach Hotel faced such severe problems in 1928 that a consortium led by the owner of Munich's Wagner Brewery had to take over its management. Subsequently, a new buyer took personal control of this shaky enterprise in time for the 1930 season. A brand new guesthouse known as the Schützenhaus, launched with great fanfare in 1928, was soon facing financial insecurities as well. Nonetheless, more visitors passed through Oberammergau in 1930 than ever before, more than 400,000, upwards of one quarter of them foreigners. Well more than eight hundred paid players and service providers, as well as around three hundred children, made the Passion Play's eighty-one performances a reality. The community had risked a great deal on a successful season, and in general its investments paid off.[118]

Oberammergau's development into a vibrant tourism center came with a price; the simple mountain village had become a socially divided community. Political diversification followed, facilitating the Nazi party's rise to prominence in this Catholic stronghold. Chapter 2 explores the emerging electoral politics in Oberammergau in the late nineteenth century. Then, the Great War and its violent aftermath eroded support for all well-established parties. With a deepening depression in 1930, a national election held during the Passion Play season saw the Nazis profiting from this disillusionment. They received an impressive number of votes from the mixed population of old-timers and newcomers who now lived side by side in the Ammer valley.

2

Voters

Newcomers migrating into the Alps helped to transform Oberammergau's political landscape and initiate a local Nazi chapter. Their role emerged in the breakout election of 1930 when the party attracted a great many votes. That year, more residents were eligible to cast ballots than the entire village population, including children. The cause of this seeming anomaly was the regulation that temporary workers counted as residents for voting purposes. Electoral rolls illustrate the effects of this rule when they include laborers clustered in various lodging houses. In one case all were crossed out again because they had moved on before election day. In 1930 hundreds of temporary service workers voted as residents because the Passion Play season was still under way when the election occurred. The unusually strong support for Nazism was in part their contribution.

Oberammergau's curious electoral history illustrates the impact of Germany's social transformation on traditional voting patterns. The political effects of industrial expansion and urbanization, followed by war, revolution, inflation, and finally depression, began to manifest themselves in the 1930 results. In Oberammergau, the Catholic Center Party, after 1918 the Bavarian People's Party (BVP), had dominated in normal times. However, liberal Catholics were already rejecting their denominational party before World War I, making a case for political divergences within the single faith. Then, during the 1920s increasing social diversity resulted in a complex party system that splintered the electorate. Oberammergau's Nazis began to reap the benefits of voters' willingness to try alternatives in the 1930 election. This community full of temporary workers and visitors saw increased support for Hitler's party that was even more dramatic than the national norm, a staggering 1,600 percent more than that in 1928.

In 1930 the confrontation between local Catholics and Nazis was certainly under way, but BVP promoters could still rely on a strongly embedded cultural bias in their favor. Oberammergau's Passion seasons deepened the loyalties of hundreds of villagers to the Catholic Church and its political arm. Voting for their denominational party was further encouraged by immersion in the Catholic way of life, although some supporters of other parties, including Nazis, were actively Catholic as well. Public witness remained an important political tool for loyalists, and the Corpus Christi procession in early summer was the annual highpoint of this open profession of their faith.

Father Daisenberger described these processions in the 1850s, when the Rosary Confraternity, a Marian brotherhood that had been founded in 1648, still provided charitable services and supported the village's protective efforts. They equipped twenty-five councilors to march alongside the bearers of banners and processional images, as well as "confraternity maidens dressed in white with blue girdles." Greatorex observed the 1872 Corpus Christi procession moving through streets "lined with young birch-trees, and strewn with grass and wild flowers. . . . The children in their spotless white led the way, the young girls followed, carrying an image of the Virgin Mother, crowned with flowers, the young men bore the many-colored banners, and in the midst [came] . . . the priest, . . . bearing the Host." They stopped at the four altars set up around the village to invoke Christ's protection for their community.[1] (Figure 2.1 shows a photograph of the Corpus Christi procession that took place more than fifty years later in 1929. Participants have reached the fourth altar set up in the square outside the Weisses Rössl Inn.)

Early in the 1930 Passion season, villagers yet again expressed their Catholic values by processing through streets lined with "fresh greenery, red cloths and pictures." Daisenberger's "whitedressed girls" and the banner-bearing youths marched with local clubs, followed by communal officials, with adult residents bringing up the rear. The power of these demonstrations to keep BVP voters loyal had certainly slipped by then. However, the political shift in favor of the Nazis, which would emerge so dramatically that September, took place slowly; it gained full momentum only when the Depression drove ever more voters to switch their faith to the expansive promises of the folkish movement.[2]

Oberammergau's political life had already begun to change when Father Daisenberger arrived as the village priest in time for the revolutionary dramas of 1848. Modernization of local government took place after the

FIGURE 2.1. A Corpus Christi procession leaves the fourth altar set up in the square outside Oberammergau's Weisses Rössl Inn in 1929.

Napoleonic Wars ended. The old chief who was part of an annually elected "six" or community managers, as well as a "representative body," the "twelve," were replaced with a community leader and other officials. Concurrently, the new Bavarian state acquired a mildly representative lower house, which was updated during the 1848 upheavals. Nevertheless, until 1906, voters, including those in Oberammergau, chose electors who in turn designated a representative for each district.[3]

With German unification came a final round of reform in local government, putting in place a mayor, a deputy mayor, and a community council elected by the citizenry. Moreover, the rights to citizenship were extended in a way that locals considered a threat to their common ownership of the surrounding woods and alps. They therefore privatized these holdings to the benefit of the shareholders, some of whom had acquired multiple interests by that point. In so doing they drew clear lines between their community's insiders and outsiders, setting up social divisions with negative political ramifications for the future. However, in 1876 Johann Lang, who had previously served a stint as leader, returned as mayor and stabilized the political situation by remaining in the top post until his death in 1900.[4]

Meanwhile, participation in Passion Play affairs became ever more intense. Villagers initiated the practice of setting up a committee to organize each season, and in time, elections for the six representatives who joined the councilors in making up this committee became raucous and contentious affairs. Play-related issues, particularly the sensitive question of choosing the top players, caused more furor than most of the political campaigns that took place every few years; the play seasons had come to occupy a central role in voters' lives.[5]

Beyond these political reforms, clubs emerged in Oberammergau, as in the rest of Germany, to organize a wide variety of communal activities. Locally, these clubs provided integrative structures that added to the sense of common purpose created by Passion seasons. They also came to hold annual elections for officers, adding to their members' voting experience. Long-standing were a marksmen's and an early version of a music club, but the real proliferation of modern associations began with the charitable Saint Lucas Club, founded on behalf of local woodcarvers. Decades later a gymnastics club was launched as something of a pioneer in Bavaria, while beyond service in the church choir came a formal singing circle. In addition, a thriving veterans' association had attracted more than a hundred members after local men served in the Franco-Prussian War. Then came Guido Lang's Tourism Club.[6]

Once Germans were unified under their emperor, national politics intruded into Oberammergau in addition to periodic elections for the Bavarian parliament. As early as March 1871, during a national election, local voters were choosing between a liberal and a Catholic candidate for the Reichstag. With the first flush of enthusiasm for a new empire they gave massive support to the liberal, whose pro-business party had contributed so greatly to the unifying process. What a difference a few years could make. The clash of cultures was well under way in 1874 when a Catholic Center Party candidate won the next national election, attracting close to twice the votes cast for his opponent. This pattern then held in the 1877 election.[7]

The arrival of both middle- and lower-class migrants after 1871 increased the political divisions in Oberammergau, although the Social Democrats (SPD) failed to establish a solid presence there until after World War I. Even liberal voters could not undermine the Catholic Center Party's strong lead in prewar elections. Bavarian parliamentary elections in 1881 and 1893 drew local attention when Mayor Lang was a candidate for elector, winning around seventy votes both times. One of his opponents in 1893 was the new priest, Joseph Schröder, who fared much better than the liberal Lang that year. Then, a citizens' club with dozens of members emerged to oppose his mayorship; he just squeaked by during his final reelection in 1899. Meanwhile, the general election of 1898 had produced an overwhelming Catholic victory in Oberammergau, although the other major parties improved their showing early in the new century.[8]

After Mayor Lang's death, his nephew Guido took up the cause of promoting liberal opposition to a still well-entrenched Catholic party. This challenge was complicated by the formation of Catholic charitable associations that bolstered the party's constituency, as did the strong faith fostered by Passion Play traditions. Celebrations in March 1907 to honor the Bavarian prince regent's birthday underscored the Center Party's importance for villagers loyal to monarch, as well as church; participants thronged streets lined with the blue and white flags of their beloved homeland. Local adulation for dead King Ludwig II was also particularly strong. Bavarian patriotism thus combined with religious activism to provide the dual pillars propping up the cause of political Catholicism in Oberammergau.[9]

Early in 1907 a general election caused "feverish activity" locally and a high turnout at the polls. Guido Lang packed in more than two hundred people at a meeting for the "German oriented voters." His speech condemned a pragmatic union of Catholics with the leftist Socialists so hostile to imperial power. The despised workers' party, however, benefited that time around from extra votes cast by temporary laborers. Nevertheless, the Catholic Center Party remained dominant, while Guido's liberals came in a sorry third. A bitter Zeno Diemer argued that unpatriotic Center Party supporters did not represent all Catholics, adding that voters should not let Father Schröder influence their political decisions. Then, despite their relative success in the election, "progressive" members of the local Socialist branch, led by a recent migrant laborer, decided to join the liberals.[10]

This SPD/liberal merger helped when Guido Lang ran for Bavaria's parliament in late May since he improved his voting totals. To cement support, according to Father Schröder, Lang campaigned widely, using his rallies and literature to disparage the priest. Similarly, one of his chief supporters used aggressively anti-Catholic tactics. In response, Lang's opponent attacked his "irreligious" position as shameful for "an Oberammergauer and furthermore a Lang from Oberammergau." Guido publicly refuted the charge that liberals were hostile to religion since "this party includes the best Christians and most upstanding Catholics in its membership." He himself had learned from no less a figure than Father Daisenberger to be both a liberal and a loving, tolerant Christian; in that spirit he had "always served the wellbeing and the honor of his homeland." The case for divergence from the denominational party could not have been made more clearly.[11]

After this campaign, Lang lost his seat on the Passion Committee, a result that he blamed on a vigorous campaign against him aimed at keeping liberals out of play affairs. However, his brother-in-law Ludwig, slated to direct in 1910, was elected "despite liberal leanings." His clash with Schröder may have spilled over into a hostile lawsuit against Guido's business relationships with the firm's workforce. The priest had apparently listened to female gossip about alleged irregularities. Despite these setbacks, the liberal faction fought on in part, Schröder suspected, through a new citizens' club founded in 1910; several members, including Lang, became councilors. Their efforts in the 1912 national and regional elections brought them elevated vote totals. However, the Catholic Center Party still prevailed and became even more dominant in a special 1913 election, whereas the liberals sank to less than half of their previous high-water mark. One further arena for political struggle in Oberammergau was the churchwarden elections, in which Father Schröder also perceived the evil liberal Citizens' Club at work.[12] (Figure 2.2 reproduces a photograph of Guido Lang together with some of his carvers in the firm's workshop.)

These fractious political divisions in Oberammergau created one set of fissures in the local population, often within the privileged circle of men controlling local affairs, in particular their Passion seasons. The very name "Citizens' Club" underscored this infighting. Local elections for the mayor and the council, as well as for the all-important Passion Committee, were sources of great divisiveness in the active citizenry, as Lang's unfortunate experience reveals. The extreme tensions surrounding the allocation of play roles was illustrated when Lang himself, now excluded from the seat of decision

FIGURE 2.2. Liberal candidate and promoter of Oberammergau's tourism economy Guido Lang appears in his woodcarving firm's workshop early in the twentieth century.

making, complained bitterly about selfish committee members who cornered "the best roles and jobs."[13]

Nevertheless, in many ways these insiders closed ranks against the migrants who moved into their village. The power-holding elite in Oberammergau remained exclusive because of traditional restrictions on citizenship and residency rights in Germany, as well as their twenty-year rule for newcomers waiting to take part in Passion service. They once again spelled out entrenched interests in a 1909 plan to divide the remaining commons among those families who were enjoying the ancient rights of access. Even when the local newspaper listed men leaving for the front in 1914, it pointed out the favored status enjoyed by Oberammergau's citizens and legal residents as opposed to that of the newcomers. Yet, as migration brought ever more settlers into the village, these clear disadvantages affected a growing percentage of the population. They watched as old-timers continued to enjoy the privileges of village life, as well as shoulder its special burdens, during the early years of the new century.[14]

Historians find themselves projecting the Nazi future into earlier stages of German history because they are so aware of the outcome. Similarly, contemplating the period before World War I brings a keen awareness of the horrors awaiting people so innocently going about their daily lives. I was reminded of this when reading about Queen Mary of Britain, who, as Princess May of Teck, attended the 1890 Passion Play and later became the daughter-in-law of the play's enthusiastic supporter, the Prince of Wales. In 1913 she hosted Austrian heir-apparent Archduke Franz Ferdinand just a few months before his assassination in Sarajevo that precipitated the war. Both royals and their spouses enjoyed a very pleasant visit, with no premonitions about the bloody end that the Austrian couple would soon face. However, it is impossible to read about this encounter without a sense of apprehension about the tragedy to come, like the dread that comes with foreknowledge of the pending war and its ultimate political repercussions.[15]

These years leading up to 1914 were successful ones for Oberammergau's population. Remaining oriented toward peaceful commerce, the residents earnestly sought to share in the general prosperity. The audiences that converged on their village in 1910 mixed future allies and adversaries. In such a place, the radical and hate-filled politics of the 1920s could only take root after violent disruptions in the lives of fighting-age villagers who were quietly pursuing their own interests until the war began.[16]

War was an experience that Oberammergau veterans like Jakob Rutz had faced during the Franco-Prussian conflict. Now, in the charged political atmosphere created by a new outbreak of hostilities, their children got caught up in the excitement; almost two hundred locals joined up in the first few weeks. By Christmas, which was so naïvely targeted as the endpoint of the fighting, that number had climbed still higher. Only a few dozen of these young men had graduated to citizenship when they answered the call to arms, and more than one-third of them were outsiders working in Oberammergau. Eventually their numbers rose to 370, including five women, out of a population of less than two thousand.[17]

We know little about the combat experiences of these villagers beyond the general information to be gleaned from war memoirs and novels such as Erich Maria Remarque's *All Quiet on the Western Front*. The loss of at least one man in five indicates that they were often in the thick of the fighting, which is corroborated by newspaper reports of wounded villagers and frequent decorations and promotions. Occasionally we glimpse the realities that lay behind these terse entries. One man was wounded for a third time in 1918; another lost his arm in a raid on Russian troops. Two members of the ancient Rutz family received medals, one for singlehandedly keeping a machine gun going. The other's unit had remained unassisted at its post in the Western trenches for several days until he extracted all of the survivors; he did not return from the war.[18]

Looking back at these years, Alois Lang, Anton's successor as Christ, remembered "how cruel was the parting" from his new bride. By late August 1914, he had sustained a nasty wound from an ordinance fragment, but he was soon employing his skiing skills in a special unit of Alpine mountaineers. Lang "campaigned in the Dolomites and in Serbia, in the Carpathians and on the Isonzo, and in the end, 1918, on the Marne." He was lucky enough to return home before the war was over, unlike a sixteen-year-old who volunteered for service only to fall into enemy hands. The eventual return of such POWs reminds us of the suffering that these men endured; they were trickling back until at least February 1920.[19]

Soldiers returning after long years of conflict brought with them intense memories of their wartime experiences. Some mourned the loss of brothers, relatives, and close friends, while others suffered permanent disabilities or remained sick. One young veteran even dropped dead of "nervous shock" after watching soldiers pass through the village in 1919. The drastic impact of such a long and vicious war is suggested by a Heinrich Campendonck painting in which a cowherd turned decorated soldier sits dressed in full armor amid his cattle. His foot is bleeding, infusing a symbolic redness into this otherwise dark and macabre scene. Similarly, the mental if not physical wounds inflicted on Oberammergau's fighting men by the Great War must have remained raw for many years after the 1918 armistice.[20]

Members of the home front also suffered both physical deprivation and mental anguish. With the loss of so many young men to the front leaving families short-handed on farms and in businesses, women and elderly parents found themselves pressed into service as a result. The decline in commercial activities and an increasingly tight food supply impoverished their lives, driving householders to rely on their own produce and livestock, as well as communally supplied groceries. Relatives fearing for their loved ones off at war soon invoked supernatural protection for them through a regular course of prayers, as well as many pilgrimages and dedicated masses. The Ettal Madonna in particular received the pilgrims' pleas for their soldiers. Despite these efforts, the death of a close relative became all too real for dozens of families as the war progressed. As early as August 1914, one young son had fallen, and his grieving mother regularly scheduled masses on his behalf thereafter. Soon Oberammergau was housing war widows and their children, creating another vulnerable population beyond the war orphans brought to stay in the village. When a young communications specialist died in 1918, a commentary added wryly that losing this talented singer had further depleted the Passion Play's cast.[21]

The beleaguered community was also receiving patriotic messages that must have deepened its hatred of the enemy. An appeal for financial support of the war effort particularly stressed the brutal Russian campaign that overran East Prussia early on, whipping up feelings with a poignant picture of refugees driven by a Cossack-like rider. The Press Club arranged "patriotic evenings" in 1916 and 1918; prominent Catholic priest Rupert Mayer spoke at the second of these events about "the World War and Christian Love." However, for many villagers the death and destruction caused by Allied forces must have made a loving response all but impossible. Like the returning combatants, Oberammergau's home community was scarred and embittered by the time their men came home.[22]

Germans soon found their world shaken to the core by a bewildering series of revolutionary events, complicating the period of demobilization when millions of soldiers rejoined battered home communities. The political implications of the lost war were made clear to Bavarian citizens even before a republic led by Social Democrats and their partners, the Progressive Liberals (DDP) and the Catholic Center Party, replaced Emperor William II on November 9; radical socialist Kurt Eisner declared a republic in Munich a couple of days before. The astonishing rapidity with which Bavaria's ancient monarchy had been swept aside struck one reporter, who nevertheless saw little real administrative change in this new setup and advised his readers to roll with the punches until new elections could take place.[23]

However, Eisner's new regime, although it included mainstream Social Democrats, was also underpinned by a workers', soldiers', and farmers' council of the sort mimicking Russian Soviets that sprang up throughout Germany during this volatile period. Soldiers' councils in Garmisch and Partenkirchen soon emerged as well, but they became the guardians of law and order rather than creating revolutionary change, a role made imperative by threats to an already strained food supply system from the expected flood of returning soldiers. Recognizing the importance of farmers in this equation, an appeal published in the county newspaper urged each community to choose a farmers' council that would assist in distributing food. The regular town officials in both Garmisch and Partenkirchen called meetings to set up these bodies; locals also selected members of a parallel middle-class council in Partenkirchen.[24]

At the urging of "Johnny" Lindemann, the head of Mittenwald's soldiers' council, the selection of a county-level people's council took place, which introduced a variety of "oversight" and advisory functions. In it were seated "12 representatives of the working class, 10 farmers, 8 small businessmen, 7 soldiers, 4 bureaucrats, and 1 member of the professions"; an extra delegate or two from the upper middle class were also permitted. Of these forty-two leaders, only one, Guido Lang, was from Oberammergau, although he was later joined by Weisses Rössl innkeeper and socialist Leo Rutz. The head of Oberammergau's Catholic Farmers' Club served on a county-level farmers' council when it was set up as well. Despite these unorthodox new political structures, in general Garmisch County's elected officials did not lose their control over local affairs. Rather, a strange hybrid of revolutionary form and conservative content emerged despite the yearning for joint governance harbored by some left-wing leaders.[25]

Meanwhile, the conciliar movement soon reached Oberammergau itself. By mid-December there existed a council made up of workers and members of the middle class, headed by Leo Rutz, but the regular leadership felt empowered to deny funds it requested because of its unauthorized nature. Late in the month, all of the local communities received orders to create either a workers' and farmers' council or a council for each group; their role would be merely to advise the traditional authorities. The workers' councils were to include blue- and white-collar workers, as well as small businessmen. Adults from the designated classes were to select their membership.[26]

Rutz was still heading the working-class section of Oberammergau's council when on February 1 he announced that it was the agency "where all suggestions und complaints of the proletarian masses always come to expression." By then, his unorthodox interference in the elected leadership's control over local affairs had created ill will, driving him to make a public statement in the newspaper. Stressing his belief in the "equal rights of all classes," Rutz asked those threatening his business because of his politics to cease and desist. In late March the council was urging potential renters to contact them for help in hunting down scarce housing; they also planned to designate two observers who would check for irregular slaughtering of local cattle. Yet, as on the county level, the conciliar movement in Oberammergau did not greatly distort the regular political setup. Veteran Mayor Bauer, though, was retiring, and the upcoming loss of so experienced a hand on the tiller at this crucial juncture must have been unsettling.[27]

While the conciliar movement unfolded in Bavaria, normal political procedures took their inexorable path toward the election of representatives at the state and national levels in mid-January. A variety of political parties began to mobilize supporters. The still-dominant Catholics had by the end of November created a successor party to the Catholic Center, the BVP. Hostile to their new regime's "revolution of disorder," these politicians added an anti-Prussian twist that denounced the centralizing aims of a Berlin-centered "Socialist republic." Christian women's groups soon held a meeting in Garmisch County to explore the "rights and duties" of the newly enfranchised female electorate, many of whom would be expected to support this new party.[28]

Other competing parties also sprang into action as the January elections approached. In Oberammergau, radical socialist Georg Murbeck, a leading figure on the Mittenwald Soldiers' Council, founded a Social Democratic Club on December 8, whose first head was small businessman Jakob Burger. This new club met, as did its liberal and Catholic opponents, before the state elections on January 12; a Farmers' League Party that carried over from the prewar period also ran candidates. So, as the violent revolutionary upheaval known as "Spartacus" week took place in the north, and as Karl Harrer, member of the racist Thule Society, helped to launch a tiny German Workers' Party in nearby Munich, Oberammergau's electorate prepared to vote.[29]

Results were encouraging for the Social Democrats, who scored 312 to the BVP's 360. Since both the liberals and the Farmers' League also did well, local Catholic voters failed to reestablish their customary predominance. Further political gatherings took place in Garmisch County before the national elections, which were held a week later. The tensions caused by such highly charged voting erupted during a Social Democratic Club meeting when a Catholic challenger made lengthy arguments that lasted into the wee hours. Perhaps he was anticipating the left-wing party's upcoming victory since it did indeed pull ahead of his BVP. As in 1871, when the liberals briefly won a great victory in Oberammergau, local voters had rewarded the new party in power, but they did so through the normal democratic process rather than the conciliar move-ment.[30]

Even before these elections gave evidence of a return to normalcy, Ober-ammergau's inhabitants began reestablishing peacetime customs with their traditional New Year's Eve procession. The demobilization of the community's soldiers was far enough advanced that plans went ahead for a big welcome on January 6. Like the villagers of Fischbachau, who dedicated a poignant votive painting of local soldiers winding their way up a snow-covered mountain to the Marian shrine at Birkenstein in thanks for surviving the war, Oberammergau's families were showing how grateful they were to have their own men back home. Carnival celebrations and numerous club meetings suggest a lively return to normal social life.[31]

Nevertheless, the villagers all faced the continuing economic problems cre-ated by diminished food supplies, housing shortages, and the need to rebuild businesses in a tight labor market. Efforts to deal with these problems continued as the revolutionary situation in Bavaria lingered on into the spring. Weeks after Eisner's party received a tiny percentage of votes in the January elections, news reached Oberammergau of the minister president's assassination. Political upheaval followed, but in mid-March the parliament established a government led by Social Democrat Johannes Hoffmann; however, it was still paralleled by a central council representing Munich's conciliar movement. Its members were to precipitate a radical phase in the revolution that threatened the economic recovery so ardently sought in Oberammergau.[32]

The fragility of Munich's political equilibrium soon became apparent when the central council set up a "conciliar republic" and drove out Hoffmann's govern-ment on April 7, 1919. Days later yet another upheaval empowered an inner group of Communists representing the soldiers' and workers' councils. Like Eisner, prominent leaders in this new junta were Jewish and even foreign. They deepened the revolutionary situation by proclaiming a general strike and assembling thousands of supporters into a "Red Army." One final shift in lead-ership late in April threatened to bring with it a military "dictatorship." How anomalous this new radical government had come to be in Catholic Bavaria is suggested in a sympathetic painting by Berta Kaiser, *Red Guard in the Marien-platz*. That famous symbol of Munich, the cathedral's twin towers, appears in the background above a beloved Marian pillar in the central square, while a red flag flies from the town hall. This guard with red armband and rifle is clearly Bavarian, but he is also alone, a foreign presence in his own city.[33]

The unsettling developments in Munich soon impacted Bavaria's outly-ing regions, including Garmisch County. On April 9 the county newspaper discussed the new republic, news of which had arrived ahead of the regime's "red posters." These provocative notices declared that the councils were now to "protect" local officials, who should keep working as long as they were loyal to the new regime. The people's council announced that area governance had to be approved by local councils, and it asked for red flags to be unfurled on "all public buildings." Yet it also urged inhabitants to stay calm and preserve the county's orderly life in the face of yet another revolutionary situation. This was quite a challenge given a telegram from the head of Munich's central council suggesting that special "councils of workers and employees" should effectively take over businesses, while the councils would manage government bureaucrats. A meeting in Partenkirchen could hardly have reassured participants when the head of the Social Democratic Club declared that "a socializing of small businesses" was off the table, but the electric works did later feature in discussions about an official takeover.[34]

Meeting to discuss this crisis, Garmisch County's farmers declared their loyalty to the "only legal regime" in Bavaria. They wanted to go on record against the "full socialization plans of 'crazies'" and "mostly foreign elements" who had set up the new republic. The county newspaper added the generalization that Jews and Eastern Europeans were persuading local workers to undermine their own state. Lacking an uncensored press, Bavarians could not express their true sentiments, but they would certainly counteract "the dictatorship of an internationally constituted minority." Actions by opponents of the new regime did indeed speak clearly enough. Lindemann, Murbeck, and others were arrested briefly, and a well-received Garmisch statement on behalf of the Hoffmann regime reinforced the farmers' position, as did a "demonstration" in Partenkirchen. Lindemann was soon expelled from Garmisch County, and Murbeck escaped, fearing armed men who had been emerging as loyalist enforcers.[35]

Confusing news from Munich kept the locals on edge as it trickled in during the next couple of weeks despite only intermittent communications with the capital. Meanwhile, life went on as the new regime's shadow crept ever closer. Hoffmann's government was soon reaching out for supporters willing to fight the dangerous revolutionaries, while Württemberger troops spread the news that they would also be intervening. As an "old Front comrade" argued in the county newspaper, ex-soldiers should join in this effort to "purge" their state.[36]

By then, the frightening news had arrived that heavily armed Red Guards had gathered in nearby Kochel so that they could deal with Garmisch's "counterrevolution." Meanwhile, a People's Guard had emerged in the county, and armed men, including veterans "once again in their element . . . as soldiers," prepared to defend their communities. The two groups would clash only a couple of days later when a convoy wound its way toward Garmisch early in the morning. Out in front of three trucks loaded with men and weapons appeared a car in which sat the fiery Murbeck; he had left Garmisch County only to return at the head of these invading troops. Commander Josef Dillis, backed up by a portion of the new guard, confronted Murbeck's car and soon fell wounded. A battle ensued, in which Dillis's men repulsed the car's occupants and those of the lead truck, killed four revolutionaries, and wounded Murbeck. Survivors ran away as the two rear trucks sped off. A subsequent manhunt reached Oberau and up the Kienberg as far as Ettal, producing eighteen prisoners.[37]

Meanwhile, posters left behind by the convoy and others displayed around town revealed the revolutionaries' plans. They intended to announce the conciliar republic in Garmisch, disarm the citizens, and set up a county-level central committee headed by Murbeck, pending elections that were to favor "only workers and poor farmers." One poster called for a general strike, another announced that "all farming implements are confiscated," and yet another socialized the tourism and transportation facilities. A "revolutionary tribunal" and even a firing squad awaited dissenters against "the Dictatorship of the Proletariat." A list of hostages included Oberammergau's Uhlschmid, who, like his fellow villagers, had barely escaped the fate reported in a letter about a successful Easter Sunday attack on nearby Miesbach. There, revolutionaries took hostages, whom they ransomed for money, and they seized precious stocks of food and wine. Particularly mentioned was the theft and destruction of "2 beautiful pigs" owned by a local cheese manufacturer. Naturally, the locals remained fearful that similar traumatic events could still occur in their own county.[38]

In response, after the repulsed "Murbeck putsch," hundreds of local men joined a paramilitary free corps named "Werdenfels" and traveled to Munich as liberators. Posters in Bavaria's traditional color, sky blue, had summoned volunteers to fight the "Communist-terroristic dictatorship set up by foreign elements in Munich." By means of a similar notice Oberammergau's leadership joined in praising the gallant county guard that had "fended off unspeakable evil from our beautiful valleys." Listing the invaders' despicable aims, they challenged workers, as well as middle-class citizens, to take up arms and protect both communal and national principles. In addition, they voiced the very real fear that their community would remain cut off from bread and flour supplies unless locals joined the fight against the revolutionary forces. A telegram from one government minister went so far as to invoke the "fate of Russia" in encouraging all able-bodied men to sign up. Hoffmann's regime stressed the need for a "genuine People's Guard" to fight the "Red Army organized . . . on the Russian model" so that the beneficial results of Bavaria's political changes could be consolidated.[39]

The mood in Garmisch-Partenkirchen became quite extreme after people had absorbed news of the red putsch and experienced its terror tactics, which encouraged locals to "wish these men to the Devil." A celebratory atmosphere therefore greeted the procession of departing troops, reminiscent of the early days of World War I. On May 1 several hundred "flower-bedecked" men, many wearing local costume, boarded a waiting train for the capital; their numbers included around a score from Oberammergau. This Werdenfels Corps arrived in Munich to join the fighting, in which more than thirty thousand troops bloodily suppressed their leftist foes. They were involved in engagements led by Franz Ritter von Epp in the Giesing area, winning the right to wear "a golden lion's head on a black background" over the Bavarian colors affixed to their sleeves.[40]

News about the hated conciliar republic's end was eagerly awaited in Garmisch County. In mid-May the men returned like heroes to exuberant celebrations, and a film shot of the corps' exploits soon made the rounds of area cinemas. Subsequently, a dramatic certificate created for them glamorized the "folkish" Alpine fighter with his traditional costume who had helped to "free" Bavaria's capital. Another such memento depicts a victorious soldier standing legs akimbo against a Bavarian flag that intersects with Munich's cathedral; he shakes one of the outstretched hands that reach up out of an unseen crowd of grateful residents. Its similarity to Kaiser's painting of the Red Guard is eerie, although here the isolating Communist regalia of an unwelcome intruder are replaced with the familiar and welcome pairing of patriotic and religious Bavarian symbols. Despite the deaths of many leftists, Garmisch County residents were proud and supportive of their Free Corps fighters.[41]

The political situation in Bavaria regularized later in 1919 and shifted firmly to the right after the Kapp putsch in 1920, which brought an end to Hoffmann's government. In Garmisch County, the people's council was dissolved early in June 1919, although a nine-person committee carried on. Then local elections took place under guidelines that opened up voting rights to recent migrants and instituted the concept of proportional representation.[42]

In Oberammergau, baker Wilhelm Rutz was chosen as mayor, while a "citizens" slate of candidates for the council faced off against a "unity" coalition made up of the Weimar Republic's BVP, DDP, and SPD supporters. This contest took on an acrimonious local dynamic that diverted much support from the generally successful Weimar parties to the citizens. They won handily with seven seats to five, denying Guido Lang and several other prewar liberals a role in the new council. In this context, Georg Lang, brother of the future Nazi mayor, began his political career as a winning candidate for the citizens and a member of the conservative liberal German People's Party (DVP). Nevertheless, in regional elections, the BVP won handily; Oberammergau was still a largely Catholic community despite the political pluralism developing there. This commitment was well expressed in the Corpus Christi procession held with great fanfare around the time of the election.[43]

Despite this reassertion of the democratic process, fears remained about leftist threats and the continued existence of revolutionary bodies. The county administrator was still worried about Communist "agitation" in August 1919 and urged arrests if needed to keep the peace. Oberammergau's workers' and farmers' council stayed around until August 20, when it voted itself out of existence. Its leading figure, Leo Rutz, was by then a councilor and a member of the county parliament. He also headed the Social Democratic Club when it decided on September 27 to hold new elections for a workers' council and similar councils for business enterprises. An advertisement for the election of the workers' council to take place in Leo's inn appeared in October, but quite what became of it thereafter is unclear, although a year later it was considered "long defunct."[44]

Development of Bavaria's Home Guard took place in this jittery postrevolutionary context. Its origins lay in communal responses to the uncertain political situation after the armistice and in particular during the conciliar republic, complementing the activities of the Free Corps Werdenfels. In fall 1919 Oberammergau counted well more than two hundred guards, who were headed by the deputy mayor. The regional body to which these local men were subordinated held a big marksmen's gathering in mid-October. There, conservative leader Gustav von Kahr addressed them, promising swift action by "our People's Guards" should a Communist threat reemerge. Franz Ritter von Epp stressed their role as guardians "of house and hearth." By the end of 1919 around 200,000 men were armed and ready to protect their communities. Oberammergau's force continued to grow, topping three hundred when the village sent representatives to a "demonstration of force" held at Munich's Königsplatz in September 1920. The new movement was clearly a product of the communal will to resist unwelcome changes in the region's traditional lifestyle.[45]

Meanwhile, a desire to fight back against the revolutionary forces at work in Bavaria had led Oberammergau's Catholic women to found the local branch of the Women's Union late in 1919. Beyond the immediate need to fend off any physical threats of Communism, Mathilde Lang's women recognized the role that spiritual leadership could play in cementing Catholic values and providing a nonsocialist way of fighting the many postwar crises. That same year villagers founded a parents' club to strengthen Christian families and bolster their education; Mayor Rutz served as its head. The existing male charitable clubs were also involved, as they happily pursued a peacetime schedule of events.[46]

Despite this largely welcome stabilization and a subsequent right-wing turn in Bavaria's political scene, the revolutionary period left deep scars. When the next general election rolled around in 1920, hatred of Communism had intertwined with anti-Semitism because of the prominent role played by foreign Jewish Marxists in the conciliar republic. A notice prepared by Garmisch County authorities captures this hostile response to local revolutionaries, particularly Murbeck, who had brought the terrifying threat of a Communist regime far too close to home. Such a regime was antithetical to peaceful prosperity; it left "nothing more for all than misery and want." However, the posting also condemns the revolution's leadership, the "foreign kids from Russia, Hungary, Galicia, and Poland [who] wanted to dominate our good brave Bavarian folk." A 1919 BVP poster dramatically depicts this hostile critique by showing Bolshevism as a "mongol" Russian Cossack extending the red flames of revolution to blue-white Bavaria.[47]

Admiration for the liberating Free Corps balanced undying hostility toward these Communist intruders, a sentiment later illustrated in a Nazi propaganda image pairing a famous photograph of the Free Corps Werdenfels as "sons of the mountains" with three Jewish revolutionaries, including Eisner, as "sons of the desert." Facing the June 1920 election, some of Oberammergau's political parties expressed similar ideas. While the fledgling Nazi party developed in Munich with the racist ideology of anti-Bolshevism and anti-Semitism at its core, local BVP leaders echoed their suspicions of "international-socialistic-Jewish ideas" so antithetical to their party's "Christian-national" message. The Prussian-based National Conservatives (DNVP) also entered this local election, claiming that they alone had translated their anti-Semitism into rejection of Jewish party members.[48]

The BVP reasserted its ascendency in this election, winning half of all votes cast; the Corpus Christi procession was providentially timed to take place right before the voting. However, the SPD still received a healthy 251 votes, and the extreme left 11, while rightists and liberals together scored close to 200 additional votes. This was tourism season, and the electorate doubtless included visitors and temporary workers, as well as Oberammergau's middle-class and non-Bavarian migrants, including a mounting number of Protestants. This variety of political choices made by the village's increasingly diverse population would characterize subsequent Weimar elections.[49]

When Bavarians next voted, the folkish Right had gained prominence from its role in the radical developments of the early 1920s. This included contributions by the Bund Oberland, a successor group to a Free Corps created by the racist Thule Society to oppose the conciliar republic. This extremist Free Corps had earlier absorbed the Werdenfels Corps, and at least one Oberammergau native joined its nationalistic campaigns in the Ruhr and Upper Silesia. A Garmisch County branch of the Bund existed; regional activities included a 1922 gathering of marksmen in nearby Murnau. The Home Guard's deputy head, Wilhelm Lechner, and Werdenfels Corps member Alfred Bierling headed the group locally until 1923.[50]

Membership in the Bund Oberland drew a handful of Oberammergau's inhabitants into the Nazi orbit just as Germany's spiraling inflationary crisis began to gather strength. Moreover, the first Nazi chapter to appear locally started up in Garmisch-Partenkirchen. At the same time, Catholics were strengthening their hold over local affairs, as the Passion season in 1922 restored the residents' faith in traditional politics; a very successful mission conducted in Oberammergau had further reinforced the Catholic base, leading to the creation of a Marian Congregation and the church-controlled Mothers' Club. It was also in this atmosphere that believing workers transformed a benevolent society into a full-fledged Catholic Workers' Club. The existing clubs, notably Mathilde Lang's group, remained active in counteracting the mounting crisis as well. By May 1923 Curate Heim had managed to add a short-lived youth club to provide village children with constructive activities.[51]

By then, the many crises of that eventful year were well under way. In January confrontation over reparations saw French troops occupying the Ruhr valley, which quickly evoked a response in Oberammergau. Officials initiated a collection for their suffering compatriots in early February; a large and very successful gathering in favor of the "Ruhr fund" also took place in the village's leading hotel. French behavior was soon being condemned as "brutality" and "shameless barbarism," while local families were asked to house young victims of "enemy sadism." The Ruhr events and a resultant influx of refugees continued to make news into the spring, while suspicions of these hated enemy occupiers persisted throughout the year; fear of French spies or agents was agitating regional officials as late as November.[52]

In May 1923 local events symbolized the growing divide in German politics. The new era was brought home when Oberammergau hosted a female politician serving in the Reichstag. However, aggressive male politics challenged the liberal Weimar republic, which had enfranchised women, when Hitler presided over a parade by the Sturmabteilung (SA) and the Bund Oberland in Murnau. Oberammergau's newspaper crowed about a visit of "military, real military" who were arriving for maneuvers and would join in the Corpus Christi procession.[53]

As Germany's inflationary crisis deepened during the fall, Communism reemerged as a regional threat, creating fears of a revolutionary upswing. Nationalists continued their militant activities with a dramatic event organized by Garmisch's Bund Oberland to recognize the very Catholic victim of Ruhr violence, Leo Schlageter. The climax came in November, when their commander unsealed a summons labeled as follows: "Secret, open on 8. 11. 23 8:30." Inside was this message: "In Munich national dictatorship declared, travel at once with local group to Munich, Bürgerbräukeller." Seventy men set off just as Hitler was initiating his beer hall putsch. They joined his abortive march through the city center on November 9; the Bund Oberland formed one of three units that crossed the River Isar toward the Odeonsplatz. These men reported how surprised they had been that Bavarian police shot at the marchers there. None, however, was among those who fell as "martyrs" that day.[54]

At least two men from Oberammergau took part, brothers from a laboring family of migrants. Their fellow villagers read about the putsch in the local paper on November 10; it must have been strange to find news of the "establishment of a national dictatorship," when surely Hitler's failure was already well known by then. Days later came a headline about the putsch's ignominious end and a brief account of the Führer's capture; police fittingly took him off in a beer truck. However, that story was crowded out by a lengthy article about Oberammergau's massive stone Crucifixion group donated by King Ludwig a half century before.[55]

The putsch had little impact in Oberammergau, where workers were busily trying to handle the inflationary crisis. One answer was the new Heimatkunst consortium of local artisans. While the Nazis were agitating in Munich, its members prepared to sail to the United States; some, including Lechner, were already there by the end of November. This controversial effort pitted councilor Georg Lang against his second cousin Anton, who received a hero's welcome in America. Georg and his brother Raimund took up the cause of the disgruntled merchants who resented the potential competition, and the village was once again divided in a hostile dynamic that stretched into the election year of 1924.[56]

National elections in the period 1924–1928 reflected a gradual calming of the political waters as Germans enjoyed an all-too-brief economic resurgence. A folkish block kept the hopes of the Radical Right alive while Hitler was briefly incarcerated after his farce of a trial in 1924. Nevertheless, their fortunes faded in the second round of elections held that November, while in Oberammergau the BVP, the SPD, and the newly arrived DNVP all rebounded. However, the electorate continued to fragment in these elections; emblematic were sixteen votes cast for a fringe party appealing to those worried about fragile savings in this postinflation climate. In 1925 presidential elections gripped the nation until the fatherly war hero Field Marshall Paul von Hindenburg was safely in place as Germany's new figurehead.[57]

Three years of peace and prosperity followed, which favored Oberammergau's Catholic community, whose many charitable and ritual activities still helped to secure its following, as did confessional schooling. Its emotional connection to the lost Bavarian monarchy was reinforced by a huge celebration marking the Crucifixion group's fiftieth anniversary on King Ludwig's birthday in 1925. The evening before, villagers continued a tradition of lighting symbols on the Kofel to honor their beloved patron.[58]

However, the continued influx of migrants, including Protestants, favored additional political diversification. The DNVP in particular could only benefit from acquisition of the Osterbichl Hotel by a National Conservative white-collar union as a convalescent home for its members from all over Germany. Moreover, in 1925 a new organization arrived in Oberammergau. Jakob Burger, once head of the Social Democratic Club, joined other homeowners to found the Real Estate Owners' Association in order to fight "socialization" and excessive taxes; under his leadership it would provide yet another political option in the next round of elections.[59]

During the following year, however, almost all of the locals agreed to oppose a despised plebiscite calling for appropriation of properties belonging to the elite, which divided "bourgeois parties" from the Left. Hatred bubbled up for the "Bolshevist plans" that lay behind this "Communistic-socialistic confiscation." Loyal feelings for the Bavarian Wittelsbachs reemerged, especially in Oberammergau, whose men had helped to build King Ludwig's Linderhof Palace. Consequently, the village counted a mere 35 positive votes, which the newspaper opined came in part from "outside workers and also . . . summer guests."[60]

This moment of common agreement was fleeting, however, and a new national election in May 1928 split the villagers once again into supporters of a wide range of parties. Nazi efforts to compete were raucous but unsuccessful, given the improved economy, which denied the Radical Right a breeding ground for discontent. The BVP fought back in Oberammergau, trouncing the Nazi party by 395 to 26. Of the established parties, both the SPD and the DNVP lost voters, while the combined vote of two liberal parties went up some. However, fewer than half of the eligible voters even bothered to cast a ballot during this peaceful period in their history.[61]

Oberammergau's citizens remained passionately engaged with local affairs, although their incentive to vote in national elections diminished once their harsh postwar experiences were behind them. The year 1924 was also one for local elections, which again proved quite divisive. Four competing lists of candidates for the community council included dozens of villagers; one spelled out the separate identity of newcomers with its title, "migrant citizens." It was a novel phenomenon for outsiders to take part in a local election, as the local paper pointed out, and the seven men on the list did not fare well compared to the long lists of contenders on the other three slates. "For All," "Progress and Work," and "Citizens" mixed classes and party allegiances, bringing men into the council who would become leading players in the political dramas of the Nazi years. In particular BVP loyalist Josef Raab, the village's chief administrator, won a seat, as did a youthful war veteran from a leading Catholic family, Rupert Breitsamter. Once again DVP member Georg Lang joined the council's ranks, as did SPD leader Leo Rutz. Hans Mayr, son of Josef, became Mayor Rutz's deputy.[62]

Four years later villagers once again committed to a normal Passion season in 1930, a decision that soon led to the selection of Passion Committee members from a pool of 154 local candidates. Zeno Diemer was the top vote getter that year, and Wilhelm Lechner's father the runner-up. Anton Lang also won a place, which gave him political clout beyond his role as a church warden. Then, late in 1929 came yet another election, this time for councilors. Whereas in 1924, 71 candidates had run, now there were 173, including a handful of women, Mathilde Lang among them. In a community of around two thousand inhabitants, this high percentage of candidates for both the Passion Committee and the community council out of the total voting population was astonishing. The need to control local affairs was so pressing that it gave rise to this intense level of political engagement. Some new men entered politics as a result, including Alfred Bierling and the future player of Christ, Alois Lang.[63]

By early 1930 a contested race for mayor of Oberammergau had become very contentious, as reflected in the distribution of almost seven thousand copies of various flyers. Deputy Mayor Mayr faced Sebastian Zwink's son Oskar as his challenger. Zwink's candidacy may well have been based on his long-standing leadership of a postwar version of the Citizens' Club. Their chief cause was the abolition of ancient residency rights in 1916, which undermined the carefully guarded distinction between insiders and outsiders. Then, postwar voting rules empowered Bavarian migrants to participate in local elections within a year (or even six months for a while) of arriving in the village. The local paper exclaimed in response that "the right of citizenship is rendered practically meaningless by this change"; established families would as a result lose control over village affairs. This was the context for the victory of the citizens' slate in 1919, as well as for the defeat of the "migrant citizens" in 1924.[64]

Four years later, as the voting for a new Passion Committee loomed, fears about control over play affairs led to a reactivation of the Citizens' Club. Members called a series of Sunday meetings to explore a plan that would create a standing committee shielded from newcomers. However, councilors opposed this idea, and their initiative failed; indeed, when the ballots were cast for Passion Committee members, eighteen voters had moved to Oberammergau since the 1922 season. Less than two years later Zwink, still head of the club, ran aggressively but unsuccessfully against Mayr only a few short months before the 1930 Passion season and a fateful national election.[65]

In 1928 a BVP campaign poster took credit for the recent good times, drawing the line firmly between a revolutionary past and the blessed present. Divided vertically, the poster's left half sets a menacing proletarian against a red banner and a ruined landscape of empty fields, tumbledown homes, and smokeless factories. To his right stands a typical Bavarian in his lederhosen and jaunty feathered hat. Under a swirling blue-and-white flag productive fields meet the plow, a sapling sits atop new construction to celebrate a housing boom, and factory chimneys belch out smoke. By 1930, however, such optimism about the regional economy and the BVP's ability to fight a resurgent left had disappeared. A more aggressive champion was emerging as Germans voted that September.[66]

The Nazis had responded to their poor performance in the 1928 election with a rural strategy that targeted small communities outside the Left's industrial strongholds. Their efforts in Garmisch County brought a small Nazi chapter to Oberammergau late in 1929, but the Passion season muted campaigning in the months leading up to the election. Yet these local Nazis managed to exceed the national trend, which brought their party to new heights of influence. While the NSDAP rose to around 18 percent of the overall vote, in Oberammergau its fortunes rose still more remarkably since their 26 votes in 1928 had become 424, close to one-third of the total.[67]

This extraordinary increase had everything to do with the fact that a Passion season was under way. Had the election been held while many temporary laborers were working on the new theater building and preparing the village for a flood of visitors, the local voting totals would have favored the Left. However, those men moved on before the season opened. Instead, a new round of more than one thousand transients arrived to serve the guests, and they were still at work in September. Their swelling of the voting population, in addition to the five hundred or so migrants who had settled in Oberammergau since 1918, contributed to the sky-high Nazi vote.[68]

As early as July 1929, an advertisement had appeared in the newspaper from a teacher's daughter, a Straubing saleswoman who was looking for work right away or during the Passion season. Further advertisements appeared that year, and then the trickle became a flood in 1930 as young workers and white-collar personnel caught on to the unique opportunity offered by Oberammer-gau's special season. Altogether, more than four hundred advertisers sought work. Of those who gave a return address, while they lived all over the nation, the vast majority were from a wide scattering of Bavarian communities, upwards of one-quarter from Munich alone. Well more than 70 percent were females; they sought domestic work, primarily as maids and cooks, or sales and office positions. The male applicants were often chauffeurs, retailers, janitors, and bakers.[69]

Also swelling the population were workers meeting the enormous demands for transportation, as well as postal and policing services. Extra trains brought visitors to each major performance, including an "Oberammergau Express." The traffic snarl caused by cars and buses was so large that fifteen managers had to be on hand. Post office workers handled a huge surge of mail, and extra police kept order among the crowds.[70]

However, it was not just the Passion Play that drew transients to the village; the hard times and traditional patterns of wandering brought in hundreds of trainee craftsmen as well, requiring the local Journeymen's Club to provide for their needs. In addition, the Osterbichl facility owned by Germany's conserva-tive white-collar workers' organization brought in additional vacationers.[71]

Some of Oberammergau's transient workers would have found employment with the temporary businesspeople who were competing with local establish-ments in 1930, like Josef Storr of Munich, who rented space to sell souvenirs. Eduard Durach, proprietor of Munich's "biggest" sauerkraut factory, opened a delicatessen, while August Belster ran a café for the Munich-based Seidl firm, the city's "biggest Konditorei." A French woman took over one shop to interest "American Ladies" in "a great choice of Lingerie, govens, [sic] stockings and parfums their being the latest novelties from Paris." Such outsiders aroused the suspicion of locals because of their supposedly shady practices; as Mayor Rutz exclaimed in 1921, "What elements there are today!" Nonetheless, they expanded the number of opportunities for job seekers, who perceived Oberam-mergau's season as a temporary refuge from an increasingly hostile working world.[72]

Oberammergau's young seasonal employees may have voted Nazi in sub-stantial numbers, but they were by no means the only supporters of Hitler's radical party that September. Members of the regular population must have voted Nazi as well, particularly migrants since they predominated in the local NSDAP chapter. After 1930, however, the party began to attract old-timers as the Great Depression gripped the local community. Experiences as searing as their participation in the war and its revolutionary consequences had prepared these men to listen appreciatively to the Nazi message, once the hard-won progress toward economic and social stability began to falter. They were joined by younger villagers who had matured during the lean wartime and postwar years. Chapter 3 examines this process by which Nazism wormed its way into Oberammergau's population, attracting both newcomers and settled villagers. The group did not develop without a struggle, however, since BVP and SPD activists fought back as best they could. It was only after years of extreme crisis that the Nazi party succeeded in Oberammergau.

3

Nazis

Standing in Munich's Odeonsplatz, informed visitors can align themselves with the massive ocher pillars of the Theatinerkirche to find the exact spot where Adolf Hitler stood in August 1914, celebrating the outbreak of war in the midst of a jubilant crowd. The future dictator's mustachioed face was caught for posterity in a now famous photograph of this huge demonstration, which stretched from the large monument honoring past war heroes, the Feldherrnhalle, up toward the Victory Arch beyond Munich University. Nine years later Hitler returned to the Odeonsplatz at the head of marching columns on his futile quest to overthrow the German government.[1]

Leaving the Burgerbräukeller where he began his putsch on November 8, Hitler headed a long procession that included Bund Oberland's men from Garmisch County. Also marching that day were the Führer's special guards, forerunners of the Schutzstaffel (SS), and Munich's own SA troopers. The putsch was in large part a local affair, although reinforcements summoned to the Bavarian capital backed up the city's men; this motley force paraded through the Marienplatz and on toward the Odeonsplatz by way of a narrow defile created by the Feldherrnhalle and the Royal Palace. Meanwhile, a group of armed comrades waited for them at a barricade set up beyond the square outside army headquarters. These members of the allied "Reichskriegsflagge" included Heinrich Himmler as bearer of the imperial wartime flag that gave his group their title.

Mounted state police were deployed at the point of disgorgement into the square, dividing the two groups of putschists. The Nazis expected these men to sympathize with their cause but were sorely disappointed.

Shooting broke out as the lead marchers reached the Odeonsplatz, and thirteen, together with a bystander, were killed. Two more putschists fell near the army headquarters. Their uprising was stopped in its tracks, but Hitler escaped to the hideout where he was later arrested.

Subsequently, Hitler shared the dock with other leading figures who had survived their failed coup. His trial gave the Nazi Führer a notoriety that later helped him to establish a national platform. Returning to his familiar haunts after a brief imprisonment, Hitler resurrected the party in 1925, arguing that Bavaria's capital was to be the "Moscow of our movement." There, the "first sacrifices" had taken place, making Munich "sacred ground." Initially, though, he faced discouraging times because of the improved economy, which briefly stabilized Germany's political situation.[2]

A building on the Schellingstrasse housed the NSDAP's office in charge of membership and funds. New recruits and income flowed in slowly until after the 1928 election, when nationally the party received less than 3 percent of the vote. However, Germany was slipping into depression, so support for the radical Nazis mushroomed throughout the country. A rising number of local chapters also sprang up in the Bavarian heartland.[3]

Nazi fortunes were already improving in 1930, when party leaders bought the imposing Barlow Palace located off Munich's Königsplatz, soon to host their militarized extravaganzas. This new headquarters, quickly dubbed the "Brown House," became the resurgent party's administrative nerve center. Control extended outward through district leaders to the officials of each community's chapter. Hitler deliberately set out to undermine the Weimar Republic by mobilizing these active chapters to contest elections and bring the NSDAP to power.[4]

Oberammergau belonged to a section of the historic München-Oberbayern district, where Nazism spread out along the railroad line from Munich into Garmisch County. However, the villagers were slow to jump on board this Nazi bandwagon. Only in fall 1929 did a smattering of local party members manage to launch their own chapter, linking up with already existing groups in the area. The following year they first introduced a small SA force. By the end of 1932, this kernel of a Nazi presence in Oberammergau had expanded into a sizeable group, although other nearby chapters were the dominant centers of party activism.

Based on their successful harnessing of democratic forces in Depression-haunted Germany, the Nazis seized power in January 1933. Once firmly in control, they sanctified the Odeonsplatz with yearly ceremonies honoring their dead comrades. Ernst Vollbehr's painting, *The Festivities at the Feldherrnhalle*, captures the first of these annual events. With impressionistic strokes of gaudy color, he recorded brown columns arriving at the site of martyrdom, where crowds salute them with the German greeting.[5]

Two years later Oberammergau's Zeno Diemer reproduced the putschists' marching route in a dramatic "bird's-eye view." Awaiting the procession that year were two new Greek-style temples linking the Königsplatz to the nearby Brown House. There, sarcophagi holding the heroic remains of all sixteen martyrs were deposited, adding a new station of remembrance for subsequent anniversary marches. Eventually, however, the war unleashed by the Nazi denizens of this ceremonial complex led to its destruction; only the weed-covered temple ruins exist today to remind visitors of the dictatorial forces emanating out into Bavaria's countryside from the new party headquarters.[6]

Hotspots in the Bavarian highlands had seen extremist action during the volatile period in 1923 that nurtured Hitler's putschist ambitions. In Murnau, a fanatical Nazi had even threatened to take over the town's policing duties. Beyond a few chapters in local towns, including Garmisch, Radical Right groups like Bund Oberland also proliferated. In Rosenheim, a local Jew's criticism of one such group led to his defenestration. Residual unrest after the unsuccessful putsch culminated in eighty of that town's Nazis menacing Jewish residents.[7]

At this time, the region's leadership, perhaps reflecting local attitudes, harbored prejudices against Jewish tourists who flooded into the area, especially at Christmastime. An early 1923 report suggested that three-quarters or more of Garmisch's business came from "the Jewish race." Distressing to the writer was the presence of both German and Eastern European Jews; the latter stood out still more because of their bizarre clothing. Polish Jews were among those visitors who were supposedly bleeding locals dry as the inflation crisis deepened. By 1926, however, this situation seemed to have improved since the Eastern Jews had stopped coming and the German Jews were more acceptable than before. Because these visitors came to be such a mainstay of the tourism industry, fears even surfaced that rowdy Nazis would drive them out of resort centers.[8]

Meanwhile, local Nazis saw their radical cause flounder during those few calm years that preceded the onset of the Depression. Still, their political associates enjoyed a fleeting success when a "folkish block" performed well in the May 1924 elections. In Oberammergau, however, a speaker for the "Hitler-Ludendorff movement" overstepped the mark of acceptable campaign behavior with "expressions [both] about Christ and Mary" and about diocesan head Cardinal Faulhaber; even fellow supporters of the folkish block took offense. Nevertheless, the party received almost one hundred votes, around a quarter of the BVP's totals.[9]

By December 1924 the block's fate had been sealed since its support eroded as the crisis atmosphere faded. Only twenty-three voters stayed with it in Oberammergau, while the BVP gained more than a hundred supporters; both the SPD and in particular the rightist DNVP also fared very well. The causes of the Radical Right had lost their appeal even after Hitler emerged from prison to resurrect his Nazi party.[10]

These discouraging years lasted into 1928, when Hitler's revived party made considerable efforts to compete in yet another general election—but without success. Members in Garmisch-Partenkirchen had reestablished their local chapter early that year, well before they kicked off the new campaign. In April a motorized column worked its way around the county to stimulate interest and distribute literature. A second tour followed, just as the voting was to take place in May.[11]

Oberammergau's BVP leaders fought back against this noisy campaigning; one advertisement asked, "What does the Catholic and Bavarian vote for?" Clearly separating themselves from both Nazis and Communists, they stressed their regional patriotism and the fact that they were "without the desire for a putsch either to the right or the left." These efforts paid off when they trounced the Nazi party by 395 to 26.[12]

Nonetheless, this Catholic victory did not obscure an advanced "fragmentation of the bourgeoisie," as the newspaper lamented. Ten other parties attracted around three hundred votes, including some for the Economic Party, promoted to answer the question "to be or not to be of the home owner." Neither the SPD nor the DNVP fared well this time, and the two liberal parties barely improved their precarious hold on the political middle. Since less than half of the eligible electorate even bothered to cast a ballot, future growth was possible for any cause that galvanized politically inactive adults and drew in voters who would be willing to desert all of the traditional parties.[13]

The Nazis employed their new rural strategy in Garmisch County within weeks of the disastrous 1928 election. Now that a chapter was established in the county capital, party members in nearby Oberau managed to launch a branch of their own in late July. This was part of an effort to root the cause in the Loisach valley, where the railroad ran from Munich to Garmisch, linking Oberau to these major urban sources of political activism. The nearby community of Eschenlohe soon joined Oberau as a dynamic center of Hitler's movement.[14]

Nazis worked all over to spread their "infection," as the county administrator phrased it. Employing confrontational tactics in meetings, they sometimes ganged up against Catholics. By mid-1929 they had also launched small auxiliary SA forces in Oberau and Eschenlohe. That August around two dozen Storm

Troopers descended on Garmisch, and their marching and singing made them "very unpleasantly conspicuous." Activists continued to travel around, boosting attendance at meetings held in various county centers. Soon they were causing distress with a campaign against the Young Plan's regularization of reparation payments, while the flaunting of party uniforms and the radical propaganda efforts were proving dangerously divisive. In the spring of 1930 the Nazis were very busy in the entire county, with Eschenlohe hosting three gatherings within a fortnight. However, plans for a broader event fell through; preoccupation with the tourist season may have dampened campaigning zeal.[15]

Contrary to what critics of Oberammergau's Passion Play might expect, the villagers were by no means instrumental in spreading Nazism throughout their county. Rather, Garmisch's revived branch had existed for upward of eighteen months, and the Oberau group beneath the Kienberg for more than a year before a small chapter was launched in their midst. In late summer 1929, thirteen men, mostly "external workers employed in the village," held a meeting to explore starting a Nazi chapter. By this time evidence for a pending economic crisis had been mounting, although Oberammergau continued to attract business ventures, while work on the Passion theater and other preparations for 1930 headed off unemployment. In fact, the community had become a magnet for transient laborers of the sort who launched the chapter. The catalyst was a longtime party member and typical transient, Ernst Nagler, a painter no doubt helping to spruce up local homes. However, making this group a reality took nine men with more substantial local ties than Nagler's. He found most of them in or near Oberammergau's Station Quarter, located beyond the Ammer, where temporary workers and new settlers had mingled since 1900.[16] (Figure 1.4 shows the Station Quarter in the foreground.)

Seven men became their chapter's founding members, joining the party en masse; two more signed up shortly thereafter. Of these nine, four left Oberammergau well before the Nazi seizure of power. One, an erstwhile putschist, was the scion of a migrant working-class family who shared their new dwelling near the station with some transient laborers; he soon left for a job in another community. Another appeared nearby in 1930, this one a sometime carpenter and in-and-out villager who had lived just inside the Ammer boundary when he became a Nazi; he, too, left town after the play season ended. Over the river on the main street into the village lived an employee of Oberammergau's bank, a resident since the mid-1920s who disappeared around 1931. Near him lodged the fourth joiner, a day laborer and recent arrival who had relocated to the Station Quarter before he also moved out of the village in 1931.[17]

All but one of the remaining five founding members were newcomers who stayed in Oberammergau throughout the Nazi era. Perhaps Nagler worked with the painting assistant who became the local chapter leader, Hans Alzinger. He lived on the very edge of the new Station Quarter, sharing the "Villa Ammerhof" with his employer, decorative painter Arno Hesse, and graphic artist Ackermann, both migrants like himself. Their neighbors also joined, the two putschist brothers, although only one remained permanently in the village. A further founding member was a butcher who arrived in Oberammergau just in time to join the new group. When he left again in 1950, he resided near the Kofel. A fourth member, a migrant carpenter, settled in his family's home in the direction of Saint Gregor.[18]

Finally, one last founder was another carpenter whose home stood in the village center, the only man fully integrated into communal life as a member of the established Bierling clan. His laboring family had, however, previously lodged next to the new station, together with railroad personnel, and an uncle lived near the putschists. His older brother, a loyal member of the Free Corps Epp and an "old fighter," did not help to launch the local chapter.[19]

Eight of these nine original chapter members were essentially working class, and all but two belonged to the village's migrant section so well represented in the Station Quarter. That profile would change substantially after 1930, but joining patterns influenced by family ties and residential proximity had emerged right away and would continue to shape the local party's development once Hitler took power. Two of the carpenters in particular were connected through family members; one ended up living briefly with the Villa Ammerhof's residents.[20]

Some of these early members were further connected through the skiing and folk revival communities. The Villa Ammerhof clique in particular, which soon emerged as the new chapter's officers, were also leading figures in both arenas. Bierling, too, was active in these cultural outlets; his uncles and father were founding members of one folk costume club, including his fellow Nazi carpenter's brother-in-law. These organizations offered an attractive opportunity for men whose migrant status or social marginality made leadership in prestigious clubs difficult. Newcomers could usually attain these desirable positions only through the integrative ties of marriage into a prominent local family or because of their high status as a bureaucrat, professional, or businessman. No wonder that early members of the still largely migrant-based Nazi party had congregated together in sporting and folkloric clubs, where they could find a warm welcome.[21]

Oberammergau's new Nazi group was poised to take advantage of the Radical Right's campaign against the Young Plan in Garmisch County. Discussions at an October meeting in the Rose Inn were positively received despite some interruptions; local Nazis made it clear that they would be offering a "sharp reckoning with the Socialists, Communists, and Catholics." Their party had made its first public mark in the village, but the timing was poor since local politics and preparations for the play would subsequently dominate communal activities.[22]

In this context, the "small but ever growing" group continued to attract mostly migrants as recruits. The influence of relatives and neighbors brought in new members. A brother of the putschists joined in April 1930, soon after their neighbor Hesse became a member and set up the entry of a close relative in September 1931. Master craftsman Hesse headed the socially diverse household community at the Villa Ammerhof, which included his wife and family, his working-class assistant Alzinger, and the elite professorial Ackermann family, as well as a cook and, in 1930, the Nazi carpenter who joined them. For centuries Bavarian households had included hired hands, maids, journeymen, and lodgers as "'housemates" of the core family, creating intimate linkages between workers and middle-class farmers or artisans. Hesse's companions formed a similarly close and cross-class relationship that continued even after the Ackermanns built their own home—on the villa's grounds.[23]

This mix of ersatz and real kinship led to a chain of joining that provided the chapter with its first leaders. Alzinger joined in 1929; Hesse in March 1930; and Ackermann followed in November 1930. In 1932 Ackermann's son was heading up Oberammergau's Hitler Youth (HJ). In April of that year mysterious ceremonies were held amid the Ammer valley's fog-enveloped evergreens; a report lauded Hesse's inspiring presence there as the local SA commander. His prominent position, combined with housemate Alzinger's role as chapter leader, complemented the younger Ackermann's leadership of the Nazi youth group. The Villa Ammerhof's extended family had cornered for itself the local party's most powerful positions.[24]

Before Hesse came on board in March 1930, a Lang who was descended from Guido's great-great-uncle Nicholas had signed up right after marrying a distant Bierling relative. His membership set off a chain of joining that included several men in Nicholas's line. However, initially Lang turned Nazi with another local who was related through his grandmother's marriage to an old Passion-playing family, as well as a migrant whose villa stood at the heart of the Station Quarter, across from the business run by Lang's new wife's uncle. With Hesse came three further members, a migrant day laborer and a professor of fine arts, Richard König, with his wife, the most socially prominent additions at this point despite being themselves recent arrivals.[25]

Alzinger emerged as his chapter's leading public figure that spring when he announced an upcoming meeting in the local newspaper. This event followed the acrimonious mayoral election, which might well have made further campaigning unpopular, as would the fast-approaching Passion season. Nevertheless, the group chose to take the bull by the horns with a talk about "Nazism, Christianity, and Internationalism." Their party's exclusively Aryan nature led to inclusion of the prohibition "Jews not welcome."[26]

A second notice launched an approach to wooing local voters that played on Catholic fears of Bolshevism, in this case by highlighting the pope's own hostility. The Nazi party alone was prepared to condemn the "Jewish" persecutors of so many Russians and to act as a "bulwark" against this threat from the East. Counteracting the general suspicion of their program's attitude toward Catholics, the group rejected its labeling as "hostile to the Church." With a dramatic flourish, they proclaimed that the "Soviets are mobilizing. Against whom?" During the crowded meeting that followed, the speaker was careful to present himself as a "believing Christian," and his "true conviction and genuine enthusiasm" were markedly successful. Moreover, the party planned more local meetings to draw in new members.[27]

Oberammergau's Nazis worked hard to promote their next event, a "mass protest assembly" against the Young Plan held in early April. Roughly two hundred attendees crowded into the Rose Inn, including a contingent from the Nazi stronghold in Murnau, as well as people from the immediate area; some sported their party uniforms. The speaker infuriated members of opposition parties, sparking interruptions by a "drunken" Catholic and a Socialist. SA members removed the two men, but the second expulsion led to an outright brawl with "beer mugs flying" that left two scrappers injured. Once the interrupted oration was concluded, the audience noisily expressed its appreciation and burst into the national anthem. These dramatic events merited a report in the Nazi publication, the *Völkischer Beobachter*, which bragged about the confrontation despite accusing their Socialist opponents of intending to pick a fight.[28]

Oberammergau's police chief reported that the audience in the Rose was made up "almost completely . . . of workers," some from outside the village. The whole affair had left "the order-loving population, especially the middle class. . . . enraged." As respectable citizens they worried that Nazi excesses would discourage Passion Play visitors. This was an anxious time in view of the fact that their economic future was on the line after so much investment in the upcoming season. It is hardly surprising, therefore, that most of the villagers withdrew into the magic circle of insiders, rejecting these intruders as disruptive and therefore dangerous threats to their community's well-being. They were fortunate that the Nazi dynamic slowed as the summer tourist season approached. A planned sequel to the Rose meeting did not take place. Instead, the local administration strongly discouraged political activities until after the election.[29]

Just before Oberammergau's Nazi chapter was founded in 1929, a new curate took up his duties. Johannes Fellerer became the radical group's leading Catholic opponent during the crucial years before 1933. His official role as Father Bogenrieder's assistant gave Fellerer a powerful platform from which to fight expressions of Nazi ideology in his parish. This privileged position was highlighted when Cardinal Faulhaber twice visited the village in the weeks following the raucous April meeting. His commanding public presence encouraged the Catholic activism that would bolster the BVP's cause as Germans prepared for a national election in September 1930.[30]

Beyond the normal ritual dramas of Catholic life, members of Oberammergau's charitable clubs had found special opportunities to show their flag. A group of journeymen set off in June 1929 for "Red" Hausham to campaign in this setting where Socialist and Nazi supporters had marched before them. Reportedly, this massive expression of solidarity easily outshone "the two hostile earlier events." Later, regional members of the Marian Congregation converged on Ettal that fall after a very active pilgrimage season.[31]

Catholic witness continued even during the 1930 Passion season. The Ammer valley was alive with rogation processions in the late Spring. Corpus Christi celebrations followed in mid-June, certainly "an overwhelming, powerful declaration of the Catholic people," as the newspaper later described them. The following month Ettal's monks opened their new outdoor Stations of the Cross on the Kienberg, a dramatic addition to the area's already well-developed Catholic landscape. The Wieskirche then hosted thousands of pilgrims at its Guardian Angel festival in September.[32]

Hundreds of thousands of Passion Play visitors arrived in Oberammergau to augment the stream of pilgrims, especially when they traveled in groups like the marching youths spotted by a reporter who thought they were Nazis. A Munich-based Jesuit had brought in these 450 flag-bearing "crusaders" to camp out at Ettal and attend the play. Catholic life in the Ammer valley could hardly have been more vibrant and outgoing in the months leading up to the September election. Looking back, the newspaper argued that the season had effectively refreshed the religious convictions of Catholic Bavarians. Britain's Cardinal Bourne went further when he compared the value of a trip to Oberammergau with a pilgrimage to Jerusalem. Catholics had in effect seized the initiative in a political struggle that they may not even have known was under way that busy summer.[33]

With the mid-September election approaching, BVP leaders advertised in their traditional manner by stressing the combined Christian and Bavarian loyalties that should once again draw believers to the polls. The party succeeded in improving its totals in Oberammergau, as was to be expected, given the swollen local electorate. However, of course, the Nazis scored remarkably well in the Passion Play village; the Socialists also recouped from a very low point in 1928. This election demonstrated how fragmented the party system was becoming, making it easy to gather up voters who had abandoned traditional allegiances.[34]

These electoral results were certainly skewed because the Passion season was still under way when people went to the polls. While an earlier vote taken while construction workers were still in Oberammergau would have favored the Left, the extraordinary Nazi vote in September relied on a new round of transients, the employees hired to serve visitors to the Passion Play. More than 1,300 "resident" voters showed up, almost twice the number in 1928 and far more than the 933 who had cast ballots in February's acrimonious mayoral contest. Nevertheless, the turnout was low, less than 50 percent, perhaps because overt campaigning had been effectively suppressed.[35]

More than 1,100 extra workers were in Oberammergau for the 1930 election, and these service personnel who staffed the village's buzzing hotels, guesthouses, restaurants, and retail establishments were mostly of voting age. An indication that they might have favored the Nazis comes from the county administrator's earlier argument that "in small communities factory workers, maids, day laborers, and the like voted in masses" against the Young Plan. Also suggestive are the mere ninety extra Nazi votes counted in July 1932, including ballots cast by visitors, as well as seasonal workers. There were enough new Nazi supporters in the village to replace the transient voters of 1930, but that left little margin for growth even at a time when massive support for the NSDAP made it Germany's single biggest political party.[36]

The startling 1930 election demonstrated how popular the Nazis were becoming both nationally and in Oberammergau. Nevertheless, their success at the polls did not reflect a noticeable flow of Passion Play actors into the party ranks. Only one NSDAP member appeared in the official program for 1930, which listed fifty-six players in the most significant roles.[37]

After the season was over, however, the electoral outcome may have persuaded prominent recruits to become Nazis. Professor Ackermann joined his erstwhile housemates, Alzinger and Hesse, together with his fellow artist, Zeno Diemer. A study in contrasts, these two middle-aged professors represented very different relationships to the village. Ackermann, a recent migrant from Protestant Saxony, was not well integrated into the community. Diemer, on the other hand, was a highly popular member of a respected old family who received the most votes for the 1930 Passion Committee. He must have played the part of the "good Nazi" uncovered by W. S. Allen in his classic study of the Nazi takeover. That is, his endorsement would have been influential when men from settled and even elite families began to join a year later. However, conditions were not yet ripe for a general move in this direction. Only one other man with deep connections to a prominent family followed Diemer's lead in 1930, artist/carver William Lechner, grandson of the first famous player of Judas.[38]

Oberammergau's Nazis continued to organize activities after the election, while their opponents remained inactive, as was usual in German party politics. First came a multimedia event made inexpensive for the unemployed. A couple of membership gatherings followed, one of which addressed the now substantial Nazi presence in the Reichstag. Much enthusiasm greeted a public talk in mid-January given by an actual parliamentarian who denounced Chancellor Heinrich Brüning. The speaker faced a questioner whose wild ideas revealed how deluded the opposition's leading politicians had become, according to the Nazi newspaper *Die Front*.[39]

After a lull in these efforts, a May meeting addressed the concerns of farmers and the middle class. Nevertheless, the party again lowered its entrance fees for the unemployed, as well as for those wounded in the war. By July Oberammergau's Nazis were returning to their leitmotiv, the party's struggle with the Bolshevik menace, at yet another meeting described as "Urgent!" They drew a full house made up of both locals and tourists.[40]

During this period migrants continued to dominate the Oberammergau party. Several were either members (or married to a member) of the growing evangelical contingent. A couple were bristling with hostility toward the villagers. The Saxon Ackermann had faced criticisms in the past and was soon to quarrel openly with the head of the local SPD. He clearly felt marginalized and rejected in his new home. Similarly, the bank clerk quarreled with influential locals, in his case the bank's managers for whom he worked. After their financing of a new venue for the Marksmen's Club had begun to founder, he felt himself blamed for the crisis. He lost his job and responded by accusing his employers of taking part in the "Berlin-centered new German ethos" now rampant in Oberammergau. This humble clerk's marginal social position was brutally exposed in the bank's public reply to this critique. He was "only" an "employee" and totally unqualified to give advice to insiders. After trying to survive as an insurance agent, he soon left the village. Both he and Ackermann experienced in no uncertain terms how alienating outsider status could become in a tight-knit community.[41]

Yet another Station Quarter resident joined in July 1931. Businessman Jakob Burger was experiencing "economic woes" that led him into the party's arms, as he later testified, but there were also social frustrations in the mix. Since migrating to Oberammergau as a child, Burger had often suffered the sting of humiliating marginalization. He was followed into the party by the husband of his neighbor Alfred Bierling's first cousin. This newcomer had served as an auxiliary policeman during the 1922 season. He set off a chain of joining that by mid-1933 involved all four of his wife's Bierling cousins and a migrant, live-in employee of one brother. Several more newcomers signed up in his wake, including two Ackermann business associates, one a prominent Protestant leader. By year's end there were forty-eight Nazis in Oberammergau.[42]

Late in 1931 the chapter began recruiting increasing numbers of young men from established families; perhaps it helped that Hitler was improving the party's social position by uniting with leading conservative politicians in the "Harzburg front," which was directed against Chancellor Heinrich Brüning. Additional insiders followed during the early months of 1932.[43]

A myriad of personal connections linked these new joiners both to established Nazis and to each other. Beyond intimate family ties were the close relationships created among schoolmates. Even Passion Play roles, which grouped men together as Jewish councilors, tradesmen, and the like, may have helped to connect a few joiners, as would club memberships. The chapter's public profile rose substantially when these well-connected villagers affirmed the Nazi cause; as the local newspaper proclaimed, "Now the great movement, which has already reached all regions of the entire state, has taken hold in our quiet mountain valley." Meanwhile, another article expressed horror at the thought that substantial numbers of actors in the recent Passion Play performances might succumb to the Nazi "heresy." Its author need not have worried, however, since only one recent recruit had been an important player, a leading apostle. Most were too youthful even to be veterans, and their roles in the 1930 play reflected the slow climb into major parts typical of Oberammergau's males.[44]

The Depression was steadily worsening as these young villagers chose to endorse a radical approach to Germany's many problems, thereby effectively rejecting both the official and the Catholic responses already under way in Oberammergau. They had experienced the gradual slide into hopelessness that began immediately after the Passion Play season was over. In fact, players had worried about their financial situation even earlier and petitioned for advances on their future earnings. That October, another petition signed by well over two hundred participants demanded the equalizing of all honoraria. By contrast, groups of players expecting higher than average remuneration argued for reclassification to increase their own pieces of the pie. They were right to focus on securing the maximum income from the 1930 performances since, by winter, unemployment was high and orders were slim. There were even some bankruptcies, possibly because of excessive business expansion in anticipation of the influx of visitors.[45]

By March 1931 a lead article in the newspaper was mentioning the need "to rescue Oberammergau" because of problems with tourism, as well as the general economic slump. Hopes raised by the high number of visitors over the summer were short lived as shrinking salaries threatened the incomes of Oberammergau's core clientele; the winter season appeared to be in danger. For struggling grocers the opening of two chain stores must also have been quite discouraging, although their response to these competitors was soon bolstered by help from the "Edeka" organization, which aimed at coordinating purchases by small retailers.[46]

For all Germans, the Depression continued to deepen in the final months of 1931. Oberammergau's rising unemployment and the series of bankruptcy proceedings brought these general experiences home in dramatic fashion. Only a confirmation that the bookings for guests at Christmastime were actually "good" seems to have alleviated this gloomy picture. However, forestry workers and laborers kept on losing jobs, and local artisans sat idle. The flow of applications for communal assistance continued unabated as winter turned to spring in the fateful year of 1932.[47]

Long traditions of self-help shaped the response of BVP Mayor Hans Mayr and his council to these disastrous economic circumstances. They drew on regional and national efforts to counteract unemployment and support the needy, including officially promoted winter assistance (WHW) campaigns. However, they also used every means at their own disposal to support locals who were seeking help, allocating commonly owned land, as well as lodging in community dwellings, to those needing homes. Increasingly, the council also paid unemployed families and even individuals, carefully assessing each application and deciding how best to help and with what conditions. They also exploited any work opportunities that would minimize the communal burden.[48] (Figure 3.1 shows Hans Mayr in his role as King Herod for the 1910 Passion Play season.)

Catholic charity paralleled official efforts to ease the Depression's impact on suffering citizens. Local journeymen housed thousands of their wandering colleagues in these difficult years. Women's Union members looked beyond supporting first-communion celebrations; in 1931 they trained their "small players" to put on a very well-received play at Christmas to raise money for

FIGURE 3.1. Hans Mayr, the future BVP mayor, poses in his costume as King Herod for the 1910 Passion Play season.

families in need. The Workers' Club similarly gave a Christmas party to lift the spirits of their "suffering brothers" and later gave out hundreds of marks' worth of food.[49]

Meanwhile, the Press Club stressed its cultural interests with a slideshow about "holy mountains" and opened a library in the village's newly established tourist center. Early in 1932 it sponsored a hair-raising talk about the Russian Bolsheviks' threat to organized religion; images of "destroyed or desanctified churches and monasteries" brought these dangers home, as did the knowledge that these same enemies were also "in our immediate neighborhood." Grateful for the warning, club members resolved to "arm" themselves for the fray.[50]

Beyond a very busy ritual round, Brother Conrad's beatification and two important anniversaries helped Catholics to make public witness of their faith. A slideshow in January 1931 honored Brother Conrad; in April villagers learned of an inexpensive opportunity to visit Padua for the seven hundredth anniversary of the highly popular Saint Anthony. Then Saint Elisabeth, patroness of the Franciscan Third Order, also enjoyed her seven hundredth anniversary; the order's yearly pilgrimage to Altötting was to mark this occasion, as would a play and later a slideshow about her in Oberammergau. Promising for their church's future was a huge gathering of regional youth at Ettal; processions of Marian worshippers in particular transformed the Kienberg into a "prayer mountain." The political implications of this rich Catholic life would soon become apparent during the extended campaign season of 1932.[51]

Escalating challenges from the Radical Right must have infuriated Oberammergau's local authorities and Catholic club members who were struggling to fight the Depression's negative effects. This threat to their long-established primacy in village affairs deepened with a series of three meetings held late in 1931 to spread the Nazi message. The first, titled "What Adolf Hitler Wants," stressed the Führer's role in setting his movement's priorities. The second responded to proliferating Bernhard Müller chain stores, which encouraged Garmisch County's Nazis to explore the new problems created by "warehouse, cooperative, and chain outlet." Aimed at inspiring resentment in the growing number of retailers who were staring disaster in the face, Oberammergau's talk was titled "The middle class at an end! Businesses bankrupt! What now?" Apparently, members of all social classes, both locals and area residents, found the topic noteworthy; the venue could not seat everyone who flocked to hear this reportedly sensible and unprovocative speaker.[52]

To build on this event's success, the local Nazis chose for their third meeting a speaker with substantial political clout in Bavaria, Munich city councilor Karl Fiehler. He was to address the still highly controversial issue of the party program's "point twenty-four" at an event called "National Socialism and Its Attitude toward Church and Religion." The chapter's leadership clearly realized that it would take more than creative plans for economic reform to woo middle-class recruits in Catholic Oberammergau. They needed to mount a frontal attack on the church officials' negative stance toward Nazi ideology, bolstered as it was by ambiguous language in the only part of the program that addressed the party's stance on religious matters.[53]

Reporting on this third meeting, the newspaper reviewed the entire twenty-five points, making its readers acquainted in the clearest possible terms with the party's anti-Semitic principles. Aims included "the excision of all foreign races (Jews) from the body politic," while, as far as religion was concerned, the key was to "fight the Jewish-materialistic spirit in and outside us." Turning to the event itself, the paper revealed that party members had chosen to explore the issues raised in point twenty-four by pitting their speaker, Fiehler, against the local champion of Catholic probity, Fellerer. They invited the curate because, as *Die Front* reported, he had recently preached against the "heretical" nature of Nazi ideology.[54]

This crowd-pleasing standoff created quite a stir. Fiehler adopted a political perspective that *Die Front* claimed had "incisively refuted the hateful attacks and slanders of the Center and BVP." However, Fellerer's lengthy response came from a theological point of view for which, according to the local reporter, Fiehler had no answers. Not so, according to *Die Front*'s account; the curate jumbled information from many varied sources with a strongly idiosyncratic twist, while Fiehler's well-received response displayed its own "conclusive logic." The Munich politician also questioned the Christian credentials of a Catholic party that was so thoughtlessly working with Marxists. According to this hostile story, the meeting took place in the Catholic journeymen's locale, where some members turned up to assist their curate and ensure that he got "a little applause." Nonetheless, Fiehler's arguments won the day for most of the audience, including journeymen who were "well on the way to converting to Nazism."[55]

Local reportage of this dramatic exchange turned controversial when the "interested" party wrote to challenge its unduly positive assessment of Fellerer's critique; the two viewpoints were as different as apples and oranges, so the curate could not defeat his Nazi opponent's logic. Incensed by this effort to play word games with his victory, Fellerer responded with questions about the reasoning capabilities of his erstwhile opponent. To give point twenty-four a clean bill of health would have required a convincing analysis of Nazi ideology's relationship with Christian doctrine, which Fiehler had failed to provide. So Fellerer had indeed established the validity of condemning Nazism as "heresy." The curate stressed in conclusion that Catholics should listen to their national leadership in rejecting National Socialism. It would hurt the village if many players in the 1930 Passion Play now deserted basic Christian principles.[56]

Curate Fellerer soon gained an influential ally when Ettal's Prior Ildefons wrote to explore the many ways in which Nazi ideology was at odds with his church's social policies and core beliefs. At risk were the continued protection of religious schools and parishes from state interference, as well as prohibitions on extramarital childbearing. Moreover, the words of Nazi ideologue Alfred Rosenberg demonstrated how far his party had strayed from Catholic belief in the Old Testament as an integral part of Holy Scripture. This, as Ildefons must have known, would be a particularly disturbing critique for the people of Oberammergau, whose playscript integrated Old Testament tableaux into the Passion story. The prior linked this scriptural crisis to the Germanic rejection of "Roman centralism [and] the international spirit." The Nazis had placed race at the center of their ideology and elevated it "way over religion." While careful to clarify that he was not criticizing the NSDAP's political program, Ildefons emphasized that Catholics could not in good conscience adopt their "worldview."[57]

His Nazi opponents seized the opportunity offered by Ildefons's arguments to set up another confrontation between their side and the Catholic majority. The prior was to debate "the basic principles of National Socialism" with Munich's Ferdinand Mössmer. However, a ban on political meetings caused them to delay this exchange until March 1932, at a time when the marathon electioneering season that would bring Hitler to power was already under way.[58]

Before Oberammergau was plunged into this electoral frenzy, a nationalistic ceremony linked contemporary torments to an earlier crisis that had evoked the fighting Germanic spirit. At the opening of a new gymnasium built for the venerable local club, much emphasis fell on the patriotic gymnastic movement founded by Father Jahn in response to the Napoleonic Wars. Then, too, a "reawakening" of the German people required training to strengthen their bodies. The architect of the building, Raimund Lang, spoke admiringly of the "magnificent gymnastic spirit" of that period, which had prevailed "over all party bickering and all tragic hardship." This was the same "apolitical" appeal to nationalism that Nazi propagandists would use in attacking what they saw as the Weimar Republic's narrowly partisan and selfish party system.[59]

The republican constitution made necessary a national election early in 1932. President Hindenburg's seven-year term was up, and this now ancient warrior faced a serious challenge for his job once Hitler chose to enter the fray. In Oberammergau, the BVP's local branch took up the president's cause and formed a special committee to mobilize votes on his behalf. Their well-advertised March 11 meeting featured discussion of the reasons "Why we vote [for] Hindenburg."[60]

Meanwhile, the Nazis propagandized and organized meetings, including the rescheduled Mössmer address titled "Economic Policy in the Next Reich." Two roomfuls of participants listened enthusiastically to an attack on both Chancellor Brüning and President Hindenburg himself, as well as on the reparations program. Despite his title, Mössmer managed to talk about mistaken perceptions of Nazism's religious principles; the newspaper later criticized his "attacks on absent people and parties." This evening ended in clear partisan fashion as the Nazi members present rose to sing the anti-Semitic Horst Wessel Lied in unison. Their party's hostility to Jews was also expressed openly on posters displayed in Oberammergau and elsewhere in Garmisch County. A locally produced version employed bold black lettering on brilliant red paper; the printed formula declared: "No Jews allowed."[61]

Once again a provocative Nazi gathering spurred a debate in the newspaper. Fellerer reiterated his attack on the "heresy" in point twenty-four, and then Mössmer countered by accusing the curate of falling back on well-worn party tactics. Only in 1930 had the Catholics taken aim at the Nazis, trotting out the "religion is in danger" canard. However, Hitler's *Mein Kampf* had already dispelled any fears of a Nazi onslaught. Finally, Fellerer shot back to reiterate his attack on Mössmer's point of view, stressing that "he can't get around the truth."[62]

In the same issue as Mössmer's spirited defense of the NSDAP platform, an elderly member of the Journeymen's Club reminded his readers that Oberammergau was the "Passion community"; their war memorial featuring Saint Michael also symbolized the church's fighting spirit. Now he had learned about a "swastika group" in the village. Nevertheless, voters should choose Hindenburg, trusting their church leadership rather than "a national-socialist speaker" on matters of religious policy; the Nazis, as well as the left-ists, were denied access to communion. This critic condemned support of Nazi ideology by Oberammergau's population in particular, although such a mistake might be tolerated "in Unterammergau or in Dachau." Nazi-inflicted damage would affect "the carving profession, tourism, and most of all the Passion Play."[63]

Two days later yet another protagonist jumped into the ring, probably Nazi member König. The professor's main thrust was to deny charges of NSDAP hostility toward Germany's mainstream churches. Rather, both sides agreed about the need to combat a whole range of troubling social problems. Return-ing to the issue of language, König defined himself as an empirical thinker rather than a believer in "doctrine, let alone a heresy."[64]

Curate Fellerer's repeated attacks also impelled Chapter Leader Alzinger to turn the tables on his opponents with yet another clever linguistic device. Yes, he agreed, Nazism was "poison" but only for leftists who were threatening the German people. Only the Nazis' efforts, as the bishop of Regensburg recog-nized, had saved Germany from the Communists. A second König entry prompted the newspaper to call for an end to the "controversy." Nevertheless, Fellerer insisted on "a last word." A battle between the various "heresies" just did not work; moreover, Alzinger had misrepresented the Regensburg bishop's position. The curate sarcastically concluded this debate by asking whether the "local leader of a party or the guardians of faith, the bishops" got to pronounce on doctrinal matters.[65]

By the time of the Alzinger-Fellerer exchange, President Hindenburg had defeated Hitler. This Nazi loss caused a flurry of debt payments in Garmisch County because of dashed hopes of an amnesty; the county administrator had discovered that "a number of the tardiest debtors" were in their camp. Testimony in Burger's denazification trial suggests that he may have been one of these dreamers; he liked the party program's section that called for the "breaking of interest slavery," hoping to save his property from bankruptcy.[66]

Nationwide, Hindenburg did not quite receive a majority, necessitating a second runoff election in April. Once again, both the Nazis and their various opponents reached out to voters in meetings, advertisements, posters, and flyers. One provocative Catholic message read: "Women, protect Germany from revolution and inflation! Vote Hindenburg!" Taking a less alarmist tack, Alzinger invited his "folk comrades" to a meeting about "people in need," where they could "gain clarity about what is what." However, only a minority of Oberammergau's electorate saw matters the Nazi way since Hindenburg received 905 votes to Hitler's 407. Overall, the county administrator concluded that the NSDAP was not firmly established in his area.[67]

This rash opinion was soon to be tested yet again in voting that followed hard on the second presidential election. Bavarian parliamentarians came up for a new term in late April 1932. The BVP pursued its traditional electoral strategy with patriotic expressions of resolve. Despite this aggressive approach, however, statewide they barely defeated their Nazi opponents, although in Garmisch County the Catholics pulled ahead more substantially. In Oberammergau meetings promoted the cause of established parties like the DNVP, but it was local Nazis who most effectively challenged the BVP; they received 434 votes to 506 votes for the Catholics. The NSDAP totals had held steady through three elections, but they did not rise above the swollen numbers for 1930.[68]

At the end of July, Bavaria's voters faced a national election to choose new Reichstag members. By then, important summer months had passed in which the depressed economy and consequent lack of jobs still dominated the political scene despite glimmers of hope. Some smaller communities were being overwhelmed by the support they provided for the unemployed, as well as the burden of an "enormous plague of tramps" traveling together along major roads. Ettal in particular had seen sixty-eight tramps on one day in May alone. A poaching case and a robbery using the cover of woods to grab a nun's purse underscored these problems. So did the suicide of a widower whose struggles to support eleven children had been foiled by the collapse of a Murnau bank.[69]

The picture in Oberammergau was in some ways even worse than for other Garmisch tourism centers. After the 1930 Passion Play season, the villagers had faced a difficult time recapturing their regular customers. Key was the provision of work, primarily on construction projects, for the ever-expanding number of the unemployed. On a smaller scale, the Saint Lucas Club was able to open a new display area for woodcarvers in the Passion Play theater, which would jumpstart this "strongly depressed industry."[70]

As the July election approached, a strongly supported Corpus Christi procession bolstered the BVP's cause, as did another to greet Cardinal Faulhaber at the yearly confirmation celebrations. In late June the journeymen celebrated twenty-five years of club life, an extra opportunity for a dramatic public expression of religious loyalties. Newspaper readers learned that, in training young craftsmen as good Catholic fathers, the club itself had become a sort of "family." Members had provided numerous entertainment activities over the years and assisted more than eight thousand traveling colleagues, half of them during the Depression. To mark their anniversary, fires burned on the Kofel in the shape of a cross and a "K" honoring the club's founder, Adolf Kolping. Neighboring clubs converged on Oberammergau for the event, turning the village into a sea of flags symbolizing the journeymen's aims, black for their Catholic faith and gold for the "golden heart of their founder." However, the official "K" had the added twist of a "Krieg," or war, against "soul-destroying" evils in such a highly charged moment.[71]

Defense of the Journeymen's Club inspired yet another public pronouncement by Curate Fellerer, which proved to be his swan song. For him, the club prepared Oberammergau's actors to express their "inner religious experience"; no one should underestimate its contribution to "the homeland and the Passion Play." With this final thrust, Fellerer left the village, a fortuitous move, as he later saw it, since out of passionate commitment to the Passion Play he might have challenged the Nazi regime. However, during the summer of 1932, Fellerer still raised an authoritative voice in favor of loyalty to Catholic institutions as the July election approached.[72]

Meanwhile, many of Garmisch County's voters were losing faith in such traditional thinking, given the extremity of the crisis. Even solid supporters of the middle-of-the-road parties were wavering. To exploit their uncertainty the extreme parties, including both Communists and Nazis, held meetings all around the region.[73]

In early June Oberammergau's Nazi chapter attracted more than three hundred attendees at one of these meetings. Then, a month later, it featured one of Diemer's sons, a successful engineer. His enthusiastic presentation underscored the personal bonds so central in drawing recruits to the group. Having returned to his ancestral home, Diemer was happy to "be able to introduce national socialist ideas to his countrymen." Ranging over a variety of topics, he pushed his audience's anti-Communist buttons and defended the party's approach to Christianity as the "renewal of a German culture." His Catholic opponents should not misrepresent Nazism as "hostile to religion," which was just the BVP's last-gasp effort to preserve its voter base. Rather, because it now enjoyed a strong Nazi presence, the "Passion Play village" could fight back against "Communist propaganda." This talk by an influential speaker launched his camp's counterattack on Fellerer's key weapon, Catholic concerns about perversion of the Passion Play. More than one party could protect Oberammergau from a future replete with threats to the community's traditional way of life.[74]

The Nazis held more meetings in late July. At one, the group explicitly targeted "the entire workforce of the brow and the fist" with a discussion about the Third Reich's plans for workers. Their BVP opponents fought back, in part with a big "protest meeting" against current administration policies, which was called by Garmisch County's Christian unions. To urge voters into the booth on July 31, one speaker highlighted the distress of elderly pensioners upon learning how badly their government had shortchanged them.[75]

The BVP continued to play on regional loyalties at a well-attended meeting held a week before election day, which highlighted the idea that protecting Catholic interests meant preserving the power of individual German states. The assembled company was infuriated by an intervention from a newly minted Nazi recruit, Raimund Lang, the future mayor. His unwelcome "dogmatic interpretations and criticisms" galvanized Father Bogenrieder himself into responding "energetically" despite the fact that he had no track record of speaking in this sort of public gathering. During the meeting, fears were expressed about a new round of cultural oppression by a strong central government. They could only have been reinforced when Bavarian Minister President Heinrich Held accused the Nazis of returning to antipapal policies that would precede an attack on Protestants as well.[76] (Figure 3.2 reproduces a photograph of architect Raimund Lang taken sometime after his debut as a Nazi spokesman.)

Two days before the election, another speaker at a BVP meeting held in Ettal referred to the postwar period of defeat and revolution. He then accused the Nazis of relying on "promises and . . . marching" to mislead voters into accepting them as the region's saviors. Hitler's poor leadership and "agitating [and] inflammatory" partisanship threatened the common good, he stated. That ended the Catholic efforts, but by July 31 their loyal electorate had been effectively primed.[77]

Meanwhile, the local Nazis hastened to counteract Father Bogenrieder's support for a Catholic speaker at the height of these electioneering efforts. While this final meeting was aimed at clarifying "the meaning of the vote for

FIGURE 3.2. Raimund Lang, NSDAP member and Oberammergau's mayor, works on an architectural project.

the German folk," the evening was to end with a discussion of the crucial question, "Can the Oberammergau man vote for Hitler?" Billed as a direct refutation of Bogenrieder's point of view, their last-ditch play for votes was delivered by Raimund Lang.[78]

During this lead-up to the July 31 election, Oberammergau's Nazis also made use of their small but active SA group. Headed by Commander Hesse, a man who, with his "chiseled" features and "white-gray frizzy hair," emerged as a much-admired leader, they had evolved into a "troop" of more than twenty men. These militants traveled by bicycle or truck to reinforce the Nazis' efforts in their region. Since most were unemployed, they could be sent "all over where they were needed," although the authorities foiled their plans to drive through the Ammer valley and blast out their radical message.[79]

A month earlier, Hesse had attended a summer solstice ceremony arranged by Martin Ackermann's tiny youth group. This comradely event held in woods made mysterious by gloomy early summer weather captured the "sunlessness" of the "German people." Struggling to get a fire going because of the damp, the HJ welcomed their chapter's leader. Then Ackermann "delivered the marvelous poem 'Summer Solstice' clearly out into the wild night." The German national anthem preceded a "fire speech" by Alzinger and the rousing tones of the Horst Wessel Lied. Between these HJ members and the SA, Oberammergau's Nazis were able to rely on a motivated group of young men as they worked to make Hitler their chancellor that July.[80]

The NSDAP used the fate of these youthful Germans as leverage in a final appeal to Oberammergau's voters; they could "help to build a new future for the youth in a free united Reich." Not to be outdone, the BVP also advertised in the newspaper's last preelection issue: "People of Oberammergau, awake! The crucial day draws near. Everyone must go to vote on July 31." Both sides were well aware that a Nazi majority would propel Hitler into unquestioned leadership, so they pulled out all the stops to get their supporters to the polls. The Nazis even deployed Storm Troopers to menace the voters as they went in to cast their ballots.[81]

The election was held as the busy social round of an Oberammergau summer continued unabated. Consequently, while almost 70 percent of the eligible resident voters turned out, they were joined by more than four hundred visitors. The outcome was a success for local Catholics since the BVP came out on top with fully 40 percent of the votes, while a grab bag of parties led by the SPD attracted another quarter, and the Nazis mustered only a third. Nevertheless, in Garmisch County as a whole the Nazis pulled slightly ahead. And nationwide they had become by far the largest party in the Reichstag, which would have made their leader the natural choice for Germany's chancellor under normal circumstances. But Hitler did not emerge as chancellor that summer, which must have been quite a relief for his opponents in Oberammergau.[82]

When Raimund Lang debuted as the local Nazi spokesman in late July, he was one of three prominent villagers who chose to join the party before the national election, each from a particular line of the old Lang, Zwink, and Rutz families. Lang was the son of a leading figure in Oberammergau's political and religious life and brother to deputy mayor and play director Georg Lang. He had returned home in 1928 to work as an architect on the new Passion Play theater.[83]

The other two recruits, who came from entrepreneurial families, also enjoyed political connections. The spacious villa that was frequented by royalty and became Cook's headquarters had been built by Zwink's grandfather; his father was the successful merchant who had challenged Mayor Mayr in 1930 after years heading the Citizens' Club. Rutz owned a prominent shop on the central square, and he had expressed his commitment to promoting local business interests by playing a leading role in the Tourism Club. Moreover, after the 1929 election, he replaced his socialist brother Leo on the council, so he became its first member to join the Nazi party.[84]

These three influential citizens joined Diemer and Lechner as Nazis of real importance in the village. They also represented the Passion-playing section of the population, although none had held a major part in 1930. Curate Fellerer recognized the significance of such influential men joining the anti-Catholic camp when he addressed Raimund Lang shortly before the architect's official coming out as a Nazi. Never one to mince words, Fellerer begged Lang "not to become a populist seducer and a traitor to your home community." However, this admonition missed the crucial point already featured in young Diemer's stirring talk. Lang saw himself and his new party as protectors of Oberammergau's unique identity, so he was impervious to fearmongering about Nazi threats to their play. He was a Guido Lang sort of Catholic who did not feel compromised by supporting a party other than the BVP. What mattered was the community's future as the Passion Play village. Moreover, to secure that future, as well as their own, Lang and his fellow joiners belonged to a group of men who were developing a plan that would also solve Oberammergau's unemployment problems—all in one fell swoop.[85]

Their hopes centered on an old idea first raised by Diemer's father, Josef, before the 1870 Passion season. At that time, he argued for attracting visitors to Oberammergau with a spa hotel and lake, but without success. Subsequently, as Guido Lang and other villagers worked to build up the local tourism industry, this concept lay dormant. However, it proved enormously attractive to the Nazi group around Lang, most of whom had inherited their interest in promoting Oberammergau as a venue for tourists. Developing a large spa complex would even allow them to separate their village's economy from Passion seasons since the local economy would no longer depend heavily on income from visitors to the play. This would shield the tradition of fulfilling the communal vow from excessive commercialization, which had attracted hostile criticism, most recently during the 1930 season.[86]

Two local men had already sought the community's support for a spa project in 1931; they made blueprints available for public inspection and seem to have gained some financial support from the council, but their plans never got off the ground. Then, in May 1932 the Tourism Club met to plot a promotional strategy for the village's regular tourism industry after the interruption caused by the 1930 Passion season. In this context the spa question resurfaced, but, so went the argument, the times dictated that private investors should underwrite such an expensive project. In response, tourism director Hermann Schilling publicly raised the issue once again. This time the village's leading administrator, Josef Raab, a councilor who also headed the Tourism Club, as well as actively campaigning for the BVP, harshly admonished Schilling for trying unsuccessfully to throw "sand in the eyes" of newspaper subscribers.

Raab had been forewarned by the previous debacle in 1931 to emphasize the "risk" posed by such a project.[87]

Raab's cautious response to the Schilling initiative did not dissuade Raimund Lang from spearheading his group's effort to make their spa project a reality along the lines of Josef Diemer's original plan. Extensive architectural plans, a mock-up, and a painting contributed by no less a man than Josef's son Zeno were soon available for public view. According to Lang, this display attracted the victims of the Depression, who could readily appreciate its many advantages. In particular, the requirement that patients stay locally in order to access treatment would, he suggested, make a very favorable impact on Oberammergau's hotels and pensions. Lang himself emerged in this context as both an expert architect who could describe the nuts and bolts of this complicated project to his fellow villagers and a leader whose vision would rescue his beleaguered community from its unemployment crisis.[88]

Despite Lang's extensive efforts, his spa faction soon came up against the opposition already faced by earlier planners. While their project excited those eager to find work for local jobseekers, it was still a huge financial challenge, and so the councilors suggested that Lang apply for state help to raise the needed funds. Only later did it become entirely clear that the mayor would not tolerate any use of communal income.[89]

Meanwhile, questions about the cultural impact of a "Bad Oberammergau" had surfaced. Some worried that such a project would undermine the Passion Play village's special nature, a charge countered in the newspaper by another leading Nazi, Professor Ackermann. Critics had mistakenly feared dragging Oberammergau down into the "mundane" entertainment world, whereas in truth the village's special values would dovetail nicely with a medical facility. Striking back quickly against the professor's accusation that a "lack of vision" was blocking this wonderful plan, a clearly offended Administrator Raab excoriated him for belittling the rightly cautious official approach to indebtedness.[90]

Zwink then weighed in on the side of the spa faction by taking a historical look at the evolution of tourism in the area, which was providing much competition during the nine-year periods between Passion Play seasons. He wielded a host of statistics to illustrate his argument that Oberammergau should benefit from new trends exploited by nearby communities. Zwink added that people tended to linger in spas, as the example of Bad Tölz illustrated.[91]

Rutz, his new Nazi colleague, followed with yet another supportive article. His aim was to diffuse worries that communal financing of a spa might undermine the all-important access to personal income derived from playing the Passion. Reminding opponents that they were actually fulfilling the communal vow, Rutz nevertheless mentioned the possibility of using the next Passion season's income to handle needed debt payments, while the spa project itself was a potential moneymaker. He added that giving up on the spa plans "might in itself negatively affect the community and its inhabitants." He deliberately echoed Raab in suggesting that there were "responsible people" who worried about failing to pursue Lang's project.[92]

This debate took place late in 1932, when the councilors were looking back at several years of disastrous employment statistics for the village; they were still struggling to finance ever-greater welfare obligations. In this context, none of the spa faction's arguments swayed them or Mayor Mayr when they refused to contemplate any public financing for the project. Nevertheless, for a while, this remarkably ambitious set of plans provided a glimmer of hope for a better economic future in Oberammergau.[93]

While Lang's spa faction was developing its plans to cope with the Depression, Germany's desperate citizens had experienced yet another national election after Nazi and Communist representatives together closed down the newly seated Reichstag. The economic context for this round of voting in November 1932 was still discouraging in Oberammergau. In particular, the leading hotel's new owner was struggling with threats of bankruptcy as tourism languished. However, a big roadworks project was starting to improve the unemployment picture, allowing councilors to divert youthful welfare recipients into paid labor. Federal incentives for employers were emerging as well, suggesting light at the end of the Depression's dark tunnel.[94]

It was at this point that Oberammergau's citizens gathered to discuss a special Jubilee Passion season in 1934, an idea that received the approval of all present. This was a momentous decision because, as the councilors elaborated, two years of unemployment and business slowdowns had been undermining their ability to bring in adequate public funds. Once again, the communal vow rescued them in the face of great suffering, and they were soon raising money by pledging anticipated income from their special season.[95]

In leading up to these November elections, Raimund Lang's very public role in the spa campaign must have been quite a boon to the Nazi campaigners. Identification with a project that would bring such clear benefits to the villagers surely bolstered their cause, which immediately after the July election had not looked entirely hopeful. In fact, the paucity of Nazi activities had encouraged the county administrator to suspect the "beginning of a decomposition" in their ranks.[96]

Once the campaign heated up, however, the Nazis sprang into action as the "liveliest" political players. A "military sporting exercise" held with area

SA members drew local men into Kohlgrub for the event and subsequent festivities. One late October night, they organized another exercise on the Laber near Oberammergau, mobilizing 180 mostly uniformed men who ranged around the immediate area and supported Nazi meetings. These and other similar events caused the county administrator to fear "a kind of preparation for a 'March on Rome.'"[97]

In Oberammergau an SA coup to overthrow the village leadership may actually have been discussed at a meeting overheard by a police officer crouching beneath a dais. Burger, now head of the local Motorstorm unit, led talk about challenging the "black hordes," but Hesse judged these plans to be premature. As the observer understood it, "the whole Passion Play, . . . the culture of the Oberammergau community," was at stake. Hesse himself later denied any knowledge of this meeting; he also described the dais as so low that the officer must have been scrabbling in the dust. It is not clear that the threatening exchange ever took place.[98]

Certainly, the local Nazi group did organize public events designed to galvanize voters in the days leading up to the November election. After bringing Hitler himself to Oberammergau, at least in the form of a movie, they featured a member of the Bavarian parliament. The Socialists also held a couple of "free" meetings, including one for their paramilitary formations and a discussion of "people's rights against dictatorship." However, the BVP still remained the primary opponents of the insurgent Nazis.[99]

This time, the Catholic party had lost its most effective spokesman with Curate Fellerer's departure; in good Christian spirit he ended his tumultuous days in Oberammergau with these public words: "I greet my friends. I also greet my enemies." Nevertheless, the faithful continued to fight the good fight. September brought another very successful Guardian Angel festival in the Wieskirche and advance notice of a regional Workers' Club conference to be held in Oberammergau. Also significant were large advertisements for a gathering in Weilheim of Upper Bavarian Catholics to defend "God and homeland." In October the Women's Union organized a huge pilgrimage and assembly in Ettal; more than four hundred women converged there to visit the cult figure. In this volatile moment when fears of leftist revolution had reemerged, the keynote speaker reminded local women of their initial commitment to fight Communism in 1919. Later that month a countywide festival for Catholic youth took place in Garmisch.[100]

Building on these invigorating events, the BVP placed a large advertisement in the newspaper for a Munich speaker, whose topic once again stressed the traditional Catholic themes: "For rule of law and freedom! Hometown, folk, and faith!" These themes were reflected in a bold poster featuring a large and typical Alpine-garbed male with the familiar blue-and-white flag. A further advertisement urged voters to "think Bavarian; act Bavarian." The importance of voting also became an issue at the regional workers' assembly attended by Father Bogenrieder. Oberammergau's Catholics had once again been primed to support their party when they entered the polls.[101]

That November, the BVP clearly benefited from its constituency's ongoing loyalty since it remained the village's largest voting block. Nonetheless, their totals fell by 185 votes from their July high. The local Nazis lost proportionally more votes and trailed the Catholics by almost 200. Their leftwing opponents, by contrast, retained all but eighteen voters, while the small number of Communist ballots actually rose marginally. Worst hit was the DNVP, which saw more than two-thirds of its previous support evaporate.[102]

This general drop in voting totals traces back in large part to the electorate's decline from the high numbers in 1930 and July 1932. It was November, a normally inactive time of year for the tourism industry. However, the economic situation was even more extreme than normal, and so the presence of both visitors and temporary workers was minimal. Consequently, these numbers represent as accurate a picture as possible of the settled population's voting decisions. For the most part, the totals achieved by the warring parties did not alter the balance of power among all of the major camps. It would take the external pressure of Hitler's takeover as chancellor to reconfigure the political relationships in Oberammergau.

Despite a substantial drop in support for the NSDAP in November's voting totals, Germany's top politicians eventually decided that Hitler should lead a new national administration. Meanwhile, Oberammergau's councilors worked to bring their community through the last Depression winter. In some ways the picture still looked grim. Lang's spa project was going nowhere, and retailers faced a disastrous Christmas season. For Oberammergau's hotels and guesthouses this crisis carried right on into the winter season. Nevertheless, employment was finally improving because of ongoing work projects. Moreover, the leading hotel announced its reopening just before Christmas.[103]

At the same time, plans for their Jubilee Passion season rolled ahead, with contentious elections for the special committee taking place in mid-December. Mayor Mayr discussed the upcoming season with Cardinal Faulhaber, who supported using the play "in the interest of Catholic faith and the community." Immediate efforts included the Marian Congregation's tenth-anniversary celebrations and various Christmas events hosted by Oberammergau's charitable clubs. The round of social events then proceeded quietly into the New Year and Carnival.[104]

Since support for the Nazi party had sunk so noticeably from the July highpoint, it was surely impossible to imagine how quickly the tables would turn after the seizure of power in January 1933. Local life was also very engrossing, so the momentous events taking place in Berlin did not immediately have much impact. The newspaper found Hitler's accession to power newsworthy but not extraordinary. Even the council did not give this latest political shift any attention, in part because its members were busy discussing a potential national initiative to fund a number of highly desirable projects, including Lang's spa, while still dealing with their extensive welfare problems. Similarly, Passion Committee members were preparing for their upcoming season with barely a hint of political engagement; only the committee's suspension for three months in the spring points to an unusual disruption of this crucial local institution.[105]

Early in February the impending political onslaught first made its way into Oberammergau when the now victorious Nazi chapter advertised a "large public rally" at which District Leader Wagner would address the topic of the moment, "Germany's rebirth." Although the chapter urged its "folk comrades [to] appear en masse," Wagner's talk drew only about 250 listeners, 70 or so fewer than had heard him speak the previous June. This time he stressed Hitler's new role as chancellor and his "government's plan." However, Wagner once again used the anti-Communist leitmotiv, stressing his Führer's commitment to "completely eradicate Bolshevism in Germany." The local Nazis then fell back on the seductive medium of radio, announcing opportunities to hear Hitler speak. Yet, while in late February local SA men were reportedly marching in Munich to mark their Führer's visit, there is no sign of a showy outdoor event in Oberammergau despite the tradition of public witness so well developed there.[106]

National politics finally impacted Oberammergau's now weary voters when they faced yet one more election in early March. This was surely a chance for the opponents of the new regime to mobilize against their Nazi foes. Consequently, the BVP leapt into the fray with a discussion of "national politics and national elections." Raimund Lang angered the party faithful at this event by intervening forcefully for the Nazi side. Meanwhile, his chapter went on the attack against its major enemy, announcing a talk about political Catholicism. They questioned those who were supposedly inflating the level of support for Catholic parties in the last election and once again attacked the BVP's willingness to build bridges to the "godless" Left. Hitler had rejected "such parties that wanted to destroy Christianity," so those Catholics in Oberammergau who wanted to avoid a Bolshevik takeover should vote for the Nazi ticket, they maintained.[107]

Soon news of the Reichstag fire was dominating the local headlines, together with stories that promoted Hermann Göring's security-tightening responses to a "civil war" threatened by the "Communist terror." Then, right before the March 5 election, a BVP advertisement entreated the local electorate to support its cause and maintain "the citizens' freedom against tyranny and party dictatorship." They would fight for "peace and order in our beloved Fatherland." In addition, Raab circulated a flyer stressing the Nazi threat to the "Christian religion . . . and the Christian education of youth." He also expressed his fears for a coming war and "cultural politics" that would undermine the cause of playing the Passion. His opponents blasted the BVP as soft on Communism and disloyal to German unity. "Only two movements exist now, . . . Bolshevism or National Socialism," and the NSDAP was the party for Christians. Both of the contending parties made radio addresses available. The Nazis again featured Hitler, who, building on Communist "guilt" for the fire, spoke about "the danger of Bolshevism."[108]

Finally, a Nazi flyer struck at the BVP establishment by using the tried-and-true tactics of the citizens' clubs. As a group of citizens themselves, they accused their opponents of "party political opposition . . . [and] party political divisiveness." BVP operatives had used a whole bag of dirty tricks to pressure the electorate, in particular the known Nazis who had even been threatened with "exclusion from the Passion Play." Continuing to attack their opponents in terms of the play so much on the minds of the villagers that spring, the flyer accused BVP leaders of failing to act in good Christian fashion to forward the "interests of a Catholic Passion village." Other long-standing residents who rejected politics as usual could protect their inherited commitment. As Nazis, they also appreciated the play's value as "German cultural property," which Hitler himself had recognized and would continue to support as a "bastion against Bolshevism."[109]

This masterpiece of electoral rhetoric wove together fears about both local and national issues by linking the play's future to the ever-present Communist menace. It once again explicitly refuted Fellerer's campaign polemics about the threat that Nazism posed to the special mission of the Passion Play village. Rather, given the prominent citizens who had taken up the Nazi cause, the curate was mistaken to assume that Catholics who rejected Nazi ideology were the only acceptable guardians of local traditions. Pro-Nazi villagers could quite plausibly challenge entrenched politicians over the right to take charge of communal affairs.

The BVP's local leaders were unable to answer this flyer's many accusations until after the election. Then they responded energetically by blaming the attack on "a few or perhaps only . . . one member of the NSDAP," whose "hate makes you blind." Nonetheless, the die was already cast, and both the Nazis and their conservative partners had doubled their votes over the November totals. The Nazis were now the strongest local party since the BVP lost votes. The left-wing parties fared a little better, down a mere three votes between them. Most of the voters were locals this time around, and the turnout was an impressive 79 percent. At least two hundred extra villagers, presumably Nazi supporters, had gone to the polls. Nevertheless, Hitler's opponents had retained most of their voting strength in the area. It was the local political scene's diversity that emerged in this last relatively free election until the end of the Nazi regime.[110]

Four days later, a new Nazi administrator was appointed to run the Bavarian state. Franz Ritter von Epp was well loved by local men like Raimund Lang and Burger, who had served under him in the Free Corps. They must have rejoiced at his new role, although Minister President Held fought the change, and only days later could Epp assume his position. Another advantage for Oberammergau was the concurrent appointment of District Leader Wagner to head Bavaria's Interior Ministry.[111]

Now that the Nazis were in charge, they flew swastikas to announce the power switch and emphasize their pride in the ascendant German nation. Locally, Hesse led an official delegation of Storm Troopers who cornered the mayor to ensure that he, too, would countenance raising a Nazi flag in Oberammergau; Mayr asked only to keep the Bavarian colors alongside. Soon these two potent but potentially divergent symbols waved above the town hall and other important buildings. Swastikas also appeared in surrounding communities.[112]

Meanwhile, despite their electoral victory over the BVP, the Nazi chapter unleashed a series of accusations against local Catholic leaders whose shady practices during the campaign had included an effort to frighten voters by pretending that "when a Hitler comes to power, the priests [will be] hung; the old women and the small children will be killed, . . . [and] inflation, misery, and war are on their way." How, they asked, could the Nazis be accused of "blind hate" by so hateful a group? Ending on a threatening note, they announced that no longer could the BVP "pursue inflammatory rhetoric, slander as well as self-interested politics."[113]

This menacing public statement must have reinforced the message sent by the disappearance of regional left-wing politicians and, briefly, a couple of suspected local Communists, welcome as that news might also have been as an anti-Bolshevik measure. The house searches for "weapons, papers, and badges" that took place locally that spring would also have reinforced this bifurcated message. However, these dangerous indignities were not restricted to leftists. Raab later described how county-level SA and police had combed his living and work areas. Fortunately for this BVP activist, he had already gotten rid of any incriminating evidence. Later memories were that leading Nazis took part in searches, reflecting the traumatic nature of this unstable time early in the Third Reich's first year.[114]

Oberammergau's new masters also moved to claim all public spaces, initiating years of public witness with a "celebratory patriotic rally" to mark the freshly elected Reichstag's first meeting. The flickering light of torches illuminated imperial and Bavarian flags hanging above the streets, through which wound a huge procession accompanied by the local band. Village authorities, club representatives, Storm Troopers, and the HJ marched together. Then, Mayor Mayr led a tribute to Oberammergau's fallen soldiers, echoing in his remarks the Nazi theme of commitment to cooperative politics aimed at Germany's regeneration. At the subsequent party, SS and SA members who were present sang the Horst Wessel Lied. Two days later the Reichstag empowered Hitler as Germany's executive and legislative ruler.[115]

These local Nazis were riding high in the first months after their seizure of power, but they still had much to do in order to "coordinate" local culture and politics. Even the council was only partially Nazified after the March election, while BVP Mayor Mayr was actually confirmed in office that April, if only for a short extra stint.

Meanwhile, new recruits flowed into the NSDAP. Chapter 4 examines Oberammergau's Nazis, particularly the core party members, most of whom remained in the village throughout the twelve years of the Third Reich. Some of the group's "old fighters," like their first leader, Ernst Nagler, had been transitory residents; men passing through the village still swelled the local chapter's ranks after 1933. However, plenty of joiners were the settled villagers, if often newcomers, whose stories best characterize the Nazi experience in their home community.

4

Joiners

When Hitler patronized Oberammergau's Passion Play in 1934, he distorted postwar assessments of the local Nazi presence, a misconception further complicated by dramatic changes in the population. Recent migrants and refugees from Eastern Europe swelled the list of party members identified by their American occupiers, leading to deceptive conclusions about the community's true relationship with the Third Reich. A fair judgment requires identifying the core of settled residents at the heart of the local chapter, separating them from the various newcomers whose Nazi affiliation took shape in other contexts. Then, piecing together all of the available biographical details about these joiners makes it possible to weave them back into the village's social fabric.

Information about the people who became Oberammergau's Nazis comes from a list generated to establish the guilt or innocence of players for a potential Passion Play season in 1946. Its details about party membership were helpfully limited by the exclusion of new residents, but many joiners who had perished, mostly as wartime casualties, were also missing. However, additional members appear in later overviews, in newspaper accounts of the chapter's activities, and in the death notices that mounted as World War II progressed.

Further information can be gleaned from the regime's membership card files largely preserved by the victorious Allies. Individual party numbers and dates of entry reflect the actual sequence of joining after the local group's initiation in 1929. These figures tell a clear story, but they also raise interesting questions about relationships among the members. Sometimes spouses or brothers joined together and were given consecutive numbers, but that leaves the question of unrelated recruits whose numbers were similarly juxtaposed. Was it by chance, for example, that two artist-professors, the despised outsider Otto Ackermann and the popular insider Zeno Diemer, were registered in sequence? Other such clusters point to connections among joiners, both before 1933 and afterward.

Beyond the tantalizing information preserved in these cards, an occasional insight is provided by an individual member's pass, which typically includes a photograph. One belonged to the already elderly SA Commander Arno Hesse, who, as a longtime activist in the Folk Costume Club, chose to be photographed in local attire. However, because the card files are incomplete, they provide no record of other joiners, leaving unanswered questions about their status.

Many pieces fell into place when a new treasure trove of data about Oberammergau's Nazis emerged: membership lists assembled by the party's secretary in 1933 and 1937, together with sign-in sheets for a series of meetings in the regime's first months. While much of this information was no surprise, these records did introduce new people into the equation who had fallen through the cracks of all other sources. Signatures in so many different hands are challenging to read; only with difficulty do some scrawls become legible with the help of powerful magnification. However, they repay the trouble taken to examine them since they connect to historic events described in other contexts. Of particular interest are flimsy sheets for a dramatic meeting in the Weisses Rössl Inn, where party members turned on each other just weeks before the bloody Night of the Long Knives.

These once-dominant Nazi activists left many signs of their presence in Oberammergau. Next to the leading junta's Villa Ammerhof, which has fallen into disrepair, the residence built by Ackermann still sports the professor's mural connecting his old and new home landscapes. Similarly, Professor Diemer's house retains paintings of his namesake saints, Michael and Zeno. Photographs abound like the one that records the Oberammergau Werdenfels Corps' anti-Communist foray into Munich. In another snapshot the youthful Alzinger wears a Hitler-style moustache as he poses with the village football team, while other party members appear in a group view of the Folk Costume Club's dancing troupe. Oberammergau's Nazis have certainly left their mark in the local store of historical memories.[1]

Identifying the enemies of these local Nazis completes the picture of the warring sides. Public records for the Third Reich's twelve years are naturally rich in details about supporters, while Catholics and leftists disappear largely into the shadows, with some exceptions when they caught the attention of authorities. Stories did emerge from denazification testimonies about confrontational efforts, including the actions of leading villagers who had lost faith in the Nazi party but nonetheless remained members. A richly bound handwritten chronicle and related documents record the efforts of local Catholics to maintain a semblance of normal parish life in the face of ever more oppressive limitations. Personal memories also illuminate private levels of disaffection and defiance. It is possible to separate Nazis and dissidents despite the complex mixing of their daily lives.

At the heart of this clash of ideologies sat various descendants of Nicholas Lang. One was Raimund, who had emerged as the major Nazi spokesman; his second cousin Anton was continuing his leadership of Catholic associational activities. Both men and their factions were intent on leading the village through the Depression, Raimund's by invigorating the local economy after a Nazi takeover, Anton's through their religiously inspired charitable enterprises. What both groups still shared was their love of Oberammergau and an active involvement in communal life, which intertwined Nazi and Catholic loyalists in a myriad of organizational and social projects. This was a delicate balance that the aggressive tactics adopted by Raimund's eventual nemesis, Motorstorm Commander Burger, would soon threaten to undermine.[2]

"Old fighters" who became Nazis before 1933 later referred to the many joiners in the first heady months of Hitler's ascendancy as "March fallen" and "May violets." In Oberammergau, a handful became members right away, over a hundred more by May 1, together with several dozen from outlying communities. Others filled the ranks of the SA and the Nazi women's group (NSF). Patterns of joining already established by the Nazi contingent helped to draw them in, but there were naturally also new motivations driving those who took the plunge now that Hitler was German chancellor. The party still brought together men and women from all social levels, mixing professionals with artisans and day laborers, established citizens with newcomers and transients, Protestants with Catholics, war veterans with untested youths. Political and confessional loyalties restrained the remaining adult population from open support of the Nazi cause, a source of much dissatisfaction for local leaders.[3]

With great fanfare the chapter held a big meeting for its growing membership in early April; the Weisses Rössl Inn teemed with Nazis, including Storm Troopers in uniform. Chapter Leader Alzinger announced his subordinate officers, all "old fighters," albeit a mix of settled and migrant villagers. Raimund Lang was to be his deputy and propaganda chief. Even Burger joined these inner circles, his loyalty rewarded with a post defending middle-class interests.[4]

Later that same month the council was officially "coordinated." All three major parties, the NSDAP, the BVP, and the SPD, had to present slates of candidates. However, seat distribution followed the March 5 election results, so the Nazis received five, the Catholics four, and the Socialists only one. Heading the Nazi list were three recent joiners; only the fourth and fifth candidates were early members, including Alzinger himself. The Catholics presented a slate of eight men headed by Administrator Raab. Alois Lang, who, like Raab, was a current BVP councilor, made the cut, but Anton Lang's son Karl, in his first political foray, did not. Only one Social Democrat, Hans Daisenberger, was to serve from a short list of three.[5]

This restructuring process over, the new councilors had to choose between two mayoral candidates. The Nazis nominated Raimund Lang, while Mayr ran again and received the support of all of the Catholic councilors, as well as Daisenberger, which created a tie. At this point, Burger tried to intervene on Lang's behalf, bursting into the town hall with twenty-eight Storm Troopers to arrest the Socialist and ensure a Nazi victory. However, as he later argued indignantly, Lang rejected his assistance, calling it "Wild West politics." Rather than ending in a coup, this impasse was resolved with a toss that favored the old BVP mayor, although Lang would soon replace him by official fiat. Moreover, Burger was excluded from representing his party locally, although he did represent the Nazis on the county assembly.[6]

By summertime, the Oberammergau chapter had swollen to well more than two hundred members. This buoyant group continued to display its numbers in public as it launched a series of special events, starting with a huge May Day celebration. Repeated mustering and marching of Storm Troopers on village streets, as well as Nazi gatherings in local establishments, made public the identity of these recruits. Of course, in other social settings the villagers were still intermingled. Nevertheless, a new line of division was emerging that would only deepen as the regime tightened its hold on local life, coordinating the organizations and clubs that had previously nurtured the population's diverse interests. Insider and outsider took on new meanings in this context as Nazis marginalized opponents and circumscribed their cultural activities.[7]

Oberammergau's new Nazi mayor was born in 1895, so he was only in his late thirties when appointed to the top office. By then, he was a seasoned military veteran, part of the most youthful group to endure four complete years of trench warfare. After graduating from Ettal's gymnasium, Raimund Lang joined an artillery regiment as a volunteer. He remained "on the front" in various capacities despite being wounded in 1915 and was demobilized as a reserve lieutenant. Returning to the political upheavals that bedeviled Bavaria, Lang assisted the Werdenfels Corps in suppressing the conciliar republic. His nephew Ernst described him as "deeply affected" by Germany's defeat and its difficult postwar circumstances.[8]

Lang resumed his studies once free of active service. However, rather than train as a sculptor like his father and brother, Raimund aspired to a professional career. After qualifying as an architect, he worked on a railroad construction project in Lower Bavaria. Returning home to help with the revamping of Oberammergau's theater, he stayed on as a "private architect," facing the same challenges as other villagers during the Depression. Lang did, however, land the job of designing the local club's new gymnasium in 1931. Burger later derided him as an "unemployed master builder" for whom early party membership would bring no penalties. He had relied on community support since his student days, and as mayor he was able to funnel official funds into his own projects. Burger saw Lang as an egocentric politician driven by personal ambition, not a real Nazi.[9]

Most saw Mayor Lang as an idealist, however. Administrator Raab later testified to this effect since he had not expected a man of Lang's "education and his family background" to become a Nazi so early. Lang's relatives were, of course, intimately connected to the Passion Play. Like Guido Lang, Raimund's father, Sebastian, was influenced by Father Daisenberger, his great-uncle. Sebastian served on both the council and the Passion Committee just when Guido was working to enhance Oberammergau's appeal to visitors; he even transformed his own home into a substantial boarding house. However, Sebastian was also a successful actor, tapped to play Caiaphas in 1900. Parks-Richards praised "his unusual histrionic ability, a fine physique, and a sonorous voice that rang out like a deep toned bell in the great theater." Sebastian's older son Georg became the play's director for the 1922 season.[10]

Raimund was therefore driven by a "certain political idealism," Raab argued. "Mr. Lang felt himself as supporter and rescuer of this play." Already upset by destructive criticism of the 1930 Passion season, he became horrified by the extent of local unemployment. Therefore, in pursuing the spa project as a long-term solution for both problems, Lang saw himself as a good Christian in the Guido Lang tradition. This orientation even earned him a designation by Nazi bigwigs as the "black mayor."[11]

Lang was also broadly perceived to be a local patriot dedicated to his ancestral community's interests. Despite being appointed to his leading role, he was, in fact, a natural as a local politician. His father's stint on the council was followed by that of his brother Georg, a liberal first elected in 1919 who stepped aside as Mayr's deputy only when his brother became mayor fourteen years later. In the last free community council election of 1929, Georg beat the 172 other candidates with the top vote total—597.[12]

Raimund's nephew later described him as a democrat who had lost faith in the chaotic Weimar system, so the NSDAP must have offered hope of restoring stability to communal politics. Committed to his fellow villagers' well-being, Lang did his best to protect them from the Nazis' excesses, including threats of imprisonment. While he harassed Administrator Raab for his refusal to join the party in 1933, on the whole Lang did not resort to "strong-arm" tactics, a point made by Raab himself later on. One opponent described him as a "strong personality who knew how to assert himself but with honorable methods." Even SPD leader Daisenberger believed the mayor to be a humanistic and generous man who ran local government competently. Observing him in council meetings, Daisenberger found him willing to listen to what others had to say rather than imposing his own policies.[13]

Lang's desire to protect the Passion Play village and its inhabitants moderated his interpretation of Nazi doctrine. When disappointed by his superiors, he was quite prepared to fight back, risking the loss of his position and more. He was even at one point perceived as leading "an opposition party against the Nazis."[14]

Ideologically, Lang remained a dedicated foe of both "Marxism" and "Jewish materialism," both forces he believed threatened the Passion players' interests. He was, therefore, not above praising their play as highly anti-Semitic, and he both tolerated and even promoted racial discrimination against Jews. Yet he opposed the efforts of Julius Streicher, the rabid anti-Semite, to display his newspaper, *Der Stürmer*, which Lang judged to be pushing too raw and vulgar an agenda. Moreover, for the most part, he did not tolerate radical and aggressive behavior directed against opponents, and he tended to let people, including his subordinates, make their own decisions about supporting the party. Nevertheless, on the eve of World War II, which sorely tested his Nazi loyalties, he still tied devotion to Oberammergau with being "the best National Socialist and thereby also the best German and patriot."[15]

Raimund Lang turned Nazi only days after the rousing talk by Franz Diemer, son of one of Oberammergau's earliest and most prominent party members; in this decision he may well have been influenced by respected Professor Zeno Diemer's affiliation with the NSDAP. Moreover, the two enjoyed personal connections when this young architect was working on regenerating the Passion theater; they also later collaborated on Josef Diemer's spa project, so dear to Raimund's heart. Zeno's grandfather had risen to local leadership just as the Passion Play was attracting serious international attention, in addition to taking on the substantial role of "chorus leader" twice. His uncle

Johann developed the Osterbichl Hotel, served as council leader, and several times headed the chorus in his turn. Like Lang's, Zeno's devotion to the special mission of the Passion Play village was a family legacy, as was his clear understanding of the community's need to modernize its tourism infrastructure.[16]

Slightly younger than Guido Lang, Diemer found himself drawn away by a successful artistic career while Lang was spearheading the village's economic improvements. He must, however, have shared Lang's vision for his home community's future, and he supported the liberal candidate's hostile attitude toward political Catholicism. Judging by the enthusiastic nationalism expressed in the guidebook written by his wife, Hermine, and by his own painting choices, Diemer became a German patriot long before he reproduced fighting scenes during the Great War. Zeno's son Franz connected him to the air force; his own depiction of an aerial battle between German and British planes captures the drama of this new arena of warfare. Zeno became fascinated by Zeppelins, painting the "Graf Zeppelin" on its maiden flight to Munich for the German Museum and a similar view for the Reichstag building. This work was particularly apt since Franz engineered the airship's "well-tried propeller."[17]

Diemer's curiosity about the latest transportation methods was balanced by a fascination with his native region's Alpine scenery and colorful inhabitants. In the 1890s he re-created a famous Tyrolean victory over Napoleon in which he showcased an extraordinary knowledge of local settings and costuming. Shortly after the war, the artist returned home to build his own frescoed house in Oberammergau; he became a beloved contributor to village culture, especially its musical life. Beyond his work for the Passion Play seasons, he also served in the church choir. However, his professional interest in the ethnically intriguing Alpine setting, his liberal Catholicism, and his wartime experiences left him open to the appeal of Nazism. His engineer son's already longstanding Nazi membership must have influenced Diemer to become an "old fighter" since the younger man joined in 1925. Other family members were reportedly early Nazis as well.[18]

Wilhelm Lechner, another prominent insider, followed Diemer into the party. After his grandfather played Judas, his extremely popular father, a teacher at the local Carving School, scored right behind Diemer in the voting totals for Passion Committee membership in 1928. Lechner's mother, born in the Wittelsbach Hotel, became a prominent businesswoman; he himself was a teacher and a successful sculptor. Like Diemer, he was in tune with the region's ethnic history and culture, praised as an "indigenous" craftsman after designing new frescoes for the 1930 season. Thoroughly integrated into associational life, he had already headed prominent clubs and was about to lead the woodcarvers' Saint Lucas Club as well.[19]

Despite his success as a businessman and local activist, there were indications in Lechner's history that he might find Nazism attractive. After extensive war service, he became the Home Guard's deputy chief. He later claimed to have led the Thule Society's Bund Oberland locally until 1923. Like Diemer, he expressed disenchantment with political Catholicism, in his case by heading a German National Club in the late 1920s. Lechner also enjoyed connections through his wife to the Protestant community, which was well represented in the fledgling NSDAP, and he lived next door to one of the party's founding members. Moreover, like other early joiners, including his neighbor, Lechner showed signs of alienation from the village administration. In late October he wrote an indignant petition about the unfair compensation of bureaucrats during the 1930 Passion Play season. By December 1 he had become a Nazi.[20]

Lechner was later described as an "eager" Nazi with ties to District Leader Wagner, a close Hitler ally. His enthusiasm led to suspicions, perhaps unfounded, that he had behaved badly toward a few potential victims of Third Reich policies. Yet a contemporary argued that "as artist and idealist he saw only the good and beautiful sides of National Socialism and could . . . not bring the occurrence of injustice into harmony with his honorable ways." Furthermore, people were certainly willing to testify that Lechner had protected them from official excesses. His own uneasy balancing act between his Catholic and Nazi loyalties was reflected in dual greetings sent for his father's fiftieth wedding anniversary. As a chorister for sixty-four years, the older Lechner was congratulated by Cardinal Faulhaber, but the Führer himself also sent a personal greeting.[21]

Raimund Lang, Diemer, and Lechner were all Catholics who had rejected their confessional party in making the political journey toward Nazism. This leading trio worked with several councilors whom Mayor Mayr had approached, so the story later ran, with a stark proposition—that they should become Nazis. As Heinrich Zunterer, Oberammergau's mayor in 1947, testified, "There existed at that time this huge question to discuss: who would agree, who would sacrifice himself . . . and join the party" to protect the villagers and their "whole tradition" once their council was Nazified. The 1930 Christ, Alois Lang, refused to cooperate, but "a few" agreed to shift allegiances. However, Zunterer erred in the timing of this decision; the men joined before an initial coordination in late April. Perhaps Mayr anticipated the need to infiltrate a Nazi-dominated village leadership after the March election.[22]

One of these Nazi joiners was Alfred Bierling. Son and nephew of prominent local businessmen, Bierling was a veteran who had ultimately served in the air force. Like Raimund Lang, he then joined the Werdenfels Corps, and like Lechner he claimed to have headed the Bund Oberland locally until 1923. As a youth Bierling played Saint John; J. F. Dickie was much impressed with his "tender face . . . so fair, so young, so innocent, so loveable." Parks-Richards agreed, praising Bierling's "gentle manner and attractive face, which lights up with a rare beauty when he is speaking." However, an American newspaperman found him sadly changed by his war experience, calling him "worn and somewhat cynical now."[23] (Figure 1.1 includes the youthful Bierling as Saint John in 1910.)

As a master electrician, Bierling expanded his business interests to include a garage for the increasingly popular automobiles. His aeronautical experience led him to establish the German Flying Club in his village, speaking at a patriotically charged exploratory meeting about Germany's need for trained pilots to defend the country in its exposed Central European location. He also participated actively in clubs contributing to Oberammergau's tourism economy. Bierling was already an elected councilor when he emerged as Lang's deputy mayor in 1933. He argued later that he joined "with a heavy heart" after being pressed to become a Nazi, although he clearly wanted to remain in charge of the ailing communal bank. Moreover, he even served as deputy head of the council's Nazi contingent in 1933. He was in touch with "old fighters" in the various clubs that he frequented and was likely influenced by close relatives already in the party. Bierling's personal history had certainly prepared him to sign up with the NSDAP.[24]

Nevertheless, Bierling followed an oppositional path of the sort suggested in Mayr's plan. A fellow councilor wrote of him in 1937 that he was not a reliable party member, and he almost lost his position when he did not support all of Mayor Lang's Nazi-inspired policies. Bierling took charge once Lang left for war, and, according to later testimony, it was extraordinary that so deviant a deputy mayor could exist in Hitler's Germany; he clearly remained a Nazi to protect Oberammergau. A police officer who transferred into the village argued that he enjoyed his new job because in his previous position "all was much harsher." Bierling would earn general approbation for his willingness to counteract unwelcome official edicts and proceed honorably during the challenging times before the American occupation.[25]

Less questionable is the claim that Rupert Breitsamter was persuaded into Nazi membership to protect the village from a hostile takeover. As Zunterer later pointed out, he belonged to "one of Oberammergau's best Catholic families." Breitsamter's father, a respected parishioner, associated closely with Anton Lang. The son inherited his father's active faith, becoming a leader in the Journeymen's Club. He was also a very popular councilor, so his desire to continue serving into the Nazi period must have been great.[26]

Breitsamter likely agreed with a close relative who later admitted to voting for the NSDAP because of the seeming promise of its agenda. However, if he did join the party with high hopes, he was rapidly disillusioned. The head of the Catholic Workers' Club later testified that Breitsamter "condemned the National Socialist teachings about race, religion, and the like, as well as any terror politics." Moreover, as one police officer put it, Breitsamter's sawmill was the "blackest" of local workshops, meriting close oversight. He therefore perceived the councilor "not as a party member but as an opponent." Breitsamter lost a prime commission because he ran an "anti-fascist workplace" and refused to lay off suspect employees.[27]

One further member of the village leadership joined the party that spring, following his brother Raimund into the fold. A sculptor with a growing reputation, Georg Lang could be seen as a "Catholic" Nazi like Bierling and Breitsamter since he succumbed, so he and others later claimed, to protect the Passion Play from hostile party members. Even more than his younger sibling, Georg was steeped in Oberammergau's legacy and an outspoken supporter of Father Bogenrieder in Passion Committee debates; he also remained a loyal chorister throughout the Third Reich. Yet opponents remembered him as "the center of the Nazis in Oberammergau," still believing in a victory even toward war's end. Lang vehemently challenged these accusations, pointing in part to "the Christian art" that he created after 1933, which the regime considered "degenerate." Sympathetic witnesses agreed; a couple argued that he even overlooked highly compromising discussions among fellow choir members.[28]

When Hitler became chancellor, Georg had been a local politician for more than a decade and in charge of the village's Veterans' Club for many years. However, according to his son Ernst, Georg did not like the hurly-burly of electoral competition, particularly of the Nazi variety; in fact, he remained a self-confessed "German liberal" until the last free vote in 1933. Once Raimund became the family's rising star in the new political firmament, Georg retreated into his role as director; on the other hand, he eventually served as the chapter's deputy propaganda chief. Nevertheless, his Nazi affiliation was not enough to break his love for the Catholic culture he had learned in the sacristan's household.[29]

Oberammergau's Catholic Nazis were joined in the party's top echelons by members of the local evangelical community, who by 1933 had even managed to build a small church of their own. Some Protestant worshippers were transient residents, including those occupying Johann Diemer's old hotel, now run by the German Nationalists. Others were either migrants or the spouses of locals.[30]

Protestant leaders included the Saxon Ackermann, who for years lived in Hesse's Villa Ammerhof. Emerging as an ideological force in Oberammergau, Otto made clear his commitment to the Nazis' anti-Semitic racial program. He may even have been the puppet master who, according to the locals, was controlling his housemate, Alzinger. A typical middle-class migrant drawn to a rural community rich in natural and folkloric charms, Ackermann threw himself into winter sports and shared with fellow artist Diemer an interest in Alpine scenery and culture, including the distinctive clothing worn in the Folk Costume Club. Like Diemer and Bierling, he was fascinated by modern travel methods, especially the motor car. After enthusing about a show that featured the prototype for a driverless vehicle, he helped to start a local branch of Germany's Automobile Club.[31]

Ackermann was soon mixing with other villagers, but he was not positively received. As early as 1923, a trip with folk dancers drew "universal criticism" because he had lured a few locals into his troupe. Then, a couple of years later, he questioned the quality of Oberammergau's all-important woodcarving industry, making himself quite unpopular. Shortly thereafter, Ackermann was likely the "professor" caught writing in a regional newspaper against plans for a new venue for the Marksmen's Club, showing once again an overblown sense of his "local knowledge."[32]

Tensions mounted to the point that Ackermann openly declared his hostility toward his adopted community, refusing even to shop in village businesses after a public accusation that he had chosen "once again to foul his own nest." This critique came from the young SPD chief, Daisenberger, and politics may have lurked behind an exchange that he pursued with his now openly Nazi opponent. However, the older man was not above evoking class distinctions, claiming that most of the educated residents deplored such mistreatment of "a man of my age and my social position." The war had ruined German youth, as this nasty attack on a venerable professor showed all too well. Daisenberger responded indignantly to this slur, adding that Ackermann had been deserting local shops for the hated "department stores" and ending on an emotional note of homegrown patriotism. Just months before the Nazi takeover nothing could have underscored Ackermann's outsider status more clearly than this vitriolic public quarrel.[33]

The professor's opinionated elitism offers quite a contrast to the behavior of the simple craftsman with whom he found lodging. Arno Hesse migrated to Oberammergau as a single Protestant worker in 1903, and he remained part of the growing evangelical parish. However, he also integrated himself into the larger community, establishing his own decorative painting business out of Villa Ammerhof.[34] Once married, Hesse followed the established local strategy of diversifying his earning opportunities. This included advertising as a skiing instructor, a sideline that he expanded into a "ski school," and later building up his villa into a well-appointed boarding house.[35]

Hesse settled in Oberammergau at just the right moment for a man whose talents lent themselves to promoting the village's tourism industry. His painting business could only grow with the building boom that preceded each Passion Play season. Moreover, Hesse arrived only ten years after the founding of the first Folk Costume Club. Drawn to this folkloric enterprise right away, he quickly rose to become its top officer. Similarly, Hesse joined the winter sports community in time to help shape Oberammergau into an attractive winter venue. When Hesse briefly headed the club in 1924, its numbers had multiplied, and a major skiing competition had just taken place in the valley. Now a leader in these popular fields, Hesse ran for local office but without success. He later found his political niche by building up the SA troop.[36]

Hesse was most likely recruited by the transient painter Nagler, who founded the local chapter and then disappeared early in 1930. Hesse's employee and housemate, Alzinger, replaced Nagler, one of a mere handful of party leaders to represent its lower-class contingent. Like so many of Oberammergau's workers, he was also a migrant.[37]

Before the war, Alzinger appeared briefly in the village but then settled permanently once it was over. Born into the same community, Kasing, as Hesse's wife, he was possibly a relative who apprenticed himself to the master painter; the two Kasing natives remained Catholics in a house dominated by Protestants. This young trainee was clearly influenced by his employer, following him into the Folk Costume Club, where he rose to deputy head in the early 1930s. He was skiing with Hesse as early as 1913 and later trained as an instructor, helping to launch the ski school. When Hesse founded his paramilitary troop, Alzinger became an SA member.[38]

Postwar testimony was almost unanimous in describing the chapter's leader as a "decent" person who remained a "simple unsophisticated worker." He was also, as a migrant, considered to have made an effort to blend in. His Nazism was genuine but that of "a blind follower without his own initiative," a politician whom others could manipulate. Yet even SPD leader Daisenberger saw Alzinger as a moderating force who protected opponents, an opinion corroborated by others who benefited from his assistance. Father Bogenrieder wrote positively about the former leader, stressing both his willingness to remain a Catholic and the mild regime that he had run in Oberammergau. This gentleness was the predominant memory of elderly villagers reminiscing about their experiences with Alzinger during the Nazi era.[39]

Alzinger's mild demeanor and permissive attitudes contrasted markedly with the disruptive personality of the man who rose to lead Oberammergau's Motorstorm. Daisenberger undoubtedly had Jakob Burger in mind when he praised Alzinger's willingness to shield antagonists from the village's "radical elements." While he and Hesse soon teamed up with Mayor Lang, Burger became a maverick whose aggressive behavior alienated him from his mainstream Nazi colleagues. This confrontational attitude grew out of years of struggle to succeed in the community to which he had moved with his family as a ten-year-old child.[40]

In 1900 Burger's parents had arrived in Oberammergau to work for the new railroad. As a "sow-Swabian," the young migrant was to remain sensitive about his outsider status. He soon began to carve out a successful middle-class career, establishing a grocery business in newly constructed quarters near the station. This was the start of expansive dealings in various basic foodstuffs and coal, notably the crucial potato market, which he attempted to dominate during the immediate postwar period. Meanwhile, he married the Protestant daughter of an Augsburg businessman, no doubt a helpful partner in his various enterprises. However, Burger's entrepreneurial practices attracted negative attention from the authorities; he had, they claimed, monopolized the trade in expensive farm products like butter and eggs. Any such suspicions of "hamstering" (or stocking up) and price gouging could give Oberammergau a bad reputation in the difficult period leading up to the 1922 Passion Play season. He may therefore have become unpopular, although the villagers were anxious to combat unfair attacks on their efforts to prepare for the visitor influx.[41]

Burger continued to build up his trading empire, adding transportation services and the manufacture of soft drinks into the mix. Like Hesse, he clearly believed in diversification but on a very ambitious scale. Leading into the 1930 Passion Play season he set his sights still higher by turning his house into "one of the most modern furnished quarters" in Oberammergau. Burger even covered the exterior of his "Green House" with huge murals of the Crucifixion and a group of apostles and evangelists beneath Mary's triumphant figure. Eye-catching in the extreme for visitors arriving by train, Burger's murals imitated those on central hotels and businesses, and their lifelike quality earned him praise in the local newspaper. During the season its editor reported admiringly on this up-to-date guesthouse where a bishop and Polish pilgrims had found lodgings.[42] (Figure 4.1 shows a postcard featuring Burger's "Green House" with its mural of the Crucifixion on the side wall clearly visible.)

Oberammergau. Bahnhofstraße mit Laber

FIGURE 4.1. A postcard captures Jakob Burger's "Green House" with its controversial mural of the Crucifixion as seen from the Station Quarter around 1930.

While Burger was working hard to expand the family business, he also participated in Oberammergau's political affairs. Before the war he followed the traditional Catholic path of membership in the Journeymen's Club, rising to leadership just as he was launching his new grocery store. Wartime service then intervened, and following demobilization Burger traveled with the Werdenfels Corps to Munich, months after he began leading Oberammergau's Social Democratic Association. This overt political involvement put Burger on the wrong side of many locals, and he soon moved on. Nevertheless, he remained, according to later witnesses, "very socially oriented and no enemy of the workers" but rather a "model employer." Burger returned to politics in 1924, when he ran for the council but fell far short of winning a seat; a second attempt in 1929 was similarly unsuccessful. Meanwhile, he had helped to found a local branch of the Real Estate Owners' Association and became its first head. His own piece of real estate seemed to be booming as the 1930 Passion Play season got under way.[43]

But Burger's successes were short lived. Praise of his efforts to replicate a typical local guesthouse soon turned into stinging criticism that underscored the very social marginality he had fought to overcome. As a man without "local savvy," he had not located the Crucifixion scene properly, which was why it lacked "harmony" and "authenticity." Far more humiliating, however, was a rapid deterioration in Burger's financial situation. Overextending himself to create the "Green House," possibly by borrowing from the community bank, he soon faced a bankruptcy proceeding; it took more than a year to sort out this serious threat to Burger's achievements. In addition, careless maintenance of his truck caused a fatal accident, so he faced judicial proceedings and ended up with a fine. In June of 1931 Burger was ejected as leader of the Real Estate Owners' Association; in October his father died. During this terrible period, he decided to join the Nazi party.[44]

Facing a denazification hearing in the late 1940s, Burger tried to re-create his motivations for becoming a Nazi well before 1933. Given his experience of bankruptcy proceedings, he stressed the anticreditor promises in the party's platform. Burger's lawyer described how his affairs "fell ever more into the hands of the profiteering circles. The profiteers had an open field in that period." Facing ruin, he hoped that the Nazi program would restore his livelihood. Needing also to explain his involvement in building up the Motorstorm, Burger traced this particular interest back to his "enthusiasm for motor sports." He insisted that this Nazi branch was "unpolitical"; a man running a transportation business needed to belong.[45]

However, Burger expressed a deeper, overtly political commitment to Nazi ideology at the time. He led uniformed troopers around the village and enforced the new regime's ways. Hearsay evidence indicates that he helped in house searches, and he certainly contributed to the BVP mayor's arrest. A probing visit to the Ettal monastery left him the object of ridicule as he turned up ancient armaments thought to be theatrical props. One telling anecdote placed Burger in a village inn when the occupants were singing the Horst Wessel Lied. A group of young men intent on their card game failed to respond properly with the "German greeting," so he threatened to "help" teach them how to do it properly.[46]

Burger also attacked Raimund Lang personally in 1935, reiterating the central party tenet that communal needs should trump individual interests. The mayor was a bad Nazi who supported mainstream economic principles and pursued "personal politics." Burger, the outsider and champion of the common man, was furious with Lang's willingness to privilege insiders in a way that undermined the emerging folk community and slighted "old fighters" like himself.[47]

How deeply Burger had thought through the "consequences of the Nazi movement" was less clear. Witnesses later saw him as "impulsive," and he himself talked about the "stupidity of my idealism." Even his support for Hitler's racial policy is unclear. While he berated Lang for failing to sustain the new prohibitions, he permitted an employee who was one-quarter Jewish to present himself as his illegitimate son when applying for army service. On war duty in the Ukraine, Burger protected locals from shipment to Germany as forced laborers; subsequently, he looked out for French POWs under his charge back in Bavaria. Yet he was one of only a few local Nazis to be prosecuted severely. The demonization of this "evil usher" seems in part attributable to his outsider status, which magnified an undoubtedly rough demeanor and overeager pursuit of National Socialist ideals. Burger's fierce conflict with consummate insider Mayor Lang also left him vulnerable to the full weight of the denazification process.[48]

Hanging above the tormented figures of Saint John and Mary in Burger's Crucifixion scene was "the noble body of the Savior on the cross." This rendition impressed viewers as a realistic portrayal, one, of course, that audiences were intent on seeing in the flesh. However, the subsequent criticisms of Burger resulting from his bold statement of loyalty to the Passion Play narrative underscored his failed struggle to belong in Oberammergau. By contrast, the man whom audiences had come to see, the player of Christ himself, enjoyed insider status by the very nature of his role. Alois Lang took up the part in 1930 and then reprised it in 1934 despite his refusal while still a BVP councilor to join the National Socialists. Only later, under pressure, would he agree to become a Nazi as a reluctant addition.[49]

Alois shared ancestry with Guido in the entrepreneurial Georg Lang line. His father built a guesthouse in 1905, which the son expanded and modernized before the 1930 Passion Play season. He also improved his artistic skills, as he explained later. "I changed over from crucifix-carving to the carving of figures in general . . . and was able to turn out several large church-figures for some churches in the Rhineland." His stature as a businessman thus complemented the meteoric rise of his fortunes as Anton Lang's successor. Alois was a natural for election to the 1930 Passion Committee; he also won a council seat in 1929.[50]

Lang was a loyal BVP member, but he shared many connections to Oberammergau's Nazi contingent. In particular, he served on the 1930 Passion Committee with Diemer. Assigned to its construction subcommittee, Lang worked with Georg and Raimund Lang, Breitsamter, and Lechner on the new theater building. His wife was a Protestant who became active in the evangelical community.[51]

Alois was born in 1891 within weeks of Alfred Bierling, who was therefore most probably a schoolmate. The two men later served in the Tourism Club, and both were active in winter sports; they eventually worked together on the council. Lang served during the war in a skiing unit, winning several medals. Later, a pioneering role in the sport's local development must have brought him close to Alzinger and Hesse, as well as Bierling. His particular interest was in training the smaller children for competitive skiing, so, like the Villa Ammerhof men, he was closely linked to youths who later joined the party and SA ranks. Lang also rose into leadership in the Veterans' Association, yet another venue that brought him together with future Nazi converts, in particular Georg Lang.[52]

However, Alois Lang also had powerful reasons for refusing to become a Nazi in 1933. He belonged to that special, rarefied category of men playing Christ, the role that had made him famous throughout the world in 1930. This prominence made him extremely nervous about international perceptions of a decision to join the party. Intermingled were personal considerations about repeating his role in 1934 and fears about harming Oberammergau's reputation abroad.[53]

As pressures mounted in the mid-1930s, however, especially from the SA, he succumbed. The same fear of tarnishing his community's image, Lang argued later, motivated this reluctant change of status. After the 1934 season he lost the right to make full use of the upgraded facilities of his family's guesthouse. The consequent decline in business made him increasingly desperate as he envisioned the player who "embodied" the Passion Play being taunted as a "bankrupt" by local Nazis. Consequently, he decided to protect himself by joining the NSDAP and securing the needed authorization. However, Lang received his permit before he became a party member, casting doubt on the genuine nature of his reluctance. Nevertheless, his credentials as an "absolute opponent" were substantial, including friendship with the only Jew to settle openly in Oberammergau during the 1930s.[54]

Alois Lang survived the council's initial coordination in 1933 together with fellow Catholic loyalist Raab. Both men then lost their positions as the Nazis filled the village's leading spots with their own supporters. Raab resisted the pressure to join the party longer than Lang, a remarkable feat because of his prominent position as Oberammergau's chief administrative official. A strong commitment to his religious faith and to political Catholicism motivated Raab's obstinate resistance until family concerns undermined his resolve in 1940. (Figure 4.2 shows Administrator Josef Raab around 1930.)

Raab was a Franconian outsider who took up his administrative role in 1915. Perhaps growing up in an area of mixed faiths near Protestant Ansbach had strengthened the bond he felt to his own Catholicism. He was soon integrated into Oberammergau's upper echelons because of his elevated position. An avid hunter, he secured one of the village's dedicated territories for himself and rose to leadership in the Marksmen's Club. Raab was sufficiently established to win a council seat in 1924 and easy reelection in 1929. He also headed

FIGURE 4.2. Administrator Josef Raab appears in a collection of
photographs published in 1930.

the powerful Tourism Club throughout the Depression years until removed by
the Nazis in 1933.[55]

As the village's chief administrator, Raab emerged as a champion of his
community's fiscal health, clashing with villagers promoting what he perceived
as risky projects, including the spa plan in 1932. Raab also became a BVP activist, serving as the local committee's secretary and helping to run its campaigns.
He even authored a flyer calling the Nazis "the greatest enemy of the Christian
religion" and a threat to the Passion Play. Clearly, he did not share Raimund
Lang's view that a Hitler chancellorship would be good for Oberammergau.[56]

With this political history, Raab could hardly hope to retain a council seat
in 1933, and he even felt threatened in his administrative position. His premises
were searched, albeit in vain, and Mayor Lang became quite hostile, putting
Raab's job in sufficient jeopardy that he hunted unsuccessfully for another
position. He survived some financial difficulties and an attempt to cut him off
socially from other villagers. Only by becoming a "passive" member of the Recreational Air Group did he fulfill Lang's minimum requirement that local
bureaucrats enter "at least a branch" of the party.[57]

Pressures to join resumed in 1937, but Raab remained true to his bedrock principles. He had by then secured a university admission for a son likely to be barred as an opponent's child. However, when another son also needed higher education, Raab agreed to apply for membership. Party loyalists derisively termed him one of the "incorrigible . . . must-be-party-comrades." As Father Bogenrieder testified glowingly after the war, Oberammergau's top Nazis certainly perceived Raab for what he was, a convinced supporter of the local church and no comrade of theirs.[58]

Oberammergau's top Nazis chose to join their new party for a variety of reasons. At the heart of each decision was a complex mix of personal and political considerations that highlighted the Passion Play village's unique identity. The old maxim "all politics is local" takes on a special meaning in this case because the villagers had developed such a strong sense of their communal mission. Even a newcomer like Burger had learned to couch his criticism of Mayor Lang in terms that included concerns about the play's well-being. As a result, joiners were motivated by the same hopes and fears that were gripping all Germans in 1933, but nationalistic yearnings and Nazi principles were leavened by village-level commitments strong enough to restrain the leadership and even preserve a modicum of democracy in local affairs.[59]

I have identified 131 core members of Oberammergau's Nazi party, all but 8 of them males. Females were much more likely to join the NSF than the party itself, often as wives or close relatives of party members. A few mostly elite migrant women became members, some even before 1933; the Protestant community was also well represented in this group. Of the male Nazis, more than one-third were "old fighters," and virtually half were settled migrants. Youth had been winning out over experience since only 4 in 10 were old enough to be Great War veterans. The trend toward middle-class predominance initiated before 1933 continued for the core membership as well. More than 40 percent were solidly middle class, while nearly 30 percent were craftsmen, including the sculptors so typical of the local workforce. Almost all the rest were workers, mainly employed in the craft sector. Oberammergau's local party cut across both denominational and class lines.[60]

While the core Nazis were drawn from all sectors of local society, other villagers in those same categories rejected party membership. The reasons some people joined whereas others did not therefore go deeper than mere social and confessional identity. Only their specific biographical details explain why Nazism attracted these particular villagers.

Often individuals were recruited through the chains of joining already established before 1933, which continued to encourage family members and close associates of the party faithful to take Nazism seriously. This process favored natives during the first hectic months of the Third Reich, netting more than twenty party members, but there were also a few chains that were mixed and at least seven that were all migrant. More than five dozen men belonged to birth cohorts with two or more joiners, a majority of which included "old fighters"; many of these same men were also schoolmates. In Oberammergau, both connections were quite significant since the bond persisted into adulthood. Neighbors provided yet another influence, most obviously when the Villa Ammerhof residents created their own joining chain.[61]

Recruits were also reachable through the service organizations and clubs that permeated Oberammergau's cultural scene. Access to the youth flowing into party and SA ranks came through the long-established Gymnastics Club and its offshoot, the Football Club, as well as the new Winter Sports Club. The wildly popular sport of skiing in particular drew hundreds of young men and women onto the slopes, many of whom later became Nazis; the SA commanders played up to this interest by providing members with competitive events. A further recruiting tool for the Motorstorm was the Automobile Club, which included a mix of "old fighters" and 1933 joiners in its membership. Also significant for this type of networking was the Folk Costume Club, with which more than thirty joiners had been associated, as well as more than a dozen close relatives of party activists, including those of several NSDAP founders.[62]

The core Nazis fell into two generations; they were either of an age to have fought in the Great War or were born after the last fateful natal year of 1899. The wartime generation predominated in the party's leadership, while the youthful group flowed into its rank and file. Paramilitary service further influenced several of the group's leaders, including Mayor Lang and Deputy Mayor Bierling, as well as Motorstorm Commander Burger and his successor. For these Werdenfels Corps men, combating the revolutionary situation in Bavaria had been extremely personal and close to home. Their colleague Lechner had, similarly, acted as deputy commander of the Home Guard. He and Bierling even extended their Radical Right experience within the Bund Oberland.[63]

Soldiers kept alive their memories of active service by networking in the local Veterans' Association. As of 1924 their annual ceremonies centered on a huge memorial designed by their chief, Georg Lang, which featured a starkly nationalistic statue of Germany's "protective saint," Michael. Dedication celebrations took place under a massive Iron Cross burning on the Kofel, while a military procession underscored the poignant lists of dead warriors on the memorial's façade. Four years later the association's seventieth anniversary was marked by dramatic ceremonies featuring bonfires on the village's surrounding hills, a play about "August 1, 1914," and much patriotic singing, including their trademark, "The Good Comrade."[64]

Veterans in the local party shared this treasured comradeship with younger joiners who experienced the war as teenagers or children. Their memories were of home-front deprivations, missing relatives, and disruptive political upheavals following the war's end. Ranging from eighteen to thirty-three years of age, the oldest were, like Heinrich Himmler, awaiting frontline service in the final months of fighting. However, these boys turned to men were mostly new to the military discipline that they came to enjoy as Storm Troopers. To enhance their experience, local commanders sought to acquire the Third Reich's beloved uniforms for them and organized soldierly activities like marches and musters, including a number of expeditions enjoyed by the Motorstorm and recorded in an album of photographs.[65]

In late May 1933, for example, Burger's troopers traveled to Bad Tölz, where the commander assembled his men and stood before them to dedicate their new flag. Official musterings of this sort were balanced by the fun of motorized excursions and the camaraderie of card games and festive gatherings. One young enthusiast later described his eager participation in "motorbike and car races." A fall event in Miesbach saw him victorious in a trifecta involving a bike rider, a car driver, and a sprinter.[66] (Figure 4.3 captures Motorstorm Commander Burger at the moment of dedicating his unit's flag in Bad Tölz.)

Youthful Nazis were coping with the Depression in their struggle to establish themselves in the working world. Thus, they became the local party's foot soldiers, although a representative group did fill spots in the top leadership. Many shared with other young Germans the brunt of the unemployment crisis. While older party members were overwhelmingly middle class, this postwar generation featured a strong contingent of workers and craftsmen. Their situation had soured after the 1930 Passion Play season and was getting progressively more desperate before the Nazi takeover, as the council's minutes reveal very poignantly. In 1932, the state of local crafts became so dire that Lechner, as head of the Saint Lucas Club, set up an exhibition hall inside the Passion theater where locals could attempt to market their products.[67]

The SA filled up with unemployed men like a single day laborer who joined the party in 1930 and Hesse's troop a year later. He was driven, Father Bogenrieder later testified, by his "hope" that the Nazis would solve the unemployment crisis. Burger's motorized troopers were similarly afflicted. He claimed early in 1934 that "a majority of my people were out of work for years." Ernst Lang recalled the public nature of their humiliating dependence on communal assistance, paid out weekly to "a strangely sad, threatening mass gathered in front of the town hall." These were "honorable men, whom I knew, workers,

FIGURE 4.3. Motorstorm Commander Jakob Burger dedicates his unit's
flag at a muster in Bad Tölz in late May 1933.

carvers, service personnel." At least sixty core party members served double
duty in the local "storm" groups, most of them young; they were motivated, no
doubt, by this Depression-induced loss of face, as well as livelihood.[68]

The older generation was certainly not immune to threats of unemployment
or at the very least underemployment, which drove many into the Nazi party.
This largely middle-class group faced the impoverishment of their clientele and
a consequent loss of income. One veteran later testified that, as a craftsman
whose business was at a standstill, he had joined the Motorstorm out of gratitude after the commander threw work his way. Burger's own bankruptcy crisis
similarly illustrates how middle-class Nazis could have felt themselves driven
into the party by personal experiences of the Depression's wrath. A like crisis
faced the purchaser of a leading inn, as well as several other Nazi joiners.[69]

Some middle-class joiners may have feared the loss or diminution of their
livelihood should they not join the victorious party. Raab's experiences with the

new mayor certainly illustrate the trouble that other less principled men might have tried to avoid. Future Motorstorm Commander Franz Kräh for one testified that he felt pressured to join in 1933 because of his bureaucratic position in the post office. Even his Motorstorm membership was in part motivated by the training opportunity it offered him as a postal worker. This type of pressure may have influenced a second round of joining in the late 1930s since the percentage of business owners, bureaucrats, and professionals in this group of new members was quite high.[70]

When Burger accused Mayor Lang of promoting his own career as an "unemployed" architect by means of his new office, the commander put his finger on another motive for becoming a Nazi: ambition. However, he missed the devotion to his community's welfare that also drove an insider like Lang. Nazi membership could indeed open up opportunities for personal advancement, particularly for marginal outsiders like new councilors Alzinger and Hesse. Men already enjoying positions of power in village affairs saw the need to protect their status by joining the Nazi ranks. Not all of the councilors, in particular, were willing to tolerate the demotion forced upon Alois Lang and Raab. Therefore, the argument that Bierling and Breitsamter became Nazis to preserve their council seats is plausible enough, although they had additional reasons for joining. These Nazi converts were men who had contested elections to serve their community, so the desire to continue working for the good of Oberammergau and its Passion Play is hardly surprising. Other dedicated leaders were already Nazis in 1933.[71]

All of these leaders had inherited a long tradition of communal self-help, which led them to perceive their special 1934 Passion Play season as the source of salvation for both individuals and the village at large. The councilors were painfully aware of the Depression-related sufferings that had forced them to borrow from the upcoming season's expected revenues. No wonder that they planned to invest in Raimund Lang's spa project and free Oberammergau from dependency on future Passion Play seasons, idealistic hopes that made them susceptible to the Nazi party's regenerative promises. Similarly affected were top bureaucrats like the local forestry office chief, Viktor Hacker, whose workers were largely unemployed. This type of idealism could motivate other less powerful joiners when they looked beyond their own personal concerns. Volunteerism was such a strong dimension of local life that ambition mixed with altruism was bound to draw recruits into so seemingly worthy a cause.[72]

Idealism turned to fear, however, when the locals considered the harm that a Nazi transformation of their community might cause. Maintaining a strong presence in the council would at least help to protect Oberammergau from radical changes harmful to local interests. Urgent, too, was control over the

Passion Committee's makeup so that their play would not be compromised. Only a few years earlier, the Citizens' Club had campaigned to keep these committees free from outsider influences. Now Motorstorm Commander Burger was just the sort of "old fighter" who would be very unwelcome in the halls of power. His prominence in the SA ranks, however, made him a likely candidate for a leadership position. In fact, he later claimed that higher Nazi authorities had wanted him appointed to office, but powerful insiders succeeded in keeping him off both the community council and the Passion Committee.[73]

Fear of radical Nazis like Burger paled before the terror that a resurgent Communist party struck in the hearts of Oberammergau's Nazis, an emotion they shared with politically active Catholics. The shadow of their postwar nightmare hung over locals horrified by the lines of unemployed workers collecting public money, not to mention a menacing flow of "wanderers" hopelessly seeking a new home. One young scion of an inn-keeping family agonized when "up to 20 and 30 people came daily to beg for a midday meal." However, it was the potentially disastrous political consequences of such misery that created a general sense of doom. Georg Lang's "baffled" and "helpless" response to the masses of unemployed urbanites he encountered in the Bavarian capital led him to conclude that these men without work would "destroy us."[74]

Already in early 1931, a homeland protection group was founded in nearby Ettal to guard their "jeopardized cultural heritage" against Communist threats. A year later Oberammergau's Press Club sponsored a frightening presentation about the Bolshevik policy of dismantling Russia's Christian infrastructure. This same threat had to be combated in Germany, the speaker argued, "even in our immediate neighborhood." The Women's Union's pilgrimage to Ettal that fall brought back haunting memories of their founding meeting in the "storm-wracked year 1919," when these valiant "activists" had taken the fight to their Communist opponents.[75]

In her 1922 guidebook, Hermine Diemer eloquently described the emotional toll of this revolutionary period. As the mother of a dead soldier, she recalled "the dreadful experiences of the war," but, reflecting her frustrated ambitions for Germany's future, she added, "and the still worse trials of the revolution." Diemer had learned to evaluate the Communist threat from Oberammergau's special perspective. "Encroaching as it did on the most secret rites and privileges, [it] threatened to overwhelm and do away with these venerable rites, with tradition, with the Passion Play itself." Fortunately, the play provided the needed "antidote" to "this poison of the revolution, with all its materialism, its terrible denial of all that is worth immortalizing. As of yore, so now we go on pilgrimage to the village still suffering from the effects of war and revolution. We wander as it were to the all-healing source."[76]

A decade later Hermine's Nazi son was reiterating her anti-Bolshevik sentiments just as the emotional resonance of Oberammergau's earlier confrontation with Communist insurrection peaked. Diemer specifically invoked the power of the Passion Play, "a carrier of German culture," to combat the "corroding efforts of Communist propaganda." Nazis and their Catholic opponents were united in their determination to head off a new revolutionary challenge, and the 1934 Passion Play season offered both sides a welcome ray of hope.[77]

Another legacy of the 1919 revolution was the linking of anti-Bolshevism and anti-Semitism. However, capitalistic enterprises that encroached on village culture and in particular the excessively commercialized 1930 Passion season also fostered prejudice against Jews as the supposed purveyors of greedy materialistic practices. Certainly, individual villagers sometimes enjoyed good relationships with Jewish visitors, as Alois Lang's case illustrates.[78] Still, the prejudice that Passion players shared with other Western Christians had left their community tolerant of anti-Semitic politics. Some were even willing to accept more extreme Nazi racial policies, although the first attack on Jewish interests in Germany, an April 1 boycott, could not have taken place in the village since no Jews worked there.[79]

What certainly did agitate leading villagers was a deep fear that "false" Jewish stories in the world's newspapers might hurt their upcoming season. An antipropaganda committee, to which both Mayor Mayr and Anton Lang were at least nominally attached, put out an "appeal" to their audience overseas. Its authors did not mince words: "Foreign and . . . German Jews have in league with Communist criminals . . . disseminated lying news stories about outrageous persecutions and the most disgraceful atrocities supposedly committed against Jews in Germany." Potential visitors should know that, in fact, all in Oberammergau was "calm and orderly," so they need not hesitate to make the trip.[80]

This document manifests a temptation to link anti-Semitic and anti-Communist rhetoric, an instinct magnified because their season was imminent. Moreover, this was, it seemed, a "smear campaign" like the one in 1930, about which emotions were still very raw, as Raimund Lang was to make clear, building on decades of concern about damaging negative publicity. Consequently, in this reprehensible act of self-defense, Oberammergau's leaders allowed their narrow communal interests as guardians of the Passion Play to predominate over a humanitarian concern for their fellow Jewish citizens.[81]

Despite sharing hopes and fears of this sort, local Nazis differed with Catholic loyalists over the best political answer to Germany's deepening crisis.

They believed that Hitler would most effectively regenerate both the nation's fortunes and those of Oberammergau. As Burger later put it, in effect: no Hitler, no 1934 Passion season. Active Catholics like Diemer and Georg Lang could therefore balance their dedication to the church and the Passion Play with openly Nazi politics. Forestry Chief Hacker was another Nazi joiner who dared to worship publicly and to wear his uniform at "church festivals." Hacker later claimed that he became disillusioned with his adopted party; as a result, he eventually became involved with resistance efforts.[82]

Men like Alois Lang, who were pressured into joining, remained similarly unhappy with the regime's policies. Lang's friendship with Jews like Meyer sensitized him in particular to the anti-Semitic measures creeping into German life. He spoke in oppositional terms with trusted associates, but ultimately Lang took the path of least resistance by protecting his business interests with a nominal party membership. The most unlikely Nazi in Oberammergau must surely have been Administrator Raab, as Father Bogenrieder later pointed out, since his entire lifestyle was devoutly Catholic. His "coerced joining" did not stop him from covert work with local youth during the war. Raab acted to protect his family's interests by becoming a Nazi, but his ultimate goal was to sustain a core of Catholic life in Oberammergau.[83]

Many joiners, however, might better be described as Catholics in name only. Kräh testified that he had little interest in going to church, although he was hardly an "opponent." Burger was never to be seen in services during the period, according to one witness. Overall, the core members were not men who had played leading roles in Catholic associations. A handful did serve as officers of the Journeymen's Club, and a few similarly in the Youth Group and the Workers' Club. Only eight received major parts in the 1930 play, while Diemer, Lechner, the Lang brothers, and Breitsamter worked behind the scenes. The rest were not to be found in important roles, and some of the migrants were not involved at all. They would remain at the party's heart for the duration of the Third Reich.[84]

Even the most enthusiastic Nazis in Oberammergau, however, ran up against the limits set by local political dynamics. In particular, the timing of the 1934 Passion season, for which planning was already under way, placed real restraints on the new leadership. Mayor Lang's eager desire to make the season a success led him to include experienced men in the coordinated community council and Passion Committee. Similarly, in 1938 he made sure that the 1940 Passion Committee included men who truly represented village wisdom. The only real outsiders were Alzinger and Hesse, who were soon clearly operating in his camp.[85]

Further restraints on Nazi policies came from the citizenry's traditional right to open consultation with their officials, as well as the power of collective action based in surviving cultural associations and the Passion Play tradition. Such residues of democracy and the new leadership's continued need to deal with day-to-day village affairs moderated their hold over the community. This local patriotism showed up in the decisions of a committee charged with naming the village streets. Rather than honor top Nazis, as was soon the norm, they drew on their special history for inspiration. Visitors would not walk down Adolf Hitler or Goering Street but along streets named after local heroes like Daisenberger. Similarly, a new settlement became the Saint Gregor rather than the Wagner Quarter. Nevertheless, for all of these limits placed on Nazi activists by Oberammergau's powerful cultural heritage, the new regime had firmly taken root and was to predominate in the foreseeable future.[86]

While fresh recruits flooded into Oberammergau's Nazi Party during the spring of 1933, their leaders were busily reshaping local culture to fit the new worldview. To compete with the traditional festivities highlighting Bavarian Catholic life, they launched a ritual calendar replete with invented or borrowed holidays. In late April the chapter used the customary lighting of mountainside fires to honor Hitler's birthday.[87]

By May 1 they were ready for a great public show of strength, mindful that adapting this workers' holiday would offer the perfect opportunity for making an anti-Communist statement. To replace a godless celebration marked by "songs of class warfare and class hatred," the leadership planned a church service to ensure "the blessings of heaven" for their new state. Once again they lit fires on the mountainside, explicitly comparing the "two symbols of the cross," their swastika, used for May Day, and "the opposite, the burning cross," honoring King Ludwig every August.[88]

Storm Troopers woke the population with drumming and singing, Bavarian, German, and swastika flags all flying. Then a big procession set off from Ettalerstrasse accompanied by local officials, the HJ, Nazi troops, and all of the patriotic clubs, together with the band. A packed service led by Father Bogenrieder was later described as "certainly the high point of the entire day." A further procession led to the village center, where loudspeakers broadcast national festivities in Berlin. That evening the Nazi chapter held its monthly meeting, which was highlighted by a Hitler oration. This splashy event stressed its "Christian" intentions, a theme that would last as long as the Passion season mandated close cooperation with Oberammergau's Catholics.[89]

Those Catholics were determined to remain active despite the new political realities. Fortuitously, just after the March election, a "remarkable pilgrimage" came to the Ammer valley. An ex-Communist had vowed to heave a large cross all the way from the Rhineland Palatinate to Altötting to make up for his political past. Journeying through Catholic territory, he dramatically embodied their own struggle with the Far Left. Meanwhile, Catholic clubs continued to meet, and some even grew in membership. The Women's Union as usual entertained the children who were receiving first communion, right before rogation processions took Catholics out into their sacral landscape and pilgrim groups began to visit Ettal. The ceremony dedicating Brother Conrad's statue in the parish church underscored these defiant acts of Catholic witness.[90]

As the Nazis moved toward single-party government, however, the Catholics would soon lose their remaining political leaders. In particular, Interior Minister Wagner condemned BVP Mayor Mayr's unorthodox reappointment in late April, although he remained in office for a few more weeks. During this precarious time both SA commanders may have been urging Mayr to remain in office as the man best suited to represent all of Oberammergau's residents and manage a successful Passion Play season. Nevertheless, Hesse and Burger pursued an aggressive campaign to remove Mayr once the Nazi councilors had failed to secure his "voluntary resignation"; the local BVP group's president had responded tartly that Mayr "was voted in legally as mayor, and he knows of nothing that stands in the way of his fulfilling the position."[91]

The two commanders did wait more than two weeks before intervening peremptorily in an effort to resolve this issue, which, they informed their counterparts on the council, "has now become intolerable for the community and also for our movement." They stated that a special meeting should take place with the "sole point of order: 'New election of the mayor.'" All five Nazi councilors joined with Alzinger and his deputy, Raimund Lang, to reject this "illegal" attempt at a "power grab." The correct procedure was to wait until Wagner visited Oberammergau to deal with the mayoral situation himself. In a further message the councilors objected to this unfriendly placing of "an ultimatum over our heads," which made them fear similar interference in communal affairs once a new mayor had been instated. Neither they nor their two mayoral candidates could accept such "Wild West politics."[92]

Hesse's and Burger's joint response can hardly have been reassuring. Citing "the will of the majority of local party members" as their reason for wanting to force Mayr's removal, they also asserted angrily their "damned duty" to monitor the party's councilors. Mayr, they asserted, had told them that he would step aside when Wagner reached Oberammergau to finalize his replacement. As a result, they agreed to "suspend a further SA action" until his visit.[93]

Just as the paramilitary commanders were flexing their muscles in this effort to dictate a resolution of the mayoral question, the village faithful were preparing for their biggest act of public worship, the Corpus Christi procession. Because it was an event calculated to antagonize the surging Nazis, this procession was to bring about a first dramatic crossing of the two sides. At the last minute, Hesse and Burger announced that their men should tag along, although the street procession was rained out, which may have prevented this intrusion from actually taking place. On the other hand, the local journeymen in particular were determined to exploit this valuable opportunity for advertising their confessional loyalties. They were in touch with Munich, where a huge convergence of their colleagues resulted in a ban on further festivities. Activists were accused of rewriting "the Horst Wessel Lied with an underlying text" and breaking new Nazi rules that forbade them to appear in uniform. From Munich arrived the offending journeymen's colorful shirts to wear in Oberammergau. Perhaps this provocation would have passed without incident had some men not chosen to stop by their meeting place after the service rather than going straight home.[94]

At this point, Hesse dispatched at least a couple of men to send the young miscreants home so that they could give up their shirts. Then Burger joined them with some of his motorized troops, perhaps at Hesse's behest, just as they came up the street from the inn. Burger later remembered a disorderly scene caused by a vocal group of journeymen "yelling and shrieking." Taking charge, he persuaded some of the young men to go home, but the remainder wanted to be taken to see Hesse. They were behaving "like wild men crying out 'Hands up,' 'Spartacus,' and so on," but he did his best to calm them down.[95]

Witnesses dismissed this story, putting the onus for the confrontation on Burger himself. One journeyman in particular, whom Burger later accused of being drunk, came in for some harsh treatment, which left an elderly woman in tears "because he was so friendly and sweet." His mother testified that he had not returned drunk that day and in any case was hardly a drinking man. Yet he and his fellow journeymen were forcibly marched up the main street to the Alte Post Inn, where Hesse quickly defused the situation by sending them home to change clothes and return the offending uniforms. However, as they set off, Burger pursued his victim once again, knocking him "into an iron garden fence." Perhaps, his mother admitted, her son had responded to the commander's taunts a little "cheekily," but he had been badly hurt.[96]

Burger did not deny this second encounter, explaining that he had been maligned with an ethnic slur that awakened old wounds and caused him to lose his temper. His status as an outsider in Oberammergau was still a source of anguish for this hotheaded man. He had aggravated a difficult but resolvable clash of wills into an incident so notorious that a public comment was required. Thus, Hesse placed a terse announcement in the newspaper to say that the journeymen had faced officially sanctioned "actions." And that was the end of the matter.[97]

Motorstorm Commander Burger's uncontrolled behavior did not undermine the truce between Oberammergau's Nazi and Catholic factions. Nevertheless, his and Hesse's raw power play against their own party's councilors paralleled this intemperate confrontation with their young Catholic opponents. Even his fellow Nazis must have begun to realize that Burger would prove to be a difficult colleague in the months ahead.

Interior Minister Wagner's flying trip to the village came only two days after the Corpus Christi confrontation. He informed the assembled councilors that SPD chief Daisenberger could no longer serve because his party had been officially dissolved. The socialist departed graciously, leaving the way open for a new vote. Now the Nazis could produce a majority, confirming their choice of Raimund Lang as mayor and Alfred Bierling as his deputy. To cement his position as the protector of Oberammergau's interests, Lang had been gathering support under the rubric "Young Ammergau" and had adopted "No excessive foreign presence" as a "slogan." Burger saw this process as a hostile act that kept him off the council during a further reconstruction in late July. Lang was even willing, Burger argued, to work with BVP and SPD opponents to achieve his own aims. In fact, Lang was dead set against any further tinkering with the membership of a body engaged in helping him to push through a series of desired reforms.[98]

With Raimund Lang in place as its Nazi mayor, the Passion Play village had fallen officially under the control of Germany's new leaders. However, longstanding traditions of local governance would mute this transfer of power, and Lang's own dedication to his community's special interests would soon lead him into a dramatic conflict with both Burger and powerful Nazis in Garmisch and Munich. Despite these problems, Lang managed to achieve a successful Passion Play season in 1934. But his first year in office was nothing less than a wild political rollercoaster ride in which he survived a threat to his life and serious challenges to his continued tenure as Oberammergau's top official.

5

Players

Fifty-six years after the special anniversary Passion Play season of 1934, I visited Oberammergau to witness the community in action for myself. Arriving in glorious summer weather, I walked out past the theater with its sea of bicycles near the players' entrance. You can't stay long during the season without seeing locals, men adorned with lengthy locks and flowing beards, dashing past on those bicycles to make their appearance on stage. Striking up the slope of the glistening valley, I was pursued by sounds wafting from the chorus and orchestra. I returned to observe the crush of visitors leaving the theater; a day later I watched another five thousand or so arrive and take their seats, a process that revealed the need for a small army of support staff to act as cashiers, ushers, and emergency personnel.

Soon it was my turn to join the audience, and with great anticipation I passed through door C to find my seat in row eleven, an excellent vantage point from which to experience the Passion Play. Cold air greeted me, despite the fact that it was August, but the mist was lifting to reveal sun and blue sky beyond the stage. As part of the excited crowd, I squeezed in next to a German monk in the jam-packed theater. With only a break for lunch, the action proceeded for the entire day. Hundreds of performers were involved in massive crowd scenes and silent tableaux, backing up scores of actors filling the spoken roles. Once again music emanated from the voices and instruments of more than 150 villagers.

I found the play completely absorbing, although I did not share in the religious epiphany described in so many guidebooks. Rather, it was the commonality of purpose handed down from previous generations that enthralled me, linking the players of major roles such as Christ with those who merely crowded around him. This was still in essence the scriptural reading that Father Daisenberger had bequeathed to his community, profoundly shaping the lives of individuals growing up in Oberammergau. New actors had replaced the cast so lovingly described in accounts of plays past, but chains of tradition still bound them to their controversial Passion narrative.[1]

More than fifty years earlier, a special jubilee season had drawn hordes of visitors, more German this time than in preceding decades, many arriving in "special trains." Then, too, the gentle beauty of shimmering meadows would have greeted these new arrivals. But in 1934, enchanting Alpine scenery coexisted with the darkened social reality of Nazi control over Oberammergau. Often it was the singing of their national anthem and Horst Wessel Lied that flooded the valley landscape, notably when Hitler spent an August day attending the play.

This Nazi takeover had only gradually impacted the local balance of power. It was well into the summer of 1933 before a full transformation of the political realities was made manifest. Even then, the spa faction's predominance within the local chapter softened the blow since Mayor Lang was steeped in Passion Play traditions. While his group had certainly developed ideas about isolating their play from Oberammergau's tourism economy, his commitment to the villagers' special role as Passion players was never in doubt. This intersection of new leadership and local customs illuminates well the compromise that for a while permitted the two cultures, Nazi and Catholic, to coexist.

Lang's became a relatively benign administration that held the most strident and insidious facets of Nazi power at arm's length. Partly as a result, he found himself engaged in conflicts that swirled around play affairs and reflected the hostility toward outsiders that typified Oberammergau's social dynamic. Tradition dominated as a Nazi-led Passion Committee chose the actors and once again staged Daisenberger's script, although they made significant revisions and tried, unsuccessfully, to modernize it. Disagreement then surfaced about the degree to which the new regime's interests should give way to communal disciplines established long before their party came on the scene. However, the value of the special season for Third Reich leaders also protected Lang when hostile forces threatened his job and even his life.

Mayor Lang lost no time in taking charge of village affairs after his abrupt accession to power in late June 1933. As a dedicated Nazi, he marveled in his first speech to the councilors that this "year of the resurrection of our German Fatherland coincides with the three hundredth anniversary of the Oberammergau Passion vow." Despite accusations about their hostility to organized religion, he argued, the Nazis had also been fighting a "plague," that is, "the enemy of Christianity, Marxism." So Lang's mayoral duty would be to protect the play in good Christian fashion with a special eye to any threats from "harmful commercial ways of thinking." He also stressed the need to look after Oberammergau's "two key industries, woodcarving and tourism." Lang ended this amalgam of Nazi rhetoric and insider wisdom with a rousing appeal for unity in the work ahead: "Long live our community, our fatherland, and our Führer." He was still blending his Catholic heritage and loyalty to the Passion Play with the new ideological light in his life provided by Adolf Hitler.[2]

After Lang's speech came a reconstruction of the Passion Committee. In addition to the sitting councilors, including four remaining BVP representatives, four Nazis and two Catholics would be chosen from lists submitted by the respective parties. This allowed BVP officials to tap Anton Lang as one of their appointees. Six of the Third Reich's primary opponents therefore remained on the committee, as well as Father Bogenrieder, so they seemed likely to enjoy a strong influence in play affairs. Moreover, Nazi-appointed committee members included leading figures in communal life. Georg Lang as play director was joined by Zeno Diemer, whose own experience with previous seasons made him a natural. One man was carried over from the elected 1934 committee, while another had served on the 1930 committee. All were men who, though party loyalists, had the Passion Play's welfare at heart.[3]

With the Passion Committee reconfigured along lines dictated by the new regime, local politicians moved to shut down Oberammergau's multiparty system. Most dramatic was the arrest of Mayr, whose dismissal had come with assurances that he would "always enjoy the respect of the council." Nevertheless, as part of a general move against their political opponents, Nazi officials took him into custody early on June 28. This arrest involved villagers, notably Motorstorm Commander Burger, while policemen actually entered his home to look through the former BVP leader's papers. Hours after his dramatic arrest, however, Mayr was released. The population rejoiced as this proud man from one of Oberammergau's most prominent families walked with his sons through the sunlit streets to prove that he was no common criminal.[4]

Despite his swift return, Mayr's party was finished as a political force since the BVP was abolished in early July. This encouraged at least a couple of their councilors to apply for Nazi party membership, a move possibly blocked at the county level. Meanwhile, SPD Chief Daisenberger announced publicly what Lang had already boasted about as a security measure, that his group had been closed down. Subsequent reporting indicates that some Socialists covered their tracks by joining either the SA Reserve or the NSDAP. The political field was left wide open for the new Nazi leadership to exploit.[5]

In his introductory speech Raimund Lang had put the village on notice that local Nazis would choose their own representatives without recourse to any normal electoral procedures. Initially, they applied this principle to the Tourism Club, which Lang now headed. Two months later they extended this reach to the Winter Sports Club, citing an extension of their "leadership principle" to "all sport and gymnastic activities." Nevertheless, it suited the new mayor to work with a diverse group of officials at this critical stage of preparation for Oberammergau's upcoming Passion season.[6]

Lang therefore made vigorous efforts to keep the council intact, but he was soon faced with the removal of all of the remaining BVP councilors. His plea for a united front at such a sensitive moment fell on deaf ears, although perhaps not completely since their replacements were men with whom Lang could work comfortably. Only one had previously been a councilor, joining Breitsamter and Bierling in a small contingent of elected carryovers. However, while the remaining additions were new to communal governance, SA Commander Hesse was really the sole outsider. However, even he and his housemate, Alzinger, already a sitting councilor, represented those party leaders with whom Lang was closing ranks. The mayor would have a malleable community council with which to complete his reform agenda.[7]

Because some of its members had been freely elected before the Nazi takeover, this new council could at least partially continue to represent the village population in a genuinely democratic fashion. Moreover, the need to satisfy local constituents would shape its political decisions, while Oberammergau's unique extra layer of representation through the Passion Committee meant that for more than a year the councilors remained in close contact with its two BVP representatives and even with Father Bogenrieder. Then, the rapid approach of another Passion season in 1940 once again drew them into consultation with their erstwhile opponents.[8]

Mayor Lang faced similar restrictions on his power if he moved too dramatically beyond traditional guidelines, while the councilors also counterbalanced his authority from their base within the community. In addition, Lang faced an angry Motorstorm faction, which felt excluded from the seat of local control since Burger blamed Lang's political "cattle trading" for his own failure to join the council with Hesse. The ruling junta would face years of tense confrontation with radical Nazis as a result.[9]

As Nazi consolidation proceeded in Oberammergau, the various village leaders continued to struggle with the Depression's negative effects. They tried in particular to rescue citizens from bankruptcy and provide for the unemployed, with charity if needed but through work whenever possible, notably construction to improve the road to Linderhof. Decades before, King Ludwig had provided welcome employment for villagers like blacksmith Jakob Rutz when he built his chateau with its fantastical underground grotto. Now Ludwig's popular retreat once again rescued local workers as Mayor Lang guided this long-desired project to fruition. Encouraging, too, was an improved tourism economy, with both overnight stays and visitor totals on the upswing.[10]

Despite Lang's desire to avoid exploiting the impending Passion season, it did offer hope of additional work and helpful public revenues, as well as anticipatory use of honoraria. However, the councilors still had to aid poor families in the winter months before the season began. One plan was to buy up the products of struggling carvers for inclusion in an "Exhibition of Woodcarving 1934." In addition, Nazi women and youth soon mobilized to launch a version of winter assistance under the auspices of the party's charitable arm (NSV), led by Mayor Lang himself.[11]

Beyond these Depression woes, Oberammergau's new leaders worried about their failure to attract active members for the associational structures designed to rival the Catholic clubs. The chief of the Nazi labor organization (DAF) captured a general disillusionment: "As is customary in Oberammergau, the most important meetings are always badly attended." Still more damaging in the Nazis' eyes was the unwillingness of enough villagers to join the NSDAP and its subsidiary organizations. By late summer officials were reporting plaintively that "precisely those inhabitants who today are holding themselves aloof from the party and behave disapprovingly of the Third Reich" were the ones absent from an enlightening meeting. During a promotional event in November, the BdM failed to draw a satisfactory number of recruits. The NSF openly advertised for new members during the winter, as did the HJ.[12]

These active, if frustrating, efforts at recruitment were bolstered by a series of public events that continued to shape Oberammergau's cultural landscape. Just after Lang's takeover as mayor, he presided over the dramatic reenactment of an "old Germanic custom," a summer solstice ceremony. Local boys and girls, both HJ and schoolchildren, took part in athletic competitions, sang, and performed gymnastics near a bonfire set up on the outskirts of the village. Taking this public opportunity to stress Nazism's Christian foundations, Lang defined the HJ's duties as "obedience, loyalty, and religiosity." In the fall came a harvest festival dubbed the "German farmers' day," and then celebrations accompanied a mid-November national vote, including a torchlight procession and a mayoral exhortation on the eve of the election. The year ended with Christmas festivities that once again focused on Nazi youth.[13]

Radio broadcasts connected locals with official ceremonies held farther afield, like the launching of Munich's House of German Art, which was blasted out by loudspeakers into Oberammergau's central square. Hitler's speeches before the November vote could be heard in various public venues. One could even attend that year's Nuremberg rally since heavily discounted travel was available to party members. Then in early 1934 Ernst Lang joined nattily uniformed boys from the region's HJ on a trip to Potsdam, where their banner was dedicated during a prototypically Nazi nighttime march, alive with flaming torches and massed flags. Lang was also among the youths who attended the famous 1934 Nuremberg rally, where he heard Hitler speak in person.[14]

Opposition to this energetic Nazi presence in Oberammergau was due in part to the continued strength of Catholic institutions. To be sure, June's Corpus Christi drama was followed by a period of truce between the two sides. Hitler's concordat with Pope Pius XI accompanied an official end to political Catholicism, while at least theoretically preserving apolitical associational life, especially the rituals that believers deemed essential to their spiritual and practical welfare. Bavarian authorities prolonged a prohibition of the Catholic clubs' normal public activities until November. At that point the Workers' Club members met to discuss the new setup's implications. They should not promote any political agenda or talk about "trade union–type questions." Furthermore, they were to obey both Adolf Hitler and "our spiritual leaders," a new interpretation of the Gospel command to "render unto Caesar" that favored passive acceptance of their new government.[15]

Oberammergau's Catholics were also plunged into a new round of intense preparations for the upcoming play season, so they had to cooperate closely with their Nazi counterparts. Mayor Lang's stewardship of Passion Play affairs was to prove quite controversial. Nevertheless, the mixed group of erstwhile political opponents managed to carry off a successful season in 1934 under his leadership.

Despite this relative calm in Nazi-Catholic relations, Father Bogenrieder echoed his political rivals' sentiments about lagging commitment when he assessed the state of confessional organizations in 1933. He was particularly worried that demanding party activities scheduled on Sundays were undermining the religious life of young men. Moreover, he deplored the fact that crucial groups, including the Women's Union, had been largely inactive.[16]

Perhaps Oberammergau's rector was overly sensitive about the erosion of his parish's associational life. He counted membership totals for the charitable clubs that were similar to those in 1931; the numbers had, in fact, also fluctuated earlier on. Both the Marian Congregation at almost fifty and the Mothers' Club at well more than one hundred had actually gained members, although they were down from earlier highs; the congregation even met in December to welcome new recruits. Mathilde Lang's group had peaked in the midst of the Depression; perhaps its subsequent losses reflected her illness in 1933, yet the new total of 130 women equaled the 1927 and exceeded the 1929 numbers. The Third Order had continued a slide from more than fifty activists in 1927 to a mere thirty-seven. But the Workers' Club, after growing to nearly a hundred during the Depression, had slipped by only a few members at the time of the Nazi takeover.[17]

The Journeymen's Club was the male organization that weakened the most dramatically since it lost more than a third of its seventy members; the allure of joining Nazi organizations was probably undermining support for this traditional group of service-oriented young men, added to pragmatic considerations about access to still elusive employment opportunities. Nevertheless, the drop merely returned its numbers to the 1927 levels, so perhaps the alleviation of Depression challenges also caused these defections. Similarly, the boys' youth group had sunk by a third to thirty-seven in 1933; the decision of religious youth like Ernst Lang and a Raab son to accept leadership positions in the HJ must have been particularly damaging.[18]

These reasonably strong membership numbers would have counted for little, however, if the Catholic organizations could not follow an active meeting schedule. Internal church groups got together most consistently, girls and mothers on a monthly basis and the Third Order quite frequently. In addition, the Press Club once again held its annual convention in February 1934, which included a slide show. The Workers' Club assembled at least occasionally, announcing one gathering in mid-November and another the following January; it also organized a Christmas party for its members. Early in 1934 the Women's Union organized a slide show about "Our Saints as Examples for Catholic Women," featuring both Brother Conrad and that year's jubilee pilgrimage to Trier. Lang herself "exhorted the many attendees to genuine cooperation and true fulfillment of duty in service to God."[19]

The journeymen stayed engaged as well, organizing an urgent "extraordinary general meeting" in November and shortly afterward a party to celebrate the 120th birthday of their founder, Adolf Kolping, the proceeds of which would go to winter assistance efforts. Chaplain Eberlein highlighted this event with a newspaper article about Kolping's successful career, stressing the contemporary relevance of his mission to rescue those lost to Christianity at a time of dramatic social transformation. Eberlein's journeymen followed up with well-attended "traditional" Christmas festivities and then a standard annual convention the following April.[20]

Through these continued public events, Oberammergau's Catholic activists demonstrated commitment to their charitable mission and fundamental religious values. Local spiritual life also continued along traditional lines. Well timed was a folk mission in late September, a successful outreach that wound up with a ceremony bringing together councilors and church officials, flag-touting club members, as well as "all schoolchildren." Anton Lang and his fellow church wardens were reelected in December, ensuring continuity in this important area of leadership. Age-old customs held firm as believers dedicated masses to their chosen saints, including the newly popular Brother Conrad, while pilgrims visited the Ettal shrine. Locals undoubtedly joined more than one thousand women converging on the Wieskirche in mid-September shortly before the "extraordinarily big attendance from city and country" at the shrine's annual Guardian Angel event. A harvest festival procession took place as usual, and later, during the spring of 1934, rogation columns headed off to their established destinations.[21]

Finally, Corpus Christi celebrations followed the initial Passion Play performances, demonstrating the continued health of local ritual life. Denominational club members were scheduled to march corporately, journeymen, workers, and young males, as well as the Marian Congregation. Once again the councilors joined this prototypically Catholic act of public witness, signaling a united communal front. No mention was made of intrusion by the Storm Troopers this time around. Rather, play visitors witnessed this traditional procession, reinforcing the pressures felt by both Nazis and Catholics to work together that summer. Nothing, not even party business, was to disturb the tranquility of their Passion season.[22]

Preparations for the 1934 jubilee had already been under way when Hitler ascended to power. As a result, his new regime's transformative effects were offset by a sequence of well-established routines leading up to a Passion Play season. The villagers had decided to launch a special season on November 9, 1932. Shortly thereafter, voting for the Passion Committee had proceeded normally so that its members could begin making the numerous organizational decisions that would ensure a successful outcome. By the time of the Nazi takeover, they had picked the director, Georg Lang; two musical conductors, including the current school principal, Anton Sattler; and the head cashier, Administrator Raab. They had also received the special blessing of Cardinal Faulhaber, who hoped for further "common work in the interest of the Catholic faith and the village community." Committee members had in addition met with famed Catholic author Leo Weismantel to discuss his historical play about the 1633 vow, which was scheduled for performance in 1933, as well as ideas about a contextualizing prologue for the play performances that never actually came to fruition.[23]

The early months after the Nazi takeover found committee members negotiating with their usual travel agencies, including Cook's, and setting up the "arrangements." Then came a three-month suspension of business activities, which must have been troubling with the season only a year away. It was during this time that Georg Lang chose to become a Nazi, supposedly to protect the play, and if the new regime was to turn hostile, this would have been the moment of danger. However, in fact, both Hitler and Goebbels had already visited and been favorably impressed by the play, and it would soon become clear just how supportive other Nazi officials would be. While fears surfaced periodically, the safety of the Passion Play tradition never seems to have been in any doubt. Even Father Bogenrieder noted how beneficial had been the "inner renewal of the German folk" as a result of Hitler's ascendancy, which had rendered the play once again "a holy source of deep German faith."[24]

The Nazi-appointed Passion Committee got to work swiftly, continuing the preparations already under way. They even summoned back Administrator Raab after his dismissal as a BVP councilor to serve on the crucial business and advertising subcommittee. All of these leaders understood the mix of tradition and innovation that had made previous play seasons so successful. They would also have been well aware of the complaints about commercialization that had surfaced in 1930. Raimund Lang was fortunate to have their support as he made difficult changes in the now customary "arrangements."[25]

The mayor was deeply engaged in altering these package deals in a way that he feared would prove quite unpopular with local homeowners. As early as June 28, he explained to committee members how he intended to rescue the play from its integral role in Oberammergau's economy. The villagers, he argued, must reject a commercial approach and return to the kind of season that their ancestors would have welcomed. They must, therefore, control prices in order to head off criticisms of the sort that had distressed them last time around.[26]

To achieve this aim, Lang soon moved to renegotiate the contracts already in place. Beyond lower package deals, he worked with railroad authorities to secure bargain fares for play visitors similar to those arranged for the centennial pilgrimage to Trier. These prices applied if the traveler acquired one of the discounted three-day stays linked to a play ticket that Lang had managed to make available.[27]

Lang expected the Passion season's beneficial pricing to improve Oberammergau's tourism industry in the off years. Building relationships with railroad personnel would, he thought, help in this effort later on. So, no doubt, would his hiring of a former spa director to take charge of the village's lodgings office.

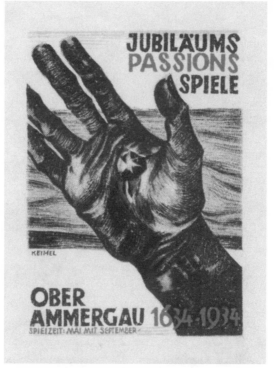

(a)

(b)

However, this visionary effort was, indeed, not popular with homeowners, who even tried to wriggle out of providing such inexpensive board and lodging. Moreover, the Passion season would still have to bring in a substantial profit, given the many demands for funds that the mayor was anticipating. Therefore, he initiated what became a prolonged fight over the level of honoraria for hundreds of villagers. His plan was to minimize their percentage of the final takings in order to divert as much money as possible toward communal projects instead. However, this sensitive issue had already caused huge problems in 1930 and would challenge Lang and his councilors for years after the 1934 season was over.[28]

Attracting the large crowds that would make the season profitable required an aggressive advertising strategy. One prong of this strategy was to provide free and positive publicity about the play through a new press secretary. There was also talk of exploiting the radio, a plan about which Lang was clearly enthusiastic. But the heart of this effort was the production of a catchy image that would appear on posters, as well as on official publications.[29]

The Passion Committee initiated a competition that soon came up with a winning design submitted by Munich artist Hermann Keimel. A starkly expressionistic image, it centers on Christ's splayed out hand etched in black, blood oozing from the nail that attaches it so cruelly to a reddish-brown cross. The poster's writing echoes its theme of black and red that makes Keimel's hand quite striking but was also to make it very controversial.[30] (Figure 5.1a reproduces Keimel's hand.)

Initially, Lang was negotiating in Berlin to turn out promotional materials with the Keimel image. However, this radical design fell out of favor with Goebbels' Propaganda Ministry, which had first understood that a whipped Christ was to be used that might "wound the German people's religious sensitivities." Even when put right about its theme, they reiterated instructions that the offending image should be replaced in particular for foreign advertising. The wisdom of this decision was confirmed by a distressing letter critical, they reported, of Keimel's "Jesuitical poster" because it "made a mockery of the German greeting."[31]

Artist Jupp Wiertz was commissioned to create a replacement, which proved to be the extreme opposite of Keimel's dark vision of human suffering. Against a hazy blue background of high Alpine ranges appear red-roofed homes and the onion-domed church clustering beneath a huge and gleaming cross.

FIGURE 5.1. (a) Hermann Keimel's image, "Bleeding Hand on the Cross," wins the competition to promote Oberammergau's 1934 Passion season. (b) Jupp Wiertz's "Germany invites You!" is chosen by Nazi officials to replace the Keimel image.

Verdant greens in the valley floor absorb the light emanating from this cross, which also plays off the forward-facing steeple. Green and purple foliage frames the viewer's entry into this valley, where the Passion theater and the parish church lie near the Kofel's familiar rocky face. A caption reads: "Germany invites you!" It is hard to imagine a cozier if more mendacious picture of the regenerated folk community snug in its beloved rural *Heimat*, secure in its traditional faith, and warming to a bright and joyous future in the Nazi state.[32] (Figure 5.1b reproduces the Wiertz design.)

However, this unwanted intrusion into his village's promotional plan enraged Raimund Lang, for whom the Wiertz image was too melodramatic. He took particular exception to what he called "this visionary cross," which misrepresented the Passion Play's entire history by comparing Oberammergau with a supernaturally inspired "pilgrimage site like Lourdes." Were Keimel's hand to be withdrawn because of its raw brutality, the villagers would like to use a different prize-winning design rather than this "kitschy" rubbish left over from the Weimar period's "lying Jewish propaganda."[33]

This brave if prejudiced effort to head off the use of Wiertz's seductive vision ended in a draw. Both his design and Keimel's saw the light of day, as well as the second-place winner in Oberammergau's original competition, a tame woodcut lacking the Keimel bite. Lang's objections reveal a man walking a fine line when working with the regime's bigwigs. He shared their basic ideology, but deep concerns about his community's welfare drove him to speak his mind when local interests clashed with the Nazis' dictates.[34]

Nevertheless, because he knew how much his superiors valued Oberammergau's jubilee, Lang worked to engage top officials in the preparations. As early as August 1933 he was inviting Hitler to attend Weismantel's historical play. Soon thereafter, Lang suggested asking a top Nazi to become the play's official patron, a potential alteration of its status so distressing to Father Bogenrieder that he protested in a committee meeting. Lang assured the anxious priest that "a certain secular protection" would not rob their play of its religious credentials. He added that Hitler's forestalling of a leftist revolution had rescued the 1934 season. Yet the community had made itself vulnerable by refusing the local recognition to leading Nazis that other places were providing, so this concession was needed. If not Hitler himself, then Bavarian Minister Hermann Esser would be a valuable patron.[35]

Esser thus joined Interior Minister Adolf Wagner, whose home in Unterammergau made him a frequent visitor to the Ammer valley, as a Bavarian magnate whose ear local officials could catch. Esser's special interest in promoting the tourism industry, Lang argued, made him a good choice. Yet this long-standing crony and Führer lookalike—Goebbels called him "a smart pocket-size Hitler"—represented the party leadership at its worst, given his virulent anti-Semitism and aggressive nature. Moreover, the author of a book first published in 1927 under the title *The Jewish Global Plague* was surely a poor candidate to promote Germany as a pacific nation. That was, however, his aim when he swept into Oberammergau in October 1933 to woo the visiting press.[36]

Wagner was hardly a statesman who could represent the village effectively to the outside world, but he was another Hitler intimate who became the ultimate source of power in Munich. His fascination with the reinvention of public festivals in the Third Reich must have encouraged him to see Oberammergau's Passion Play as an object worthy of his patronage. Ernst Lang was struck by this repugnant leader's "red face . . . [and] swollen eyes." He recalled Wagner's jaunty getup, including a "leather cap" suited to rides in an open convertible, as well as "riding pants with . . . laced up motorcycle boots." Nevertheless, his war service and severe injuries, which left him with an artificial limb, made criticism difficult for Lang and his contemporaries.[37]

Despite their disturbing personalities, such powerful connections proved quite helpful. Yet that attention could also be a mixed blessing. Goebbels, for example, had been particularly impressed with the play's crowd scenes leading up to the Crucifixion, which he saw as an expression of the "eternal" Jewish character. Perhaps as a result, his ministry was eager to promote the performances as a folkish sort of anti-Semitic propaganda. However, in a diary comment Goebbels wrote after his 1930 visit, he referred to Oberammergau as "a delicious little place," which may help to explain the ministry's intervention in support of Wiertz's despised image of rural bliss. More propitious, perhaps, was the interest shown by the Nazis' chief ideologue, Alfred Rosenberg. He was hoping that members of Cook's tours would linger in Germany once the play's lure had brought these foreign visitors into the country.[38]

Local officials needed this sort of ministerial support in part to counter damaging misperceptions that might undermine their efforts to attract an international audience. Naturally, suspicions abounded that Germany's new rulers would dictate unwelcome changes to the play's staging. As early as May 1933, worries surfaced about the *New York Times* picking up the false idea that all of the roles would go to Nazis.[39]

That August foreign newspapers mistakenly reported that Goebbels was angling for an Aryan Christ, "a blond man with blue eyes" clothed in swastika-covered garments. Similarly, the "Apostles were to be the Aryan-Germanic type. Only Judas will be portrayed as a pronounced Semitic type." An indignant Swiss reader duped by this rumor exclaimed: "Christ as a swastika follower. One holds one's head and can't decide whether to get mad about the[ir] tastelessness . . . or the impudence with which they dare to ridicule Christ and his disciples . . . a few weeks after the conclusion of the concordat between Germany and the Catholic Church." Surely, he added, the propaganda minister would not interfere in this way.[40]

Even the Nazi organ itself was propagating a strange misconception reported in *Figaro* that the players were mostly Jews. However, because they had left Germany, Nazis with Semitic features were replacing them at Esser's behest. Later, *Figaro* added the specifics that "the player of Judas was to be a Jew" who would be subjected to "whistling." As the season got under way, a Danish paper expressed the idea that Alois Lang was a "fighting Christ." "Anton Lang was Stresemann's Germany, suffering and submissive. Alois Lang is Hitler's Germany, the nation awakening, which knows that victory can be won and the future beckons." The paper also argued that the Judas player would complement Lang's performance by imbuing his character with "an almost modern, communistic shape."[41]

While this report may well have seemed positive in the context of Third Reich culture, a critical reaction in a Swiss newspaper was unambiguous. Responding specifically to the Wiertz poster, its writer exclaims sarcastically: "Germany calls! So, Germany, not Christ." The article continues in the same vein: "Johann Georg Lang as Germano-Saxon-SA-man-heroic Christ. Thank you very much! Then it would be best if Oberammergau were made into Bayreuth, Baldur [von Schirach] crucified with musical accompaniment by Richard Wagner, text by the poet of the Horst-Wessel-Lied." Warning his fellow Catholic citizens against attending the play, the writer ends on a serious note of criticism directed against Nazi racism; their Christ had sacrificed himself to benefit all races. Such critiques were powerful, although they wildly overestimated the influence that Nazism was to have on the jubilee performances. To counter them would take all of the promotional tools that Oberammergau's leaders could muster.[42]

On the face of it, efforts to assuage suspicion about Nazi meddling with their play might actually have suffered from Esser's visit with international press representatives to cover the long-anticipated selection of the cast. Assembling uniformed males to greet them, Lang thanked the season's official "godfather." Esser then dined with the visitors in Oberammergau's best hotel, hoping to convince them to report accurately about the play's role, that is, the promotion of Germany's commitment to "world peace." They would, he hoped, return home with a reassuring understanding of the new state's desirable qualities.[43]

Esser returned to a swastika-hung Oberammergau for the first performance in May 1934, hosting British reporters at Alois Lang's establishment.

Curiously, the villagers once again allowed a prominent official to meddle openly with their season's ritual highlights despite the sensitive question of interference already plaguing them. A further visit by Bavaria's minister president in July even saw the Passion orchestra rendering the Horst Wessel Lied at Lang's guesthouse.[44]

Appearances were actually quite deceptive where Nazi influence over the play itself was concerned. Certainly, the picture was not as rosy as Britain's pro-German *Times* suggested. One article reported that "the strange combination of a brown shirt with flowing locks and a full-grown beard" was "a rare sight." Another enthused that "little in the village of Oberammergau and nothing in the Passion Play has been affected by the changed conditions of Germany. The tercentenary performance . . . is completely free from the political distortions rumoured in England. . . . There are in the streets formal evidences of the new regime, a salute now and then, a flag here and there, but a more peaceful and friendly place would be hard to find in Europe."[45]

Nevertheless, the actual process of allocating parts and service assignments was remarkably free of Nazi interference. To be sure, for the first time the full Passion Committee was to vote openly within the confines of a closed meeting, in what observer Sophie Rützou calls "the National-Socialist spirit." However, when its members paid their customary visit to the parish church before finalizing their selections, they once again accepted the traditional mandate to choose only the best actors. Furthermore, all of the evidence suggests that they followed this well-established approach to making decisions, which, after all, would determine the play's success as an artistic enterprise.[46]

The first step was as usual to classify the available roles in a series of separate male and female "classes" tied to a payment schedule. Top pay on the male side went to the play director, the musical director, Lang as mayor, and the three major acting parts, Christ, Caiaphas, and the prologue. In the second class came Judas and Peter, as well as Annas and Pilate, together with the lead singers and the chorus, the musicians, and the stage manager. A youthful John made it into a third class along with other leading players and service personnel. The remaining apostles shared a fourth class with other midlevel players, while lesser parts were relegated to the fifth and sixth classes. Most of the service categories and the male crowd ended up in a bottom seventh class. Women were divided into five classes, with Mary and Mary Magdalene in the top group, singers in second place, and players in the lower classes, with the crowd and wardrobe assistants bringing up the rear. Separate classes also existed for young adults and children, as well as medical personnel. Salaries ranged from 100 percent to 50 percent of the top rate, which was 2,000 marks for men, 1,400 marks for women. With only minor adjustments later on, these far from popular salaries were successfully maintained.[47]

Equally important in deciding who would fill these various roles were the guidelines to be applied concerning residency restrictions. In the end the Passion Committee was remarkably flexible in reinterpreting the old rules. Although Georg Lang stressed the need for a migrant to "first live in the whole atmosphere of the play," the cutoff date for new residents was set at 1924. They also lifted restrictions on participation by eligible employees despite fears that their absence from work might flood the village with unwanted replacements. Consequently, while many of the newly minted players were clustered in the low-level service categories, they were able to benefit from the truncated but nonetheless eagerly awaited honoraria.[48]

Esser swooped in with press representatives just as the Passion Committee began applying their revamped classification system to filling the most coveted and best-paid roles. At this point, the committee members showed no interest in elevating key Nazis into these top classes. Certainly, the administrative posts in the two highest categories were partially filled by party men, but they were either repeats from 1930 or in Mayor Lang's case predetermined by his official position. Their inclusion of Raab in particular, a clear ideological opponent, underscores the emphasis they placed on competence over political orientation. All three class one players were repeating their parts from 1930 and, like Raab, were identifiable as Catholic opponents. Anton Lang returned as prologue, his brother-in-law was to reprise as Caiaphas, and the deposed BVP councilor Alois Lang reclaimed his role as Christ. Similarly, the important Herod part was once again filled by ex-mayor Mayr despite his dramatic arrest a few months earlier.[49]

The committee members were following traditional guidelines in making these and all subsequent choices, the most influential of which was an actor's successful rendering of that role during the previous play season. Almost half of the sixty individuals listed as top cast members in 1934 were repeating roles; a further ten moved into parts similar to those they had filled in 1930. Consequently, there was much unanimity in the voting process, although a few problems surfaced, notably the choice of a new Judas. The eventual pick was not a Nazi, but Raimund Lang did stress his likeness to the popular image of Judas. Two early joiners were serious candidates for Saint John.[50]

Close to a quarter of these players had joined the NSDAP by 1934, including a couple of NSF members and a handful of "old fighters." Party allegiance, however, was secondary to proven acting ability in these cases since more than half of them were reprising roles or moving into similar parts. Fellow party members who secured new roles were young, no doubt hoping to work their way up to the highly coveted major parts.[51]

Nazis made up 14 percent or so of the more than 850 villagers who received payment for their participation in 1934; more than twelve hundred were involved overall. Almost a third of these Nazi players were "old fighters," including some of the recent migrants for whom newly permissive residency rules opened up access to Passion service, mostly on the lowest levels. The Villa Ammerhof leadership in particular provided a crowd member, an usher, and two cashiers. Involving a wide cross-section of locals thus led to a substantial Nazi presence in both cast and support personnel.[52]

Beyond the party members involved, there were also Storm Troopers since forty-five of Hesse's men were to receive honoraria, but only some of them were enrolled in NSDAP ranks. Dozens of men listed in the Motorstorm were also Passion workers, but the possibility that many were actually unwilling carryovers from a junior branch of the Stahlhelm veterans' group makes their activist status questionable. All five men listed as SS in 1934 were also engaged with the play, although it is not clear that any but one was officially part of Himmler's paramilitary force. Finally, some underage players would have belonged to the HJ or the BdM.[53]

Because Nazis were integrated into all sections of the population, it did not take malice aforethought to include them with Oberammergau's other players. Consequently, their participation does not support the idea that officials favored their fellow party members. Nor was there any serious effort to elevate Nazis into desirable, lucrative roles since so many "old fighters," including leading figures, were relegated to the lowest class of Passion workers. Rather, the peculiar rules of this communal enterprise scattered activists naturally into the various categories that best suited their talents and social standing. They carried out their jobs cheek to jowl with their counterparts who had chosen not to join the party, following the custom of mixing people from all political backgrounds in local affairs.

Mayor Lang and his Passion Committee certainly blended tradition and innovation in preparing for the 1934 season. When necessity dictated that they modify entrenched practices like their arrangements, they bent. Otherwise, they built on decisions already made in 1930. Some policies proved to be widely unpopular, notably the reduction in honoraria. On the other hand, including so many recent migrants must have pleased that section of the population, if not most of the old-timers. And the leadership was not done with stirring up controversy. In a response stretching back to their ancestor, Father Daisenberger, and beyond, the Lang brothers met serious criticisms leveled against the playscript with a plan for its rejuvenation.[54]

Their idea was to have author Weismantel make needed revisions, but he had balked at this assignment, reportedly pointing out that "amateurish work could not be further revised." Daisenberger's text needed to be thoroughly "translated" and rendered error free. As Max Lenz pointed out in a Silesian newspaper, it was "clumsy," "undramatic," and "contradictory"; characters were drawn in "black and white"; and recent discoveries about the Crucifixion story, together with a synthesis of the various Gospel narratives, ought to reshape its message. Consequently, Weismantel set out to write a new text based at least in part on research he was pursuing in Berlin. Lenz approved of this effort: "The writer has a high purpose: he is striving [to write] the German Passion." Raimund Lang later argued that this endeavor was to be the salvation of Oberammergau's legacy.[55]

The question of using some version of their new text then surfaced at a Passion Committee meeting. Father Bogenrieder demurred, arguing that it strayed too far from its biblical base, so he was read excerpts to calm his fears. However, no final decision was made until this whole affair had blown up into a major confrontation that drew in Unterammergau's mayor and even Minister Wagner himself.[56]

The next step was to present Weismantel's new text to the top players. As Lang later informed the Passion Committee, 70 percent had "enthusiastically" endorsed it, but then a furor had arisen over this misunderstood attempt to save the play. In particular, two actors and Principal Sattler had secretly visited Wagner in his nearby retreat. Showing him the offending playbook, the three enlisted his assistance in blocking its use. A disappointed Lang was particularly upset that the defectors included a "former Saint John now playing Pilate" and even more so the principal, now also serving as musical director. He suspected that the two actors involved were exacting retribution after receiving lesser parts than they had anticipated. Apparently, all kinds of rumors were circulating about funds flowing out to Weismantel and perhaps to the Langs as well. Threatening to suspend the committee members if they did not bolster his position, the mayor demanded that they put the story straight with Oberammergau's population.[57]

However, the crisis did not end there. Mayor Dominik Schwab of Unterammergau protested to Wagner that several newspapers had written about the "mockery" involving "a corrosive Center member [acting] against an ancient religious specimen of folk art in the mountains." This was because Mayor Lang was spreading the news that, far from supporting the three critics, Wagner had endorsed Weismantel's text. Moreover, Lang was falsely claiming to have a majority of villagers on his side, the exact opposite of the actual situation. Cunningly, Schwab added that this publicity was undermining Wagner's "person as Minister of State." But he also feared that Oberammergau's established population had lost any commitment to their own customs, as well as to Hitler's instructions that neither the Passion Play village nor Bayreuth should alter "their ancient inherited nature." Sadly, a tiny minority of locals was using party ideology as "cover" for a challenge to mainstream interests.[58]

Schwab also approached Wagner's deputy, Max Köglmaier, reiterating his major complaints with an additional dramatic twist. Not only were most of the villagers and Wagner opposed to the Langs' plan, but they were also "lovers of good art and German [culture]." To add insult to injury, he understood that the brothers were planning to replace Daisenberger's picture in Oberammergau's promotional literature with that of BVP member Weismantel. In response, Köglmaier contacted the councilors and expressed his boss's hostility to any lingering public discussion over reforms that the minister had clearly told Mayor Lang to abandon.[59]

By then, however, the Lang brothers' reform efforts had been defeated, and rehearsals with the traditional Daisenberger text must have been well under way. The two had found themselves trapped by a convergence of wary traditionalism and Nazi promotion of unadulterated folk culture. However, resentments lingered, as Raimund Lang revealed after the season was over. People unschooled in Oberammergau's history, he groused, had intruded into his community's most intimate and ancient affairs. There was only so much meddling by outside Nazi officials that this homegrown mayor could tolerate.[60]

Rejection of the Weismantel text did not free Oberammergau's leadership from any need to quash suspicions that their play would be altered. In fact, they found out that opponents of Nazism were spreading rumors about "anti-Semitic" intentions to violate the script's traditional makeup by removing its Old Testament tableaux. In a public statement they rejected any idea that politics had played a part in discussions of the text's future, which had been going on for many years. They mentioned that Weismantel was working on minor alterations, and, indeed, small if significant and supposedly artistic improvements did take place. Yet, given the tumultuous outcome of the original plan to rewrite the text, it is hardly surprising that claims by contemporaries, notably Anton Lang, denied any "changes in the libretto."[61]

The aim of these textual adjustments remains controversial. Shapiro draws attention to the chorus's interpretation of an initial tableau depicting Joseph's betrayal by his brothers. Its lines harshly condemn the brothers/Jews to physical annihilation as opponents of "God" and his "only Son," but they omit softening words about "pardon, grace, and endless joy" included in earlier versions. This vengeful rhetoric, added to the play's already antagonistic portrayal of "the Jews," fitted well with Nazi ideology.[62]

However, it is hard to imagine that Weismantel and the Lang brothers could have anticipated the literal extermination that would follow in the

1940s. Moreover, evidence suggests that the Langs would not have condoned such vicious treatment of their fellow humans, some of whom they had come to know personally in the family boarding house. Rather, it seems likely that they wished to counter threats posed by those twin modern evils, "Jewish" Bolshevism and "Jewish" commercialism. Despite this aim, however, they touted the preservation of their play's Old Testament tableaux in 1934 as proof that Nazi ideology had not shaped Weismantel's efforts. It is also possible that Wagner believed their chosen playwright to be half-Jewish, one reason for the minister's hostility toward his involvement.[63]

Beyond these textual alterations Georg Lang's staging may have reflected Nazi ideology, according to Frederick Birchall, writing for the *New York Times*. Citing "a new note in the presentation," he went on to argue: "Never have Oberammergau's Jewish mobs been more virulent, never have the Pharisees and scribes who invoke the mob been more vehement than this year. Never has Pilate seemed more scornful of Caiaphas and his fellow-priests, Annas and Nathaniel. Pilate stands out pleading with the persecuting hierarchs—an Aryan who is their noble foe." He goes on to assert that the "presentation differs, of course, as it always has, from the actual Bible story." Nevertheless, even Birchall minimizes the Nazi regime's negative "influences." He praises in particular the play's especially capable direction and its unique "verisimilitude" created by highly effective major players.[64]

With Father Daisenberger's largely unaltered playscript shaping their rehearsals, Oberammergau's villagers once more swung into high gear to prepare for the coming invasion of both German and foreign tourists. One description of this effort concentrated on the women, whose role in providing board, lodging, and amusements was vital. Already, female carvers were busily preparing "their charming Christmas crib pieces and angels and wooden animals" for possible sale to visitors. Other women were making clothing for the actors. Elisabethe Corathiel agreed that all of this work was essential to making the season a success. Beyond so many activities needed to equip homes for entertaining guests, younger unmarried women were joining their male counterparts in rehearsals.[65]

Just when these busy villagers most needed calm to complete their preparations for the season, dissension assailed them once again. On the one hand, shortly after the nasty confrontation over their playtext, Cardinal Faulhaber chose to attack Wagner over deteriorating conditions for Catholic youth in Germany. As he informed the minister, despite his patriotic impulses he was hesitant to promote Oberammergau's Passion Play with potential visitors, including Catholic bishops. This was because, he added, "I cannot imagine

Catholic youth groups from Italy, Switzerland, and other foreign countries coming to Bavaria and moving around with pennants and uniforms, while the children of our own people get denied the freedom of club life." These visiting groups would receive a "devastating impression" from the restrictions placed on their German counterparts. Beyond annoying the top Nazis involved, however, Faulhaber's protest was unlikely to change any facts on the ground.[66]

Far more threatening was a clash developing between Oberammergau's Nazi leadership and Burger's excluded Motorstorm faction, one that could destroy Mayor Lang's effective management of the upcoming season; it even put both men's lives in danger. Burger was so polarizing a figure by spring 1934 that great animosity had developed against him. Long forgotten were any shared interests that had initially linked the Motorstorm commander with local party officials. Rather, those Nazis perceived as planning a "radical course" for Oberammergau were identified with Burger, while Alzinger and his deputy chapter leader, Mayor Lang, were seen to be standing in their way.[67]

Burger had by then developed a personal animus against the Lang brothers; he later argued that their efforts to revise the playscript had heightened his own opposition to men whom he regarded as greedy materialists. However, he was also suspicious of the Langs' failure to support the Nazis' rearmament efforts; the mayor in particular did not, he complained, want him to prepare his troopers for future service in a regenerated German army.[68]

On a more personal level, Burger resented Raimund Lang's efforts, as he saw it, to keep alive issues from his past, notably his bankruptcy woes and the attack on journeymen during the Corpus Christi debacle in 1933. He continued to blame the mayor for scuttling any chance of his taking part in local politics. The unfortunate surfacing of a cartoon drawn by Ernst Lang which parodied Burger and his deputy as the faces of "German justice" only worsened this situation. It also implicated Lechner, whom the commander suspected of encouraging the younger Lang's satire. Still another of Oberammergau's leading Nazis, Deputy Mayor Bierling, also fell into this anti-Burger camp.[69]

Beyond Burger's problems with the local leadership was a growing rift between his Motorstorm members and Hesse's "good" SA, as Mayor Lang later described them. Both paramilitary organizations had been recruiting during the first months of Nazi rule. As a result, the SA numbered around 80 men; the Motorstorm theoretically had 143, but only about a third were active Oberammergau troopers, and almost four dozen more hailed from the surrounding communities. Nonetheless, such a rapid buildup would have created a competitive situation, given the finite pool of potential recruits. And there may have been some crossovers from the SA to the Motorstorm, including those whom

Burger later labeled "Lang backers," implying that they were less than loyal to their commander.[70]

Estrangement was certainly the issue for a large group of young men whom Burger tried to incorporate into his own storm ranks after a failed SA effort to absorb them. These were the local Stahlhelm unit's founders, who aimed to "create an opposition" to the paramilitary forces. A festive launching ceremony was announced for late April and then delayed until June. Meanwhile, the national organization had been politically "coordinated," and at least one local member had left the village for a while in May to escape possible action against him by Minister Wagner.[71]

It was late in 1933 when Oberammergau's SA failed to follow up on a national initiative to absorb Stahlhelm youths; they may also have tried to co-opt older Stahlhelm men, a move ordered by Ernst Röhm in January 1934. In this context, a clash erupted between the group's members and their SA liaison officer in a local beer hall. These independently minded villagers then resisted the attempt to transform them into motorized troopers. Burger's version of events had the mayor's agents within his unit blocking their inclusion, but not before he had listed them in an effort to acquire funds from the council early in 1934. The Stahlhelm's final manifestation, known as the National Socialist German Front Soldiers' Association, enjoyed a shadowy existence locally until 1935.[72]

Tensions continued to rise during the spring of 1934, with Burger's Motorstorm at the epicenter. In mid-April a public scuffle took place one night at the hotel run by Burger's deputy. Supposedly, "the uniformed SA" and "the people of Oberammergau" "came to blows," although Mayor Lang later denied any involvement by the village's top officials. Implicated was a Munich-based officer, Wilhelm Schmitt, who shortly thereafter was executed during Hitler's massacre of SA leaders known as the Night of the Long Knives. A version of the story places Schmitt inside the hotel, where he was part of a "boozing" session. Burger was sure that he and his men were the targeted figures.[73]

As April turned into May, Mayor Lang and his villagers were all too aware that the opening festivities for their upcoming Passion season were only days away. However, fears of the supposedly revolutionary aspirations of SA luminaries like Schmitt were also brewing during these tension-ridden months. In this context Oberammergau's own conflict exploded publicly once again. Lang had gotten wind of efforts by Burger to agitate SA men over the sensitive question of the honoraria; he also appeared to be working toward a power grab against both party and communal leadership. The angry mayor asked Alzinger to organize a chapter meeting at which he could discuss this incipient crisis.[74]

Party members gathered on May 2 in the Weisses Rössl Inn's cavernous interior to hear Lang speak about Burger's "kind of terrorizing." As emotions intensified in the "good part of the SA," the situation became so overheated that the men drove the despised commander out of their midst. Lang later argued that "a tolerable relationship between Burger and the local population was absolutely not possible since they still rejected him as führer."[75]

Burger had even been losing control over his own men as he faced angry crowds inside the Weisses Rössl Inn. Only his most loyal supporters had obeyed instructions to join a muster in front of the inn's entryway. Refusing to back his "extreme line of politics" was an estimated score of troopers, including at least a couple of junior commanders who turned their subordinates against the chief. One such "grumbler" asserted that membership in the Motorstorm had been rendered thoroughly disreputable. These "mutineers" and "inciters" enjoyed clear connections to Lang, part of what senior SA officials called "the entire black brood with your black mayor." From this perspective they had joined an "oppositional party" hostile to the Nazis' interests.[76] (Figure 5.2 shows a muster of Storm Troopers in the square outside the Weisses Rössl Inn.)

Burger complained to his superiors about the May 2 fiasco, with the result that Mayor Lang, Chapter Leader Alzinger, and SA Commander Hesse were all

FIGURE 5.2. Local and visiting Storm Troopers muster outside the Weisses Rössl Inn, occupying the square used to set up the fourth altar for the annual Corpus Christi processions.

summoned to Munich to face the music. Initially, they met with "a panel of top SA leaders" set up in the district headquarters; Wagner's administrative deputy, Otto Nippold, was also present. Lang found himself in a heated exchange, becoming quite eloquent in defense of communal interests, which, he argued, "lay closer to my heart than the achievement of the particular goals of a few activists." In condemning the local "radical elements," Lang used a derogatory term to describe Burger, drawing still more heat on himself.[77]

As a result of his defiance, Lang was threatened by one SA magnate with imprisonment in Dachau, the standard response, it seems, to difficult comrades. However, all three men escaped with a "reprimand," which gave Burger a theoretical victory at best. A visit with Wagner revealed that the officials had been restrained because of Oberammergau's upcoming Passion Play season.[78]

Nevertheless, Lang was obliged to return a few days later to confront Nippold once more. He had come back home in despair after the first encounter, anticipating a new summons that might cost him his job and possibly a stint in Dachau. During this subsequent meeting, the mayor defended himself by drawing on his close connection with Propaganda Ministry officials over the promotional efforts for the Passion Play. He asked Nippold to call them before thinking of committing him to the concentration camp. This ploy worked, and the crisis was finally over.[79]

Lang survived these intense encounters with Nazi magnates—but at an immense emotional cost. Seeking out the mayor in a Munich hotel to deliver an official message, one fellow party member found him in a state of collapse. "Now all is over," he sighed. Administrator Raab also visited Lang late in the day of his first drubbing and found him "completely broken and despairing." Thinking he had come home "to straighten out his affairs" before returning to an uncertain fate, the mayor was close to suicidal, Raab feared, because he dreaded losing his position. However, once the two men had strategized for the upcoming meeting, Raab found him regaining his confidence. Lang must have been comforted to hear about a massive show of support for his leadership that took place while he was back in Munich on May 8.[80]

Alzinger had spread the news of Lang's bravery back home, so an idea emerged to demonstrate on behalf of the beleaguered mayor who had undergone such a struggle for Oberammergau's sake. The fear that, should Lang be deposed, Burger would be in line for his leadership position also drove the population to this dramatic step. First, the village marching band assembled in the Station Quarter, where it encountered the local police chief, who was armed with orders to break up any demonstration. However, the drum major, a bearded giant and Great War veteran, quickly called for a drumbeat and "gently but surely brushed aside" the police as his column was set in motion. Former SPD

Chief Daisenberger, a well-established band member, remembered that "we did not let ourselves be stopped."[81]

Encouraged by the oppositional musicians, party members mingled with the general population as their procession snaked through the village streets. It was late in the day and possibly even nighttime since one participant described burning torches that illuminated the band members' scores. Eventually an estimated 1,000–1,500 villagers took the extraordinary step of appearing together in this show of defiance. As Daisenberger reported later, the whole place "stood full of people." Burger was left helpless to resist this snub since his armed supporters from Garmisch arrived too late to make a difference, perhaps deflected by Deputy Mayor Bierling. The entire affair was a great success, underscoring how devoted most of the locals were to their mayor. Three of the councilors even wrote to Lang afterward to point out the implications of this "public witness," which promised a hopeful future for their sorely tried leader.[82]

Oberammergau's May demonstration signaled clear support for Mayor Lang's restraint of the threatening Motorstorm faction. One participant, in fact, claimed that it was actually directed against Burger's "clique," uniting "reactionary" Nazis with the "blacks." And indeed the crowd openly expressed its hostility toward the despised commander and his deputy when the marching band members fell silent outside their homes. Burger subsequently described the turnout as hostile to himself, tying it both to Lang's vendetta and SA ill will. He particularly resented a boycott of his lemonade stocked by the local inns, which the Storm Troopers participated in during the Passion season and kept going the following year. A witness later argued that Burger's championing of the immigrant population had triggered regular party members into using "lies and slanders in an attempt to destroy his very existence."[83]

The boycott was likely fueled by resentment of the harsh official treatment experienced by Oberammergau's paramilitary groups as a result of the May troubles. Both SA and Motorstorm were closed down to some extent; uniforms were even confiscated but soon restored. Hesse never recuperated as SA commander, while his unit managed to fully reemerge only in 1935 under new leadership. Burger's star was fading, too; he was permitted to reconstitute his Motorstorm out of the remaining loyal elements and to initiate disciplinary treatment of the "mutineers." However, his active force remained tiny even after he resigned as its commander late in 1934; it was also controlled from outside the village until late in the following year. In addition, even local party members were forbidden to meet as usual until further notice.[84]

Meanwhile, as the Passion Play season got under way, Burger and Lang clashed anew. The mayor had established a firm policy of downplaying Oberammergau's ties with the Third Reich during the performances. Yet Burger and a Nazi councilor wanted to wear party badges in their public role as ushers. They also planned to distribute posters of "the German greeting" sent over by the county office for display around the village. Lang made it clear that no such proclamation of party loyalties would be tolerated that summer, although he later softened this requirement with respect to combining badges with the blue uniforms assigned to all of the support personnel.[85]

Once again the mayor found himself summoned to Munich because of his efforts to restrain Burger's Nazi enthusiasms. This time he and a local SA commander faced overbearing questions from officials in the Bavarian Interior Ministry and the Gestapo, but he talked himself out of trouble in his usual direct manner. The two men returned after a "simple warning" from Deputy Köglmeier, but Lang's companion remained convinced that the frightening encounter had constituted a threat to Lang's life as a potential victim of the Night of the Long Knives. Lang later recounted that Köglmeier had warned him about impending danger, suggesting that he "be on his guard" with the SA. Moreover, he had clearly established himself as a "black" mayor in the eyes of Munich's party leadership. Yet it was Minister Wagner who aided Hitler in setting up the massacre, and it was Wagner's deputy, Nippold, who protected Lang from inclusion on the execution list in the nick of time.[86]

At the same moment, Burger and his deputy were also under threat from the Gestapo because, he charged later, of Lang's "brutality." Burger's radical behavior was calculated to give the SA a bad name as revolutionaries, and therefore he had been identified as part of the "Röhm revolt." The Motorstorm commander was at Linderhof when a phone call alerted him to the danger; he decided to hide out until it had passed, choosing as his refuge the Hundingshütte, a remote mountain cabin built by King Ludwig II near the Austrian border and subsequently turned into a café. Both he and Lang, therefore, survived this looming menace but had reason to continue their feuding into the hot summer months.[87]

The unwelcome drama of the Night of the Long Knives, which was highlighted in the local newspaper, took place near Oberammergau just a few weeks into the jubilee season. Mayor Lang had finally managed to quiet Burger's radical threats for the moment, it seemed, but this new crisis might well threaten the delicate balancing act that was sustaining a steady flow of foreign tourists. Lang immediately issued a statement about any possible negative consequences of these "internal political conditions," reassuring the worried villagers that official news reports would declare their play "unaffected." And indeed, the audience was gratifyingly large at the subsequent performance. Within a week the

Passion Committee members' fears would be assuaged by the information that "happily" there had been no ill effects from the executions.[88]

Up until this point, the community had been doing everything possible to avoid putting off the usual international audience. Lang may have disliked the behaviors described by a sarcastic Adolf Stein for a German newspaper. American visitors chased after actors' curls, while the British sought to hire major female players as maids to "offer the guests tea and a halo at the next 'garden party.'" Germans, Stein added, do not come to see the "stars." However, the mayor recognized the importance of an Anglo-American presence at the performances. Therefore, he worried about foreign news reports, and he acted to head off any local actions that might undo the positive publicity put out by Oberammergau's contracted travel agencies. The idea was to convey "the beautiful idea of National Socialism" in a way that would counteract "misconceptions."[89]

Lang was still worrying about overseas coverage after Hitler attended the play in August. He wanted to guarantee favorable accounts that would highlight the trip's grounding in a shared concern for the "Christian ethic" that the villagers were pledged to maintain. Mayor Lang once again sat on a knife edge, needing the Führer's patronage while agonizing over the impact of his visit on Oberammergau's supporters abroad.[90]

Despite all of these efforts, the jubilee performances did not attract the normal influx of foreigners. American visitors were particularly few and far between, their numbers shrinking to a little over one-fifth of previous seasonal totals. Many factors no doubt contributed to this dramatic decline, including the Depression's terrible impact, but a story written by Peter Jens is intriguing. He stresses the "hard" way in which Alois Lang played Christ, which did not please elderly American women, who found him "not sweet enough." The British audience was larger, making up more than a third of the entire foreign presence. As usual, they often arrived in large group tours.[91]

Also different was a shift away from the glittering assemblage of notables that had peaked in the "year of prominence" in 1910. Only a few royal and noble visitors appeared, notably the King of Siam; Alois Lang's guesthouse was refurbished to house this special guest in style. However, the Catholic episcopate from both the New and the Old World was well represented; in particular, several bishops traveled over from the United States. Concerns about the fate of denominational clubs in the new Germany do not seem to have deterred them, although one motoring group canceled a "special journey" because of "attacks on the Catholic youth."[92]

Ordinary Germans, many tempted by Lang's special railroad fares and reduced prices, made up the most important audience in what became "the year of the folk pilgrimage." Pilgrim groups were organized as before, like the Saarland contingent, which was also to visit Altötting's Marian shrine. As many as five thousand Upper Silesian pilgrims arrived on special trains as well. However, this being Nazi Germany, there was also a steady stream of "larger and smaller Hitler Youth troops, . . . for whose accommodation in the theater the Play officials took special care."[93]

Not every visitor left with positive memories. One parish priest criticized artistic lapses in the play's staging, like Christ's "theatrical" and "whiny" presentation, which was "so hard, cold, soulless." While he was unhappy with the Mount of Olives and Last Supper scenes, this complainant's full critique was directed at the whipping of Christ, who was left "white as a freshly bathed Swan lying on the ground," hardly a realistic depiction of so bloody an experience. The performance was "threatening to sink into rank commercialism." This two-pronged attack struck a raw nerve with Mayor Lang, so he responded tartly that the priest's complaint was a holdover from "the old Marxist Germany."[94]

Of course, the ultimate visitor to Oberammergau's Passion Play was the Führer himself. Hitler's day in the village should have been a highly gratifying success for Mayor Lang and his Nazi contingent, but a dark cloud fell over the festivities when they precipitated yet another confrontation with Burger. He and his unit turned up to provide their leader with a "safety squad" at the hotel where he spent the midday interval. However, the effrontery of this "unworthy" bunch, not all of them properly dressed in uniform, proved intolerable for the regular Storm Troopers. Fearing the worst when he heard about this disaster, Lang rushed to the players' dressing room, but his effort was in vain. A fight had already erupted. One Motorstorm member was injured, and another had been humiliated; "further insults" were hurled before the drama subsided. The mayor had to take firm measures so that no future outbreaks would threaten the rest of the season.[95]

Burger took this new reversal of fortune badly, arguing later that no other clash with Lang had disturbed him more. He happened to encounter the Berlin Gestapo chief during Hitler's visit, who encouraged him to make an official complaint about Oberammergau's unorthodox power relationships. However, Minister Wagner, on finding out about his intentions, wrote to head off any new trouble during the Passion season. When a Nazi councilor sought Burger out to dissuade him from trying to "overthrow" Lang, the disgusted commander brandished this letter; he had been foiled once again in his efforts to bring down the hated mayor.[96]

Despite Hitler's perceived efforts to slip quietly into the Passion theater, his arrival did not go unnoticed. To be sure, a New York Times reporter described how the Führer, in "the role of a casual tourist, . . . arrived without fanfare, appearing with a ticket which was part of a block anonymously issued to 'a Nordic travelling group.'" Yet, excited onlookers greeted the "well-known column of automobiles" that brought Hitler and his party to the village from Ettal. Sitting among "his beloved folk" rather than in the exclusive section, Hitler then tried to become "a Passion Play pilgrim, full of desire for total concentration. He wanted to remain incognito in order to avoid disturbing the rapt attention of all the other visitors." This effort, too, was fruitless since the audience, realizing that their Führer was present, sent out a chorus of greetings interrupted only by the orchestra's opening strains.[97] (Figure 5.3 shows Hitler standing in his car as he passes through the village center on August 13.)

This enthusiastic reception, described in one newspaper as exceeding all previous welcomes in Alpine communities, reflected the propagandistic aims of a visit carefully timed to impress Catholics who might doubt the sincerity of

FIGURE 5.3. Adolf Hitler rides in his automobile through jubilant crowds filling the streets of Oberammergau when he attends the Passion Play on August 13, 1934.

Hitler's own faith. President Hindenburg had died only a few days beforehand. Now Nazi officials were organizing a plebiscite for August 19 to endorse their plan to name the Führer both president and chancellor, which made wooing Catholic voters a high priority. His appearance in Oberammergau also provided Mayor Lang with an opportunity to reassure the Anglo-American public about the Nazi leader's willingness to protect Christian values.[98]

Oberammergau's special visitor attended the day's performance until the lunchtime interval, at which point Lang appeared to acknowledge his presence. Hitler's car then drove through flag-bedecked streets lined by the HJ and the BdM; the usual bouquets of flowers were extended to him as well. Enthusiastic crowds soon burst through all of the restraints to coalesce around the Führer as he made his way to a central hotel, where the innkeeper's young son gave him the Nazi salute. A great horde of visitors gathered outside and went wild as Hitler stepped out onto the hotel balcony, whereupon "the Horst-Wessel-Lied rang out over the entire square and thousands of hands provided the Führer with the German greeting." In Ernst Lang's opinion this multitude had become a "hysterical shrieking mass."[99]

Lunch over, Hitler returned to view the second half of the performance. Afterward he went backstage, where he was caught on camera standing with Georg and Raimund Lang amid a throng of actors. This was an exciting opportunity for party members in the cast; Ernst Lang, who was well positioned to observe both the Führer and his audience, saw that "the believing Nazis . . . had tears in their eyes." For oppositional performers, however, this command appearance must have been quite uncomfortable. Mayor Lang did head off one potentially embarrassing incident when he granted Father Bogenrieder's request to be "spared the necessity to meet with Hitler. He knew that it would be unpleasant for me."[100] (Figure 5.4 shows Hitler standing with the players on stage after the day's performance.)

Nevertheless, even opponents could be thankful that Hitler had repeatedly expressed his willingness to protect the Passion Play in its traditional form. Writing later about this event, Anton Lang argued: "Oberammergau will always remember one day in August when 'Der Führer' was among the spectators; at the close of the performance he spoke to the players gathered around him behind the curtain, and his reference to the future made everyone recognize the importance of a faithful continuance of the pledge of our ancestors. Oberammergau . . . must preserve its Passion Play unchanged in spirit and production." His cousin Raimund also rejoiced over Hitler's strong support, which, he was heard to say, gave him needed ammunition "against the SA leaders and radical party members who considered the play a disgrace and wanted to replace it."[101]

FIGURE 5.4. The Führer speaks with Director Georg Lang, Mayor Raimund Lang, the player of Christ, Alois Lang, and other players after attending the Passion Play.

During the 1934 Passion Committee's final meeting in mid-December, a Nazi spokesperson thanked both Mayor Lang and Hitler for Oberammergau's productive season. The Führer in particular had "saved German culture, destroyed Bolshevism and so permitted the staging of the Passion Play." This gathering ended with a triple "Sieg Heil." However, the villagers had already expressed their traditional thanks for another completed season in fulfillment of the now three-hundred-year-old vow. Marching to Ettal, the players offered up a prayer for the future: "May the Mother of God, Ettal's miraculous mother, as she has in so many other difficult times of storm and struggle, continue to spread her protective mantel over [our] quiet valley." The local newspaper echoed this dual invocation of their new Nazi and traditional Catholic protectors by proclaiming the visits by Chancellor Hitler and Cardinal Faulhaber as the season's highlights.[102]

However, the convergence of ideologies mediated by Oberammergau's jubilee season was about to fall away, as did the locks of hair that an enterprising photographer caught being shorn after the last performance was over. In the following years, Nazi activists would chalk up many victories as they worked toward social dominance. Yet dissention split the village community along fault lines that were both social and political. In particular, efforts to destroy Catholic life, emanating primarily from beyond local boundaries, further separated the

two major groups. Before war struck in 1939, the full traditional round of processions had been tampered with, and their scope reduced. Catholics fought
doggedly for their rights but had to give ground to the Nazi ownership of public
life. Mayor Lang remained at the heart of this drama, his Nazi convictions still
moderated by a strong local patriotism and communal sensitivity.[103]

6

Leaders

Oberammergau's villagers can draw on a centuries-long tradition of musical excellence to support the Passion Play, as well as many other cultural activities dear to local hearts. Every decade the chorus and orchestra send their notes soaring out into the valley basin, as Alban von Hahn recorded a hundred years before I experienced this same phenomenon. From high atop the Kofel, he caught the sound of voices "carried by the wind." Music has also been a dominant feature of parish life, centered around the church choir. Moreover, no procession would be complete without its marching band, dressed since the Corpus Christi of 1965 in striking period costume: navy jackets, red waistcoats, and brown plus fours above white stockings, all crowned with a conical blue hat. Their very presence adds to the public witness of these events.[1]

So extraordinary a flowering of local talent has depended in part on a sequence of local schoolteachers who were chosen for their musical abilities and asked to prepare and conduct the chorus and orchestra during play seasons. In the late eighteenth century Johann Martin Reichard skillfully trained the church choir, which came to be accompanied by local musicians. One of his many pupils was Rochus Dedler, the man who would draw on his extensive education in Rottenbuch Abbey and Munich to write the score for Weis's Passion script. Dedler was able to conduct his final version for the 1820 season. Serving as schoolteacher in his turn, he also left behind religious compositions, as well as music for a special New Year's Eve procession with a large star, the Sternrundgang. Most beloved has been the *Primiz* mass, written for a youthful Daisenberger's induction into the priesthood. Much of this legacy is still in use, modernized by experts like Zeno Diemer.[2]

A series of teachers worked with local singers and musicians after Dedler's death in 1822, cementing the link between instruction and conducting. Howitt commented on this dual responsibility in 1850, noting that the present incumbent "had taxed his musical skill for the production of the music." She was intrigued with his singers' exotic appearance as, "like the antique chorus, they sang the argument of the play." A subsequent commemorative print shows the current teacher at work, surrounded by his orchestra playing their stringed and wind instruments. In 1900 Burton admired the delivery of their "soft, sweet, and sad" music at a time when teacher Feldigl had taken over as conductor. For the 1930 and 1934 seasons school principal Sattler played this role.[3]

Local men emerged to lead the chorus. Zeno Diemer's grandfather and uncle both served, and then until 1910 Mathilde Lang's father took on this job; her grandfather, a soloist in midcentury, had studied under Dedler. After the Great War, singers turned for leadership to Zeno's son Guido, a trained professional. Beyond involvement in the play, skilled villagers would perform both folk and classical pieces in private concerts attended by honored guests. The Singing Circle launched in 1866 was eventually headed by Diemer himself.[4]

As a teenager Zeno had played the drum for Oberammergau's marching band, an institution that drew on a remarkable wealth of orchestral talent for a small village. Local chronicler Friedl Lang points out that Dedler's compositions favor wind instruments, suggesting that particular competence had developed in this field. Early descriptions of the band hint at an origin in the Home Guard, although its musical scores were considered "ceremonial" rather than overtly "military."[5]

A tradition developed in which band members would lead visitors around Oberammergau on the eve of each play performance. As early as Greatorex's day they would assemble in the Ettalerstrasse, much to her annoyance, and set off "from the front of our garden. . . . First come the firemen, then the musicians, and now they parade through the streets, to the Passion theater." The band would also awaken playgoers early on the day itself; a dramatic print captures them striding out near the church with their instruments, led by a youthful drummer.[6]

Oberammergau's marching band was organized by the village's Music Club, an early manifestation of which emerged during the Napoleonic Wars. A century later the musicians founded the modern club, which would support their many contributions to the local tourism industry. Beyond Passion service, the club members played in a variety of concerts and introduced bandstand performances, which became popular with visitors. In 1925 they staged a Zeno

Diemer play dramatizing a historical incident linked to the Sternrundgang, which remained a beloved custom. The professor also presented them with a new star and additional music. In addition, the musicians assisted in the celebrations, processions, and performances of other clubs, while religious festivals, notably Corpus Christi, were enlivened by the sights and sounds of Oberammergau's band. The young drummers photographed with their adult comrades point to yet another club imperative: training replacements from the next generation.[7]

Shortly after the Music Club's revival, the band's long-standing conductor stepped down after a failed bid to seize control of the Passion orchestra. Mathilde Lang's cousin Ferdinand Rutz took over the band and doubled as the orchestra's assistant conductor. After his untimely death in 1919 and years of band leadership by his successor, the role passed on to Ferdinand's son Heinrich shortly before the Nazis' seizure of power.[8]

"Heini" Rutz soon resumed his father's efforts to end the tradition that put a carefully selected teacher in charge of the Passion's musical performances. Within a broader crisis caused by the general unhappiness with the inadequate honoraria, this question of Rutz's conducting during the next play season rather than a specially hired school principal took center stage. Rutz was supported by his fellow Music Club members, easily identified as old political opponents of Oberammergau's Nazi officials. They made sure that the years after 1934 would be tumultuous ones indeed.[9]

Mayor Lang was able to rest on his laurels only briefly after a successful Passion Play season. He had known all along that reducing the cost of a stay in Oberammergau would be unpopular. Friction developed during the season itself after tickets were discounted and the price of the related three-day arrangements was slashed. Lang was obliged to exhort homeowners who were complaining about meager returns to consider the policy's value for enticing visitors back in future years. Those who demurred were showing "how little communal feeling" they had developed.[10]

Closely linked with this discontent were the low honoraria paid for Passion-related service. By prioritizing the use of proceeds from the play for local projects, Mayor Lang had ensured that individuals would have to accept modest personal recompense. Nevertheless, given the general unemployment woes, he did agree to grant advances to deserving players. Pressed again later, however, Lang declared that "the earlier Marxist-egotistical point of view must fall also in the case of . . . honoraria and be replaced with communal sensibilities."[11]

Looking back during the final Passion Committee meeting, the mayor thanked its members for supporting his effort to curb spending and preserve the village's options in the face of an uncertain economic future. However, he remained in a precarious position, facing the growing opposition of "a wide circle" over the honoraria question. The head of the ambulance brigade even decided to resign, it seemed, because of unhappiness about his own meager salary for Passion-related obligations; some of his squad were quitting as well. Much more serious, however, was the development of an open split over this issue in the local population.[12]

At the heart of the crisis were Oberammergau's musicians, whose contributions to local culture and the entertainment of visitors had become indispensible. Pressure continued to mount on busy performers as the community struggled to compete effectively with nearby spas and bring their tourism industry back from Depression lows. In addition, the impending 1940 Passion season gave them little breathing space. This was hardly a propitious moment for a quarrel that withdrew Music Club members from active duty just when they were so badly needed.[13]

Their clash with Mayor Lang had been developing even before the season was under way because of a decision to compensate the musicians for play service with a flat lump-sum payment. Yet the Passion Committee worried that the musicians might not have sufficient "communal spirit" to keep performing when denied any "extra remuneration." The season successfully completed, anxiety surfaced about Lang's efforts to tie a higher payment than originally contemplated to meager compensation for future band performances. In November Lang rejected a counteroffer by Conductor Rutz, hoping to work out their differences in the future. Only a few days later, Rutz was asked to create a string orchestra, considered more suitable than the band for taking on most of the spa support functions.[14]

Relations between the Music Club and Mayor Lang deteriorated over the next couple of years. The leading members had opposed the Nazis before 1933 and remained suspect during the Third Reich. Chairman Anton Rutz and club officer Hans Daisenberger were both left-wingers, while a former secretary and the present cashier were BVP supporters; cashier Sepp was even heard openly criticizing the regime. Other musicians were political opponents as well. The local police indicated that the quarrel involved "earlier black-red supporters"; Lang himself publicly "described the members as Marxists and black and red." Of course, most of the villagers had been either BVP or leftist sympathizers. Now the community was sharply divided, with Nazis in the minority. Dissidents could count on much support in their prolonged battle with the mayor.[15]

Once Oberammergau had lost Principal Sattler after his two stints in the role, this quarrel soon focused on the selection of a new conductor for the 1940

Passion season. Mayor Lang chose to hire a personal friend in Sattler's place. Considering Josef Laumer well qualified to train the chorus, he clearly intended to assign the new principal the conductorship, as more than a century of tradition dictated that he should. Still, the musicians informed Lang that they wanted one of their own, Heini Rutz, to inherit the top spot because local talent should be preferred whenever possible.[16]

This championing of Heini Rutz as conductor raised the crucial issue of his training and competence. If he were to replace an outside expert hired to guarantee professional musical performances for the Passion Play, Rutz would have to prove himself equally capable. In discussing this challenge, Lang argued that the "better" candidate ought to get the job. His struggle to resolve the crisis set up years of conflict between Rutz and Laumer.[17]

Tensions mounted to the point that Anton and Heini Rutz were summoned to a council meeting, where they were asked about an emerging "movement" against official policies. News had spread concerning a plan to circulate petitions directed at Minister Wagner and launch a hostile "Dedler organization." The leadership strongly objected to this challenge and moved to head it off.[18]

Central to their efforts was a move to replace Anton Rutz with a new "führer," but instead he was "unanimously" returned to his once and future post. Nonetheless, an antagonistic relationship with the mayor soon led to Rutz's demotion by regional authorities, although he escaped a guilty verdict after charges that he had called Lang "a liar" for suggesting that he remained an SPD loyalist. A Nazi "commissar" took charge of the club, but the issue of Heini Rutz's 1940 role would not disappear.[19]

Principal Laumer soon found himself victimized by a campaign to force him out of the job that, he argued, had convinced him to leave his old position for Oberammergau's. Failure of their concerted efforts to secure Laumer's withdrawal in favor of Rutz drove Music Club members to extreme measures. The exasperated local administration had to watch helplessly as they undermined the putative conductor's professional standing and engaged in "sabotage of his work." A couple of dissident Nazis were even accused of using "inflammatory rhetoric" against the unwelcome newcomer, and one publicly derided both Laumer and Lang, part of a general open hostility toward both men. Finally, in the summer of 1938 "excrement" found on the entryway to the principal's home was blamed on "a few musicians."[20]

Still, the Music Club members were not content with attacking Laumer; they also initiated a crippling "strike." Particularly distressing was their refusal to support the customary Sternrundgang that would usher in the year 1937. Not only did they withhold their beautiful star, but they also left an HJ band to accompany the procession. The council's efforts to provide "a new large star" were not appreciated, and an appeal by Mayor Lang to mobilize the local musical community fell largely on deaf ears. Moreover, crucial preparations for the 1940 Passion season were jeopardized by the musicians' refusal to take part in performances that normally trained future players. The goodwill that had underwritten their many public appearances had dissipated.[21]

As this damaging struggle continued into 1937, Lang cast around for a workable solution to the conductor question. At first he had agreed to make Rutz and Laumer coequals in their leadership of the instrumental and choral performances, delaying any decision about the top position. However, in August 1936, a high official designated Laumer as the local "trustee" for Oberammergau's musical life. Then, at Christmastime, Heini Rutz resigned from his leadership position, deepening the "open break." So tense was his confrontation with Laumer that Rutz stormed out of a meeting with the principal. To calm the waters Mayor Lang offered Rutz a paid role in charge of the village's string and wind sections. He would share the right to direct the "communal performances," and once again a final decision about who would conduct in 1940 was delayed. However, these concessions were met with hostilities, including "a new trick" involving the DAF, whose leader agreed to "protect" the Music Club's interests by absorbing the group into his association.[22]

Lang read this move as an attempt to trap officials into capitulation. He was particularly outraged by efforts to establish the "equal guilt" of both sides. Then, in March, the councilors voted to replace the Music Club's musicians with a "professional spa band." In late June Lang was still at his wits' end, so he fell back on the old custom of holding a community meeting, at which he could explore the rights and wrongs of the conflict. An estimated three hundred villagers attended this dramatic gathering to hear a three-hour speech by their mayor.[23]

After tracing the confrontation's entire history, Lang reiterated the need for traditional "voluntarism" in play affairs; failing that, he argued, "we have lost the right to put on the Passion Play." Future honoraria would not increase, and all of the personnel must take part in "normal performances outside the Passion years," with remuneration only for extraordinary contributions. In fact, the mayor pontificated, failure to remain active would exclude an individual from Passion responsibilities altogether. Laumer would, he added, help with the preparations for the 1940 season; a panel of experts would decide the knotty conductor question.[24]

It was shortly after Lang's marathon speech that Anton Rutz lost his job as the music club's "führer." The mayor had made it clear that he held Rutz responsible for his musicians' "revolver politics" and their resultant "strike." Dismissing old-style "barter politics," he scorned the idea that a "camaraderie" existed among the Music Club members, which he compared to bonding in pre-Nazi labor actions. The newly accepted wisdom found such dealings destructive of the general good. Moreover, beyond any loss of Passion service for noncompliers, Lang added the possibility of official sanctions, an attitude so ominous that the musicians later reported fearing that they "repeatedly stood with one leg in a concentration camp." Nevertheless, the quarrel continued into the following year.[25]

In this context Oberammergau's leadership began to choose a 1940 Passion Committee, making resolution of the never-ending tensions an urgent matter. Heini Rutz, it "emerged," wanted a better salary; consequently, they discussed giving him a position as "communal musical director" in the hope that then "the musical section would function again." If cooperative, their pay would be increasingly generous. Laumer and Rutz would share the responsibilities, and both would attend the Passion Committee's music subcommittee meetings; filling the top post was again delayed. The councilors were not uniformly happy with this generous arrangement but empowered Mayor Lang to pursue it in the hope of solving their problem.[26]

As this year progressed, Alzinger's deputy forged a deal that would make Rutz conductor if he scored top marks for his professional training. Meanwhile, Laumer was to direct the music for Weismantel's historical play. However, this agreement fell apart when the Nazi second-in-command moved away that summer, and the hostile feelings that remained led to Laumer's public humiliation caused by the desecration of his home. The councilors were still working on a contract with Rutz in November. Ultimately, the war must have intervened and forced a cancellation of the 1940 Passion season before this long battle could be resolved. Rutz disappeared into the armed forces and continued to lead the village's scant musical performances only on the sidelines.[27]

Mayor Lang and the local police clearly read the conflict with Oberammergau's Music Club as political when identifying their leaders as "black and red." Daisenberger's prominent role could only bolster this interpretation; the former SPD chief and councilor remained under close watch. Just when the Heini Rutz question was heating up, he was described as harboring a "hate-filled attitude against the NSDAP." Not only did Daisenberger remain friendly with loyal Catholics, but he would also gladly join any "counterrevolutionary efforts" against Hitler's regime. Lang also blamed Chairman Rutz for his club members' lukewarm response to the Nazis' seizure of power. From this perspective their "revolver politics" was inspired by partisan loyalties left over from the pluralistic Weimar Republic. However, in the single-party system of the Third Reich, such hostilities had to be diverted into ostensibly nonpolitical agitation.[28]

From the musicians' point of view, it was a mistake to treat their quarrel with Lang and Laumer as politics by other means. Leading players testified later that the Rutz conductorship was indeed their sole concern. If partisanship had entered into the struggle, Mayor Lang was to blame. Daisenberger himself insisted that confrontation "arose out of the peculiarity and sensitivity of the practicing artists." He even acknowledged Lang's unprecedented attempt to equate the band conductor's job with the top musical slot. Nevertheless, this tussle did pit erstwhile BVP and SPD supporters against their sworn Nazi enemies.[29]

The strike mounted by Oberammergau's musicians is particularly remarkable because it took place in the threatening environment of the Third Reich. Individuals clearly recognizable as "nonparty members" and opponents defied not only their village's Nazi-dominated administration but also its NSDAP hierarchy. Local Chapter Leader Alzinger was an active participant, especially when a couple of his own people chose to support the musicians over their party comrades. In addition, Alzinger's deputy leader was Mayor Lang until 1936. Moreover, as a local führer Lang could have brought all opposition to a speedy halt by choosing to wield the punitive weapons at his disposal.[30]

Nevertheless, despite mentioning "state and party" penalties for dissidents, Lang relied primarily on Oberammergau's ultimate motivation—securing one's right to participate during the 1940 Passion season. However, this reticence could hardly mask the reality that Lang and his fellow Nazis had come to dominate Oberammergau's cultural scene. As a result, the Catholics were thrown on the defensive by prescriptive attacks on their own associations and celebrations. By means of an aggressive mix of economic and social policies, their new leaders had constructed a parallel and increasingly intrusive way of life for local inhabitants.[31]

Successful imposition of this Nazi culture required an end to the internal conflicts that tore apart the local NSDAP in 1934. Even monthly party meetings remained suspended after the May debacle. Feuding raged on between Mayor Lang, party leaders, and their "good SA" on the one side and Motorstorm Commander Burger with his few loyal troopers on the other. Over the summer resentment flared over Burger's mistreatment of so-called "mutineers." Lang decried his "clumsy" handling of disciplinary measures that in a couple of cases led to expulsion from the force; other dissidents faced a month-long suspension. The SA "boycott" aimed at Burger's economic fortunes continued despite his repeated pleas for mayoral intervention.[32]

The Passion season over, Burger had lost important sections of his business empire and soon decided to resign his command. He was further humiliated by a notice set up near his house that read: "Jakob done in." By mid-1935, however, Burger reckoned that the boycott was receding as people woke up to the "injustice" of it all. Nonetheless, the rump group of his Storm Troopers still operating in Oberammergau were subordinated to Oberau's commander.[33]

Burger poured out his pent-up frustrations and feelings of despair about this negative turn of events to Raimund Lang, whom he held responsible for his misfortunes. He characterized the mayor as dishonest and self-serving, failures that made Lang a terrible Nazi. He was in particular neglecting the welfare of Oberammergau's laborers, an issue dear to Burger's heart. Moreover, the mayor had privileged his own supporters and even partisan opponents over early joiners of the party. He could also be blamed for the lost monthly party meetings. Lang was, Burger concluded, unhappy that locals were looking to the Motorstorm commander for a change of leadership.[34]

Burger contacted a raft of higher officials with his litany of complaints against Mayor Lang, but the results of this vendetta were disappointing. Hitler's deputy, Rudolf Hess, sent a messenger to assure party members that "the local leaders have done their duty." Both Lang and Alzinger had been cleared by a high-level inquiry after assertions by the Burger faction had been "found groundless." The case was therefore closed, but not for Burger himself, who faced disciplinary actions, which he appealed. A subsequent hearing left the matter unresolved. Burger's official difficulties continued until 1938, when Hitler issued a general amnesty.[35]

The year 1935 was one of recuperation for Oberammergau's SA and Motorstorm formations. Founding chapter member Bierling took over the SA, while Mayor Lang recommended Franz Kräh to head the Motorstorm troopers. At an informative meeting in November Kräh stressed that both groups had resolved their difficulties. He urged "former members of these associations, who had left precisely because of these troubles, perhaps because it had gone against their moral sense," to come back into the fold. However, these were men who had been declawed by the Night of the Long Knives. Kräh later claimed that his leadership was devoted entirely to sports, and indeed such activities, as well as marching and collections for winter assistance and other Nazi-sponsored causes, did dominate the Storm Troopers' public profile.[36]

Oberammergau's Nazi officials were now firmly in charge of their paramilitary wing, which included a tiny SS group. However, volunteers for Himmler's elite force were hard to find. A new local commander named late in 1937 was charged with building up the membership but had no noticeable success. The SS would be no more of a threat to Lang's and Alzinger's agenda than the Storm Troopers.[37]

Also contributing to Oberammergau's vibrant Nazi culture was a dramatic improvement in the local economy. Beyond taming revolutionary threats, this centerpiece of Hitler's domestic agenda was designed to win the hearts and minds of both middle- and lower-class Germans. Initially, the bid to end Depression-level unemployment centered on large construction projects like the new highway to Linderhof, photographed as a dramatic asphalting project in the 1934 official guide. In the Ammer valley itself, a massive effort to contain the river aimed at ending the periodic floods. Then a series of communal building enterprises took shape, funded by both the government and Passion Play income.[38]

First came the completion of the new suburb in Saint Gregor. Together with an Alpine swimming pool complex conceived by Mayor Lang, ten homes in austere Nazi-chalet style were finished by 1936. A laudatory article described their "simple, appropriate" design as "born out of the new era's spirit." A large army barracks followed in 1937, also engineered to fit both Nazi and Alpine construction styles. Finally, a similarly devised new school building opened late in 1938, part of a complex intended to provide an "Ammergau House" and spa park.[39]

At first, public works like the Ammer river project reduced local unemployment, although anxious wintry months followed the Passion season. Then, as the 1930s progressed, Oberammergau's economy improved sufficiently to require importing laborers, including men from Breslau and Upper Silesia who built the military barracks. Local construction businesses also profited from various projects that included expanding private enterprises. One was the addition of a "Tiroler weinstube" to Hans Mayr's boarding house.[40]

As the Depression lifted in Germany and elsewhere, Oberammergau's woodcarvers also enjoyed a renaissance. Help came in part from local sources, such as the winter assistance program's order of badges like the 150,000 crude carvings of a swaddled baby or multiple babies nestled in a crib, each bearing the initials WHW. But orders from abroad were also significant. Consequently, by early 1937 the carvers could be described as "fully employed."[41]

Soon, however, concerns about overseas markets resurfaced, as the emerging Sudeten crisis disrupted trade with Britain and the United States. Merchants tried to restore this lucrative connection by launching a "lively" advertising blitz, but to no avail. Only after Prime Minister Neville Chamberlain's infamous meeting in Munich did foreign sales pick up again—for a time. Hitler's expansionist policies were soon discouraging international trade with German firms as the world spun toward war in 1939.[42]

This revival of Oberammergau's carving industry fed off improved tourist flows into the village. To improve business between Passion seasons, the local leaders were busily upgrading infrastructure and encouraging cultural programming. With the winter season in mind, they also worked to improve skiing venues. In addition, they designed a series of summer and winter prospectuses with attractively decorated covers to pull in visitors.[43]

Central to this promotional campaign was the spa venture proposed by Mayor Lang and his now powerful faction. However, their vision remained an elusive dream. Instead of the hoped-for major facility, they had to settle for Lang's Saint Gregor swimming pool complex and later the new "Ammergau House" to host cultural events. On this basis the local authorities touted Oberammergau as a "spa location." However, war intervened before the construction of their entertainment center could get off the ground.[44] (Figure 6.1 shows the 1937 summer prospectus, which highlights Lang's spa-like new complex.)

Closely related to these public improvements were the dozens of subsidies made possible by Passion Play money to upgrade guest quarters in private homes. The council also recognized a growing need for well-appointed boarding houses, in addition to "first-class" hotels and pubs. Coffee- and wine-drinking facilities were another favored development; Alois Lang added this type of bar to his budding hotel in 1936. The tourism trade had doubled, councilors

FIGURE 6.1. An elegant woman graces the cover of Oberammergau's 1937 summer prospectus advertising Mayor Lang's new spa-like Alpine swimming pool complex.

reasoned, and hundreds of soldiers from the new barracks would soon be looking for recreational opportunities.[45]

Oberammergau's flourishing tourism industry was bolstered by the presence of specifically Nazi visitors, including various bigwigs who frequented major hotels. The winter season was also improved by SA-sponsored sporting events like the major ski meets organized by Motorstorm Commander Kräh. Hundreds of black-clad SS Death's Head guards from Dachau made a more sinister contribution when they filled the village for a couple of September days in 1936, ate lunch in the village center, and wrote postcards like regular guests. However, it was largely the Strength through Joy (KdF) organization's group excursions that brought serious extra business to local boarding houses and restaurants.[46]

Founded by DAF chief Robert Ley in November 1933, the KdF program was soon exploiting Oberammergau and surrounding attractions. Using the German railroad's low fares, a train full of Munich sightseers became the first arrivals. After a chance to ski or look through the museum and theater, they took a sleigh ride out to Linderhof and Ettal and dined in local establishments. Thereafter, sponsored groups came from a catchment area that included northern Germany, even Berlin, and, ultimately, the Sudetenland. Ernst Lang observed white-collar workers bused in from the north for a two-week stay. Locals found especially intriguing the "female office workers, . . . their strapping figures draped in mountain attire," quite a contrast to the elegant and modish woman who graces the cover of the 1937 summer prospectus.[47] (See Figure 6.1.)

The KdF negotiated cut-rate prices for these quintessentially Nazi tourists, which distressed local businesses, but they did boost the total number of overnight stays. In 1937 almost ten thousand tourists passed through Oberammergau, although their numbers were sharply reduced once a key competitor, Austria, joined the Third Reich. Co-opted local clubs were put to work amusing the KdF visitors with musical and dancing performances, including competitions, as well as theater and "country" entertainment. Northern Germans learned about regional "manners" through a series of greeting and farewell occasions.[48]

The KdF also provided the villagers with recreational activities. In fact, Oberammergau's specifically Nazi cultural atmosphere flowed primarily from their events, not always to the approval of the old-timers. One particularly dreadful performance by an outside troupe, which had "nothing to do with German art and culture," took place in 1938. Deputy Mayor Bierling had to intervene after the spectators grew increasingly indignant. There was "whistling," and "in between came cries—like: 'Bring down the curtain,' 'a scandal,' and so on." Perhaps more edifying were the wide-ranging courses offered by the KdF office's growing staff, as well as various musical and sporting activities. Fortunate locals got to join in hiking and climbing excursions; a few went on substantial vacations, while others took short trips to places like Innsbruck and Munich.[49]

Much of this amusement intruded into Catholic culture, as symbolized by the provision of a train ride to Munich on Mary's ascension day, dubbed "People's Excursion Day." Similarly, a special Christmas event took place in 1935 for which music and singing were supplemented by Mayor Lang's rendition of "Christmas legends." The targeted audience was Nazis and the members of subordinate party organizations.[50]

The KdF's sponsor, the DAF, came to organize the labor force previously represented by trade unions; it soon absorbed the middle-class employers' organization as well. In Oberammergau, the DAF was run by a local mechanic who arranged introductory meetings after the Passion season to attract more villagers into the fold. This was an important moment for such a humble worker, although his leadership was already drawing complaints from unhappy locals.[51]

The DAF's organization into "cells" and "blocks," each with its designated leader, underscored how intrusive the government's control of working affairs had become; it even included special delegates in the biggest private businesses. Rising to an eventual membership of well more than five hundred, this was one of the most extensive networks that the Nazi Party built in Oberammergau. When in 1936 Ley decreed that its members could no longer belong to "confessional special clublets," that is, the Journeymen's and the Workers' clubs, he exposed the DAF's aggressive efforts to reorient the cultural landscape.[52]

Mayor Lang headed a similar effort by the NSV. Entering a field dominated by the Catholic clubs, this charitable initiative offered an acceptable cover for people needing to join some kind of official group. The NSV therefore recruited a large membership grouped into its own organizational units. This "German folk community for true socialism" soon absorbed the WHW, for which both the HJ and the Journeymen's Club were collecting in 1933; later they added a summer program (KLV) that brought city youth to the countryside for a vacation.[53]

The NSV's efforts to assist needy families centered around an annual series of "casserole" dinners, the savings from which citizens could then donate to the cause. The WHW's advertisements reflected the Nazis' eye for a good propaganda angle; a typical example centers on a mother and child responding to disembodied outstretched arms. Its touching caption reads: "No-one should go hungry! No-one should stay cold." Another approach used in 1936 was to compare the miserable sums collected by Weimar "socialism" with the Third Reich's successes, adding that "you" were needed to keep up the Nazi side.[54]

The government's weight clearly lay behind all of this giving and was enforced by an array of local luminaries who solicited contributions on the streets and in house-to-house visits. Party officials alternated with members of the various paramilitary corps, while representatives of all of the youth groups were frequently deployed. Early on, an HJ march promoted the concept of winter assistance; accompanied by a loud band, the youths carried two notices echoing the program's slogans about support for their neediest fellow citizens.[55]

In addition, Nazi officials administered intense social pressure by selling easily distinguishable "holiday badges" and "collectibles" during the frequent collections. Nevertheless, these proofs of good citizenship were clearly designed to appeal to consumers. In 1935, Hitler's "favorite" bloom, the Edelweiss, hung in one badge above a typical Alpine scene. The 1936 summer program was promoted by a well-received "porcelain butterfly," followed by six figures made in a variety of materials, one of which was an aluminum "Führer head." This concept of a collectible series took off in 1937, when the WHW turned out 21 million pieces of a ten-unit group of "costumed folk." The next year came ten porcelain members of the armed forces, for which the proud owner could acquire a specially made container.[56]

The NSF organized services parallel to those of the NSV and assisted with its "mother and child" initiative. Sometimes the group met together for charitable "working evenings," and it oversaw a mounting store of goods destined for the disadvantaged. Ongoing training sessions for mothers promoted both their own and their offsprings' welfare, while related courses taught cooking and sewing skills.[57]

Recruitment for the NSF was an enduring challenge. In particular, activists strove to involve their counterparts in the remaining Catholic clubs. Launching a "mothering course" in 1935, the Nazi women targeted their "comrades from the Women's Union." Two years later they were complaining that "very many" people had avoided their latest get-together, which could have dispelled mistaken ideas about the group. In a further membership drive they stressed the benefits of participation, which included deepening relationships with other local women.[58]

Members of the NSF and the BdM also began to honor fertile mothers in annual celebrations connected to Hitler's birthday, manifesting the racial ideology that underwrote their activities. A modest ceremony in 1935, featuring entertainment by the girls, was surpassed in 1936 by a party for seventy-three mothers, which was held in a beer hall. Some of the girls even visited the homes of elderly women unable to attend the gathering. Events in the following year included remarks by a member of the Third Reich's ideological corps, the SS.[59]

Like their adult counterparts Oberammergau's girls struggled to attract recruits to their cause. A poignant appeal late in 1934 asked why girls remained aloof and assured potential members that religious commitments should not stand in their way. The BdM followed up with a play intended "to show the many other still standoffish girls and the[ir] parents" how much knowledge and sporting fun they could benefit from by participating. "All young girls belong in . . . a single front" was the ultimate message of this promotional effort.[60]

Overseen by a local teacher, those girls who did join were organized into two sections; there was also a group for younger girls. The BdM was eventually assigned a headquarters for cultural activities. "Home evenings" included singing with musical accompaniment on "guitars and flutes." In their "tiny dining room" a group of future Germanic housewives ended a cooking course by entertaining several regional officials; these powerful men had descended on the BdM clubhouse to partake of a typical three-course meal.[61]

Snapshots taken of the Third Reich's public events in Oberammergau capture both older and younger Nazi girls lined up with their male HJ counterparts. Beyond a role in collecting for the WHW and other charitable drives, these children took part in the frequent processions that marked Nazi holidays and competed in athletic meets. They also played a central role in the Christmas festivities organized to delight the party faithful.[62]

The HJ attracted members far more readily than the BdM, although at first it struggled to draw recruits into the organization. Young boys like Ettal's Michl Pössinger enjoyed its cozy evenings with "model building" and the odd film, as well as opportunities for "small-caliber shooting or in the holidays camping and skiing." The HJ soon benefited from policies aimed at closing young people off from the confessional clubs; exercises scheduled to conflict with church services also undermined their loyalty to traditional Catholic culture. Symptomatic of this power shift was the official decision late in 1935 to confiscate the Catholic youth group's recreational area to accommodate the HJ.[63]

These young Nazis who marched through village streets with the paramilitary columns enhanced their acts of public witness with the adoption of a special uniform. Early on, they borrowed the popular Alpine look of lederhosen with knee socks and added a white, long-sleeved shirt with a swastika affixed to an armband and a dark tie. But their association with the SA suggested making a brown shirt standard, finished off with a "black chest strap, neckerchief with leather knot," and perhaps an "HJ camp cap."[64]

Oberammergau's boys obtained a headquarters where they could enjoy their own "comradeship" and "home evenings." Cultural activities included taking part in plays and musical performances. In particular, the HJ's drummers, with their special striped epaulettes, featured large in Nazi processions.[65] (Figure 6.2 reproduces a photograph of an HJ band.)

Preparation for their future role as Hitler's soldiers sharpened the edges of this male experience well before HJ membership became compulsory in 1939. Their whole ethos was permeated with the martial discipline that typified Third Reich culture. To be sure, two years after Hitler had reinstated universal conscription, it was still necessary to remind Oberammergau's boys that "the point of a militarized sporting body lies not only in political education and sporting competitions but also in military upbringing." Nonetheless, these warlike activities had early on attracted boys like Ernst Lang, who saw their training for soldiering as the "route to hero status." His trips to rallies where he could parade in uniform before party magnates also thrilled this bedazzled youth leader. Although Lang himself was soon expelled from the local group because of his cartoon attacking Motorstorm Commander Burger, boys just like him continued to serve eagerly in the HJ.[66]

Weeks spent by Oberammergau's teenagers at the region's "Camp Highland" provided a bridge to their future two-year stint in the armed forces. In 1937 tent life and "soldiers' rations" were organized by local units of the 1st Mountain Division to simulate actual campaigning conditions. The mountain-

FIGURE 6.2. Hitler Youth activities in Oberammergau include musical performances by local boys.

eers also worked to make sure that the boys truly understood their military responsibilities. This symbiotic relationship between Garmisch County's youth and the warriors stationed in their midst could only have led to heavy recruitment into divisional ranks.[67]

Despite their extensive efforts, Oberammergau's Nazis only partially succeeded in establishing cultural dominance over the local community. Mayor Lang and his political allies faced determined opposition from the Catholic loyalists, who were eager to protect their own cherished rituals, at least in a circumscribed fashion. Accordingly, while the Nazis pursued a hastily constructed annual round of festivals, the Catholics also flooded the streets when tradition called for these acts of public witness.

The Nazis enjoyed ample opportunities to don a uniform and celebrate their calendar's special days. May Day remained a high point, preceded by a fiery swastika lighting the night sky on the preceding evening. Summer solstice celebrations, harvest festival, "takeover day," and Hitler's birthday all became chances to make a noisy appearance in the village. Special occasions also called for festive excitement and parading, like the Saarland's "freeing" in 1935, the ceremonial opening of Saint Gregor's settlement and its adjacent swimming pool complex in 1936, and the occupation of Oberammergau's new barracks by the 1st Mountain Division's signal corps in 1937.[68]

Early in 1938, the party leaders got ready to mark "9 years of the NSDAP in Oberammergau." They kicked off a series of events that included contributions by Zeno Diemer and local archivist and secretary Zwink, who had prepared a slide show about the village's past. For Zwink, "all culture emerges from the human connection with ancestral blood, with the home soil, etc." Devotion to one's own locale, he argued, was "a cornerstone of the Nazi worldview." The gathered leaders also reaffirmed their chapter's history, emphasizing service on behalf of its "godly" mission to fight "Bolshevism's" murderous intentions. Only a few days later the Third Reich absorbed Austria, the first of many aggressive steps taken that year to tighten control over enemies both at home and abroad.[69]

Despite the Nazi chapter's domination in Oberammergau, local opponents of the Third Reich found it possible to stay aloof in relative peace. This benign state of affairs resulted from Raimund Lang's mild regime. The mayor may have been feuding with dissident musicians, but he fiercely defended the common good, as he perceived it, and protected his constituents when outside forces threatened.[70]

Lang's principles were sorely tested, however, when his desire to husband the proceeds from the Passion Play clashed with Wagner's plans to include

Oberammergau in financing the Ammer containment project. He risked his job once again by trying to persuade the minister that these funds would be better spent elsewhere. Wagner even threatened to retire the entire council rather than drop his demands. In the end they all felt pressured to join in this massive construction effort.[71]

Lang was later credited with saving both fellow party members and opponents threatened with imprisonment in concentration camps. He himself claimed to have protected Curate Eberlein from the dangers brought on by his antagonistic preaching. In this context former leftists could take cover in Nazi organizations and the Stahlhelm, or they remained "withdrawn" during the 1930s. Even SPD Chief Daisenberger felt obliged to join the DAF and the NSV, but this was a move that fooled no one; he even remained free to debate openly with the mayor without prejudice, as well as to join councilors in their customary socializing and skat games after meetings. He and a small group of notorious adversaries did, however, remain on the active watch register; Lang designated a few, including Daisenberger, when he had to prepare his own list. Since one man was his sister-in-law's brother and others, like the SPD chief, were well integrated old-timers, he found himself once again caught between local loyalties and his duties as the Nazi mayor.[72]

Certainly, a few villagers did end up incarcerated for transgressions against Third Reich regulations, and one died in a concentration camp during World War II. A former BVP supporter faced a brief jailing over his negative comments about the dedication ceremonies for the two temples containing putschist remains near Munich's Brown House. Several men, one a former SPD supporter, had to appear before a "special court" to answer charges that they had "praised the current situation in Russia and Communism." All were fortunate to escape judgment. Laborers in Oberammergau on construction detail also included suspicious characters; one had been jailed for more than two years on a charge of "preparations for high treason."[73]

Despite some isolated cases, most of the dissidents were able to keep their heads down and stay safe, if not economically buoyant, in Oberammergau. Some felt pressured to join the NSDAP after its ranks opened up in 1937. Alois Lang later testified that the SA made the requirement for party membership "quite plain and clear" if he wanted to secure business advantages that his family desperately needed; Lang also joined the National Socialist Motor Corps (NSKK.) Administrator Raab eventually responded to this blackmail because of his son's need for a university place.[74]

Mayor Lang himself allowed his employees to evade party membership, and even teachers reported enjoying "full freedom in the school and in private life."

As late as 1937, Lang appointed a leading Journeymen's Club member to be the community's official gardener despite his known affiliation. The Forestry Office, run by Viktor Hacker, was similarly free of any "Nazi spirit." Under his administration, officials "sabotaged as much as possible the DAF's orders," although all of the employees were enrolled with the labor organization in 1935. In general, Oberammergau became infamous for the avoidance of "German greetings."[75]

Father Bogenrieder later testified that, despite his lenient regime, Mayor Lang adopted cautious relations with the local church to avoid "endangering himself and possibly also me." In fact, Bogenrieder complained in 1936 that administrative officials were setting a new trend by avoiding the major annual processions and special services at which they had traditionally appeared en masse. The mayor was even wrongly accused of shutting down the Corpus Christi events in 1937. However, Lang followed custom by including the parish priest on the 1940 Passion Committee, together with other "nonparty comrades" like Anton Lang's son Karl. Even Daisenberger was listed as a possible representative of the musical community. Once again, Oberammergau's remarkable local institution undermined the Nazis' efforts to banish Catholic traditions from the village.[76]

Not surprisingly, Lang came to fear hostile actions by the Nazi bigwigs. More than anything he worried about the play's safety despite Hitler's own expressions of support. He even sent Secretary Zwink to look for *Völkisher Beobachter* coverage of a Hitler speech. The Führer had described their play as "a German cultural achievement," but the paper's management denied that the speech ever took place. Of particular concern was ideologue Rosenberg's militantly anti-Christian philosophy. The major bulwark against the play's enemies remained its value to Goebbels's propaganda efforts.[77]

Loyal Catholics in the Nazi ranks found cover for their active participation in public rituals when devout men like Georg Lang and Councilor Rupert Breitsamter fudged the boundaries between party and parish. Forestry chief and "nominal" party member Hacker also pointedly marched in the big church processions as a bureaucrat "in uniform." He even helped to prevent Storm Troopers from blocking the distribution of a pastoral letter from Cardinal Faulhaber. Later Breitsamter intervened when local police tried to stop Catholic youths from making the famous papal letter "With Burning Anxiety" available to parishioners.[78]

Yet another champion of Catholic interests emerged in the figure of Deputy Mayor Bierling, who became quite distressed by Lang's support of an initiative to secularize the confessional schools in 1937. Party members and Storm

Troopers were even pressuring parents to fill in supportive ballots at home. As a father, Bierling identified with the hapless opponents of their school's transformation and would not defend his boss's policy. Consequently, Lang had him put on leave and tried to remove him but without success. "Almost the whole community" agitated on Bierling's behalf to block his permanent retirement from office. Of course, he had been duly elected before 1933 and was therefore as close as it got in Hitler's Germany to a genuinely democratic representative.[79]

Although these Nazi Catholics supported Oberammergau's parish life, the union of Nazis and Catholics caused by the concordat and in particular by the 1934 play season broke down during subsequent years. As early as 1935 the police were reporting unhappily about the village's "two camps," identifying the "bigger group" as oppositional. Discontent was expressed by this refrain: "Once again we have the Third Reich to thank for that." However, caution dictated that most of the public's resentment was concealed behind "gestures and secret expressions."[80]

Almost two years later, a series of extremely popular celebrations demonstrated the residual strength of clerical influence in Alpine Bavaria. In particular, the induction of a new priest in Oberammergau drew a flood of visitors from the surrounding countryside, perhaps, officials thought, as an organized effort to show how effectively the Catholics could still be mobilized. "Objectively regarded," the police chief opined, "the event was a powerful advertisement for the church." Attendance far exceeded that of previous such ceremonies.[81]

Traditional decorations marked this act of public witness. "The church, the rectory, and a few private houses hung out the white-gold church flags," driving out any Nazi competitors. A large procession displayed "club and church banners." In its midst a few children had to be prevented from selling religious prints. Also noticeable for their support of the new priest was Oberammergau's marching band, whose dissident stance against local officials was just then reaching its climax. Soon six thousand visitors crammed into the Passion theater to hear a fiery sermon advocating martyrdom in support of the Christian faith, if needed.[82]

Parallel efforts of party and parish to attract support for their harvest festivals in 1937 only underscored the relative success of such priestly "propaganda efforts." The following year a springtime mission once again revealed the magnetic pull of Oberammergau's Catholic church. Maytime services demonstrated village loyalties, as did Christmas celebrations in this last winter before the war.[83]

Despite persistent support by so many of their parishioners, the clergy faced an increasingly uncertain future as Third Reich politicians circumscribed their authority. From the start, Father Bogenrieder saw himself fighting the "enemies of Christ and the Church." Particularly difficult to keep in line were the males, so many of whom were fully engaged with Nazi activities. Curate Eberlein was caught complaining early in 1936 that "the men are cowardly because they no longer attend church so as to avoid being regarded as black."[84]

The youthful priest took on preaching duties at Oberammergau's big weekly service, showing "ever clearer" signs of oppositional tendencies in his sermons. One Sunday in July 1935, he chose the following as his "timely" text: "Beware of the false prophets in sheep's clothing—for they are rapacious wolves." Eberlein's confrontational message was clear despite his careful wording; he seemed in particular to reference Rosenberg. Consequently, visiting party members complained to Alzinger about his apparent freedom to get away with "such inflammatory preaching." Eberlein did, however, bow to the powers monitoring him for a while, although "his preaching was always somewhat pointed," the police reported the following year.[85]

Soon Eberlein was at it again as he discussed the Communist campaign against priests in revolutionary Spain. He anticipated this murderous anticlerical rampage spreading to Germany, where believers were struggling to defend their faith while losing the right to "freedom of the press." Eberlein then "yelled out" these words: "The pastoral letters are subjected to the strictest censure, and in the other presses one can characterize Christ as a crook-nosed and flat-footed Jew." Yet he was still able to deliver a series of sermons in mid-1937 about "Catholic martyrs and hunted priests," having just declared himself "ready" to join their ranks on behalf of the beleaguered church. Fortunately for Eberlein, with some help from Mayor Lang, he never became one of those imprisoned for their oppositional stance.[86]

Oberammergau's priests defiantly publicized intermittent pastoral letters as a way of galvanizing local opposition to the Nazi regime. Bogenrieder read out a series of these letters emanating from episcopal conferences in 1935 and early 1936. In June the police chief groused that he still detected these priestly efforts to manipulate their parishioners. Bogenrieder had actually risked arrest by bringing a letter from Bavaria's bishops to his flock's attention despite a strict police injunction; although the reaction was mixed, it was more supportive than critical. The reading of further letters was still provoking the Garmisch County faithful in 1937 and "alienating [them] from the . . . National Socialist worldview." At this point Oberammergau's clerics satisfied this obligation by merely passing on the letters' content without comment. But this quiescent state of affairs did not last. After youthful activists were prevented from handing out copies of a papal communication on church premises, they were arrested. Eberlein and "several elderly women" had to negotiate their release at the police station.[87]

Pastoral missives helped to keep the Catholics angry about Nazi interference in traditional practices. Persistently upsetting was the deliberate scheduling of Nazi-sponsored activities for the local youths to coincide with regular church services. This policy accompanied the gradual erosion of membership in the confessional clubs, several of which were ultimately closed down; the seculari-zation of community schools also diminished Catholic education. In this con-text Bogenrieder worried about the failure of most parents to provide their children with a good Christian environment, blaming the allure of "entertain-ment," "sport," and "mountains" in particular.[88]

One extra worry arose with the newly enforced labor service in 1936, which for "most had increased their indifference to religious living." Another was the councilors' withdrawal from church events, which further delegitimized these activities in the eyes of the general population. The erosion of Sunday as a day of worship and rest was another blow to the priest's efforts. In fact, the police chief described Bogenrieder's congregation as "mostly women and older men"; that is, the working population was largely absent. Subsequently, Bogenrieder railed against "the old religious liberalism, which more than ever has come to life under the new conditions."[89]

Nevertheless, apart from the worrisome men, the parishioners remained quite diligent about attending mass, while charitable giving remained gener-ous. Biblical instruction continued with special meetings drawing dozens of people throughout the mid-1930s. The parish library was still popular, and subscriptions to church-issued news outlets rose sharply. Oberammergau's Catholic faithful were loyally supporting their priests in the face of increas-ingly hostile Nazi initiatives.[90]

Some charitable clubs also continued to function within the confines of the parish church. The Third Order grew slightly in the late 1930s and sustained a schedule of lectures, although the Press Club's fate is unclear. Women's groups survived, other than the Marian Congregation, however, which was closed down in 1938 after organizing regular gatherings for around fifty members for several years. In particular, the Mothers' Club flourished, while Bogenrieder organized female youths during the mid-1930s into a "Catholic girls' club [called] 'Loyal for Ever.' "[91]

The independent members of the Women's Union were less fortunate. Although they stabilized their membership levels until 1936, after which time the figures become unavailable, their activities narrowed to focus on charitable efforts for first communicants. To be sure, a party in 1937 resembled the vibrant celebrations of old; two dozen or so children attended the union's trademark event, which included child actors performing "best-loved plays" to the intense joy of their audience. Primarily, however, the Women's Union seems to have cooperated with the church-based mothers during the Nazi years.[92]

Still less fortunate were the Catholic males, whose healthy membership in three clubs when Hitler took power sank quickly as the temptation to forsake their confessional groups became acute. As early as 1933 a few past leaders joined the party. Nevertheless, the journeymen resumed some activities after the 1934 Passion season, and in 1935 both they and the workers held meetings during Saint Joseph's month of March. A small version of the youth group was still going that May, but it was active mostly inside the church, where its members only occasionally donned a uniform. In particular, party members complained about Eberlein using two youths to assist at Good Friday services. During the Corpus Christi procession that year, all of the Catholic clubs were forbidden to use "badges, pennants, and flags."[93]

Anton Lang's teenage son Gottfried was busy during this period connecting youth group members to the broader organization of young Catholics. He "went from house to house collecting subscriptions to the weekly newspaper, *Junge Front*, which was, we thought, a strong voice against Nazism. I think I was able to get about 40 subscriptions." This was a rewarding way of meeting anti-Nazis who might even express open hostility toward the Third Reich.[94]

In 1935 Lang joined fellow activists on a trip to Rome. "We camped there, wore off-white shirts with big silver buttons, and stood in cruciform formation in front of St Peter's to receive the pope's blessing. Then with banners flying we marched to the Colosseum, where our leaders made speeches reminding us that, like Peter and Paul, we also had to suffer for the ultimate victory of Christ." But the travelers faced official harassment when they returned home to Germany; Lang himself had attracted the Gestapo's attention, and he was obliged to leave for the United States in 1937.[95]

That was also a hard year for the male clubs, which Bogenrieder described as lifeless. Technically, the club for young adults was not closed down until early 1938, together with the "confiscation of their library and cash reserves." However, all action had by then retreated into the church, where Eberlein ran "youth get-togethers in the sacristy" in spring 1937. More than a dozen ten- to sixteen-year-olds had attended one of these gatherings, which the police suspected were not, as reported, purely spiritual affairs. Eberlein then moved his youths into the church for weekly meetings, drawing fifteen to twenty attendees until the July school vacation. However, Bogenrieder doubted the value of these efforts, in particular because of a police officer's brooding presence. When Eberlein resumed his weekly meetings "in the heated sacristy" the following January, he attracted "mostly the members of the dissolved Catholic Young Men's Club, the Catholic Journeymen's Club and two soldiers" from Oberammergau's new barracks. However, the police presence soon discouraged this new initiative until a larger group, still including soldiers, met in May.[96]

More resilient than the once vibrant Catholic associations were the parishioners who were determined to keep alive their customary ritual calendar of feast days, processions, and pilgrimages. Loyalists refused to work on special Bavarian holidays like All Saints' Day despite Nazi prohibitions against closing. As late as 1937 the Garmisch County faithful still insisted on attending services and maintaining churchyard rituals on this important feast day. Oberammergau's Catholics were no different, staying away from local workplaces. Bogenrieder was especially pleased that visiting laborers agreed to suspend construction work on the day. He was less sanguine about any possibility of maintaining this defiant attitude in the future, given official efforts to prevent businesses from releasing their employees.[97]

Rogation columns set off as usual each spring, one to visit Kappl on Saint Marcus's Day and, later, three more to traditional venues. A June procession to Ettal "to bless the crops" was ongoing as well, as were the harvest festival celebrations. Pilgrimages to Ettal and the Wieskirche retained their vitality, notably for Mary's ascension day at Ettal and the Wieskirche's Guardian Angel festivities. As late as 1939, more than twenty groups of pilgrims made it to Ettal, more than half of them female, perhaps because of women's relative freedom from Nazi organizational life. But one big loss to the pilgrimage scene was the death of "Rom Kathl."[98]

For Oberammergau, the highlight of each year's ritual round was still the Corpus Christi procession, which in 1934 had been a great success, coming as it did early in the Passion season. The weather cooperated, play visitors enjoyed taking part, and the usual Catholic associations remained at its heart. In 1935, however, locals were dismayed by a ban on displaying associational paraphernalia. Only here and there were Bavarian flags to be seen until the homeowners received orders to remove even them. The following year, a Sunday procession had to suffice because of bad weather on the customary Thursday. Only church buildings and Anton Lang's home sported the "white-gold Church flag." The next spring, bad weather seems to have precluded outside processions. However, this loss was suspicious enough for Mayor Lang to face accusations that he had suppressed them.[99]

In June 1937 the Garmisch County administrator assessed the implications of "extraordinarily big and lively" crowds during Catholic celebrations. There was ample evidence, he argued, that priests in Alpine Bavaria were influencing their parishioners to remain "thoroughly passive, if not hostile toward the National Socialist state leadership." Locally, it was Curate Eberlein whose activities, especially with young Catholics, came under suspicion. He was certainly lucky to escape arrest, likely with help from Mayor Lang.[100]

The following year Nazi leaders were emboldened by a series of international successes, and both Catholics and Jews were to feel the negative effects. In March came Austria's incorporation into the Third Reich, while later the ill-fated Munich conference led to the seizure of Czechoslovakia's Sudeten highlands. Meanwhile, local Catholics suffered the loss of their greatest lay champion when Anton Lang died that May. He had spearheaded the effort to keep alive traditional holy days, and he dared to reject an "invitation" from Mayor Lang to join the NSV, citing his long-standing support of the Catholic charity Caritas. The Nazis found this a good time to restrict the easy access to public streets that activists like Anton Lang had continued to enjoy.[101]

During the period right before Oberammergau's Corpus Christi celebrations in 1938, monks drew crowds into the parish church for a mission week. Rogation processions set off as usual in late April and May, while special Maytime services attracted spillover attendance. Then, the big annual event, scheduled that year for mid-June, promised to repeat the publicity coup of previous years. However, two weeks beforehand, Garmisch's district administrator wrote to Father Bogenrieder forbidding marches along major routes because of a burgeoning number of automobile drivers. A human mass clogging key arteries would, he argued, seriously impede traffic.[102]

The priest sent back an indignant response, detailing the procession's customary route with annotations that minimized its use of busy streets. A "short" stretch of Ettalerstrasse would take participants off this main road over an Ammer bridge to the first stop, the letter states, from which a "footpath" leads to Station Road. There they "cross quickly" to reach their second stop and then the Passion theater. Only when they entered Dorfplatz and Dorfstrasse to reach the small plaza near the Weisses Rössl Inn would they displace traffic, which could be diverted to the parallel Schnitzlergasse. Alternatively, they could use Schnitzlergasse and avoid the traffic. However, Bogenrieder added tartly that cars were delayed far more dramatically on a daily basis by the "tempo" of local cows returning from their pastures. He ended with this devastating riposte: "The devout folk would hardly understand if their processions . . . were not as well treated as the cows."[103]

Nevertheless, instructions to move two of the altars to side streets arrived ahead of the holiday. Bogenrieder was able to insert a small article in the local newspaper describing the permitted route and encouraging his faithful to take part. "The Corpus Christi festival is the Savior's high feast. . . . Our prayerful participation in the procession should be a fearless expression of our faith." Perhaps his flock did not realize how bravely Bogenrieder had attempted to shepherd their ancestral tradition. However, despite these efforts, the summer of 1938 marked a turning point in Oberammergau's parish life as the Nazi authorities initiated a series of inroads into well-established public rituals. Soon afterward, Curate Eberlein's efforts to maintain a vestigial religious organization for the Catholic youth faded. The situation could only deteriorate from that point forward, although many parishioners remained faithful to their traditional beliefs and practices for the duration of the Third Reich.[104]

In June 1936 Oberammergau's police chief reported that the "Jewish" composer Max Peter Meyer had marched conspicuously in the Corpus Christi procession, "head held high" as he joined his fellow Catholics on their holiest of days. Meyer was Father Bogenrieder's only parishioner to face the escalating hostility of Nazi authorities toward German Jews in subsequent years. He and his Protestant wife had converted to Catholicism after moving from Munich to Oberammergau in 1935. They continued to find refuge in their adopted parish's confessional life, and they enjoyed close ties with Ettal's abbot as well.[105]

Meyer had "befriended" Alois Lang while staying repeatedly at his hotel; in fact, he had been one of its original visitors after Lang modernized the family's guesthouse before the 1930 Passion season. Lang later persuaded this Munich-based Jew to relocate in Oberammergau. He had been anxious to find a safe haven "in the countryside," contemplating either Tutzing or the Passion Play village. Meyer even checked to be sure that he would get a welcoming reception, both socially and from the official leadership. Receiving Mayor Lang's go-ahead, he moved into the Waldhaus in the Saint Gregor suburb. He became his new community's only resident identified as a "full" Jew during the next three years.[106]

The Meyers and the Alois Langs remained fast friends. Meyer later testified that "we were always together. I was a constant guest in his house." He even discounted Lang's eventual decision to join the party, stressing his clear opposition to Nazism. Only the deteriorating situation for Jews began to separate the two couples, as Meyer downplayed their friendship "out of purely rational grounds." He had become quite a recluse, although he liked to visit the cinema and the parish church.[107]

Until Kristallnacht Oberammergau offered Meyer a sheltering environment despite the hostility toward Jews that local Catholics shared with their Nazi counterparts. Although worshipping with the "mixed" couple after their conversion, they still shared with Passion Play audiences a confrontational reading of the Gospel story that pitted its Jewish antagonists against Jesus and his Christian followers. While they had certainly refused to strip the 1934 playscript of its Old Testament dimensions in light of Third Reich ideology, they were not unduly sensitive to the anti-Jewish campaign raging in Germany during the later 1930s. Even so prominent an opponent of the Nazis as Anton Lang concentrated on defending his Catholic community's interests, particularly their customary right to perform the Passion Play.

Just as Meyer was moving to the village, performances of a controversial play highlighted the whole question of Oberammergau's relationship to Nazi anti-Semitism. Surprisingly, Alois Lang took the leading role in *Ernte* since its storyline, according to the local newspaper, allotted the titular harvest "to the Jews." However, the village authorities were indignant when the staging of this play led to a "lying report" in Czechoslovakia that Oberammergau was replacing the Passion Play with "a trendy anti-Semitic skit." In fact, they argued, *Ernte* was entirely free of hostility toward Jews, a shaky judgment indeed. For them and perhaps even for Lang, evading the pervasive anti-Semitism spewed out by Hitler's regime in its propaganda and political rhetoric was a tall order.[108]

Even before the ensemble of *Ernte* took the stage in July 1935, it became obvious that a ratcheting up of anti-Semitic propaganda was under way in Oberammergau. That spring the newspaper included a nasty piece from Julius Streicher's virulently anti-Semitic *Der Stürmer*, while Mayor Lang attached the exclusionary tag "Jews not permitted entry" to announcements about a couple of NSV meetings. Later, as the local NSDAP chapter returned to a regular meeting schedule in July, its members took up the issue of "blood and soil" at a talk that advocated stripping Aryans of their racial identity for even "thinking 'Jewish.'" In August Lang issued a rule denying Jews any access to the new swimming pool complex. Then, following the promulgation of the Nuremberg Laws came a slide show titled "Jewish Intellect" and an announcement that limited flag displays to the swastika, except for Jews who had their own "colors."[109]

Discussion of "the Jewish question" followed at November's party meeting, where a local teacher openly attacked a perceived lax attitude toward the regime's new Nuremberg policies. He condemned the "thoroughly inappropriate humanity and sensitivity," as well as the "sympathy," shown toward Jews by his compatriots. Germans needed a persuasive education about "the true mentality of the Jewish race" to justify what might seem like "overly harsh" countermeasures borrowed from the other side's arsenal. "One cannot fight the Jews with the delicacy of a noble Aryan soul," the speaker added, reminding his listeners of their enemies' use of every "lie and slander" in fighting the NSDAP before 1933. Switching to the central Nuremberg issue of the Jews' racial makeup, he rejected any concept that a "German Jew" could exist even "in the tenth generation." Moreover, Jews were hungry for power as the "chosen people."[110]

The next monthly meeting featured a racially oriented talk by a local SA doctor. Meanwhile, Hitler's program to segregate Jews from their fellow Germans escalated, reinforced with "ancestral tree forms" that obliged "Aryans" hoping for success in their Nazi-dominated society to establish an untainted ancestry. Filling out these forms required collusion by the parish priests, whose vital statistics records provided the necessary "proof."[111]

By August 1936 local Nazis had switched the topic to Jewish predominance among the Soviet Union's commissars, fanning the widespread anti-Bolshevik fears and elevating hostility toward the Russian enemy. A year later Mayor Lang picked up the theme of Third Reich racial ideology while making his lengthy address to Oberammergau's residents about the Music Club crisis. Proudly linking "our National Socialist fundamentals" with "the play's original concept," he argued that "we do not perform Jewish skits because . . . [their] ritual is foreign to us. The Passion Play is also no Jewish play but rather, as many leading men have already declared, the absolute opposite. It is the most anti-Semitic play that we have. In order to stage it, we rely on our inborn, truly German sensitivity, which is supported by a genuine Christian belief." Yet another heated discussion about "racial politics" came late in 1937, whipping up further hostility toward the Jews.[112]

Despite these substantial efforts, Oberammergau's political leaders were not entirely successful in imposing the regime's ideological program on their fellow villagers, including party members. Even Mayor Lang objected to putting Streicher's *Der Stürmer* on public display in 1937. He clashed with the powerful minister himself, arguing that "the cultural level of this paper [was] not suitable for Oberammergau." Lang also balked at a subsequent initiative to display "Jews not welcome here" notices at the village boundaries for similar reasons. However, this "tasteless" effort promoted by the SA prevailed despite his appeal to a higher authority. The mayor would likely have disapproved of the crude and visually provocative images presented in an odious slide show about "the eternal Jew," which played to a "packed" theater in this same period.[113]

Like their mayor, Oberammergau's population did not wholeheartedly accept the Nazis' interference in their daily lives. Ackermann, for one, noted that he had fielded numerous complaints from summer visitors about avoidance of the German greeting. He then repeated a story recounted by a shocked party member, who said that, in his area, those failing to use the correct salutation would be ejected from local establishments as if they were themselves Jewish.[114]

Policies against Jews who brought business into Garmisch County were also unpopular. Commercial farmers, for example, had come to rely on a Weilheim-based "cattle Jew" when selling their livestock. In 1937 the authorities shut down his business to the great distress of his former clients, including farmers in Unterammergau. One of Oberammergau's butchers, also a party member, actually defied the restrictions on trading with Jewish firms to continue his dealings with a Wolfratshausen cattle trader.[115]

The county's tourism industry also suffered from an anti-Semitic campaign to end the regular flow of Jewish urbanites into centers like Oberammergau. Local innkeepers and boarding house owners had continued to host known Jews, including "traveling salesmen." Alois Lang, for one, enjoyed the return custom from Jewish guests; Meyer ran into a Munich-based bank director, like himself "a long-standing visitor of Lang's establishment"; in addition, someone "from Frankfurt, a dealer in cigars, 5 or 6 families, were always returning." In another local inn, a regular testified to staying there "many times, 10 to 15 times a year."[116]

As late as January 1937, "12–15 Jews from Munich . . . spread themselves out in the winter sports venues" around Ettal to the annoyance of some observers. Months later a police report found that Jewish guests at the Ettal monastery's hotel "appear to feel comfortable there." Meyer's acquaintances even returned to Lang's hotel for the Christmas season that winter, although Ettal did not attract any more Jews. Only in 1938 did Oberammergau's summer season get under way without most of the usual Jewish guests. The Jewish owner of a village property also found a local purchaser that August.[117]

Because Jewish visitors often enjoyed intimate contact with their host families, respectful and even friendly relationships developed like those between the Langs and the Meyers. Rejecting Nazi propaganda about Jewish threats to national and international health, Ernst Lang's parents, he later recalled, valued the presence of "cultivated and likeable" fellow Germans in their boarding house. A Munich-based bureaucrat had visited Oberammergau so regularly that he had watched his innkeeper grow up and felt quite at home in his establishment. A bank director who repeatedly stayed there described socializing with his host in this locale, which was also frequented by Nazis; they had enjoyed lively conversations "in the private quarters or in a sideroom." The Jewish daughter-in-law of a famous musician also remained a welcome guest in the inn even after Kristallnacht, enjoying her host's "unaltered affection and . . . friendship."[118]

Visiting Jews also got to know villagers in the NSDAP, whose commitment to their welfare survived Third Reich pressures. Deputy Mayor Bierling's decades-long acquaintance with one such man led him to buck the Nuremberg prohibitions by marrying him to an Aryan bride. Even committed Nazi Raimund Lang gave the nod to Meyer's relocation into the village as a refugee from Nazified Munich. By contrast, Motor Commander Kräh later decried his inability to protect Jews mistreated in his native Munich, which disturbed him greatly; he also lost acquaintances to emigration. His perceived helplessness illustrates how easily Germans became passive observers of the escalating hostilities directed at their fellow Jewish citizens.[119]

During the months leading up to Kristallnacht, even a "close friendly relationship" like Meyer's with Alois Lang became strained. At that point the Meyers would no longer be left in peace in their Waldhaus. The long arm of the Nazi regime was about to reach out and tear their lives apart.[120]

Meyer was at home when the pogrom reached Oberammergau. Nazi officials had been busy, seizing the chance to rid their area of Jews once and for all. They therefore prepared a form that "pledges" the signatory to "leave Garmisch-Partenkirchen with the next available train and never again return." It went on to require the unfortunate victim to accept the Aryanization of his "land, buildings and possessions." To obtain the signatures of all of the regional Jews and ensure their immediate exile, the county leader hauled them into his office on November 9.[121]

Meyer later described his own experience with this aggressive policy. Morning was just dawning when he was "attacked by a mob," as he characterized the SA squad who arrested him. When he responded to the "horde" that had turned up at his home, an Oberau officer manhandled him, dislodging his spectacles. Because of this, Meyer never identified the raid's other participants, arousing speculation about just which villagers had joined the official party; later, councilors mentioned only that the "local SA" had colluded with county-level troopers. The man who struck him commanded both Oberammergau's forces and those of other nearby communities.[122]

Meyer himself was soon incarcerated in the Dachau concentration camp, one of thousands brutalized as a result of the pogrom. A few months later, he made his escape into exile, primarily in Britain, where he ended up teaching music and affiliated with the London College of Music. However, Mrs. Meyer remained for a time in the Waldhaus since her Aryan status protected both her person and the real estate wisely purchased in her name. In general, the agony of this one family does not seem to have disturbed their fellow villagers. The local police chief reported worries about the pogrom's economic implications, balanced by an "understanding of the other measures by a preponderance of the population." Countywide, there were doubters, some perhaps influenced by news from abroad. In fact, given the necessary conformity with Nazi doublespeak, it is hard to know what the locals were thinking, but they certainly did not intervene in any way to prevent Meyer's removal from their midst.[123]

Hitler's regime unmasked its murderous intent toward Jews in the Kristallnacht pogroms. By November 1938, however, foreign governments had made appeasement their preferred approach to Nazi Germany, as the Munich conference had so recently illustrated. Only four months later, German forces would enter Czechoslovakia to occupy the entire country beyond the Sudeten highlands. Preparations for yet another campaign followed, with the official outbreak of World War II taking place as Nazi forces crossed into Poland on September 1.

War changed the character of Oberammergau's villagers as they became ever more inexorably drawn into the Third Reich's many campaigns. Soldiers left to fight in the various German forces, primarily on the murderous eastern front and in antipartisan warfare around the Balkan Peninsula. Their relatives kept the home fires burning as best they could while bombed-out refugees, important armaments industries, and forced laborers relocated to the Ammer valley. However, the locals retained their powerful sense of identity as Passion players, which toughened the leadership's relations with increasingly dangerous Nazi overlords. Headed by Alfred Bierling after Mayor Lang left for active service, the community refused to plunge fully into Nazi Germany's murderous depths.

7

Warriors

By September 1939 preparations for the next summer's performances were well advanced in Oberammergau, but Hitler's plans stood in the way. His Polish offensive might have led to a rapid victory, yet the Germans remained at war, and any hope of rescuing the upcoming Passion Play season was soon abandoned.

Initial successes turned into long years of warfare as men and eventually boys were enlisted into active combat. The worst fighting came after Hitler's "Barbarossa" invasion of the Soviet Union launched close to four years of ideologically driven slaughter; death notices soon became common currency in the local newspaper. Soldiers and civilians alike were caught up in the increasingly cruel grip of a dictatorship that crushed both dissenters and racial enemies. Under cover of brutal occupation regimes, Nazi forces were free to commit the mass murder of Jews and other Holocaust victims that would taint all German citizens.

When Hitler began the Second World War, he drew each participant into a series of experiences that intersected with the grand drama of massive campaigns. Gradually, individual stories buried at the heart of wartime Germany have emerged into the public record. These memories, combined with contemporary documents and postwar testimonies, inject a human, and particularly female, dimension into military and institutional histories, balancing their overwhelmingly male emphasis.

Service on the front lines was, to be sure, experienced by millions of German men, including hundreds from Oberammergau. One was Ernst Lang, who campaigned with a sapper unit through Poland, France, and the Soviet Union, remaining for long years on the vicious eastern front. However, an early incident in Galicia brought him closest to Holocaust-related atrocities, judging from Lang's own account of his wartime exploits. The SS's Ukrainian allies were attempting a mass slaughter; they had trapped some local Jews in a burning synagogue. Racing to free them, the humble army officer faced down an enraged SS commander in charge and forced this would-be murderer to make himself scarce.[1]

Lang's fellow villagers also fought on the many fronts opened up by Third Reich armies. The local connection was primarily to the 1st Mountain Division, whose signal corps was housed in Oberammergau's new barracks. Men joining this division applied their well-honed mountaineering skills to campaigning in the Caucasus, as well as in Greece and the Balkans, where soldiers used brutal occupation tactics developed in the east. Divisional units even assisted with a massacre of Italian soldiers immortalized in a book and movie titled *Captain Corelli's Mandolin*.[2]

Overall, however, Oberammergau's fighting males were primarily engaged in the murderous years of campaigning on the eastern front. They experienced death tolls that escalated during Barbarossa and remained high until the even more dramatic losses of the war's final months. Photographs of young soldiers affixed to local tombstones reflect this disaster, while a series of tablets hanging on the church's south wall memorializes these fallen warriors.

Back on the home front, Oberammergau's women, children, and elderly males struggled to survive in difficult and crowded conditions. Their situation worsened with the arrival of a Messerschmitt research institute for jet and rocket technologies. A camp full of forced laborers joined POWs already employed in local businesses, deepening the villagers' uneasy complicity in the Third Reich's exploitative use of occupied populations. This was a period full of painful experiences for both soldiers and homebound villagers; their reminiscences complement the documentary evidence that so often glosses over lived realities.[3]

All of these sources converge in depicting a surprisingly benign wartime regime in Oberammergau. Talking to people who knew prominent Nazis familiar to me only from the written record, I was struck by their willingness to emphasize the positive. Postwar testimony similarly describes a mayor and councilors unwilling to follow their superiors into an increasingly savage tyranny. This was partially because of a tendency to whitewash the actions of well-known local figures and to avoid giving hostile witness in the denazification hearings. Nevertheless, the Passion players' acutely developed self-image did help to inoculate their leaders against succumbing to the Third Reich's worst excesses.

Largely responsible for this local regime's character was the personality of Acting Mayor Alfred Bierling, who took over once Raimund Lang disappeared into army service. Bierling's own wartime memories and a set of values internalized from playing the Passion moderated the behavior of this freely elected official. Even Bierling's fellow councilor, Chapter Leader Alzinger, represented an unassuming presence rather than a looming menace. As a result, their village never became a Nazi stronghold in which ruthless policies were enforced.

Twenty-five years after the festive launching of World War I, Hitler invaded Poland. The people of Oberammergau may have shared his expansionist aims, but, like most Germans, they certainly were not eager for a new war. Too many bitter memories remained for both civilians and veterans, some of whom would once again have to take up arms. Their nation's strategic interests also dictated caution, with Communist threats still lurking despite the truce created by the Nazi pact with the Soviet Union.[4]

One villager who had failed to anticipate Hitler's warlike intentions was Raimund Lang. As Administrator Raab later testified, he even exclaimed, "I would be crazy if I believed a war to be in the cards." Similarly, when Lang's deputy, Bierling, presented the mayor's nephew Ernst with mobilization papers, his body language betrayed a reluctance caused by fear for the new generation's safety. Ernst's parents clearly agreed, based on their own experiences during the Great War, which included the loss of two of his mother's four male siblings.[5]

Anxiety about a fight breaking out over the Sudeten crisis had already reduced the locals to holding their collective breath until the Munich conference produced a peaceful outcome. Then, as the Polish campaign got under way, authorities had to suppress oppositional voices. The hope was for a speedy end to a conflict that frightened the villagers because any "weakening of the belligerent powers" could bring back "the Bolshevistic world revolution."[6]

Oberammergau in particular had everything to lose from an extended war in 1939 because its timing was much more damaging to the Passion Play tradition than a conflict begun in middecade. Only a quick resolution and a return to peace with Britain and France, now technically at war with Germany, would save the season. As the year drew to a close, however, Mayor Lang and his Passion Committee members had to face the inevitable. Despite a successful outcome in Poland, hostilities were going to force the postponement of all of the anticipated performances. For Lang, whose every effort had gone into maintaining his community's dedication to their ancient vow, this was clearly a devastating blow, as it was for the general population.[7]

Culpable here, according to the mayor and others, were the hate-filled British, whose supposed commitment to "morality and humanity" had not prevented them from undermining this opportunity to "bring together peoples in a reconciling spirit and in peace." Locals who had long enjoyed warm relationships with their British visitors now rapidly turned against them. Yet they clearly hoped that a normal pattern of brief wartime interruptions would be repeated. Afterward they could reconcile with their erstwhile foes, as had happened after World War I. Little did they know that a 1940 season was lost forever and that six years of destructive conflict would consume the lives of Oberammergau's villagers.[8]

During those long years their community experienced a roller coaster of emotions as the conflict's impact grew ever more dramatic. A constant theme was the desire for peace, but as campaigning realities shifted, thoughts about how best to achieve that peace changed accordingly. However, the dreadful memories of 1918 encouraged people to work toward a successful outcome; this new war should at least improve their lives.[9]

Initially, hostility toward the British translated into determination to bring them into line. This deteriorating relationship fed on suspicions that "the head of the English Secret Service" was complicit in Georg Elser's attempt to assassinate Hitler during celebrations of the November putsch. Then, a successful summer campaign in 1940 encouraged rising expectations as German troops occupied Western Europe. Yet the villagers, while gratified, still faced the nagging question of the undefeated British, "who bear the unique responsibility for this war."[10]

During the rest of the year, they anticipated defeating Britain in short order. By late December, speculation had it that either the enemy might capitulate or Hitler would invade. A bombing raid on Munich had further soured the local mood, soon to be reinforced by the stories of more than two hundred refugees arriving from bombed areas in northern and western Germany. They were the first of a stream of refugees bringing dire news about the chaos and carnage that British raids were inflicting on urban centers. No wonder that hopes continued for a speedy defeat of so destructive a foe.[11]

Attention soon shifted eastward in 1941, although initially the talk was still of a British defeat or perhaps a peace deal. There was, however, concern that American interference might complicate the path to peace outside of Europe. Mussolini's Mediterranean bunglings caused some discontent, and even when German armies intervened successfully in that theater, "a certain war-weary feeling" persisted.[12]

By late April, rumblings about the concentration of forces to strike Soviet Russia had begun, so the actual invasion on June 22 could hardly have been a surprise. Authorities reported a favorable reception in Garmisch County, where the logic of a war against Bolshevism perked up a depressed population. Yet they encountered a hostile reaction in Oberammergau; the specter of 1918 again raised its ominous head, and the locals feared that the invasion could well prolong this undesirable war. By late July, however, they were catching the anti-Bolshevik mood and optimistic about their country's ability to prevail rapidly. August confidence about a speedy victory before winter turned to anxiety in September. But spirits remained high that fall, once the vital significance of a war against Communism had sunk in. Declawing their Soviet enemy was an urgent enough task that it even justified a longer conflict.[13]

Japan's attack on Pearl Harbor ushered in a new phase of the war. Locals interpreted this provocation as contributing to victory in the European theater since the Americans would hold back their own armaments and weaken both the British and the Soviet forces. However, the mood in Garmisch County was soon depressed again. Soviet armies were continuing to fight back, and the war was clearly far from over.[14]

Nevertheless, Oberammergau's belt-tightening population remained certain that Hitler's policies were fending off "extermination from the East." In 1942 they were buoyed by positive news about Field Marshall Erwin Rommel's African victories, by an effective U-boat campaign in Atlantic waters, and by Japanese forces dramatically sweeping through Asia. Additional successes in their eastern theater, they surmised, should lead to a rapid conclusion.[15]

But the news turned sour, and opinions shifted once again. Expectations for an easy defeat of the Soviets had been misguided; even the decision to initiate a war with Russia was a mistake. By year's end officials found villagers in a "hopeless" mood. The conflict was dragging on indefinitely to the particular detriment of less-privileged Germans.[16]

The year 1943 brought more negative feelings about the eastern theater, where German forces were in retreat after the disaster of Stalingrad and a failed expedition into the Caucasus mountains. In Garmisch County an unwelcome realization of war's "harshness und cruelty" was sapping still lingering hopes for a positive outcome. By then, Allied forces had landed on European soil in Italy. Bombing raids on Munich began to worry the locals, who were fearful that their community would not be exempt; the nearby downing of a U.S. bomber could only have heightened those anxieties. That summer a defeatist attitude was manifesting itself in the county. Oberammergau was the leading community by year's end in "expressions of defeatism," partly perhaps because English speakers were listening to the BBC.[17]

The great new expectation in 1944 was for a miracle weapon capable of knocking out the Allies in time for a German victory. To some extent that idea persisted into summertime, when news of the D-Day landings reached Oberammergau. Rockets had been launched against their British foes, but could they really work—and in time? Hopes and fears mingled during the rest of that year as bad news came in from all quarters. By the last wartime months, however, the villagers were accepting defeat and thankful to be on the verge of release.[18]

Those villagers who lived out the war on the home front experienced these alternating hopes and fears without any direct involvement in the fighting. The primary brunt of the wartime horrors was borne by the men who disappeared to join Germany's armed forces. Once Hitler reintroduced universal service in 1935, young males had to spend time in training; as of 1936 this required period of military preparation was to run for at least two years. In 1938, local soldiers found themselves in units enforcing the "peaceful" annexation of Austria and Sudeten areas of Czechoslovakia.[19]

Many villagers joined their resident troops in the 1st Mountain Division. Highlanders like Alois Lang had performed so impressively in World War I that the Weimar leadership decided to continue a small unit. In 1935 these men helped to form a mountain brigade that three years later became a full division based in the Garmisch area shortly after its signal corps had occupied Oberammergau's barracks. Symbolized by an Edelweiss, this Alpine-based force was a natural fit for youths who had grown up with mountaineering and winter sports.[20]

A general conscription ahead of the Polish invasion continued this flow of able-bodied villagers into the war's maelstrom. Even a record of action throughout World War I did not protect middle-aged men like Mayor Lang from the pressures to reenlist. Just after graduating from Ettal's gymnasium in 1914, he had immediately entered trench warfare; yet despite his four years at the front and subsequent action in the Werdenfels Free Corps, he soon disappeared into the army again. In fact, there was some initial grumbling that married veterans had been tapped for service while younger men were still at large "in the cinema and at dances." Soon enough, though, increasingly youthful males were detailed into the armed forces.[21]

Seen through the lens of eastern front horrors, the Polish and Western European campaigns emerge in retrospective accounts as positively halcyon despite some low points. The 1st Mountain Division troops took part in the rapid envelopment of Poland's army, traveling through "marvelous" Germanized Slovakian highlands before hurrying toward the city of Lvov. As one of their commanding officers, Max Pemsel, later characterized it, "[T]his chase is so truly dear to the hunters' hearts." Then days of fierce and bloody fighting outside the city were about to end in an outright attack when Russian forces arrived to occupy their prearranged zone. To be sure, Pössinger, like Ernst Lang, encountered anti-Jewish atrocities, which he claims were committed by Poles. He describes his own unit's intervention on behalf of menaced Jewish civilians, yet the guilt for these attacks extended to the incoming German forces, who tolerated and even participated in them. Further ideologically driven killings took place in Lvov when the mountaineers passed through during Barbarossa; one unit in particular served in the occupation detail and exploited the discovery of slaughtered Ukrainians to turn local anger against their "Jewish-Communist" enemies. Massacres of local Jews followed in this context.[22]

First, however, came the German invasion of France and its northern neighbors in 1940. The 1st Mountain Division entered French territory northwest of Sedan, passing by the historic fortress of Rocroi. After defending a position on the "green hell" of the Oise-Aisne canal, divisional troops fought their way out toward the Marne river in grueling summer conditions. Racing over the Marne, they continued south in hot pursuit, crossing first the Seine and then the Loire. To recuperate from these tough campaigning weeks, the mountaineers were sent to guard the French border, where they were able to luxuriate in attractive highland surroundings lit by glorious summer sunshine. After training to land in the British town of Hastings during Operation Sealion and then to carry out an equally ill-fated plan to scale Gibraltar, they spent winter days in mostly friendly territory, from which they could travel to French tourist attractions like Paris.[23]

Ernst Lang experienced a similar shift from fierce combat to cozy duty in France. He was still there when the Barbarossa campaign began, enjoying "the idyll of an undestroyed town in Burgundy, surrounded by vineyards and in a [beautiful] landscape."[24] By contrast, the 1st Mountain Division was torn away from its French pleasures in time to assist with the spring invasion of Yugoslavia, which preceded Barbarossa. Entering Slovenia and later Croatia and Bosnia, divisional units met little opposition and even a positive reception by ethnic Germans. However, they were soon preparing for Field Marshall Gerd von Rundstedt's sweep through the Ukraine as part of that massive assault's southern thrust. This was a new and very deadly mission that would take them hundreds of miles east to the Sea of Azov.[25]

Once past the border with Russian-held Poland, the mountaineers immediately faced a baptism of fire that presaged the murderous fighting to come. Intense conflicts alternated with rapid movement through the Ukrainian countryside as troops once again raced to envelop their opponents. Passing beyond the Dnieper river involved a frightening and highly exposed trip across a "long swaying bridge over the 17 meter deep waters," which led them into the Russian steppe.[26]

There, the weather conditions turned against the division's forces. First mud and then freezing snow and ice slowed any forward progress, causing a process of "demodernization," as historian Omer Bartov has described it. A snapshot of the muddy road along which four horses are seen dragging an ambulance epitomizes this regression. Soon the troops were digging in near the Mius River during an "implacable winter," occupying frontline trenches reminiscent of World War I. Subsequently, they manned positions on the Samara river until spring brought more mud in advance of a return to summer conditions.[27]

Hitler committed his southern forces to attacks on Stalingrad and the Caucasus in 1942. So, as part of Operation Blue's Army Group A, the 1st Mountain Division headed thankfully toward the lofty Caucasus region, where they could once again put their mountaineering and survival skills to good purpose. Symbolic of this new assignment would be a daring climb to the top of Mount Elbrus, the range's dominant peak, where carefully selected troops planted their flag. Hitler, however, was not amused by this unprofessional detour from the actual fighting on so crucial a front.[28]

The Elbrus formed part of a mountain chain intersected by well-guarded passes, which divisional units seized one by one, sometimes using oblique tactics to outmaneuver and literally climb around the Soviet defenses. Eventually they had established operational lines extending over a fifty-mile stretch of territory, setting up what the division's commander, General Hubert Lanz, described as the "unique . . . experiences of these weeks in rock and ice." However, all of the efforts to free the route leading out of this highland fortress collapsed; the needed reinforcements did not materialize with which to build on their initial successes.[29]

That fall most of the divisional forces were reassigned to campaign in an area of dense and "ancient" woodland cut by deep valleys, which separated the German invaders from the Black Sea coast. However, they were foiled by a fearless enemy and persistent rain that created a muddy "morass." The soldiers could see the port city that was their goal, but they never reached it. Rather, months of costly fighting led early in 1943 to a retreat back toward the Azov coast through flooded rice-fields and lagoons.[30]

Campaigning in Soviet lands introduced the mountain troops to ideologically driven policies directed against the local peoples. In that context Nazi officials characterized enemy soldiers, partisans, and frequently even noncombatants in terms that both dehumanized them as racial inferiors and conceptualized them as dangerous aggressors, facilitating mass killing. This was certainly the attitude of a divisional commander who gave a talk in Oberammergau. He called his enemies "beasts." Yet, while on Soviet soil, the mountaineers mostly engaged in frontline conflict rather than the even more brutal tactics developed in occupied areas.[31]

After ending their initial dash across the Ukraine, however, the invading mountaineers entrenched themselves amid the locals, who were hunkered down in "miserable villages." One such occupier captured the bleak reality of a snowbound hamlet in his photograph of clustering, thatched farmhouses. Pössinger claims that his soldiers treated these noncombatants fairly. Rather than drive them out, the men settled in with the residents whose homes they occupied; he even observed a friend from Oberammergau delivering a baby in the Mius area. However, a contrary account suggests the forced removal of the villagers instead.[32]

The 1st Mountain Division also enjoyed some genuine support from Ukrainian peasants as opposed to hostility from the industrial population; similarly, the civilians of Karachay, living high in the northern Caucasus, cooperated in the fighting against Soviet troops. Lanz describes the "friendly greeting" of these "freedom-loving" people," a point reflected in a photo of a smiling young woman and her impassive father in Utschkulan. They reminded Pössinger of Alpine natives not only "in look and behavior but also in culture and building style."[33]

Nevertheless, hints of Nazi interference with such positive relationships cast doubt on the veracity of this cozy picture. One suspects, for example, that the captured "commissar" photographed by one soldier met a speedy death because of the standing order for such killings; a "sharpshooter" receiving a "hunter's greeting" may also have been summarily executed. Historian Roland Kaltenegger claims that Nazi policies "carelessly squandered" the friendly impulses of the people of Karachay. Yet even greater fears about their own government's persecution drove many locals to accompany German forces when they later retreated out of Soviet territory.[34]

One source of bitter feelings was the mass co-option of Eastern Europeans to work as forced laborers in Germany, but this process took place in the Ukrainian regions soon left behind by the division's eastward race. Back in the Kiev region, however, former Motorstorm Commander Burger turned up to run a soft-drink factory for the troops at headquarters, Middle East Command, providing employment for many local workers. He was later credited with flouting higher authorities to give them "physical and spiritual succor." Known affectionately as "Pappi Burgi," he forcefully prevented "hundreds of deportations" to the Reich.[35]

Burger's apparently positive role seems like an aberration in the horrific context of Hitler's Eastern holdings. Bartov has concluded that "the war in the East offered the German soldier endless opportunities for committing authorized and unauthorized acts of murder and destruction, robbery and plunder, rape and torture, for which he was rarely punished and not infrequently praised by his superiors." On the other hand, individual scruples ran up against a merciless and often deadly enforcement of official orders. To what extent Bartov's description applies to the 1st Mountain Division's experiences in Soviet territories is unclear, but it accurately characterizes their subsequent stint in Greece and Yugoslavia.[36]

In 1943 the division was deployed to secure the vulnerable western coast of Greece from a possible Allied invasion. Units of its 98th Regiment took part in slaughtering thousands of "traitorous" Italian soldiers who resisted a German takeover on the island of Cephalonia, as well as others on Corfu. Their commander, historian Mark Mazower argues, "liked to boast that he had turned the 98th into a 'regiment for Hitler.'" The division's new general was also fiercely loyal to the Third Reich. General Lanz, by contrast, now his superior officer heading the 22nd Mountain Army Corps, tried as a believing Catholic to avoid unnecessary killing. He had worked to negotiate a peaceful demobilization of all of the Italian troops in Greece before the island defenders chose to resist instead. This was, Lanz believed, a "mutiny" that required firm handling but not the mass executions ordered by Hitler. Nevertheless, the massacres proceeded, and Lanz also tolerated the imprisonment of thousands more men whom he had encouraged to expect repatriation.[37]

The mountaineers were primarily reassigned to the Balkan Peninsula in order to control the local populations. There they experienced antipartisan warfare so intense that it broke down individual reluctance to join in the murderous pacification efforts. Superiors pressured the officers and men actually fighting partisans to follow their brutal orders against these "bandits" and "criminals," although some did take readily to their task. At its worst this debilitating process led to soldiers killing civilians, even those not suspected of assisting their enemies.[38]

General Staff Officer Karl Wilhelm Thilo stated that, in Greece, partisans were not aggregated into large formations. Consequently, these "small . . . groups of rebellious men and women" favored "ambushes using 'peaceful' shepherds and peasants. . . . Even children were co-opted as scouts and lookouts." The Germans' response, he argued, was to "take hostages from suspected communities and bring about deterrence with the public threat of shooting them. At any rate, [this] succeeded in gradually creating some peace and order." However, Mazower captures a much darker reality caused by this blurring of fighting and noncombatant categories in the Greek countryside. As "restorers of order," soldiers extended the violence to burning whole villages thought to be in league with partisans. They also killed multiple hostages and launched "reprisal" actions to avenge German deaths and even lesser offenses. While men were the primary victims of mass executions, women and children also died. Some of this slaughter involved "wanton cruelty."[39]

Writing about similar divisional operations in Yugoslavia, Thilo hints at the racial attitudes that underlay such massacres. He describes how the "centuries-long fighting of the local [Montenegran] folk against gruesome oppressors has shaped the character of the people. Bloody feuds were and are their life element, their fighting customs are ruthless and gruesome, human life has little value." As Muslims, he adds, they also killed out of "revenge." The mountaineers were also dragged down by brutal orders that shaped their murderous treatment of both partisans and local residents in the lofty and barren Durmitor region, where they tried unsuccessfully to encircle partisan forces and destroy them.[40]

In Yugoslavia, unlike in Greece, the mountain troops were facing Josip Broz Tito's formidable and organized "folk army."[41] However, Pössinger describes a confused mix of foes, "partly in uniform, partly in civilian clothing." He excuses the summary executions of enemies who had brutalized fellow Germans and slaughtered their Croatian and Slovenian allies, and he explains away "angry" and even "unjustified" actions pursued against noncombatants suspected of harboring partisans.[42]

As Mazower discovered, other than the eager killers among them, the 1st Mountain Division officers were disturbed by their antipartisan role. One judged the slaughtering of an entire community as "unworthy of a German soldier." Because they could not hide behind their superiors' sanitizing language, which managed to turn massacres into normal combat, some of the soldiers involved were also upset by a "disgrace which had nothing to do with fighting a war." A divisional priest late in 1943 dared to report that their involvement "is producing a difficult inner burden on the conscience of many men."[43]

Yet the terror of operations in a partisan-laden context lacking the clarity of regular warfare helped to sell the logic of "reprisals." Moreover, the fierce military justice system perpetrated by the Wehrmacht's Nazi leaders kept ordinary soldiers on task in order to avoid the severe punishments handed out to dissenters. They "lacked the courage to desert."[44]

These months of antipartisan duty in the Balkans included increasingly harsh measures against the Jews caught in their jurisdiction, climaxing in an "action" to ship Joannina's Jews to a concentration center that was gathering victims destined for Auschwitz. By then most of the mountaineers had been sent to bolster Hungarian troops when their government's support for Hitler collapsed early in 1944. Pössinger describes an atmosphere in which SS units were hunting down Jews, causing him to protect the "rich" family with whom he stayed in their "villa." Divisional units ended up in Germanic areas of Siebenbürgen, near the town of Sighet made famous in Elie Wiesel's memoir about his own experiences of the Holocaust. There they assumed positions in the Carpathian highlands to face the oncoming Russian forces. However, they were once again summoned back to their old role as occupiers of western Greece before the onslaught began, arriving in time for the forced transfer of Corfu's small Jewish population to Auschwitz in June. Dealing with partisans once again led them into fierce combat situations.[45]

Many of Oberammergau's 1st Mountain Division soldiers would have taken part in this series of campaigns as infantrymen, but the housing of their signal corps in the community's own barracks also drew locals into service as specialists providing communication links, even in extreme conditions. Whether on the chase across Soviet territory or in the Caucasian mountains and Balkan fastnesses, these troops connected fighters with their commanding officers. One small unit, for example, was photographed at work on the slopes of Montenegro's Durmitor mountain in 1943. Such units must also have facilitated the flow of orders and reports linked to the killing of partisans. Like all other villagers still serving with the division after their transfer from frontline action in the Caucasus, they were obliged to operate in the general context of demoralizing and brutalizing campaigns.[46]

Casualties in the Balkan theater were light compared to the massive losses on the eastern front, where deaths spiraled from the very moment that troops reached Soviet territory. Only ten of Oberammergau's men had died by the end of 1940, but that total doubled in 1941, and then sixty-seven more succumbed in the next three years of fighting, including Mayor Lang's young nephew and namesake. The seventeen confirmed deaths in 1945 were in addition to fifty-three missing in action; further losses were attributed to war-related causes. By then, the 1st Mountain Division was back in action against the unstoppable Soviet armies as they rolled through Eastern Europe. However, villagers also fought and died with units scattered throughout the many theaters of war during those final dreadful years.[47]

Beyond serving in the cruel Russian and Balkan campaigns, Oberammergau's men apparently did not seek out ideologically driven units. The villagers' indifference to the SS continued into the war years, although a few newcomers joined Himmler's armed formations. The local party secretary did choose to associate with the SS's civilian branch and work outside the Dachau concentration camp in a furniture design office that employed inmates. There, however, witnesses later testified, he helped to free a few men and tried for more.[48]

It is not clear how much the soldiers and their loved ones at home knew about the full extent of wartime atrocities committed in their name, most particularly the killing of millions in death camps strategically located in occupied Polish territory. Certainly, Oberammergau's fighting men traveled to and fro as best they could on the special trains that gathered up lucky leave takers from their frontline stations. Communications about the Holocaust could take place in this context once either combatants or villagers got wind of it. However, knowledge about the mass killings was dangerous in wartime Germany, and it stayed within the confines of a trusted circle of intimates rather than triggering any attempt at intervention. Conceivably, it helped to stiffen the will of those locals who assisted Jewish fugitives needing their protection.[49]

Life for most villagers, however, was circumscribed by apprehension about their nearest and dearest rather than about fellow Jewish citizens. Periodic leaves and letters arriving from the front—or the lack of them—created awful anxieties for relatives left at home. Joy at a soldier's homecoming, as captured by a Munich newspaper in a series of photographs showing "three apostles" returned temporarily to the bosom of friends and family, was tinged with sadness at the knowledge that men on leave must soon return to their wartime assignments. Worries naturally rose with the Barbarossa invasion; concerns about the troops' preparation for a long hard winter were soon exacerbated by stories about frozen extremities. Of course, loved ones dying became the ultimate fear that the eastern front's escalating slaughter made all too likely; a few families even lost multiple members.[50]

Returning soldiers encountered a rapidly changing community that was dealing with increasingly intrusive wartime conditions. Initially, the reduced manpower was readily apparent; a now buoyant carving sector was hard pressed to fill orders because so many workers disappeared into the armed forces. Even lost international business connections were replaced, at least temporarily, with orders from Scandinavia and a brief suggestion of trade opening up with the Balkans. Ultimately, however, domestic sales kept the remaining carvers very busy indeed.[51]

The situation had also changed, of course, for Oberammergau's tourism industry. Together with a 1940 Passion Play season, plans for the village's new cultural center had faltered once the war got under way. Only the furtherance of normal tourism could continue, naturally without foreigners from now hostile nations. One intrepid British couple was still visiting Oberammergau late in August, but afterward only the British family of a film star employed as a radio newscaster for the Nazis remained as established residents. A turnaround would have to rely on domestic visitors alone.[52]

Late in 1940, a new pool of guests began to improve the fortunes of Oberammergau's hosts. Refugees arrived from regions threatened by enemy bombers, initiating an ever-greater flow from targeted cities that included mothers with their underage children. During the following year, these urbanites formed the largest contingent of visitors, but their numbers declined after the summer, although there were again many relocated families from threatened areas in 1943. Meanwhile, the KLV program brought groups of children to Oberammergau, often school classes led by a teacher. Co-opted "camps" housed upward of two hundred mostly female evacuees during parts of 1942 and 1943, but after a few months all of the girls' camps, with one exception, were again disbanded.[53]

These novel visitors were joined by a variety of foreigners from all over Europe. One large group arrived as a direct result of Nazi ideology when, in May 1940, officials relocated them from the Italian south Tyrol. These elderly "folk Germans" were part of a demographic realignment that was intended to advance racial purification.[54]

Much more common, however, was the arrival of foreigners to be employed as both voluntary and forced laborers. As early as 1939 some Czech citizens had reported for work in the area, only months after the occupation of Prague. A few Yugoslavs were employed for a while in Unterammergau, and there was talk of Germans from Poland helping local farmers. In late 1940 Bessarabian Germans did arrive for a time in nearby Ettal.[55]

These apparently voluntary workers set in motion the practice of using foreigners in Garmisch County, just as local men were siphoned off into the armed forces. But after the fall of France, POWs were apportioned out as an additional labor pool. Dozens were soon working on Oberammergau's streams, just as Russian prisoners had done a quarter century before. Some remained in a POW camp, while others were held in nearby communities. A poorly clad gang of Poles was similarly brought in by the German railroad for temporary work. Small numbers of untrained Polish men and women also worked on local farms that year, singled out by a "P" on their chests and isolated by language barriers.[56]

In Garmisch County, these laborers were joined by Russian POWs before the end of 1941, and soon more than three dozen Italians were working in the district's big stone quarry. The particularly desperate straits experienced by Eastern Europeans led a few of the Russians to attempt flight. Some of their French counterparts had also tried to flee in early summer 1941, and they responded unhappily to the Barbarossa invasion, which threatened to extend their imprisonment. Later, however, they were allowed to switch to "civilian laborer" status, working for the most part in agricultural settings and local forests. Ten Frenchmen were employed by the post office late in the war; some even served as drivers.[57]

In a strange historical twist, the Nazis actually created multiracial communities in Germany's heartland despite their pursuit of racial purification. Up to this point, Oberammergau's population had remained quite homogeneous despite the worldwide draw of their Passion Play seasons. Therefore, even the addition of so many northern Germans represented a new mix of "racial comrades." Subsequently, the influx of men and women from occupied Europe caused a very undesirable racial intermingling in Nazi terms. Certainly, many foreign workers were kept segregated in camps and on public works projects. French POWs and forced laborers, however, became integrated by means of their civilian jobs as they moved about the village and both ate and lodged at private workplaces or in local homes.[58]

Responses to these newcomers varied. Some of the bombing refugees made themselves unpopular in Garmisch County. Relocated mothers in particular were accused of neglecting their offspring and lacking any interest in taking up work. Moreover, mothers were leaving nearby Unterammergau as existence there was "too blah." Oberammergau must have been equally unexciting and even alienating for women accustomed to living in large cities, and their boredom could hardly have pleased the locals. The KLV girls also felt isolated from their new community. One of them later described their "marches (naturally in uniforms) through the village" as a "provocation" to residents who, she thought, perceived these outsiders falsely as "little Nazis." Even the Tyroleans had minimal contact with the villagers. Only a handful got to work outside their "repatriation home"; a couple of jobs found for them were even summarily withdrawn by one of the spiteful women who inflicted a humiliating and unnecessarily spartan regime on these unfortunate senior citizens.[59]

Regional officials reacted dispassionately to the fate of POWs and civilian workers, commenting without any humane sympathy about their desperate escape attempts and the demoralization that followed the news of Barbarossa. Oberammergau's police chief complained about the skimpy clothing of the Polish laborers but only because they were ill prepared for winter work. Their interpreter was trying to persuade the NSV to improve their situation.[60]

A few individuals showed a degree of concern. One shopkeeper earned herself a prison term for handing out provisions without the proper stamps; her daughter explained to me that she had given food to needy foreign women. Father Bogenrieder's special services, which were held every other Sunday at least in 1940, provided spiritual comfort. Countywide, doctors were coddling sick foreigners, according to Gestapo complaints in 1942.[61]

As time went on, for the French POWs and forced laborers at least, the situation improved once they became incorporated into civilian life, earning wages that they hoped in part to send back to France. Those assigned forestry duties kept the same hours as local workers, with whom they lodged and ate; Mayor Bierling directed that they receive extra rations because their duties were so challenging. Frenchmen attached to the postal service testified later that they were well treated. One added that his working conditions were the same as those of his German counterparts.[62]

A crucial flashpoint in the relationship between the villagers and all sorts of newcomers was unstable provisioning despite Nazi controls placed on the flow of goods. Rationing came along with the war itself, regulating access to basic foodstuffs; it was by manipulating this system that the kindhearted grocer ended up in jail. Nevertheless, there were soon shortages. This being Bavaria, complaints about beer rations surfaced as early as mid-1941, a staple that "for the farmers and workers is . . . liquid bread."[63]

That same year fruit and vegetables became scarce at times, while fish had long been severely rationed. Moreover, the lack of sufficient meat to satisfy more than a hundred hearty Tyrolean appetites caused a crisis in black-market slaughtering. In general, just the suggestion that meat rations were facing reductions could cause an outcry. By 1942 the provisioning crisis was deepening—eggs were scarce, bread was inferior, and tobacco and fat were in short supply. Even the price of poultry was soaring. As a result, complaints surfaced that the distribution of staples was even more unfair than during World War I. Moreover, business owners initiated a barter system by demanding provisions in exchange for their goods. No wonder that criticism about greedy visitors emerged in this tense context.[64]

While Oberammergau's citizens struggled with difficult wartime changes, they continued to function within the context of a grudgingly Nazified society. To ensure strong support for the regime and especially its Führer, leaders organized two rounds of "mass meetings" in the early war months. At the same time, however, they faced a shrinking pool of adult males. Party members and Storm Troopers were mostly young and therefore subject to conscription; even the community council lost key players to war service. Most significant was the disappearance of Mayor Lang himself, which left his successor, Acting Mayor Alfred Bierling, to manage an increasingly disrupted community.[65]

Consequently, meetings and musters would soon thin out beyond the usual poor attendance; maintaining a full schedule later became impossible. Remnants of the new Nazi festivals persisted into the last of the war years. A somber note was the addition of services held to honor lost warriors. First, their comrades buried them near the battlefield as best they could. One man found a final resting place outside "a Ukrainian schoolhouse"; others lay in a line of graves, each marked with a simple wooden cross, set out in ancient woods beneath the Caucasian heights. There slabs of rock were used to cover the dead. To mark their passing, back at home it became customary to construct a "hero's grave" in the church, where the usual mourning wreaths could be delivered and mountaineers stationed in the village bestowed a military salute. A March day was designated nationally to honor Germany's dead soldiers; it was marked annually by Oberammergau's "grieving community" with a moving ceremony. Conducted by the troops of the local garrison, it featured an officer's address at the war memorial.[66] (Figure 7.1 captures this event when it was held in 1943.)

During the first wartime years, apart from the troops lodged in their barracks and two companies from other units housed in private homes, Oberammergau was full of women and children. These soldiers in their midst provided cultural and sporting activities that must have enlivened a dull homebound existence. However, women kept busy working for the Red Cross, the KLV, and the NSV, among whose agents were the two Tyrolean minders. Several guesthouse owners were hosting the KLV "camps," while the NSV's efforts employed locals to house and feed refugees as well.[67]

Women drawn out of the community into active service were replaced by the revolving groups of mothers who arrived with their children from bombed

FIGURE 7.1. Soldiers from Oberammergau's barracks honor their fallen heroes in front of Georg Lang's war memorial on March 21, 1943.

regions. We get a glimpse of these women as they helped to provide an NSV-sponsored "communal kitchen" in 1943. Teenage girls arrived as well to contribute their required labor service out of a camp set up for them in the Schützenhaus. Dressed in folkish attire, they paraded in full song through the village and offered "variety" entertainment.[68]

The other active social group left in the village comprised children of both sexes. In fact, refugees swelled their numbers, requiring the addition of two extra classrooms. Membership in the HJ, the BdM, and their junior branches became the norm, as refusal to participate became increasingly difficult at least for boys. Official police warnings for miscreants were followed by the threat of actual weekend confinement. A big "induction" ceremony in March 1942 underscored this pressure to become new members of "the German family."[69]

Officials organized extracurricular activities for the Nazi youth, providing space for their meetings and cultural events in the abandoned centrally located schoolhouse; dozens of little girls were searching for a similar clubhouse in the final wartime months. Programs emphasized secular amusements, including the sporting competitions that Father Bogenrieder feared were weakening teenagers' loyalty to the church. The young people were also pressed into community service, as well as performances that showed, one report crowed, how liberated children had become, no longer hanging back "behind mothers' skirts." Boys took part in compulsory training exercises for their inevitable future role as soldiers, which were still provocatively scheduled on Sundays.[70]

Despite all of these efforts to win them over, Oberammergau's swelling population remained only partially Nazified. The citizens often expressed distrust of or outright hostility toward their Nazi leaders, although in the early wartime years the Führer himself remained immune. When Hitler's popular deputy Rudolf Hess disappeared after his flight to Britain in 1941, the mood clearly soured. Eventually, after reeling from the Stalingrad debacle, Garmisch County residents were exchanging hostile "rumors and jokes" that included negative comments about even Hitler himself. Nevertheless, some of the locals remained loyal to him into 1944, as expressed in particular through their joyful reactions when he survived the July 20 assassination attempt led by Claus Schenk, Count von Stauffenberg.[71]

The regional Nazi authorities tolerated much negativity, commenting frequently about the various criticisms expressed by ordinary citizens. Even war weariness and defeatism appeared in their reports without apparent consequences for those harboring these illegal sentiments; in mid-1942 they were already noting the receipt of foreign broadcasts as the source of such unhappiness in Oberammergau. A later report found many Garmisch County residents "hanging their heads" in despair when the news about Stalingrad worsened. Late in 1943 Oberammergau's villagers in particular were still showing "defeatist views," partly because they feared bombing by Allied aircraft. Nonetheless, they could also understand English, allowing them to receive the "enemy propaganda" beamed into Germany. Mayor Bierling himself paid attention to these forbidden radio signals, from which he followed the war's course on a map publicly displayed in his office. He also refused to act on denunciations of his villagers' listening habits and in one instance protected a fellow councilor who risked arrest for his persistent efforts at "enlightenment" from abroad.[72]

Central to Oberammergau's defiance of Nazi authorities, even in wartime, was the loyal Catholic population's insistent pursuit of traditional religious practices. This effort was spearheaded by Father Bogenrieder, particularly after Curate Eberlein left in 1940; the priest maintained a precarious existence in tension with Nazi officials and the Gestapo. He had to operate within a general context of suspicion expressed by the county police chief when he reported that clerics were "quietly opposed to the Third Reich." The outburst of a "very religious" Mittenwald woman who accused the Nazi leadership, including Hitler, of lying seemed to confirm the Catholic flock's hostile attitude.[73]

One source of priestly influence was confessions; another was the continued reading of pastoral letters, issued especially in 1941, when the locals had to deal with the threatened removal of Catholic symbols in school classrooms. A subsequent pronouncement condemned mass sterilizations but ignored the euthanasia program already openly attacked by Bishop Clemens von Galen. In Oberammergau, even the provision of a well-stocked parish library seemed threatening enough that officials confiscated the books and permitted the reopening of only a reduced collection.[74]

The potential for retribution was soon made clear when, early in 1940, Munich's Gestapo arrested one of Garmisch County's parish priests and then his two chaplains on seemingly false charges of tuning in to the forbidden radio broadcasts. Later, another priest was detained for defending the sacred nature of rogation customs, which were, he insisted, hardly "fun like KdF trips or the circus." Even holding a successful outreach week could bring in the Gestapo, as happened to monks in Mittenwald who were raided on the charge of "hoarding groceries." All of the Catholic priests in Garmisch County must have been aware that even pursuing the church's normal activities put them in danger of confrontation with the secret police.[75]

As the priest's outburst about rogation ceremonies indicates, witnessing for their church in public spaces remained a particular source of tension with Nazi officials. Father Bogenrieder later stressed the danger for parishioners who took part in "processions, pilgrimages, etc." But he even included regular church attendance, declaring that those "who do not see this as an open announcement of [one's] . . . own worldview and an outspoken statement against the aims and plans of National Socialism are ignorant of the history of the last twelve years." Even a money drive held by girls in a nearby village to decorate the altar during May observances triggered a police report to the Gestapo.[76]

Authorities may have wanted to eradicate church activities, but the wishes of a huge public restrained them. Instead, they placed increasing limits on customary processions, forbidding corporative marches even for schoolchildren and the fire brigade, as well as the display of flags, canon fire, and the generous strewing of high-quality grass on local streets. After blaming traffic jams for the curtailment of customary routes, their next step was to use wartime labor requirements to shift each procession from its traditional day to Sunday.[77]

Father Bogenrieder had to obtain permission for all of these rituals and establish them as long-standing traditions; the parish was also forced to accept responsibility for the participants' safety. In the face of this harassment, the priest adopted a formula that listed the date on which each event should have been taking place as a form of protest. He even obeyed diocesan orders to reinstate the communal pilgrimage to the Wieskirche in 1944 after a nine-year hiatus. This reflected a growing interest in visits to beloved shrines; Ettal in particular attracted ever larger pilgrim crowds as wartime fears escalated.[78]

Beyond his dealings with Nazi authorities, Father Bogenrieder also found social life difficult during the Third Reich. He decried the retreat from good Christian living that was infecting his Catholic flock, although his annual reports actually reflect substantial success in maintaining church attendance and even religious instruction in the secularized school. Outside his church, Nazi society marginalized the priest, as a story he told after the war makes clear. Standing on the platform at Oberau's crowded train station, Bogenrieder was surprised when the commander of the 1st Mountain Division's signal corps greeted him openly. Waiting travelers fell into a hushed silence because this action was very unusual for "so high an officer in such a time." The two men could more freely interact on the streets of Oberammergau, although Nazi-oriented junior officers refused to observe any "customary niceties."[79]

Father Bogenrieder must truly have appreciated those villagers who gave him a genuine welcome. One such supporter was Administrator Raab, who, he said, "provided much worthwhile service to the church" despite his nominal party membership. Hundreds of parishioners helped their priest to keep Oberammergau's Catholic rituals alive. As late as 1944, he was anticipating up to three hundred people at the various rogation processions and estimated as many as a thousand participants at that year's Corpus Christi celebrations.[80]

Believers also maintained a subdued form of internal parish life. The Women's Union still provided needy first communicants with outfits, but there is no longer any mention of the beloved plays and parties. The more church-bound Mothers' Club held increasingly frequent meetings, although Bogenrieder judged them to be largely "passive." Their membership grew during the wartime years, as did the Third Order's loyal adherents, who continued to hold frequent meetings. Church-based charitable clubs managed to raise money, particularly Caritas since even in the face of competitive NSV efforts, it reached the remarkable level of more than 2,000 marks in 1943.[81]

Children were, of course, a prime concern because of the exclusive role that official Nazi groups were supposed to play in their lives. Father Bogenrieder managed to retain good contacts with schoolchildren throughout the war, and he was able to organize gratifyingly popular "rallies" for loyal Catholics at various points. Older girls in particular felt free to witness their faith, and so the priest managed to establish monthly "Marian instructional sessions" for them, as well as more frequent Bible-study lessons when working conditions allowed.[82]

Administrator Raab secretly provided males with a counterpart in his own home, where the youths—including older boys—could meet for "religious discussions." During the last couple of wartime years, this goal was achieved in part under cover of an HJ group dedicated to learning signal skills. Training was provided by two junior officers, former monks who had studied theology; lodging with Raab, these men could use their evenings to work with the boys. Raab later argued that "through these meetings Oberammergau was preserved as a nucleus of Christian youth, which represented a strong force in the [postwar] reconstruction."[83]

Indignant Catholics opposed any undue official interference with established religious practices. As early as 1940 Garmisch parishioners withheld their children from HJ activities out of "bitterness" at their priests' imprisonment. The county administrator admitted that the locals were "still very strongly committed to the old customs." He found this superstitious mentality all too well expressed a year later when Adolf Wagner, in his capacity as head of Bavaria's Ministry of Education and Cult Life, decided to act against such obdurate traditionalism. Wagner ordered the removal of crucifixes and Catholic imagery from school classrooms, as well as normal school prayers. Outraged parents moved quickly and aggressively to restore their "belief symbol."[84]

Oberammergau's Catholics tied these protests to their suspicion of Nazi magnates, for whom, they suggested, a newly luxurious existence had made any dependence on God redundant. Referring to the ongoing conflict with Soviet Russia, which had already caused so much sacrifice, they questioned the point of a war with "Bolshevism" if their own schooling became similarly "godless." They even reinterpreted Hess's recent flight to Britain in light of this crisis, arguing that he could not tolerate "the spiritual suppression of the German people."[85]

Father Bogenrieder reported at the time that crucifixes disappeared from local classrooms for a good week before popular pressure forced their restoration. To achieve this result in nearby Ettal, the unhappy Catholics made "threats like desertion of the party organizations, withholding of donations to the winter assistance collections, and notification of relatives stationed in the field." In Oberammergau, credit was due in particular to the rock-solid determination of the parents, undoubtedly most of them mothers since fathers were away fighting.[86]

Some Bavarian communities acted dramatically to bring back their crucifixes, reflecting what Minister President Siebert characterized as "almost a revolutionary mood" in the state. However, such confrontational action would have been unnecessary in Oberammergau, given the sympathies of the local leaders. Mayor Bierling had, after all, put his job on the line in 1937 by opposing the local school's secularization; as a parent, he had a personal stake in Catholic education. Bierling's own inclinations were, therefore, in line with the firm resolve of his constituents to preserve all remaining Catholic influences in their school. Moreover, Unterammergau's mayor later claimed that he had offered to help Bierling bring about the restoration of the crucifixes. Even Chapter Leader Alzinger remained committed to Catholic values by presenting all three of his children for baptism during the wartime years, including one in 1941. As a result, official support for the purging of religious expressions in school classrooms was absent in the Passion Play village.[87]

Anger only gradually subsided after the crucifixes were successfully restored. In Oberammergau, a tactless Nazi representative briefly fanned the embers of discontent by reopening the subject that November. The general opinion remained that "every German should be able to believe as he pleases and should also in no way be prevented from practicing his religious customs." This entire crisis demonstrated that Nazi culture had failed to win out in the Garmisch area since the Catholics were ready to fight officials publicly when their families' welfare was at stake.[88]

In one further arena, however, such open defiance was impossible. Germany's remaining Jews faced a rapidly worsening situation after Kristallnacht. Much of the evidence of their particular experiences in Oberammergau comes from survivors' testimonies at denazification trials and the memories of involved villagers, which could well provide an overly optimistic picture. However, certain individuals with ties to Oberammergau found a degree of protection there.

Most in need of that assistance were "full" Jews who lacked the cover of an Aryan spouse, preferably a husband. During much of 1940 one such Jew, a sick elderly man whom the Munich-based Gestapo was tracking, stayed in the home of a local official. Mayor Bierling and Raab may both have contributed to the survival of another elderly Jew, a former visitor who drew on decades of acquaintance to find a home with Anton Lang's family during the final war years and afterward; she was protected by the removal of the "J" on her papers.[89]

Oberammergau also hosted the "fully" Jewish spouses of Aryan husbands, like the wife of a local man who lived in Munich but visited her husband, at least into 1940. Similarly, the daughter-in-law of a famous German composer later described the warm reception that she and her mother received in a major local inn even after the Kristallnacht debacle despite the fact that she was a foreign Jew born in Prague. When in 1940 a Jewish woman from Düsseldorf became fearful despite protection from a "mixed" marriage, she took refuge in Oberammergau with her child. Perhaps because of the new requirement to wear a prominent Star of David in public, she later went "wandering" with her husband. However, she placed the child with a friendly local family, although a year later the parents had to break short a visit after drawing unwelcome police attention, possibly because of a denunciation. By contrast, Mayor Bierling protected a sick Jewish wife staying covertly in the village when officials threatened to confiscate her lodging; she was still resident there after the war.[90]

Partially Jewish Germans operated within a special limbo status that could become life threatening as the Holocaust progressed. Some males, particularly "quarter" Jews, served in the armed forces during the war. One such man, Pössinger's junior officer from the local signal corps, had to survive the order to place him in dangerous frontline situations where his bloody end could "wash clean his disgraceful descent." He ended up fighting with the French resistance to escape a degenerating situation after Stauffenberg's failed assassination attempt.[91]

Back at home, a half-Jewish woman survived the Third Reich working as a bookkeeper with the Lang firm. Arriving months before Kristallnacht, she kept her "mixed race" background to herself until the police found out in 1941. That same year, Mayor Bierling agreed to officiate at the marriage of an Aryan woman and a long-time, half-Jewish visitor to Oberammergau, overlooking papers that concealed the bridegroom's heritage. He had developed excellent relationships with a couple of local innkeepers, one of whom hosted his wedding celebrations; the daughter of the house was a bridal attendant. And he was not alone in remaining welcome in Oberammergau's inns, as a Garmisch-based bank director testified. Despite his minority status, he continued to stay in the village periodically until the regime's "very end."[92]

Intimate connections also created opportunities for mixed-race Germans to retreat into a secure environment. A party member's relative by marriage found refuge in his home, together with her mother, after her own residence was destroyed by a bomb. Forestry Chief Hacker claimed to have become the sympathetic protector of a frightened hunting enthusiast who, late in the war, wanted to establish a retreat from the Gestapo in case he should need one; Hacker promised him access to the department's remote mountain lodges.[93]

In 1943 Oberammergau became the victim of massive Allied air raids over German cities. No bombs ever fell on the village so fortuitously tucked away in its highland valley. However, that very remoteness made it an ideal site for vital war industries forced to relocate because of the bombing. In the spring a Munich-based communications manufacturing firm had co-opted space for its operations. Efforts to use the Passion Theater as a war production facility ensued. First, BMW eyed this large and seemingly empty building to produce airplane motors. Then came the massive Messerschmitt aircraft concern, which was busily spreading production all over the Bavarian countryside; Oberammergau could host "the principal offices and the engineering design and development work." The village officials ultimately managed to head off such use of their beloved theater, even though, it was rumored, Professor Messerschmitt had received instructions from Hitler himself to take it over. Rather, the 1st Mountain Division's soldiers moved out of their barracks, and hundreds of Messerschmitt workers began taking their place.[94]

Augsburg-based Messerschmitt AG was by 1943 a vast enterprise dedicated to providing the Luftwaffe with the Me-109 fighter and a new "high-performance, single-seat, twin-jet fighter," the Me-262. The firm had also launched a variety of sometimes highly experimental projects. Because of Messerschmitt's importance to the war effort, Albert Speer's armaments ministry took almost complete charge of its operations as of March 1944, and early in 1945 a key Himmler deputy, SS General Hans Kammler, was assigned oversight of the jet fighter's progress.[95]

This pathbreaking aircraft had been cleared for manufacture in April 1943, a time when Allied bombing had become an increasing threat to city-based plants. In fact, Messerschmitt's Regensburg branch suffered extensive damage during air raids in 1943 and early 1944. The firm therefore found a variety of creative ways to disperse all of its facilities needed for producing the Me-262. As a postwar American enquiry established,

[O]ver an area from Stuttgart to Linz in northern Austria, and from Nürnberg south into the Bavarian Alps, subassemblies were made in caves, tunnels of the Autobahn, . . . clearings in the forests, small buildings, etc. Many small assembly lines, just a small steel building with one pair of rails for conveying and an overhead crane, were set up in woods for final assembly. Some of these were near the Autobahn, which was used as a runway after concreting the center grass strip and painting it green.

In this context Messerschmitt decided to relocate its all-important design branch to Oberammergau.[96]

The Upper Bavarian Research Institute, as this new facility was named, took over the vacated army barracks and began excavating a nearby mountainside to create underground space for operations, as well as air raid shelters. In this sprawling complex, engineers were able to develop improvements for existing aircraft and explore a range of new variants, including the P1101 fighter, a "good turbo-jet, high-speed fighter with a swept-back wing," which provided useful features for U.S. aircraft after the war.[97]

Additionally, the institute set up a working group in Linderhof to further the design of a "flak-rocket, tailless, mid-winged plane, rocket driven" known as the Enzian, one of several related missiles promoted by the Air Ministry. This new project was a response to ever-heavier bombing raids and the lack of an effective defense using manned aircraft, which suggested "the need for a pilotless directed missile of high speed and climb." Manufactured elsewhere and tested in Peenemunde, only sixty Enzian rockets ever saw the light of day before the war's end.[98]

The Upper Bavarian Research Institute's workforce grew steadily to one thousand in 1943 and peaked in the range of three thousand a year later. Beyond the plant's specialized employees, hundreds of common laborers were deployed to build and maintain infrastructure. Females constituted around 450 of the skilled workers; some were employed as "technical specialists such as detail-draftsmen, calculators, etc."; the rest as white-collar staff. Most were German women except for a few skilled French and Italian workers. Other than a contingent of roughly a hundred Eastern European women, the rest of the workforce was largely male, including foreigners from well more than a dozen different nations.[99]

Some of these workers were even there "voluntarily," according to the American enquiry, because a portion of the French and possibly the Lettish and Dutch draftsmen had transferred after losing their positions in Messerschmitt's branches. Close to 150 more foreign workers seem to have been semivolunteers, including POWs granted civilian status. Almost all of the hundred or so maintenance workers were Russians and Yugoslavians supplied "by the German

Board of Work." They were joined at the height of the building phase by around five hundred construction workers drawn from various occupied countries. Many Russian, Italian, and Yugoslavian laborers were still in Oberammergau at the close of the war.[100]

Given the potential for the cruel treatment of "slave" laborers in Nazi Germany, the situation of Messerschmitt's multiethnic workforce seems relatively benign. As the postwar American enquiry notes, these foreign workers had to put in the same long hours as German employees, and they received identical payment according to set scales. However, most were assigned to common labor with little opportunity for advancement. Messerschmitt eventually provided barracks for them, although they ate meals with the German staff in the plant's cafeteria. Mayor Bierling later testified that he had tried to ensure the provision of adequate food, including the all-too-scarce vegetables, for this foreign contingent. Nevertheless, questions remain about how generally well fed they were, particularly since they had few ways to supplement their diet. Clothing may also have been inadequate, as suggested by the refusal by a group of Croats to work during cold weather because their shoes were so dilapidated.[101]

Inevitably, the tensions inherent in this coerced lifestyle erupted from time to time. One Frenchman had to be taken into custody after behaving in a "very cheeky, foul, and presumptuous" manner, which involved his smuggling a knife into the workplace. Longstanding ethnic tensions surfaced one May evening in 1944, when a dozen or so Croats fought with a larger group of Easterners, with the result that two Croats were rushed to the local hospital with stab wounds. It all started over the amorous relationship between a Russian woman and one of the Croat workers; eventually, bad blood between these two ethnic groups became so untenable that the Croats, swearing to avenge their fallen compatriots, had to be housed separately.[102]

Official policy restrained Messerschmitt's foreign workers from mingling with the local population, although they were thrown together in the workplace. Most particularly the East Europeans were not permitted to live in village homes. Even at the plant they had to wear special "olive-green work clothes." Like all locally employed Easterners, they were also supposed to wear a sew-on badge, but this system broke down in the last wartime months, as did the use of identity papers for the remaining foreign workers, who moved about freely in their leisure hours.[103]

Theoretically, employers were obliged to contain their racially questionable laborers, but even Messerschmitt became rather ineffective. Early in 1944 complaints emerged about "a gang of Russians" ranging around at night. Help was promised to end "this outrage . . . by night and fog." However, even the huge new camp located at the southern edge of the village did not restrain inmates who "could go in and out freely," according to one survivor. A curfew was briefly declared in November 1944, although, as the war drew to a close, the Ammer valley's large foreign workforce became increasingly restive and hard to control.[104]

Despite opportunities to kick the camp's traces, Messerschmitt's foreign laborers remained cut off from communal life as they perched uneasily on the outskirts of the village. With such a big camp on their doorstep, however, the locals became deeply implicated in the Third Reich's mistreatment of occupied peoples. The huge plant where these foreigners worked caused other radical changes to local society. Although Oberammergau had avoided this kind of subordination to a single predominant employer during a previous crisis in the 1840s, it temporarily became a company town as villagers flocked to the firm for work. The exigencies of armaments production in the war's desperate final years were strong enough to sweep aside the village's traditional economy.[105]

Even before the Upper Bavarian Research Institute arrived in their barracks, Oberammergau's population had grown and diversified under Nazi rule. Yet the community was still recognizably a woodcarving and tourism center, albeit with its craftsmen serving as soldiers and its hotels turned into a variety of "camps." Even the reassignment of large woodcarving firms to making prostheses for those wounded in the war was a natural adaptation, while refugees became guests of a sort for their host families. However, the demands of a massive facility employing thousands of people fundamentally changed the nature of local society. The independence of its small business core eroded as tradesmen and retailers inevitably reoriented toward serving the new inhabitants, while hotels, guesthouses, restaurants, and private homes all became grist for Messerschmitt's aggressive efforts to procure needed board and lodging.[106]

Oberammergau's motley population grew still further until the village began to burst at the seams. In addition, after the fall of 1943, the wartime predominance of women and children was reversed as men employed at the institute moved to the Ammer valley. These engineers and technical staff working to restore German air superiority were more aggressively pro-Nazi than most of the villagers with whom they now shared a common fate.[107]

Mayor Alfred Bierling sat at the heart of Oberammergau's transformation from a refuge for bombed-out urbanites to an armaments research center. For more than three wartime years, he had dealt with the many demands that Nazi officials had placed on his village even before the Messerschmitt intrusion, with its culturally questionable and inhumane consequences. Bierling judged all of the new demands on his community from the vantage point of a man steeped in the region's Catholic traditions and with decades of experience playing major Passion roles and more than ten years of political leadership.

Bierling was especially outraged by threats to the Passion theater because they represented a secularizing perversion of its true purpose. As he argued, "the theater is in its way a house of God; similarly, they could seize and desanctify a church." His successful intervention brought him the unwelcome attention of Munich's Gestapo. By contrast, he could not protect the villagers and their guests from Messerschmitt's invasive presence; both the 1st Mountain Division's soldiers and most of the refugees living in Oberammergau were summarily forced to relocate. While the refugee population was highly mobile, this was no doubt a harrowing experience for already traumatized people fleeing places like Berlin, Düsseldorf, Cologne, and Hamburg, where the massive Allied bombing raids had been so deadly. Bierling characterized the whole process as having "put the earlier lodgings situation totally on its head." He felt unable to counter the new forces at work in his jurisdiction and was forced to give up, for example, on the case of a mother with two children whose husband was imprisoned overseas. Bombs had destroyed their Berlin home a couple of years before, and they had ended up in Oberammergau only to face yet another dislocation.[108]

Nine months into his fight against the depredations of the Upper Bavarian Research Institute, Mayor Bierling became a central player in a dangerous clash with Messerschmitt's engineers and other members of the swollen local population. In midsummer 1944 two U.S. aircraft crashed in the vicinity of Oberammergau, and the fate of the surviving crewmembers of both planes caused a heated confrontation. Numerous community residents, including the Messerschmitt workers, who were all too familiar with the devastating impact of enemy forces, had experienced Allied raids. Moreover, they were, of course, working at full throttle to find ways of destroying those very planes and regaining German control of the air. Especially after the recent D-Day invasions, the locals had developed a new fighting spirit with the promise of decisive "revenge" weapons directed against Britain. Leading Nazis fanned the flames of that desire for vengeance by ordering the execution of any surviving crewmen of downed planes. Some hotheads supported carrying out this death sentence on any enemy fliers who fell into their hands.[109]

The two planes crashed at a time when the villagers were on heightened alert for air raids as Allied bombing fleets dominated the Bavarian skies. As early as October 1941, a stray dropping of bombs near Eschenlohe had shaken the county's population. A serious raid on Munich early in 1943 had reawakened people's fears, but it was later that year when the real danger emerged.

Nearby Innsbruck was attacked in December at a time when enemy flights were passing overhead unchallenged, even in daylight. Great waves of bombers hit Bavarian cities in the following months, causing fears that their ordnance might fall on Oberammergau now that its wartime industries made the village a potential magnet for enemy fire. Officials began plans to step up protective efforts, notably the building of a huge air raid shelter, but nerves were definitely on edge that summer.[110]

The first crash involved a fighter plane that came down in moorland near the Lang farming complex on Oberammergau's northern edge. Its pilot was lost, but the navigator parachuted safely into a group of haymakers and surrendered peacefully; he was nonetheless menaced by at least one soldier working in the fields until a local pub owner took him under his wing. The crash soon attracted a crowd of other villagers, including some Messerschmitt employees, who were at the forefront of those eager to follow the orders to kill downed fliers. Police officers arriving on the scene managed to usher him safely into the village, but then Messerschmitt agitators succeeded in roughing him up.[111]

At this point Mayor Bierling arrived to intervene "very energetically" by organizing the threatened navigator's removal into his personal air raid shelter. But Bierling was a worried man; he had received instructions to lead "the civilian fight against the enemy and particularly against the hostile fliers," but he disagreed fundamentally with this policy. Fearing for his job when it became obvious that he had defied orders, Bierling consulted with Raab, who assured him that a World War I pilot like himself had to act honorably; the mayor could insist on respecting his unwelcome visitor's POW status from that perspective. Raab then summoned a flight official from Altenstadt to extract the navigator from this dangerous situation.[112]

Bierling was right to be anxious since he received explicit instructions to carry out the directive in the future. Yet, when a day later a large bomber came down and its occupants were turned in to the local authorities, he once again intervened. After a lively discussion in which Messerschmitt people again showed their desire for revenge, the locals decided to summon the Altenstadt officials once more. As a confidant later reported, Bierling's actions had endangered "his life and the existence of his family," as well as his health. Yet, as a true product of local culture, the mayor had exclaimed: "If we in Oberammergau permit the fliers to be hurt, then we could never more play the Passion in good conscience." He was fortunate to evade arrest by SS officials sent from Munich, although he had to endure a nasty confrontation with regional magnates. Bierling later stated that he was able to continue as mayor only because of support from regular army personnel who did not appreciate attacks on airmen. However, such "humane" sympathy for downed fliers was also common in the Garmisch area.[113]

This same humanity was exhibited once again during a curious incident that occurred two days after the second crash when one member of the bomber crew was detected high up in Oberammergau's mountains, where plane spotters had established a headquarters. Since it was Messerschmitt employees who first informed them about the escaped American, the team suspected brutal intentions on their part and got rid of them before locating the fugitive. He turned out to be disoriented and exhausted after mistaken efforts to find safety in Switzerland. The spotters fed him well and helped him to freshen up before taking a nap. Sharing the English language, the prisoner and one of his captors also exchanged niceties, including names and addresses. Eventually the local police took him away to the strains of a "farewell yodel."[114]

During Mayor Bierling's final months in office, he presided over Oberammergau's motley wartime society until Germany's "collapse" on May 8, 1945. Plans developed by a small resistance group to undermine SS and army rearguard actions against the oncoming U.S. forces complemented Bierling's concerted efforts to hand over his community peacefully. Successive mayors then struggled with a harsh postwar environment in the U.S. zone until elections were held in 1948 and restored the now denazified Raimund Lang to his old job, just in time to shape the preparations for a 1950 Passion season. Currency reform and the newly created federal republic led to a regenerated economy in West Germany. In this context, the Passion Play village seemed to be back to normal, but its reprieve was short lived; the legacy of Oberammergau's Nazi past would not disappear.

8

Allies

Outright resistance to the Nazis was a dangerous and even deadly game, particularly in wartime. One young soldier associated with a dissident household in Oberammergau observed the Gestapo's response to oppositional expressions on a fateful day at Munich University. He had studied under Kurt Huber, the mentor of a student group known to history as the White Rose. Horrified by the atrocities committed under cover of the eastern front, they had disseminated a series of writings aimed at inspiring outrage in German citizens. While distributing another typewritten appeal, the group's leaders were reported to the local authorities. After a friend had shown him this offending broadsheet, the young Huberite witnessed just how swiftly the regime cracked down on its critics.[1]

Several White Rose leaders were hastily tried and executed that February of 1943. A year later, after Stauffenberg had failed to kill Hitler in his headquarters, thousands of leading Germans fell victim to the Führer's gruesome acts of vengeance. During the war's final months, summary justice threatened anyone who blocked the efforts of Nazi officials and marauding SS units to stave off defeat. Fear of a death sentence haunted anyone seeking to end the fighting peacefully, even in the remote Ammer valley.[2]

Until this point, resistance in Oberammergau had centered on the efforts of Catholics to protect their way of life. Late in 1944, however, victorious Allied forces swept inexorably in Germany's direction, and Nazi leaders tried to organize all of the remaining males into a "People's Home Guard," but the villagers were quite reluctant to support these desperate efforts to defend their Alpine homeland. Rather, a few of them launched a resistance group with the primary intent of sabotaging both party and SS preparations to greet the oncoming armies with force.[3]

Central to these plans was Forestry Chief Hacker, an expert in managing mountainous hunting areas. Despite his lively Catholic faith, Hacker had become a Nazi in 1933 but later turned against the party, although he saw no point in giving up his membership. Instead, according to subsequent testimony, he criticized the regime in conversations with anyone whom he found trustworthy, as well as through his very public support of church activities. This was why he protected his forestry workers from a Nazified environment, and in particular from DAF initiatives.[4]

Hacker's resistance unit was named after a large black bird sometimes seen in the mountains, the Auerhahn. He established this "fighting group" out of his forestry staff, as well as other trusted contacts. One of Mayor Bierling's brothers was involved, as were Partenkirchen resident Wilhelm Grovermann and the Jewish man to whom Hacker had been offering a safe haven. Believing the war to be almost over, the plotters identified a retreat where they could imprison their "bloodthirsty and dangerous" county leader and his entourage, who, they believed, clearly wished to prolong the fight.[5]

Additionally, the members of Auerhahn prepared to deal with any other Nazis who might use remote forestry outposts to confront the incoming Allied forces. For their own protection, they also developed plans for a hasty withdrawal, which included storing arms and supplies around the area. Meanwhile, they had to sit out a long Alpine winter since deep and persistent snow made their plans too dangerous, particularly with ever-greater numbers of hostile military and SS forces lingering in the vicinity. What they feared most was tracking of the group's movements, leading to terrible consequences for their loved ones. But April continued in snowy splendor, and U.S. troops drew ever closer to the Ammer valley as Auerhahn awaited its chance to act.[6]

General Alexander Patch's Seventh Army was approaching Auerhahn's immediate region, aiming to head off the creation of a "national redoubt." Supposedly, Nazi leaders intended to retreat into this "Alpine fortress," where they could make a final stand against the Allied forces. In fact, Propaganda Chief Goebbels and the SS's security branch had been spreading information about this largely mythic plan to confuse enemy intelligence and press agents. Their success was measured by Supreme Allied Commander Dwight D. Eisenhower's decision to accept this concept while strategizing his invasion path into Germany's heartland. Consequently, one thrust moved to cut the country in two, preventing any transfer of leaders and troops south from Berlin. A second headed toward the broad Alpine stretches identified as belonging to the redoubt, sending General George Patton's Third Army eastward of the Seventh's trajectory into the mountainous environs encompassing Garmisch County.[7]

Also placing their faith in the redoubt were leading Germans, particularly SS Chief Himmler, whose inadequacies as a military strategist trapped him in a naïve acceptance of this chimeric scheme. Perhaps Himmler influenced his immediate deputy, Kammler, who received orders to relocate the Third Reich's crack rocket-design team, led by Wernher von Braun, to Oberammergau. There Kammler's men were busily negotiating a takeover of well-placed mountain retreats suggestive of just the opposition to enemy forces that a redoubt would involve. He himself took up residence in the Bavarian capital.[8]

Toward the end of April, as the Allied forces were fast approaching, Hacker's group burned down the Hundingshütte, King Ludwig's fanciful lodge where Motorstorm Commander Burger had found refuge in 1934. Nazi leaders like Himmler and Göring might, they understood, be headed for one of Dachau's outlying concentration camps set deep in the woods stretching from Garmisch County into the Tyrol. Key to their protection by SS guards would be this lodge, which was furnished in rough medieval fashion to re-create a favorite scene from the first act of *The Valkyrie*, an opera by Richard Wagner. The king's beloved retreat was located near the Austrian border in a remote spot under the mighty Kreuzspitze, where he could observe the natural beauties of his beloved Alps. Hacker's effort to neutralize this potential last bastion against the oncoming Americans offered the further inducement that it would become a "symbol" of the group's commitment to "active intervention against party and SS."[9]

To carry out these incendiary plans despite the lurking SS presence, Hacker and a companion set off on foot during the night of April 27. Hours later this trek brought them to the spot where they successfully carried out their mission. Fellow resistance fighter Grovermann then managed to drive into the valley and pick them up, maneuvering them successfully back to Oberammergau.[10]

Hacker's Auerhahn resistance group came into existence because the locals began to accept the inevitable fall of Hitler's Third Reich. At the end of April, U.S. troops freed the Ammer valley's highland inhabitants from Nazi rule and set up a halting postwar restoration of everyday life in the U.S. zone. Benign oversight by the zone's overlords also encouraged local officials to think about restoring Oberammergau's special identity as the Passion Play village with a regular season in 1950. The community was returning to normal—or so at least it seemed.

Oberammergau's villagers had long been praying for peace when U.S. forces reached them on April 29, 1945. Nazism's Catholic opponents had already reacted negatively to the failed plot of July 20, 1944, revealing dashed hopes of bringing down the "Hitler regime." That outcome, they had anticipated, would facilitate a "bearable" and "speedy end to the war." Then fear crept in that the party leaders were out to protect their own interests, indeed their very lives, by fighting to the last.[11]

Well before April, the locals were aware that Germany was about to experience another catastrophe of historic proportions. The mood was regretful; misguided decisions had ruined their country's foreign policy, which could have made them preeminent among nations if it had been shaped along Bismarckian principles. At this point, fear was rife about Soviet victories on the eastern front, so all hopes rested on an occupation by the Western Allies.[12]

Meanwhile, daily life limped on in wartime mode, with increasingly drastic military recruitment stripping the community of needed public and private workers. Looking ahead, Raab worried about providing the most basic services, notably the gathering of wood for the next winter's heating. Later he had to defend the handful of remaining bureaucrats from service in the People's Home Guard. Private retailers and innkeepers faced staffing problems, illustrated when the only remaining apprentice of one village baker, a disabled veteran, received his conscription papers. To forestall closing his shop and depriving Oberammergau of vital bread supplies, a plan emerged to retain the apprentice long enough to allow an Italian baker to train as his replacement.[13]

In addition to drastic workforce reductions, the local businesses were scrounging for supplies. Declining cargo traffic also made provisioning difficult. The population was depressed as families struggled with the grief caused by sky-high numbers of dead and wounded, as well as the anxiety of losing ever more men to the war machine. Tensions surfaced in November 1944, when the local women were required to contribute their sewing skills at a center in Unterammergau; they complained that outsiders were permitted to sew in Oberammergau and complied only when threatened by the police. Even the village children faced upheaval when their school was requisitioned to house wounded troops. A couple of rooms in the Passion theater became the new schoolhouse for the final wartime months.[14]

Into this unhappy community intruded a highly unwelcome group of visitors just months after Kammler requisitioned Alois Lang's hotel in early February 1945. The still youthful SS general represented the Nazis' prototypical Aryan in both looks and self-assured cruelty. An academically trained engineer, he had risen to prominence through his work designing Auschwitz as a killing center. He came to control Germany's missile technology, first at Peenemunde and later at Nordhausen, with its infamous "Dora" slave labor camp. He also oversaw the V-2 rocket attacks on Great Britain, which could, had they been more timely, have undermined the D-Day invasions. In his capacity as "rocket czar," Kammler began closing down development in the Ammer valley of the Enzian and other rockets early in 1945. By late March he was in charge of revitalizing the entire air force and soon succeeded in pushing aside party leaders Speer and Göring to become one of the most dominant underlings Hitler had ever created.[15]

Kammler descended on Oberammergau early in April as hundreds more people arrived to squeeze themselves into the Messerschmitt-run barracks. Perhaps he intended to use Braun and his most valuable technicians as bargaining chips with the Allies after he had relocated them from Nordhausen to the village, where he could "protect" them with a troop of SS enforcement officers. Most of Braun's men traveled by train in their "Vengeance Express," but their boss himself arrived in a fleet of vehicles, with which he hoped later to escape over the border. Summoned a few days later to Lang's hotel, Braun overheard Kammler and his aide discussing a dive underground as a monk in Ettal. He then encountered the general in Lang's bar and was plied with the monastery's own liqueur. Afterward, Kammler left him in the care of his deputy, SS Major Kummer, and disappeared. Fearing his men's continued imprisonment under SS control, Braun persuaded the major to let them find lodgings all around the Ammer valley, a ploy that allowed them to slip away into the Tyrol.[16] (Figure 8.1a pictures the Lang hotel in the immediate postwar period.)

By late April the local population was facing an extremely fluid situation, with movements both in and out of the area. As the German armies disintegrated, a constant flow of defeated men rode or walked through the valley on their way home. Some were hoping to find "asylum" from Soviet forces in the redoubt, while others found themselves driven along by force of battle. In Oberammergau, soldiers joined "shattered" SS troops; Father Bogenrieder counted five hundred of Himmler's blackshirts ominously settled near the Passion theater before they moved on ahead of the incoming Americans. Some sought to "camouflage" themselves as ordinary soldiers tucked away in lodgings. Even Messerschmitt's employees were preparing to leave, as the firm was told to expect a move into the Tyrol. This led to what one described as a period of "chaos," with personnel moving around and records stashed in various scattered locations. An SS general also established himself at this eleventh hour in Linderhof. With him was a company of youths from the Mittenwald officers' school, which was charged with "defense to the last man" of the road that led, ultimately, to the Ammerwald concentration camp.[17]

Reluctant members of the People's Home Guard were at this point expected to spring into action in defense of local communities. Previously, two months after Hitler had decreed the creation of this force in September 1944, the

(a)

(b)

FIGURE 8.1. (a) Otto Ackermann-Pasegg sketches Alois Lang's hotel soon after the U.S. occupation of Oberammergau. (b) Otto Ackermann-Pasegg sketches his own home, now a headquarters for U.S. troops, and the nearby "Villa Ammerhof," once shared by Oberammergau's pioneering Nazi officials.

Ammer valley's commandant was still trying to enroll stragglers as he organized swearing-in ceremonies. A profound unwillingness to resist the enemy only strengthened as the American armies drew near. Nevertheless, various local formations were established, including members of the voluntary fire brigade; the plan was to recruit women as firefighters so that full service would continue. However, those who could avoid call-up begged off. The few remaining village officials sought exemptions because their duties made them unavailable for training exercises. One elderly innkeeper even moved away from the area after rejecting his orders so that he could evade any possible punishment.[18]

In addition, Auerhahn leader Hacker worked to place his own loyalists in commanding positions within the Home Guard. One took charge in Graswang, and another headed an Oberammergau company, which allowed him to assist his boss in hiding their weapons at the forestry office. Hacker also persuaded him not to turn in those unwilling to sign up with the guard since these men were exactly the people who would be the most supportive of their plans later on. In fact, the company was largely made up of "antifascists," and even a second company's leader was cooperative. The forestry chief had maneuvered himself into a strategic position from which to influence the outcome when the moment of decision finally came.[19]

Those who felt obliged to join the Home Guard trained halfheartedly, using weapons borrowed from soldiers still quartered in the village. On a visit to Oberammergau, the county leader showed his disappointment with their pacific behavior. Reviewing the troops as their regimental commander, he delivered "a fiery speech to awaken a fighting spirit" in them. His rhetoric ran to wild generalities during this period. In the spirit of those who had defeated the primitive "Huns, the Arabs, the Mongols or Turks," Germans were fighting for the "defense of the West." But, in Oberammergau, such high-flown ideas were wasted. The men "listened quietly; a belief or an operational readiness was not there." In particular, they did not want the weapons awaiting them in the county capital, so they simply avoided ever picking them up.[20]

Early on April 28, Hacker returned from burning down the Hundingshütte just as waves of retreating soldiers flowed through Oberammergau. Clearly, U.S. troops were close behind. Meanwhile, developments had been complicating his efforts to engineer a peaceful surrender. Three days earlier an official order had arrived to mobilize the Home Guard. However, a day later, the locals managed to neutralize a small formation still in Oberammergau who agreed with their plans to surrender peacefully. The plot thickened when, on April 26, a young commander arrived from divisional headquarters in Garmisch-Partenkirchen "to organize and to take over" all local defenses. Refusing to see reason and renounce his mission, he insisted on following orders despite the "senselessness" of resisting the Allied onslaught.[21]

A day of frantic telephoning with Garmisch-Partenkirchen ensued, but to no avail. Mayor Bierling therefore met with the captain in charge of a "motorized department" of the mountain troops now in Oberammergau. He had already refused one request to pick up the Home Guard's weapons and another to truck in the wherewithal to blow up the barracks, choosing instead to collect needed provisions on the community's behalf. Now he, Bierling, and a couple of other men discussed how to deal with the new military complication, which, they all agreed, meant preparing "some reliable noncommissioned officers" to intervene. The mayor would send over a trusted accomplice to alert the captain when his men were needed.[22]

Fortunately, this plan became superfluous when, before the U.S. forces arrived, the regional commanders relented. They replaced Oberammergau's remaining troops with the Mittenwald officer cadets positioned in the southern defenses leading to Ettal and Linderhof. Nevertheless, the situation was still dangerous since the question of guarding the village's northern entrances was unsettled. Beyond this, Bierling was suppressing orders that he should facilitate the destruction of the huge Echelsbacher bridge, which spanned a deep gorge only a few miles to the north.[23]

Failure to carry out the command to mobilize the Home Guard was, as the mayor already knew, a daunting proposition; he was still recuperating, in fact, from a nervous collapse induced by his earlier battles with Nazi authorities. Nevertheless, on April 28 Bierling visited the northern defenses with Hacker's loyal company commander in order to make his own position absolutely clear. Representatives of the army, the SS, and the Home Guard all listened to the mayor's argument for handing over Oberammergau without a struggle. As a result, his arrest was planned, but he was once again saved by the rapid advance of the U.S. troops.[24]

One further event took place on April 28, after Hacker had returned from his nocturnal expedition. The forestry chief summoned a group of around thirty "trusted" locals who would help him engineer a peaceful handover of the village. Meeting later with Bierling, Hacker was able to reiterate their support for the beleaguered mayor's efforts to save his beloved community.[25]

General Alexander Patch's Seventh Army moved rapidly through the Bavarian countryside during the final days of April. Early on April 29, an advance unit was spotted approaching the Ammer valley, and soon U.S. tanks were lined up to cross the still-intact Echelsbacher bridge and make their way into Oberammergau. By then Hacker's agent had defied orders to activate his company in the antitank defenses despite fears that a unit of Werewolf resisters had arrived to execute the organizers of any handover. In addition, a sudden "illness" hit the village's elderly men, who were "cured" only after the occupation forces were safely in control. To everyone's great relief, remaining army units departed in the face of the oncoming enemy advance; any stragglers were firmly whisked off local streets. However, a slight scare arose when a "work service unit" drew up unexpectedly in the central square and had to be rapidly removed.[26]

Warning telephone calls had tracked the U.S. forces as they progressed southward. Consequently, Mayor Bierling was ready to greet the leading tanks once they entered Oberammergau around 11:30 A.M. He and a Hacker loyalist in the Home Guard approached the column and were referred to a German-speaking U.S. soldier. They immediately conveyed their community's peaceful intentions; only the tank trap defending the route to Linderhof would provide resistance. That established, both men conducted their occupiers into the village.[27]

After these forces had successfully occupied Oberammergau in a matter of minutes, their commander initiated an attack on the unfortunate cadets from Mittenwald, which left several dead. One was later recovered "with still-open violet-blue eyes in his defensive position. He had, before he died, propped up the photos of his loved ones in front of him in the snow and lighted a candle." This young corpse stands as a fitting symbol of the Nazis' casual sacrificing of their teenage supporters in hopeless defensive outposts all over Germany. His unit was easily pounded into submission by machine guns and then artillery based in Unterammergau, with shells passing over Oberammergau to reach the southern outskirts of the village. That left SS and army remnants hidden in the woods, whom Auerhahn leaders rounded up for arrest by the Americans. They also cornered a remaining SS general who had fled Linderhof and hidden himself away in a Graswang villa. He was soon under lock and key in the county capital, as were regional party magnates who surrendered after arriving on skis from a remote retreat.[28]

After the U.S. tanks entered Oberammergau, the occupiers took immediate steps to consolidate authority over the locals. At the town hall, tensions were mounting because Mayor Lang had made his way back home and announced that he would soon resume his old job. This enraged Bierling, who complained that his leadership had sufficed during the difficult wartime years. Yet it was Lang who cooperated with the military commanders who were taking charge of local administration. A few hours later, while the town hall buzzed with activity, Lang became "provisional" mayor; he and Raab worked into the evening to orient their American counterparts in communal affairs.[29]

Oberammergau's capitulation led to a series of demands on the local population. Most urgent was an immediate order to disarm, advertised by a poster stuck up near the town hall. A curfew was soon in place as well; only a few special passes exempted key personnel. The requisitioning of homes followed, as the 10th Armored Division's troops and their equipment passed through for a couple of days, leaving reserves in the village. They began a displacement of families, who were obliged to search for new lodgings, where they sometimes had to stay for years. Ackermann recorded this process when he sketched his own co-opted home and the nearby Villa Ammerhof. Within this context a charming incident played out when a Colonel Donovan Yeuell made his way to Anton Lang's boarding house; he had stayed there while attending the 1910 Passion Play, as his signature in the guestbook revealed. Yeuell wanted to sleep that night in his old room, which was currently used by a family member. However, she vacated it in order to accommodate this unexpected visitor from a past that must have seemed almost unimaginable amid the chaotic beginnings of a U.S. occupation.[30] (Figure 8.1b shows Ackermann's sketch of his own villa and the nearby Villa Ammerhof during the early weeks of the U.S. occupation.)

A series of increasingly junior officers took charge of Oberammergau in subsequent weeks, as the U.S. occupiers settled down in the village and local authorities cooperated "smoothly." Initially, the volume of soldiers was large enough to employ eight priests. Afterward, this troop presence ebbed and flowed, while an intelligence school was established in the barracks, employing hundreds of civilian German personnel. In addition, an array of representatives from leading American aircraft companies, including Lockheed and Boeing, ensconced themselves in order to investigate Messerschmitt's wartime activities.[31]

As U.S. servicemen occupied Oberammergau, they encountered local men returning from action with Germany's battered armies. Less fortunate were other local soldiers imprisoned by the victorious Allied powers, particularly the Soviets, in sometimes terrible circumstances. Many would come home only months or even years after the war was over.

However they ended up, these soldiers had already shared the experience of a shattering series of defeats. Moreover, the replacement of massive casualties had often meant separating individuals from the army's "primary groups," made up of men from the same region. Pössinger calls them his "trusted circle of comrades . . . with whom I shared home and dialect." The very language of his memoir illustrates how impenetrable were these tight-knit forces sharing a colloquial way of speaking and distinct regional customs. Yet, both he and, to a lesser extent, Ernst Lang struggled with the dislocation of a transfer into a "foreign" unit, which further demoralized German fighters.[32]

Soldiers still campaigning with the 1st Mountain Division faced an increasingly desperate situation as they fought both Russian and Titoist forces in what one commander later called "a witch's cauldron." Encircled south of Belgrade in October 1944, divisional troops seized a last opportunity to save themselves by bursting out of this trap "like a raging mountain stream." After regrouping to the west, the division was hastily relocated to western Hungary, where they endured the war's last winter staring down Russians. Subsequently, these fortunate survivors ended up surrendering to American occupiers in mountainous Austrian Styria; they were demobilized after a brief imprisonment.[33]

Consequently, while dozens of local soldiers disappeared into Allied prisons, the 1st Mountain warriors and a few other lucky men found themselves near home or actually in the village as their war came to a close. Among them was one young husband who had been "miraculously" stationed just a few hours from Oberammergau by train. His wife was able to visit him and hand over civilian clothes to facilitate a later escape. He walked through the mountains to avoid any hostile locals or occupying troops and arrived safely.[34]

After years spent on the eastern front and an assignment training sappers in Saxony, Ernst Lang was moved to Mittenwald—out of the path of the Russian forces. This relocation left him close to Oberammergau when the U.S. troops overtook the area, and he was eager to present himself as a civilian while attempting to reach his village. A nasty scare followed when he encountered a U.S. patrol near Eschenlohe; salvation came from the greed of one soldier who stole a knife lying on top of his backpack without uncovering the officer's paraphernalia that hid beneath. Lang was able to take cover in a local apartment and days later made it home.[35]

One young noncommissioned officer spent the last wartime weeks in his home community commanding the mountain troops assigned to block Patch's advancing army. Together with a cousin who had been invalided out of the air force, he worked to undermine his unit's willingness to carry out its orders; they were, in fact, the defenders who were replaced by the officer-trainees decimated by U.S. shelling. Beyond these grateful survivors, a few lucky servicemen had actually worked throughout the war as overflight spotters on the Pürschling heights once beloved by Ludwig II.[36]

The U.S. authorities moved immediately to quash any armed opposition by identifying all of the fighting troops in Oberammergau, which amounted to around 1,500 men. Many were the locals who had made their way back home, but others were outsiders caught in the village. All were required on pain of death to come forward and face interrogation, but, thanks to Mayor

Lang's vigorous intervention, only nonresidents were taken away as POWs. The community members received identification papers that authorized them to stay at home, although final processing took place later on.[37]

Before long ex-soldiers and civilians alike came to appreciate the grim reality of occupation. Certainly the villagers' prevailing mood had been hostile to continued Nazi rule and thankful that U.S. troops were invading their region. Nevertheless, as that spring's late snowy weather gave way to summer, the fears and challenges of a foreign armed presence were embittering. Father Bogenrieder summed up this helpless hostility with the words "Vae victis!"[38]

The priest was reacting in part to incidents, including several rapes, that portrayed the occupying troops as victors. Most ubiquitous were thefts of, as he put it, "Passion village mementos," which included the blatant theft of his own expensive watch, which he himself indignantly witnessed. Other desirable objects, like cameras and field glasses, disappeared in their turn. The Americans also requisitioned various accoutrements of daily living such as radios and pianos, while treating the furniture where they lodged with scant respect. Further reported incidents included the smashing of beer mugs or public lighting by angry soldiers and the use of headlights to illuminate hunting expeditions.[39]

Worse than the possible loss of valuable household and business equipment was a general anxiety about in some way falling foul of the Americans' expectations. Danger lurked in one crowded home as a lodger decided not to turn in her weapons during the collection, thus putting this entire household at risk. Similarly, the occupiers' discovery of a picture of Hitler was a potential disaster. One young woman clashed with a GI after criticizing a musical performance because it "sounded like Negro music." Another soldier then pointed out to her that "we Americans have won the war with this Negro music and you have lost it." She was later arrested.[40]

The most important issue, however, was the identification of perpetrators tainted by the Nazi regime. Perhaps party members did not expect to be targeted, but very quickly Mayor Lang was removed from office, while even his replacement, Raab, lost the job for a couple of months during the summer. In late May automatic arrest orders netted party officials like Georg Lang, to his family's surprise. Lang and a couple of other leaders were held in the Seventh Army's internee camp at Ludwigsburg; Motorstorm Commander Burger was taken to a camp in Garmisch and later to Moosburg Camp, where Chapter Leader Alzinger also ended up behind bars. Their colleague Lechner spent time in yet another camp at Heilbronn.[41]

American officials subsequently moved to identify low-level members of the Nazi party and its subordinate organizations so that, at least in theory, they could be limited to "common labor." The U.S. intelligence school generated a list that included both SA and SS members, leading to a demand for full attendance, including any implicated women, at a film titled *Nazi Atrocities*. Those missing had to attend a repeat showing. Other penalties might include the confiscation of clothing and valuable household items like radios and even the loss of one's business. Nevertheless, dissatisfaction soon emerged about spotty enforcement of the new rules and illogical decisions about which party members should be judged most guilty.[42]

This piecemeal approach followed a disturbing breakdown of law and order after the war ended, later characterized by Mayor Raab as "fearful chaos." For example, the large numbers of free-ranging horses left by army units and even the Home Guard were one target of petty theft that was, however, soon quashed. Beyond that, Oberammergau's hundreds of forced laborers were implicated in raids on local businesses and homes. "They took suits, underwear, shoes out of the shops without paying, bicycles from private houses," Raab recalled. Hard hit were a couple of centrally located hotels and a big clothing store, as well as homes on the village outskirts, but they also looted grocery stores. Even locals took part in ransacking supplies destined for the army's hospital; luggage waiting at the train station and in the adjoining beer hall was also picked through.[43]

While both foreigners and villagers were implicated in these crimes, saner counsel prevailed in most cases of homegrown looting, and the goods were recovered. Then the U.S. commander restricted the freedom of movement of the Eastern European laborers, reversing a permissive attitude adopted by French workers briefly placed in charge of local policing. Nevertheless, some nighttime break-ins seem to have continued until the Easterners left for home in mid-June.[44]

The locals showed scant sympathy for these exploited foreigners stranded in Oberammergau when they tried to supply themselves with food, clothing, and transportation. Unauthorized raids on private and military property infuriated officials like Mayor Raab and the police, as well as Father Bogenrieder. Yet, when the U.S. commander decided to step in and restrain the laborers, he explicitly guaranteed assiduous support that would include regular meals served at their camp. And as they prepared to journey home, Raab did try to organize a clothing drive for them and other victims of Nazi exploitation.[45]

Temporarily, the barracks vacated by the Messerschmitt workers were filled by other groups of forced laborers from the East, including a large contingent of White Russians and Ukrainians. The United Nations took over camp administration, reflecting both the need to provide a protective environment for these abused people caught so far from home and the recognition that this new transit unit was international in character. In 1946 some of the camp residents were even middle-class "folk" Germans who had been displaced during the Nazi effort to achieve a racially pure society.[46]

Accommodating this large transient population, as well as U.S. personnel and their German civilian staff, was complicated enough, but refugees from bomb-torn communities also crowded into Oberammergau to join those already living there at war's end. Fluctuating numbers of traumatized urbanites filled spaces carved out for them in local residences. In July, officials counted a thousand Munich residents, as well as hundreds more from Prussia and other parts of Germany; subsequent counts fell as these displaced people began returning home. Nevertheless, a November list of those seeking transportation included close to fifty separate destinations, including Berlin and other northern cities like Cologne, Dresden, and Breslau.[47]

One last category of newcomers began arriving in Oberammergau once ethnic Germans were targeted for expulsion from their homelands in Eastern Europe. A small number of Sudetens turned up late in 1945, joining the few Czech Germans who had already settled in the village. Thereafter, the trickle became a flood as hundreds of expellees crammed themselves into all sorts of accommodations. The community was bursting at the seams as its disparate and dispirited population struggled with the new realities of postwar German life.[48]

Meeting the special demands of Oberammergau's "visitors" during the first months of occupation was by then a well-worn process, if one that some locals were reluctant to perpetuate. However, defeat caused an unprecedented breakdown of vital links to outside suppliers of basic foodstuffs; communication and transportation services were all suspended. Moreover, the incoming U.S. troops arranged for their own provisioning at local expense. Consequently, villagers, refugees, and Messerschmitt laborers all faced a crisis with potentially catastrophic implications.[49]

Fortunately, Mayor Raab was able to exploit family connections to organize an emergency shipment of the most basic provisions, hauling them in with abandoned military vehicles. However, even this means of transport became precarious when fuel ran low; Raab found himself negotiating for the use of several wood-fired trucks instead. To ensure that all of the residents had access to a basic diet, several restaurants were pressed into service as canteens, obviating any immediate need for a "community kitchen."[50]

A strict rationing system carried over from wartime controls, distinguishing among people fully dependent on buying provisions and others either partly or fully self-sufficient. Even most of the permanent residents could not feed themselves completely despite having gardens and the ability to raise livestock. Ernst Lang, for example, found a cow waiting for him, purchased by his father in anticipation of the family's needs. Those with advantages were carefully calculated into the rationing equation, as well as groups with special needs. There was even a "household" or "Werdenfelser" card, while access to the highly valued tobacco was addressed separately. But the scarcities continued, particularly of vegetables and even meat for a while.[51]

Not surprisingly, a black market emerged during this time of limited resources; Mayor Raab reported in February 1946 that it "flourishes in all corners despite the ban and high penalties when caught . . . with the most unbelievable objects." A barter system soon developed as well, in which Oberammergau's carvers exchanged their products for desirable commodities. As Richard Lang, the eventual owner of Guido Lang's firm, later put it, "The currency which talked then was cigarets, cigars, candy, coffee, chewing gum. One littel [sic] angel went to the soldiers for two packs of cigarets, two angels for a pound of coffee or cocoa." Ackermann highlighted the cigarette cartons when sketching life under American occupation. A photograph of Lang captures the carver adding to his stock of winged angels in his workshop.[52]

Village authorities moved to employ capable males, including former party loyalists, on urgent road works projects and gathering wood in nearby forests. Long before winter returned to Oberammergau, the village authorities started worrying about providing their public facilities and expanded population with adequate heating materials; hundreds of the most helpless local families would be needing assistance. By November, Mayor Raab was arguing worriedly that "only with communal understanding and sacrifice" could they fend off disaster.[53]

For all of these reasons, morale in Oberammergau fell to a low ebb once the humiliating consequences of occupation became apparent. Moreover, the villagers were still mourning their lost loved ones, including the many still listed as missing, as well as agonizing over the fate of several hundred POWs. Certainly the community had escaped any bombing, in contrast to urban areas like Munich, so physically devastated by war's end. Nevertheless, the whole place had become uncharacteristically shabby and ill kempt.[54]

Mayor Raab was soon attempting to restore Oberammergau's public face to its usual high standards, spurred on by the U.S. military. A particular concern was the behavior of local children, who were running loose, as a charming Ackermann sketch illustrates. They had found a way of earning treats for themselves by bothering GIs with the sale of "postcards of the most terrible sort." To prevent this breakdown of order, Raab implored parents to control their children, and he anticipated setting up classes for them over the summer months. The occupation authorities subsequently provided acceptable teachers and written materials for the students, a slow process that was still under way the following year.[55]

Physical improvements, however, moved quickly, although a surly unwillingness to serve the public interest continued. Fearing a lackluster response when he sought donated female labor to transform old army uniforms into civilian garb, Raab stiffened his appeal by referencing the sacrifice of the ex-soldiers now asking for help. Similarly, his call for donations to help carry a new wave of refugees through the winter included threats of forced requisitioning. The mayor tried to arouse his villagers' conscience to meet this new challenge, banking on the fellow feeling of German Christians for their needy compatriots. He added a special plea unique to the self-perception of Passion players. Oberammergau's population, he exhorted, had to demonstrate its fundamental commitment to the highest standards of "brotherly love."[56]

Despite the many discouraging features of postwar village life, some regenerative signs emerged. Catholics anxious to resurrect traditional religious practices thankfully secured permission to hold their Corpus Christi procession. The American authorities restored the ancient right to Thursday ceremonies, although bad weather forced a customary shifting of this joyous and well-attended peacetime celebration to the following Sunday. A festive service honoring the church's patrons, Saint Peter and Saint Paul, further marked the community's new freedom. Religious instruction was permitted, as well as the resumption of Catholic youth meetings. Journeymen took up their club's business as soon as late July. "To the joy of the readers," their parish library was back up to its old strength, and the local Caritas branch successfully raised generous sums for the needy.[57]

The restoration of Oberammergau's disrupted economy was a greater challenge. Men essential to reviving the woodcarving sector were absent in POW camps, although trade with GIs did create a market for traditional products like "littel angels." Soon complaints about price gouging surfaced, so the occupation authorities raised the specter of regulation to prevent overly wide disparities. New rules required the labeling of all goods, including those sold out of "a private woodcarver's home."[58]

Still more challenging was any revival of the tourism industry. The requisitioning of local hotels and pensions, as well as accommodations in private homes, had completely disrupted normal peacetime business. Owners were permitted to require rent from their lodgers, which resulted in exorbitant prices at times. The U.S. intelligence school's representative was outraged in particular by the charges demanded for "a small single [room] without running water, without any comforts." Controlling such inflation would be an ongoing struggle.

Meanwhile, the villagers saw little hope of returning to the flourishing trade of prewar years.[59]

Oberammergau's faltering economy made it impossible to replace its lost 1940 Passion Play season during the first peacetime summer. Garmisch County's military chief launched this idea at a council meeting in late July despite looming questions about the speedy return of all too many imprisoned locals. The councilors immediately formed a Passion Committee, which promulgated the usual rules for participation and drew up a list of eligible players. However, U.S. officials required them to identify any ex-Nazis in this process so that they could be denied "important parts," which meant the rapid training of new actors to replace implicated cast members in some of the most crucial roles.[60]

Military authorities turned to the top army leadership for help in facilitating the 1946 season. This complicated endeavor, with its implications for a very broad public, required that "approval for such preparations should emanate from the highest headquarters." In addition, POWs would have to be located in the four Allied prison systems and their release prioritized according to "the relative importance of each character in the play." Naturally, so lengthy a process left the villagers in limbo, hoping for a decision that would give them time to prepare for a complete summer season. Players had to be selected, and rehearsals launched several months before an opening day projected for June.[61]

Mayor Raab became increasingly worried that these torturously slow official deliberations were threatening the whole plan. Ultimately, in late January the Passion Committee had to make the heart-wrenching decision to cancel their 1946 season. As the committee judged the situation, public transportation systems were not yet sufficiently restored to bring in Passion guests, and the villagers were in no situation to host them. Moreover, the process of freeing the POWs was not advanced enough to provide adequate cast and support personnel. Although this loss distressed the local population, Raab reported, they were nonetheless accepting of their fate.[62]

Meanwhile, Oberammergau's villagers had made rapid progress toward the restoration of their community's democratic government. A couple of weeks after their arrival in Bavaria, the occupation officials were replacing Mayor Lang with Administrator Raab. Two weeks later they replaced all Nazi-appointed councilors with relatively untainted popular leaders from the village's various social groups.[63]

At this new community council's inaugural meeting, the local commander wished them well and assured the mayor of his support for their community's "successful future." He went on to say how excited he was to land an assignment in "so beautiful a town as Oberammergau" and charged his listeners with reviving their battered economy. Mayor Raab then spoke about the restored "spiritual, cultural, and economic freedom." While villagers had once voted Hitler into office, now they would use democratic means to guarantee that no such regime could ever again find support. Moreover, he added, "We in Ober-ammergau have the double responsibility to nurture and forward our great [religious] tradition, the Passion Play, and the carving craft." Raab then broached a matter close to his heart, the renewed appearance of all of the councilors in the Corpus Christi procession; his invitation was unanimously accepted.[64]

A month later, this fledgling democracy met its first obstacle when Mayor Raab was temporarily removed from office because of his technical status as a party member. Once fully reinstated, he presided over the reactivated commu-nity council. At its meeting on New Year's Eve, Raab previewed an announce-ment penned for release to his constituency. Stressing the horrendous loss of life caused by the Nazi regime, he exhorted the villagers to draw from their "regained freedom of thought, action, and desire" to work toward social renewal. Their new leaders should help them "to guard and continue Oberam-mergau's tradition to their own benefit and the benefit of the community." After so many tumultuous months, the councilors parted with many good wishes for the New Year.[65]

On January 27, 1946, Oberammergau's voters participated in the first free election for more than twelve years. As early as the previous August, General Eisenhower had promulgated a limited right to local political organization through which the Germans could prove themselves capable of democratic behavior and, as he put it, "redeem yourselves both at home and in the eyes of the world." Months later, the village's first public political meeting was called by the Communists on November 29; it attracted around twenty-five people. Organizational efforts followed in December by both major postwar parties, the SPD and the CSU (Bavaria's variant of the emerging Christian Democratic Union). In early January the SPD drew about fifty people to its open gathering, while a much larger CSU event drew five times that attendance. A similar number also turned out to hear Hans Luther, ambassador to the United States and one of Weimar Germany's chancellors, speaking about the "American State Constitution and Democracy."[66]

Whipping up intense interest in the election, these meetings clearly dem-onstrated the popularity of the conservatives, who would achieve a resounding victory at the polls. Four out of every five voters chose the CSU slate, for a total of approximately 1,200 votes, with all but thirty-two of the remaining votes cast for the SPD list. Turnout was also boosted by a spate of pamphlets containing "anonymous verses" directed against particular candidates. These voting returns were good news for Mayor Raab, who was reconfirmed in office four days later by the newly elected councilors. The CSU's predominance during this first postwar election contrasts with earlier postwar results in 1871 and 1919, when the SPD briefly triumphed in Oberammergau. No such nod to the Left seemed desirable this time around, just as a revival of traditional Catholic practices was underpinning the "Christian" political movement.[67]

When Oberammergau's voters flocked to the polls, they already knew that they had lost any hope for a 1946 play season. The Passion Committee members recognized just how abnormal a living situation they still faced, and the villagers reluctantly agreed. They could not have known, however, that close to three years would pass before they would see any real improvement in these conditions. In fact, their problems actually worsened as new rounds of expellees crowded in from Eastern Europe. Moreover, both settled residents and newcomers had to work through a denazification process that challenged hundreds of Nazi supporters to defend their behavior during the Third Reich. Meanwhile, they participated in an incremental reconstruction of Germany's democratic institutions from the local level on up that would culminate in the creation of a federal republic in 1949.[68]

During these years, adults and particularly children faced an inadequate diet of 1,500 calories a day or even substantially less. In 1947, the already scanty rations were cut still further, and concerns surfaced about the health of schoolchildren, especially those in the lower grades. In 1948, however, they were judged to be growing within normal parameters. Yet, during the winter of 1947–1948, the situation seemed truly desperate, and the Bavarians' frayed nerves found expression in a brief strike to protest the "critical" situation. While in Munich a huge crowd gathered at the Königsplatz, in Oberammergau the protest was "calm," although trade union members resorted to threats in pressuring recalcitrant employees to participate. Soon U.S. General Lucius Clay raised the calorie count to more acceptable levels. However, it was not until a new currency had transformed Germany's economic situation that food supplies began to improve. In March 1949 Garmisch County authorities declared triumphantly that the full complement of needed rations had been achieved.[69]

During the lean years, public health officials worried about the consequences of "general undernourishment and weakness." Tuberculosis lurked as the major challenge, although diphtheria was also a worry, and incidents of typhus broke out as well. In 1946 a typhus epidemic involved twenty-four people in nearby Eschenlohe. Cases continued to emerge in 1947, and another smaller epidemic developed on Oberammergau's outskirts on a single farm, where seven people had become ill by August 1948. There was a single case in the village itself that fall, indicating the need for improvements in the local water supply.[70]

Substandard housing conditions exacerbated the precarious health of Oberammergau's residents. Refugees and expellees in particular crowded into inadequate lodgings, including the old Messerschmitt barracks. To provide the needed accommodations, some party members suffered expulsion from their homes into "less comfortable" lodgings, often for years. They received such meager compensation that even paying for these "emergency quarters" was a challenge. One couple was first forced into "two attic rooms" but then got permission to build a small annex onto their still requisitioned home. A single room served as both bedroom and kitchen, while the other was a bedroom/bath combination. When all of the home's inhabitants took their weekly soak, its unfortunate owner had to retire at night to his "hot and damp" quarters.[71]

For most of the residents, however, cold posed the greatest threat during several difficult postwar winters. Mayor Raab's early efforts to mobilize wood-cutting parties recognized the challenge that heating posed right from the start. In 1946 former Nazi activists in particular were required to go out into the forests to gather the needed supplies of wood. Nevertheless, not all of the rooms were heated, and the American occupiers enjoyed the right to those with a central heating system. Expellee families with young children were also supposed to have access to heatable lodgings.[72]

Beyond this postwar crisis in living conditions was the question of reconstructing Oberammergau's economy despite the presence of U.S. personnel and the large number of expellees. Certainly, the transformation of Messerschmitt's plant into the intelligence school provided work for some of the local residents. However, if Oberammergau were to regain its traditional economic structure, independent businesses had to be revived on a large scale.[73]

Until 1948, a huge impediment to recovery was the depressive effect of an unreformed currency, which encouraged an underground economy just when supplies and retail goods were scarce. In addition, a portion of the village carvers and businessmen remained out of commission either as POWs, party members in camps, or Nazi loyalists restricted to work as "common laborers" until their cases were fully resolved. Only relatives or surrogates would be able to keep their ventures alive. On the other hand, some of the remaining evacuees and locals wanted to start up small businesses, so the councilors thoughtfully vetted their applications. Often they found a need for new enterprises although they were careful to prevent undue competition with established concerns and to deny extra advantage to already economically secure families.[74]

One traditional pillar of Oberammergau's economy, woodcarving, still profited from the presence of U.S. troops, but the concerns about price gouging for very inferior merchandise indicate that standards had slipped; the councilors set up an oversight committee to resolve any complaints. Earlier, sales had benefited from a lively tourism sector, but now the village's homes and guesthouses remained largely unavailable to visitors. To be sure, in late 1946 U.S. officials complained about superior rooms being held back from refugees "in speculation of well-paying tourists." Nevertheless, overcrowding continued to be a controversial problem.[75]

Letters began arriving from abroad expressing interest in a trip to Oberammergau if conditions warranted, which of course they did not. Even in 1947 an effort faltered to bring as many as forty American visitors to the village; their tour would also have included visits to Rothenburg ob der Tauber and Munich, with a quick look at King Ludwig's palaces. The mayor would still characterize Oberammergau's tourism branch as "to a great extent closed down" in 1949.[76]

Survival in these dark years was facilitated for local Catholics by the positive upswing in their religious life. Despite losing a 1946 Passion Play season, they managed to revitalize the basic rituals so badly eroded during the Nazi years. A fitting symbol for this new era in parish history was the two hundredth anniversary celebration in 1949 of the church's Baroque refurbishing. By then, they had for some years been enjoying their newly regained freedom to take part in traditional acts of public witness like the Corpus Christi processions.[77]

Only in 1947, however, was permission granted to include the "customary" appearance of the village's brass band on the eve of Corpus Christi. Musicians once again wound their way through local streets while followed by a large throng. However, popular participation in this beloved event was so enthusiastic that the U.S. military personnel feared they were facing some kind of "demonstration" egged on by "martial" tunes. On the contrary, wrote the mayor in an effort at mollification, these musical pieces were harmless tunes heard on the radio, and the crowds were merely expressing their "happiness" at seeing a longstanding ritual restored. Oberammergau's fame as the Passion Play village also attracted outsiders, for whom the band's evening march served as a "greeting."[78]

The following year, regional pilgrimages were also attracting visitors. Upward of five thousand pilgrims celebrated Mary's ascension day at Birkenstein to mark the shrine's founding 275 years before. Ettal was once again the site of a regional Women's Union meeting, and at the Wieskirche the rosary brotherhood's customary celebrations attracted pilgrims from a wide area. Not surprisingly, given the immense numbers of wartime casualties, the shrine of their protector, Saint Anthony, in Partenkirchen was also the site of much activity. And to cap off this resurgence of the old ways, when typhus threats lifted in the area of Bavaria's national shrine at Altötting that fall, special trains resumed operation "on a regular basis."[79]

Despite this eagerly awaited resumption of traditional practices, Father Bogenrieder expressed his fears that the Third Reich had exacerbated a much longer process of decline in "the Christian family," rendering young people morally weak, self-indulgent, and badly behaved. Of particular concern was the indifference of Oberammergau's newest residents to parish life. Yet some did seek the customary protection of beloved saints, leaving candles in red glass holders near one of the church's Madonnas and at the Lourdes grotto.[80]

The priest was also alarmed by new competition offered by Seventh Day Adventists and in particular by a Methodist minister attached to the U.S. forces in Oberammergau. He was attempting to bribe refugees to attend his meetings with American provisions, and by 1948 local members of "sects," notably Methodists, did exist. Mainstream Protestants included several hundred expellees from the Batschka area of Yugoslavia. The community was therefore much more diverse in religious terms than before 1933; in addition, a special Orthodox ministry was established temporarily for the hundreds of Russians in transit. Certainly, the percentage of non-Catholics now living in Oberammergau fluctuated during these postwar years, but they often made up more than a quarter of the total population.[81]

Facing this challenging environment, Bogenrieder tried for years to bring in a helpful mission to stimulate his flock's spiritual commitment; he was eventually successful in 1949. Meanwhile, he agonized over a possible decline in the membership of clubs like the Marian Congregation, which were short on new recruits. Encouraging was the quick revival of the Journeymen's Club, now known as the Kolping Family. Members staged a play as early as 1946, and two years later they celebrated a special mass as they restored the Laber cross high over Oberammergau. Their numbers were continuing to rise at decade's end. Similarly, the former Workers' Club had reemerged as the Catholic Workfolk, although the fifty members in 1948 were no spring chickens. Hope for the parish's future lay mainly with the reconstituted youth groups, which attracted dozens of new recruits of both sexes to Christian activism.[82]

A top priority for Oberammergau's parish clubs was to help the many needy families and individuals crowded into their village. Mathilde Lang's Women's Union once again worked tirelessly, bringing huge containers full of donated goods to the church. These efforts contributed to the local Caritas committee's success since, as Father Bogenrieder pointed out, in his "poor and starving region" the parishioners could not donate food. The committee members therefore concentrated on meeting their impoverished population's many other basic needs. However, Caritas's international connections led to the arrival of canned food from America's Catholics; a shipment arrived late in 1946 with all kinds of delicacies, including the elusive vegetables and meat and even some coffee. Rules dictated that the distribution of these desperately needed supplemental rations was to be strictly nondiscriminatory but would favor the neediest social groups.[83]

Oberammergau's charity-minded Catholics teamed up with the Protestants, the Red Cross, and local leaders to face a new challenge that loomed early in 1946. Up to that point, their community had accommodated many hundreds of refugees from Germany's destroyed cities and soldiers trapped in the village at war's end. Most were being returned to their places of origin, but those coming from eastern areas cut off by the new territorial lines cemented by the Soviet Union could never go back home.[84]

Then, the fledgling United Nations permitted large-scale expulsions of ethnic Germans living in Eastern Europe, and many soon arrived in the U.S. zone for repatriation. Consequently, Oberammergau received peremptory demands to open up any remaining small spaces for these new unfortunates. The unattached were expected to double up, and families would be confined to a single room. Hundreds also ended up in the old Messerschmitt barracks.[85]

Oberammergau's situation was further complicated by the special needs of surviving Jews attempting to continue their lives in Germany. A few made efforts to take over businesses still run by ex-Nazis. One new resident, for example, wanted a local cinema confiscated on his behalf; this Aryan partner in a mixed marriage had lost his livelihood because of Nazi persecution. He and his wife were the couple who ended up traveling to evade Gestapo oversight during the last wartime years. Such requests were hardly welcome, as demonstrated by the negative response given an official request to house "150 Jews of German extraction." Later, the authorities also waved off a huge contingent of three thousand Jews from Silesia that passed by looking for lodgings.[86]

However, Mayor Raab actively sought the return of Oberammergau's only Jewish resident and "beloved fellow citizen" in the mid-1930s, Max Peter Meyer. His skills as a singing teacher allowed him to fill a gap in the community school's faculty for a time, yet his request for a permanent position, which he claimed had been the reason he came back to the Waldhaus, met with little sympathy.[87]

The reception was still colder for a family who by virtue of their persecuted Jewish members exercised a legal right to seize the home of two Nazi activists. Years of fuss ensued, including bitter complaints by the homeowner's tenant about her eviction "within two hours." The council's efforts to resolve this issue brought it a strict rebuke from the Bavarian Jewish Relief Organization. Their "illegitimate behavior . . . against racially persecuted individuals" was reprehensible; any

efforts to hand back the requisitioned lodging to its Nazi owners were incompre-
hensible, particularly since they were notoriously anti-Semitic and had behaved
badly toward these new occupants. Perhaps councilors had not fully understood
the extent to which Jews had been slaughtered by the Nazis.[88]

Most of the new arrivals, however, were ethnic Germans from the Sudetenland, Yugoslavia, Hungary, and Romania. Anticipating this new wave of
migrants, Mayor Raab worked to arouse the tired consciences of his villagers.
"These poor Germans" needed the willing assistance and sympathy of their
new community because they had been forced to leave their entire lives and
livelihood behind.[89]

One eight-year-old child who ended up in Oberammergau later told this
story from the viewpoint of her own expulsion from the Sudetenland. Families
had been forcibly thrown out of their homes, which had been portioned off to
the Czechs, and the local men were then hauled away. All of the remaining family members—in her case, her grandmother, mother, and two sisters—left their
Egerland farming village near the Bavarian forest for a transit camp in Mies.
Clinging to the few possessions left to them, her family then boarded cattle wagons lined with straw for a trip to Dachau. There the Mies contingent was directed
to various Bavarian locations for resettlement; her family arrived in Oberammergau to take up residence in a single room made available in Pension Mayr.
Only the following year was her father able to join them in their new home.[90]

The first contingents of these expellees had reached Oberammergau in the
depths of winter, but whole shipments arrived that April, not only the Mies
party, estimated at 150, but also a group of well more than 100 former Brünn
residents, followed by 80 or so from Abertham. Evangelical "Danube Suabi-
ans" from the Batschka region also arrived in substantial numbers, as did other
Easterners from Romania and Hungary. The totals peaked at roughly 1,250 and
only later sank to just over one thousand long-term residents.[91]

Some of the expellees faced dim prospects for improving their living conditions and obtaining work. In particular, Yugoslavian farming families languished in the UN camp with no hope of returning to their old profession, yet
because rents were low, many later clung to their quarters when offered alternatives. Wandering in that area of the village, Elisabethe Corathiel sympathized
with a "peasant woman" tending chickens. Her "lean legs stretched out straight
in front of her, the poor, thin, rusty black dress she wears emphasizing rather
than veiling their outline, her pinched face, of uncertain age, framed by the
white kerchief which completely covers her head, her hands folded, not lazily,
but patiently, resigned, in her lap."[92]

Other groups, however, did find improved lodgings, like the Sudeten child
who moved into a barracks complex on the Hubertusstrasse. This, while still

cramped, offered her family and others a small apartment each. And some managed to find employment opportunities, which came to include the U.S. intelligence school, as well as a small shoe factory and a reconstituted glove factory set up by skilled workers from Abertham.[93]

These ethnic Germans arriving in Oberammergau joined other newcomers, as well as long-term residents, in facing a U.S.-designed denazification process that evolved in fits and starts during the first postwar years. A vetting process launched in March 1946 gradually separated out the innocents from their more or less guilty neighbors. All locals eighteen years old or older perforce filled out an extensive questionnaire to which various officials and a "political" committee added evidence about any complicating factors like denunciations or material exploitation of NSDAP membership privileges. Each completed questionnaire was then submitted to a county-level tribunal for evaluation. Gradually, lists of cleared or amnestied individuals, invitations to open hearings, and announcements of guilt publicized the outcome for all eligible Germans.[94]

The first lists of innocents appeared in July 1946, with more following during the next couple of years, but the number of cases was overwhelming. Delaying progress still further was a lack of fuel, which caused the tribunal to disperse during the early months of 1947. To expedite the processing, a variety of groups with extenuating circumstances received a "Christmas amnesty." Similarly, the most youthful Nazi activists were soon amnestied.[95]

Garmisch County's tribunal initiated hearings at the end of August 1946. Its chairman promised "firm" yet fair proceedings, while deploring the "flood of exculpatory witnesses, who make white sheep out of so many well-known Nazi wolves." To be fair, however, much of this evidence does mitigate the negative picture of party members, some of whose activities were genuinely defiant of Nazi dictates. The tribunal soon began announcing the identities of the upcoming defendants in the hopes of attracting knowledgeable accusers. However, many hostile witnesses were reluctant to give testimony; one discontented assistant prosecutor even argued that "anti-fascists" were so fiercely grilled that they might as well have been on trial themselves. Fear of retribution may also have held them back from this "radical" judicial body. The resultant weight of positive evidence led to complaints that the tribunal was actually "too mild." Even the occupying authorities saw a slide in the direction of "leniency" as most of the activists were classified at the lowest level as "fellow travelers."[96]

Oberammergau's Nazis only gradually came up for either written or public hearings. However, two leading figures whose party membership was mitigated by their oppositional efforts were on trial late in 1946. Former Mayor Alfred Bierling received many encomia about his benign wartime administration and brave acts of defiance against senior Nazis; he was labeled a "fellow traveler" and given minimal fines to pay over the following months. Forestry Chief Hacker similarly received much support for leading the Auerhahn resistance group, with the result that he was fully exonerated, although American authorities later reversed this decision.[97]

Other leading figures with mitigating circumstances faced hearings in May 1947. Rupert Breitsamter, for one, was praised by a tribunal member for his "good service" to the larger community during the Third Reich. His fellow BVP councilor, Alois Lang, received a couple of glowing testimonials, including the enthusiastic support of his friend Max Peter Meyer. Just returned from his time in exile after Kristallnacht, Meyer described his many years of visits to Lang's hotel and stated that these trips had cemented their close relationship. He credited Lang with persuading him to take refuge in Oberammergau and praised Lang's willingness to reject Nazi ways of thinking despite being pressured into becoming a party member.[98]

By contrast, also that May, one of Oberammergau's chief Nazis faced a largely antagonistic trial that cost him substantial penalties and sent him back to a work camp. Incarcerated in 1945 Jakob Burger subsequently found employment as a laborer while awaiting his hearing. A sudden call to appear before the tribunal, he later claimed, gave him no time to mount an adequate defense. The accusatory local officials and witnesses told a damning story about Burger's behavior as Motorstorm commander. The tribunal's chairman, who openly expressed his frustration with witnesses reluctant to tell the full story of Nazi atrocities, also condemned Burger's claim that hard times had driven him into the party: "The people always say they were under duress." While one woman was testifying, the chairman could no longer contain his hostile feelings and cried out that "because of such elements her son had to lose his life and other people's sons lose a leg." It was a press report about this trial that labeled Burger as the "evil usher," referring to his job during the 1934 season.[99]

Nevertheless, an appeal launched shortly after his reincarceration softened this harsh picture as Burger mobilized character witnesses on his behalf. One former employee explained away his boss's supposedly negative actions and listed the difficulties he had had to face because of hostile party forces. He agreed with others who described Burger as a "very socially thinking, thoroughly upstanding, and rational human being." A further witness lauded him for championing "equal rights for all," even newcomers to the village. Yet another referred to the awkward social skills of this "good-natured" man. Burger's popularity with his Ukrainian employees earned him praise, as did his care of French prisoners in the final wartime months; he eventually risked blocking their removal by the SS before U.S. forces arrived to save them. Even the former head of Oberammergau's political committee dismissed overly harsh judgments of Burger, who was "impulsive" rather than "ideological."[100]

Oberammergau's remaining Nazi leaders whose cases remained on the tribunal's docket were fortunate to have them resolved in undramatic written proceedings, which usually left them with "fellow traveler" status or less. One opponent complained in mid-1948 that he had watched while minor Nazi players were punished, but "I myself became disappointed" as the "big" fish wriggled off the hook. He had given up his job as a prosecutor in disgust after observing "the lawsuit of the Passion Play actors of Oberammergau," at which Breitsamter, Alois Lang, and a fellow performer had received only minor sentences.[101]

One of those lucky former Nazis was Raimund Lang, who received his clearance to resume a normal life just in time to take part in a new election for mayor and councilors scheduled for late April 1948. By then, democratically elected county-level representatives had been operating for two years. The Bavarians had adopted a new constitution drawn up by a special assembly, which led to elections for representatives to the new parliament in December 1946. Meanwhile, in Oberammergau, Mayor Raab had been replaced by his deputy, Heinrich Zunterer, who was reconfirmed in office by a special council vote early in 1947.[102]

A variety of political parties emerged to contest these postwar elections. Still dominant in Oberammergau, Garmisch County, and the Bavarian state was the CSU. However, the Social Democrats also reconstituted as worthy opponents, while both Communists and liberals also garnered some support, as did a new "Economic Regeneration Union" (WAV).[103]

Then, in 1948 came the new round of local elections after a flurry of political meetings. The CSU's primacy was coming to an end as various challengers organized their own lists of candidates. Alfred Bierling, Hans Daisenberger, and others consolidated as a "Neutral Citizens Unit," and Raab campaigned for the liberals (FDP), while the KPD still made its presence known as well. A new addition was a "unity" bloc of refugees, which garnered five councilors, as did both the CSU and the Neutral Citizens. Two more councilors were to represent the FDP. No mayoral candidate won outright on the first ballot, but Lang prevailed during a runoff held a week later. The local wisdom was that he "got all Nazi refugee and evacuee votes."[104]

As with earlier elections, this contest stimulated the production of multiple flyers and posters. The "Neutral Citizens" introduced themselves in a circular as apolitical men out to serve their community and its Passion Play; rescue local crafts in danger of becoming "kitsch"; and improve the lot of their fellow villagers both materially and spiritually. A large green "unity" poster laid out

FIGURE 8.2. A KPD poster for the 1948 elections lampoons the
still-dominant Catholic party (CSU) by turning its socially prominent
religious and secular supporters into fierce vultures.

this group's list of basic demands from their adopted community under the
rubric "What we want!" A CSU poster played on the traditional blue-and-white
coloring to declare its members as both Bavarian and German Christians. One
SPD effort pictured a wall across which was inscribed: "Build housing first." In
addition, the FDP promoters favored primitive imagery of people fighting and
breaking eggs, with these captions: "Watch out for the eggs" and "Let the others fight. We want work and reconstruction. Help us out." The KPD fancifully
rendered its CSU enemies as vultures, while their eye for a vivid image shaped
other posters like the one promoting a unified Germany and imploring viewers to "fight with us for it all."[105] (Figure 8.2 shows the KPD's imaginative
rendering of the CSU's secular and spiritual leaders against a Bavarian blue
background.)

After the electioneering was over, many citizens remained furious that discredited former Nazis and ethnic German newcomers had saddled them with Lang as their new mayor. They launched an appeal that challenged his denazification status and, therefore, his ability to resume elected office. Supposedly, Lang and former Third Reich allies had used discredited Nazi-style "tactics to ruin their political opponents. . . . Greenhorns fixed the posters during the night, guarded the posters and removed the posters of the political opponents. When an opponent at an electoral assembly tried to dispute something, he got interrupted by shouting and whistling. . . . To camouflage their real intentions they hired some unpolitical known people as dummies."[106]

Critics blamed Lang's resurgence on the U.S. commitment to democratic liberties. One fulminated in imperfect English: "And everything under the protection of a democracy. For the Americans freedom means everything and a matter of course, so they will not recognize that it can be dangerous, too. But we got it to feel, what dictatorship means, and therefore we do not want this regimen a second time. . . . I would not wonder if Nacism in a few years would take over power again." Moreover, argued another opponent, "'democracy'— that means for these people poverty; 'Nazism,' however, more or less [means] prosperity." Therefore, a majority of the local electorate put its faith in this "new arising Nazi danger."[107]

Lang fought back successfully against the effort to unseat him. He defended his work as mayor, which had caused difficulties for him with Nazi officials and even put him at risk of execution during the Night of the Long Knives. In particular, Lang highlighted his own efforts in 1934 to restore the Passion season to its original "Christian spirit." Far from being one of "the bad elements of the party," he had always served Oberammergau honorably. Leading officials backed Lang and disputed the negative descriptions of his campaigning. Even an opposing candidate for the mayoral position, Raab, supported his well-orchestrated operation. Many voters had concluded that the former mayor's professionalism made him the "best" hope for their community's future.[108]

Weeks after Oberammergau's fateful election, a restructuring of the German currency and assistance from the Marshall Plan finally offered a chance at economic regeneration. A new federal republic followed in 1949, uniting the U.S., British, and French zones into a democratically grounded West German state. Both developments underwrote the community's decision to launch a Passion season in 1950, which coincided fortuitously with a Holy Year drawing pilgrims to Rome. With Mayor Lang in place to lead this effort, the villagers could draw on his "energetic" management and expertise gained from the 1934 season.[109]

One of Lang's most urgent challenges was providing beds for Passion visitors, a logistical nightmare that heightened the uneasy relationship with Oberammergau's newest residents. In fact, the locals were forced to address press accusations that they had tried to drive out these problematic migrants, and, indeed, some did leave before 1950. The primary effort to free up rooms for visitors, however, involved the construction of dozens of additional dwellings in time for the new season. This helped to validate Joseph Maria Lutz's claim that Oberammergau "is one of the most cultivated, most comfortable and . . . most beautiful holiday resorts in the whole of Germany. Not only in hotels and inns but in almost every private house do we find cosy rooms, comfortable common-rooms, and courteous, kind hosts."[110]

Oberammergau's infrastructure was also in need of regeneration. One urgent job was to fix the local streets after army vehicles, including heavy U.S. tanks, had torn them up. A general sprucing up was also needed; the usual preparation of local homes to serve as boarding houses would have been especially challenging after years of wear and tear. Observing "dilapidated" scenery and even "a rubbish-tip" on the edge of the village led Corathiel to exclaim: "Such a decline in Oberammergau's standard of neatness seems almost unbelievable." There was much work to do.[111]

The Passion theater also cried out for massive improvements since the wartime storing of provisions had left it in sorry shape. Corathiel observed the resulting "patches of moss which have eaten their way into the concrete." Yet, a year before the Passion season, performances of the Munich Philharmonic Orchestra's choir, together with two other choirs and internationally renowned performers, were able to be held on stage. Meanwhile, the stock of costumes needed to be upgraded, as did the backdrops used in the scene changes. But these enormous pieces of material had been woven on "special" machines that were now cut off from use in the Soviet zone; new ones, if required, would have to be improvised out of standard lengths of cloth.[112]

All of these efforts took place in the context of a now buoyant German economy, as advertisements in the official 1950 guidebook illustrate. An Esso man salutes the reader on its back cover: "Esso friends in good hands!" Announcements appear for Agfa photographic wares, and a two-page spread promotes close to twenty outlets for "art in Munich." A sign of the times, however, is "The M. A. N. Prefabricated House, a cheerful home for all purposes," available for inspection adjacent to the theater.[113]

More advertisements promote Oberammergau's businesses and those of the surrounding area, although some are for name brand items carried locally, like the Klepper raincoat, so useful in the uncertain Alpine weather, or the Vivil natural peppermints, with which visitors could find "breathing consciously . . . refreshing for body and spirit and [which] keeps you fit to follow the grand play." Reflecting a growing automobile market, the Cologne branch of Ford Motors competed with Fiat, as well as Daimler-Benz. To assist still hurting carvers, the guide also promotes an inexpensive "souvenir of the Passion Play carved in wood and painted, . . . a symbol of folk art in Oberammergau, as expressed in its play and the traditional craft of woodcarving."[114]

To promote Oberammergau, officials decided on using Goebbels's once despised image of the enchanted and tranquil highland village under its shining cross. Similarly, Gustav Barthel's "little guide" includes an etching that echoes this wistful image of the community's setting in a serene landscape, framed by parish church and Passion theater. Barthel enthuses over the region's many months of glorious weather. "Mountains and forests, villages with their houses and churches, monasteries and places of pilgrimage, all seem to have been made only to bask in the sunshine, which alone brings to light their brightest beauty." The members of a devout peasant family representing the local population "seem to radiate an atmosphere of confidence, joy and peace." In fact, so little has changed in "Old Bavaria" that "unalterable and unshakable tradition" prevails. Consequently, "strolling along the village street of Oberammergau . . . on a warm summer evening one gets an impression of perfect rural peace."[115]

Recovery from the war in a spirit of "love, peace, and reconciliation among the nations" is also the major theme of the messages provided by Bavarian officials in the 1950 guidebook. Minister President Hans Ehard sets the resumption of the play "after a long interval due to the war" in the context of its origins during the horrors of the Thirty Years War. He ends with this heartfelt appeal: "May the Passion Play today, when the world and Germany are still suffering from the aftermath of two wars, help to reestablish for individuals and for nations, the pax Christiana as a way of living and a binding law." Mayor Lang stresses the many extraordinary challenges that faced Oberammergau's villagers as they took up the "torch" handed them by their ancestors after years of war and recovery. "On the stage, the older players have joined hands with the younger generation, whose bitter experiences enrich their interpretation of the Play." Meanwhile, homeowners have prepared to "welcome all with generous hospitality."[116]

Within the context of the growing Cold War, these public expressions reflect an official view that Oberammergau could contribute to spiritual and material regeneration both in Germany and in the broader global community. Ehard compares the years of murderous fighting to a time when "all Europe, and Bavaria in particular, was being ravaged by war, and its dogs, famine and pestilence." In the aftermath of the horrors that he passively describes as perpetrated on Bavarians, Ehard argues that the Passion Play offers "for many visitors from all corners of the globe, an appeal to search the soul." However, these introductory remarks and the various articles that follow in the guide make no specific mention of soul searching over the many crimes committed during the twelve years of the Third Reich. Nor is there any consideration of the play's possible role in fostering a degree of anti-Semitism that led, at the very least, to a passive acceptance of the Holocaust.[117]

Also glossed over in Oberammergau's guidebook is the former relationship of some of the cast members to the NSDAP. Yet this very issue caused quite a stir as the Passion Committee began selecting players for the major roles in 1950. In his executive capacity Mayor Lang made a controversial decision. He would disregard the wishes of Oberammergau's conservative faction and overlook political choices made during the Third Reich. Other committee members backed him in accepting the now denazified status of certain cast members, so, despite some dissent, they issued a "clarification" to that effect. Indeed, the top actors were a mix of rehabilitated Nazis and their opponents, reflecting the fact that they had always been a politically diverse group in the past. Consequently, there was a flurry of negative press coverage, including one rather colorful story of a woman who responded loudly to the announcement of the Passion Committee's choice: "Have the Nazis won?"[118]

The U.S. occupying officials supported a rapid normalization of Oberammergau's players as part of their efforts to keep the new Passion season on schedule in 1950. Expecting the play to have a positive impact on GIs stationed in Germany, they reserved more than 30,000 seats for them. Top American leaders, including General Eisenhower, attended, as did German President Theodor Heuss, Chancellor Konrad Adenauer, and Bavaria's Minister President Ehard. Both secular and spiritual leaders from all over the world supported Oberammergau's renewed fulfillment of the ancient vow. The villagers continued to enjoy the elite validation of their Passion Play that had helped to make it famous since 1850.[119]

Once the season was under way, ordinary travelers arrived in large numbers by bus, train, and car. Both foreigners and Germans flocked to Oberammergau, many once again taking advantage of arrangements that linked a three-day stay to a play ticket. As before, Cook's "World Travel Service" and American Express brought their British and American clients to the village. Beyond attending the play itself, these visitors once again shopped enthusiastically; a souvenir particularly beloved by Americans was a scarf designed by Ackermann. However, complaints soon surfaced that too much "kitsch" was on sale in the village, like the "miniature lederhosen as piggybanks with pictures of Oberammergau." Commercializing the Passion Play remained a problematic issue.[120]

When the 1950 Passion season drew to an end, more than half a million visitors had passed through Oberammergau to attend the play. By all measures the Passion Committee's risky choice to fulfill the community's vow had paid off. Problematic for future seasons, however, was its decision to reprise the 1934 version of Father Daisenberger's text, making only minor improvements like restoring the lines that softened the guilt of Joseph's brothers.[121]

Jewish concerns about a revival of performances that might still arouse anti-Semitic feelings merely led to revisions of the text's preface. "Sometimes," it reads, "in earlier times and at other places, it has happened that spectators were stirred to take sides against Judas or the Jews; that, surely, was to misunderstand the very meaning and essence of such Passion Plays. For they are not a mere representation on the stage of historical happenings, however much these may be necessary to the play and the faith behind it; the performance of the play is meant to awaken awareness of the evil within us and to point [out to] us the only way to overcome it." This "spiritual mission" also represented, according to an article in the guide by Hans Heinrich Borcherdt, "a great work of art which, rooted in the soil of Bavaria, is one of the crowning achievements of German culture."[122]

Convinced of their positive role as healers of the ghastly wartime hatreds and divisions, Oberammergau's citizens had thankfully retreated into their familiar prewar patterns. Only in subsequent decades would they be forced to accept the need for fundamental alterations of Father Daisenberger's Passion text and staging in order to eradicate its anti-Jewish dynamic, a process still under way today. For similar reasons, the history of Nazi-era Oberammergau has only gradually come to light despite the potential it offers for examining in intimate detail the relationship of both activists and opponents of the Third Reich. I explore the insights gained from my extensive study of the community's encounter with Nazism in the conclusion.

Conclusion

Decades after the Third Reich fell in defeat, I began searching two communal graveyards for the central players in Oberammergau's Nazi story. Many are interred beneath the Kofel's craggy heights in a new burial ground carved out during World War II. Others joined family members in the community's traditional cemetery surrounding their parish church.

Wandering one day from grave to grave in this ancient yard where villagers had performed their play until 1830, I was forced to take shelter from a rainstorm in the church portal. From that vantage point, I glanced obliquely at an image attached to a nearby gravestone. Staring out at me was an elderly member of the high priest's entourage wearing a large turbanlike headdress. But when I ventured out again after the rain had stopped, this prototypical figure from Oberammergau's Passion Play had morphed into a young soldier in full army uniform, one of Hitler's youthful warriors whose official photographs hang uneasily in many a family plot.

This unnerving mirage reminded me that in Oberammergau, the Nazi regime's powerful dictatorial intrusions were refracted through the special lens of a local culture forged by Passion Play traditions. Even fierce soldiers were also actors whose lifetime of roles had shaped their individual sense of identity. Both Nazis and their opponents, both insiders and to a lesser extent migrants like Motorstorm Commander Burger, thought from the play out. A local man writing to plead for his imprisoned Nazi father captured this worldview: "He was unthinkable outside the communal lifestyle and grew up with the tradition [of the play] so [completely] that consequently the deepest gulf . . . divides him from the typical National Socialis[t]."[1]

All too many Nazis were these "true Oberammergau" men, for whom the play became "the leitmotiv of his whole operation." They joined the party despite or even because of their loyalty to the community's special traditions. Raimund Lang, for one, saw Nazism as instrumental in his efforts to save the play from capitalistic exploitation. However, that same set of values empowered him and others to fight back against their Nazi superiors when they threatened the community's bedrock principles. Similarly, Alfred Bierling was able to find the courage to defy inhumane orders not just as a former pilot but also as a Passion player. Later on, Josef Raab used that same communally shaped self-perception to mobilize consciences on behalf of forced laborers and German expellees, if not needy Jews; the blind spots of the villagers' restraining impulses also carried over into the postwar period of reconstruction.[2]

My mistaken glimpse of a character from Oberammergau's Passion Play grew out of almost thirty years of familiarity with the special village traditions. It underscored the validity of my decision to pursue an intensive community study, limiting the number of individuals whose complex social and cultural interactions I sought to re-create. Only in this way would I be able to understand their various relationships to the Third Reich. However, in developing this personal relationship over so many years of intimate acquaintance, I have been forced to struggle with the dual temptations that I have come to think of as the twin perils of Scylla and Charybdis.

One tempting extreme is the "nasty girl" syndrome made famous in the 1990 movie dramatizing the revelatory work of Anna Rosmus about her own community's Nazi past. As I teach my courses about Nazi Germany and the Holocaust, I find myself repeatedly confronted by unspeakable acts of cruelty and slaughter that I can only condemn out of hand. The responsibility for these murders lies incontrovertibly with the perpetrators, whose deeds are all too well documented. Again and again I find myself encouraged to extend this judgment to the villagers tucked away in their remote Alpine fastnesses whose story I have been reconstructing.[3]

Intensifying this quandary for me is the knowledge that, while Oberammergau's citizens operated in a dictatorial environment, their residual democratic institutions modified the regime's iron grip. Vestiges of a previously well-developed representational leadership restrained Nazi officials like the two mayors and allowed the villagers a modicum of space within which to make moral choices even during the increasingly dangerous years of the Second World War. For some of the locals, those decisions shaped their responses to Jews, which ranged from ideological racism to the protection of vulnerable individuals. Far from reflecting Goldhagen's Germans, who remained culturally distinct from other Westerners in the blind depth of their anti-Semitism, Oberammergau's villagers were able to draw on a varied and complex set of beliefs and values that had been nurtured by sharing the Passion story with visitors from all over the Western world. Yet they did very little to intervene when the Nazis murdered their helpless fellow citizens and so many millions of other Europeans.[4]

Echoing Thomas Mann's assessment of the ongoing challenges posed to individuals by the Third Reich, Lucile, Irène Némirovsky's character in *Suite française*, contemplates her town's German occupiers leaving for the Soviet Union in 1941. " 'It's a truism,' she tells herself, 'that people are complicated, multifaceted, contradictory, surprising, but it takes the advent of war or other momentous events to be able to see it. It is the most fascinating and the most dreadful of spectacles, she continued thinking, the most dreadful because it's so real; you can never pride yourself on truly knowing the sea unless you've seen it both calm and in a storm. Only the person who has observed men and women at times like this, she thought, can be said to know them. And to know themselves.' "[5]

In coming to "know" the individual villagers whose moral fiber was continually tested during the years of Hitler's ascendancy, I have been cautioned by the reluctance of my students to condemn even the executioners whose actions we read about in Christopher Browning's classic work, *Ordinary Men*. That response reflects the other temptation created by gaining insight into locals as complex actors: apologism. Flawed people emerge from the historical record, setting up questions about how much we can expect of them, caught up as they were in a myriad of personal and communal concerns that intensified with the coming of war in 1939. To be sure, many tried to push back against a dictatorial regime by testing the ragged edges of Nazi tolerance on behalf of threatened local traditions. But most also responded weakly to a limited, albeit sufficient perspective on the Third Reich's many atrocities. As Claudia Koonz has recently pointed out, this debate connects to unsettling evidence about the "potential for decent human beings to collaborate in evil."[6]

There were, of course, some Nazis in Oberammergau who remained enthusiastic ideologues during the Third Reich. Other villagers gave the regime their "consent," but it was mostly of the grudging sort that emerged out of selfish impulses summed up by this thought: "Why not? I'm no risk taker." Yet, as Koonz has persuasively argued, this "selective compliance" came with a strong dose of ideological reshaping. Based on a belief in "ethnic righteousness," Nazi Germany was "a state so popular that it could mobilize individual consciences . . . in the service of moral catastrophe."[7]

In Oberammergau, no one could truly claim to have taken part in the organized resistance typified by the Kreisau Circle's leading members, Helmut and Freya von Moltke, oppositional activities for which Helmut paid with his very life. Rather, the villagers fell into categories that Detlef Peukert identified more than twenty years ago as "shades of grey." Yet, when Freya von Moltke spoke with Alison Owings several decades after her husband's execution to discuss the couple's years of resistance, she did not excuse herself from the personal responsibility that accrues even to Oberammergau's non-Nazi population. "Sometimes," she argued, "we too said 'Heil Hitler!' It was not worth risking a lot only because one didn't say it."[8]

I will give Freya von Moltke the final word about the many Germans, including Oberammergau's villagers, who navigated the Nazi regime's turbulent seas. Her conscience led her to a brutal assessment: "'I say that no one who survived in Germany is guiltless. Such a person does not exist. Such people do not exist. People who lived through the Nazi time and who still live, who did not lose their lives because they were opposed, all had to make compromises at whatever point. And among them, I also count myself.'"[9]

Abbreviations

JM	Jungmädel
JV	Jungvolk
KLV	Kinderlandverschickung
KPD	Kommunistische Partei Deutschlands
KdF	Kraft durch Freude
NSF	Nationalsozialistische Frauenschaft
NSDAP	Nationalsozialistische Partei Deutschlands
NSV	Nationalsozialistische Volkswohlfahrt
NSKK	Nationalsozialistisches Kraftfahrerkorps
SS	Schutzstaffel
SPD	Sozialdemokratische Partei Deutschlands
SA	Sturmabteilung
WHW	Winterhilfswerk

Notes

PREFACE

1. Shapiro, *Oberammergau*, 28, 227; Günzler and Zwink, *Berühmtes Dorf*, 166–67; Joseph Maria Lutz, "The 1950 Play and Its Performers," In *Oberammergau* (1950), ed. Community of Oberammergau, 56.

2. Mann, *Joseph and His Brothers*, v.

3. I have been strongly influenced in this assessment of German democratic traditions by Anderson, *Practicing Democracy*.

4. Goldhagen, *Hitler's Willing Executioners*; Shapiro, *Oberammergau*, 28, 140–41, 160–62.

5. My analysis builds on classic works in Bavarian history, notably Pridham, *Hitler's Rise to Power*; Broszat and Fröhlich, *Bayern in der NS-Zeit*; and Kershaw, *Popular Opinion*. Similarly, a large literature treats the story of Catholics in the Third Reich, notably Conway, *Nazi Persecution of the Churches*; Dietrich, *Catholic Citizens in the Third Reich*; and Phayer, *Protestant and Catholic Women in Nazi Germany*. The importance of a regional approach for studying Catholic culture emerges in Möller, Wirsching, and Ziegler, *Nationalsozialismus in der Region*; Heilbronner, *Catholicism*; and Stephenson, *Hitler's Home Front*. Heilbronner found a deteriorating Catholic society, but in the "priests' corner" of Upper Bavaria, where Oberammergau is located, a flourishing Catholic milieu rich in popular rituals still existed before and during the Nazi period. This makes Oberammergau valuable for understanding the relationship of Catholic activists with Nazism. My analysis also builds on local studies starting with the classic by Allen, *Nazi Seizure of Power*. Analysis of small Catholic communities appears in Rauh-Kühne, *Katholisches Milieu*; and Rinderle and Norling, *Nazi Impact on a German Village*. I draw on the voluminous general literature about the Nazi era as appropriate in the chapters that follow.

6. Shapiro, *Oberammergau*, 137–86, 234–35. In particular, Friedman's *Oberammergau Passion Play* does not draw on much of the rich documentary evidence available to reconstruct the villagers' complex story during the Third Reich.

7. Two fairly recent books have made pathbreaking contributions to this historical grounding: Rädlinger, *Zwischen Tradition und Fortschritt*, and Utzschneider, *Oberammergau im Dritten Reich*. I am grateful for their pioneering work, from which I have benefitted substantially.

CHAPTER 1

1. Anton Lang, *Reminiscences*, 101, 144–45.

2. GAO: ZA/Passionsspiele: "The Ober Ammergau Passion Play, 1900," *Times* (London) (Feb. 6, 1900); Browne, "Where Faith Abides," 266.

3. Schumacher, *Meine Oberammergauer*, 112, 117.

4. Parks-Richards, *Oberammergau*, 112–15, 123; Krause-Lang, *Erinnerungen*, 88; Moses, *Passion Play*, vii–ix.

5. Daisenberger, *Geschichte* (1859), 4–5; Zainer, "Kult und Kampf," 5–25.

6. Daisenberger, *Geschichte* (1859), 16–17, 20–28; Glasthaner, *Wirtschaftliche, rechtliche, und soziale Verhältnisse*, 5, 12–13, 20, 28–33 (1521); BHstA: KL Ettal #47 (1571), #49 (1672), #50 (1738), and #61 (1781).

7. Parks-Richards, *Oberammergau*, ad section; Daisenberger, *Geschichte* (1859), 30–33, 76, 137, 143, 186–87; BHstA: KL Ettal #49 (1672); GAO: Einwohner u. Hausbesitzerverzeichnis 1930; Pk-Sammlung #12–13; Feldigl, *Oberammergau* (1910), 37, and (1922), 150; Florian Lang, Ammergauer Häuser scrapbook.

8. BHStA: KL Ettal #49 1672); StAM: Kataster 8791 (1810); Daisenberger, *Geschichte* (1859), 156, 181–85, 189; Feldigl, *Oberammergau* (1922), 150.

9. Daisenberger, *Geschichte* (1859), 20, 76, 156, 158, 179, 184, 186–87; GAO: Einwohner u. Hausbesitzerverzeichnis 1930; Parks-Richards, *Oberammergau*, 90–91.

10. Eduard Devrient, "Ein Bericht über das Passionsspiel in Oberammergau," Beylagen in *Augsburger allgemeine Zeitung* (Sept. 14–20, 1850), in *Beyträge*, vol. 3, ed. von Deutinger, 129.

11. *Lang's Führer* (1910), 61, and (1905), 15; Diemer, *Oberammergau* (1900), 202; Parks-Richards, *Oberammergau*, 197; Central File.

12. Central File; StAM: LRA 131441; Guido Lang, *Lang's Illustrated Practical Guide*, ad section.

13. Feldigl, *Oberammergau* (1910), 34–37, and (1900), ad section; Parks-Richards, *Oberammergau*, 200 and ad section; von Schaching, *Oberammergau*, 25; GAO: Pk-Sammlung, #14–16; *AZ* passim in the interwar years.

14. Heilbronner, *Catholicism*, 12, 15–16, 29, 35–37. The social milieu of Heilbronner's chosen subject was clearly very different from that of Oberammergau, although his lack of interest in the details of common Catholic behaviors and beliefs in his part of Baden makes it difficult to judge how different. The weakness of the Center Party there contrasted with its dominance in Oberammergau.

15. Daisenberger, *Geschichte* (1859), 10, 63–64, 122. Rauh-Kühne, *Katholisches Milieu*, 139–40, emphasizes the "ritualizing" of family life, which complemented the public witness of pilgrimages and processions. Daisenberger, *Historisch-topographische Beschreibung*, 27, lists Oberammergau's "entire population" as Catholic in 1880. By 1915, however, thirty non-Catholics were living in the village, as recorded in PAO: Schublade 17: Kirchliche Statistik Deutschlands: Königreich Bayern, 1915.

16. Friedrich Springorum, "Ways to Oberammergau," in *Oberammergau* (1950), ed. Community of Oberammergau, 29; Bogenrieder, *Oberammergau* (1930), 19, 51.

17. Brauneck, *Religiöse Volkskunst*, 73.

18. Harvolk, *Votivtafeln*, 86; Jablonka, *Freiwillige Feuerwehr Oberammergau*, 15, 17; Salberg, *Geschichte*, 16.

19. *AZ* 18/51 (June 28, 1924), 2; 20/110 (Sept. 23, 1926), 1; 23/106 (Sept. 14, 1929), 3; 24/99 (Sept. 4, 1930), 1; Kriß, *Die Volkskunde*, vol. 1, 161; Finkenstaedt and Finkenstaedt, *Die Wieswallfahrt*, 169–73; Finkenstaedt, *Wies*, 46.

20. Blackbourn, *Marpingen*, which also, illustrates some of the tensions that this Marian worship created in the context of the new German Empire.

21. *AZ* 1/75 (July 13, 1907), 2; 14/37 (Aug. 5, 1920), 1; 22/59 (May 24, 1928), 1; 22/61 (May 31, 1928), 1; 22/65 (June 12, 1928), 1; 24/5 (Jan. 16, 1930), 3; 24/55 (May 17, 1930), 3; 24/82 (July 22, 1930), 2–3.

22. Glasthaner, *Abtei Ettal*, 88–90; *AZ* passim for masses and the yearly "Bittgänge" and 16/76 (Sept. 23, 1922), 1; 24/109 (Sept. 27, 1930), 3; Feldigl, *Oberammergau* (1922), 29; Daisenberger, *Geschichte* (1859), 96.

23. Anton Lang, *Reminiscences*, 33, 68–69; Krause-Lang, *Erinnerungen*, 100–101; Central File; *AZ* 19/57 (May 21, 1925), 1.

24. *AZ* 19/35 (March 28, 1925), 1; 23/59 (May 23, 1929), 1; 28/4 (Jan. 11, 1934), 2; Kopp's gravestone; GAO: AII/26.

25. *AZ* 20/12 (Jan. 30, 1926), 1; 25/7 (Jan. 17, 1931), 3; 25/93 (Aug. 13, 1931), 1; 25/133 (Nov. 14, 1931), 3; 25/152 (Dec. 31, 1931), 5; 26/8 (Jan. 23, 1932), 2; 26/5 (Jan. 16, 1932), 2; 26/11 (Jan. 30, 1932), 3; 26/32 (March 19, 1932), 3; 26/92 (Aug. 13, 1932), 3; 26/124 (Oct. 29, 1932), 3.

26. Christian, *Person and God*, 85, 181; Hahn, "'Joseph Will Perfect,'" 54–65.

27. Orsi, *Thank You, St. Jude*; *AZ* passim. In surveying the masses listed in the *Ammergauer Zeitung* for 1926, I identified at least eighteen commissioned by Oberammergauers to Anthony.

28. Fischer and Schnell, *Die votiv- und Wallfahrtskirche St. Anton*, 2–3, 14–15; Kleinschmidt, *Antonius von Padua*, 356, 371–73, 385–86, 389–93.

29. *BF* 13/12 (Dec. 1931), 97; 16/8 (August 1934), 58–59; Kleiner, *Bruder Konrad und Altötting*, 40–42; Hoedl, *Bruder Konrad*, 34–37.

30. Theopold, *Votivmalerei und Medizin*, 150.

31. *AZ* 9/3 (Jan. 9, 1915), 3; 10/2 (Jan. 8, 1916), 2; 10/135 (Dec. 9, 1916), 3; 16/70 (Sept. 2, 1922), 1; 18/48 (June 18, 1924), 1; 21/31 (March 17, 1927), 1; 21/95 (Aug. 25, 1927), 2; 23/137 (Nov. 26, 1929), 1.

32. *AZ* 1/22 (Feb. 26, 1907), 2; 9/73 (June 26, 1915), 4; 16/19 (March 8, 1922), 2; 19/30 (March 14, 1925), 1; 21/56 (May 17, 1927), 1; 22/32 (March 17, 1928), 1; 24/31 (March 18, 1930), 1; 26/69 (June 18, 1932), 1–2; 26/74 (July 2, 1932), 3; 27/36 (March 25, 1933), 3. Rauh-Kühne, *Katholisches Milieu*, 141–57, examines in great detail the myriad of clubs that developed in urban contexts to perpetuate the Catholic milieu during the early twentieth century.

33. *AZ* 13/74 (Sept. 27, 1919), 1; 13/93 (Dec. 6, 1919), 1; 13/95 (Dec. 10, 1919), 1; 25/93 (Aug. 13, 1931), 1; *BF* 1/1 (Jan. 1919), 2–4; 1/2 (Feb. 1919), 1, 4–6, 9, 19; 1/11 (Nov. 1919), 78–79; 2/9/10 (Sept.–Oct. 1920), 37–38; *Fünfundzwanzig Jahre Katholischer Deutscher Frauenbund*, especially 15, 30–31, 119; PAO: Pfarrchronik von Oberammergau.

34. *AZ* passim for first communion ceremonies; 16/15 (Feb. 22, 1922), 1; 18/41 (May 24, 1924), 5; 18/48 (June 18, 1924), 1.

35. *BF* 15/5 (May 1933), 38; *AZ* passim and 20/105 (Sept. 11, 1926), 3; 22/53 (May 10, 1928), 1; 25/49 (April 28, 1931), 1.

36. *BF* 1/11 (Nov. 1919), 78–79; 15/4 (April 1933), 31; 15/5 (May 1933), 38.

37. *AZ* 27/59 (May 20, 1933), 1.38. For an extensive discussion of the modern transformation of local Catholic culture in Bavaria, see Waddy, "St. Anthony's Bread," 347–70.

38. Brunner, *Das Passionsspiel zu Oberammergau*, 12.

39. MacColl, *Ober-Ammergau Passion Play*, 27–30, quoting a letter in the *Times* (London) of June 27, (n. d.); Doane, *To and from the Passion Play*, 13, 15–18, 28–96, 122–23; Blackburn, *Art in the Mountains*, 27–32, 171; Foreman, *Pilgrimage to Oberammergau*, 8–10.

40. Tweedie, *Oberammergau Passion Play*, 56–57; von Oettingen, *Die Passion*, 9; Sellar, *Passion-Play*, 20.

41. Cresswell, *Retrospect*, 3–4; Deutinger, *Wallfahrt nach Oberammergau*, 15; Howitt, *Art Student in Munich*, 51, 53; MacColl, *Ober-Ammergau Passion Play*, 34; Greatorex, *Homes of Ober-Ammergau*, 2; Parks-Richards, *Oberammergau*, 26.

42. Cresswell, *Retrospect*, 16; Howitt, *Art Student in Munich*, 54.

43. Farrar, *Passion Play at Oberammergau*, 46; Doane, *To and from the Passion Play*, 123.

44. Holland, *Impressions*, 6, 25–26; Howitt, *Art Student in Munich*, 61; Devrient, "Ein Bericht," 139; Cresswell, *Retrospect*, 13; Scheffer, *Ein Besuch in Oberammergau*, 15, 20; Blackburn, *Art in the Mountains*, 37–38, 55; Schwarzmann, *Reise des Pfarrers Elias Schwarzmann*, 37; Athawes, *Representation of the Passion*, 2; Frick, *Das Passions-Spiel in Ober-Ammergau*, 10; Koch von Berneck, *Oberammergau*, 16.

45. Devrient, "Ein Bericht," 128–29; Blackburn, *Art in the Mountains*, 37–38, 55; Clarus, *Das Passionsspiel zu Ober-Ammergau*, 34; Howitt, *Art Student in Munich*, 61; Regnet, *Nach Oberammergau*, 29; Greatorex, *Homes of Ober-Ammergau*, sketches and 43; Howe, *Oberammergau in 1900*, 5–6; Holland, *Impressions*, 6, 25–26; Doane, *To and from the Passion Play*, 123; Fuller, *World's Stage: Oberammergau, 1934*; Höhl, *Führer zum Ammergauer Passionsspiel*, 111–12.

46. Holland, *Impressions*, 25; Blackburn, *Art in the Mountains*, 38, 41, 43, 169–70; Schröder, *Oberammergau* (1910), 117; Molloy, *Passion Play at Ober-Ammergau*, 12;

Scheffer, *Ein Besuch in Oberammergau*, 15; *Augsburger Postzeitung* (Aug. 2–4, 1850), Beylagen 142 and 143, in *Beyträge*, vol. 2, ed. von Deutinger, 554–55; *Neueste Nachrichten*, 260–65 (Sept. 17–22, 1850), in *Beyträge*, vol. 3, ed. von Deutinger, 42; Bogenrieder, *Oberammergau* (1930), 19, 51; *Aehrenlese* 2/41–52 (1840), in *Beyträge*, vol. 3, ed. von Deutinger, 354; Lampert, *Das Passionsspiel in Oberammergau*, 18.

47. Schumacher, *Meine Oberammergauer*, 18–20; Jerome, *Diary of a Pilgrimage*, 105–106; Holmes, *Travelogues*, 123–25, includes photographs of simple accommodations around 1900.

48. Schwartzmann, *Reise des Pfarrers Elias Schwarzmann*, 37–52.

49. Holland, *Impressions*, 4; MacColl, *Ober-Ammergau Passion Play*, 46–47; Tweedie, *Oberammergau Passion Play*, 73; Burton, *Passion-Play at Ober-Ammergau*, 94–95.

50. Eichbaum, *Country Parson*, 35; Burton, *Passion-Play at Ober-Ammergau*, 95, 120–21; Greatorex, *Homes of Ober-Ammergau*, 11; Regnet, *Nach Oberammergau*, back cover; Howitt, *Art Student in Munich*, 63; Cresswell, *Retrospect*, 15; Tweedie, *Oberammergau Passion Play*, 79; Molloy, *Passion Play at Ober-Ammergau*, 22–23.

51. Klinner, *Joseph Alois Daisenberger*, 67–87; Otto Huber, Helmut Klinner, and Dorothea Lang, "Die Passionsaufführungen in Oberammergau in 101 Anmerkungen," in *Hört, sehet, weint, und liebt*, ed. Henker, Dünninger, and Brockhoff, 164–70; Otto Huber, "Zwischen Passionsandacht und Gesellschaftskritik: Die Passionsspiele von Pater Othmar Weis," in *Hört, sehet, weint, und liebt*, ed. Henker, Dünninger, and Brockhoff, 186–95.

52. Howitt, *Art Student in Munich*, 45–46; Devrient, "Ein Bericht," 169; Günzler and Zwink, *Berühmtes Dorf*, 31–32, 40; Deutinger, *Beyträge*, vol. 3, 1–2; Huber, Klinner, and Lang, "Die Passionsaufführungen," in Henker, Dünninger, and Brockhoff, *Hört, sehet, weint, und liebt*, 170–171; Scheffer, *Ein Besuch in Oberammergau*, 5–7; Lampert, *Das Passionsspiel in Oberammergau*, foreword; Doane, *To and from the Passion Play*, 7–8; Farrar, *Passion Play at Oberammergau*, 23–24; von Hahn, *Nach Ober-Ammergau*, 6; Höhl, *Führer zum Ammergauer Passionsspiel*, xii; Shapiro, *Oberammergau*, 113–14, 231–32.

53. Blackburn, *Art in the Mountains*, 22–25; MacColl, *Ober-Ammergau Passion Play*, 76; Scheffer, *Ein Besuch in Oberammergau*, 8; Howitt, *Art Student in Munich*, 34, 46–48; Steinbrecher, *Führer zum Oberammergauer Passionsspiel*, 32.

54. Blackburn, *Art in the Mountains*, 64–65, 87–89, 111, 160–61; Steinbrecher, *Führer zum Oberammergauer Passionsspiel*, 38–39; Howitt, *Art Student in Munich*, 59, 64; Winkler, *Von München nach Oberammergau*, 61; Molloy, *Passion Play at Ober-Ammergau*, title page; Doane, *To and from the Passion Play*, 135; Parks-Richards, *Oberammergau*, 103–105.

55. Lampert, *Das Passionsspiel in Oberammergau*, foreword, 12–14, 67; Steinbrecher, *Führer zum Oberammergauer Passionsspiel*, 38–39; Scheffer, *Ein Besuch in Oberammergau*, 10–11; Fuchs, *Oberammergau und sein Passionsspiel*, 4; MacColl, *Ober-Ammergau Passion Play*, 79.

56. Holland, *Impressions*, 23, 29; Steinbrecher, *Führer zum Oberammergauer Passionsspiel*, 38–39, Blackburn, *Art in the Mountains*, 129–32, 147–48; Lampert,

Das Passionsspiel in Oberammergau, 12–14, 35, 50–51; Winkler, *Von München nach Oberammergau*, 52–53.

57. Molloy, *Passion Play at Ober-Ammergau*, 33; Lampert, *Das Passionsspiel in Oberammergau*, 12–14, 35, 50–51; Scheffer, *Ein Besuch in Oberammergau*, 10–12.

58. Lampert, *Das Passionsspiel in Oberammergau*, 12–14, 36; Steinbrecher, *Führer zum Oberammergauer Passionsspiel*, 38–39; Blackburn, *Art in the Mountains*, 147–48; Howitt, *Art Student in Munich*, 62; Scheffer, *Ein Besuch in Oberammergau*, 25; Holland, *Impressions*, 23.

59. Blackburn, *Art in the Mountains*, 131, 134; Howitt, *Art Student in Munich*, 60; Lampert, *Das Passionsspiel in Oberammergau*, 15, 35, 63; Jaron and Rudin, *Das Oberammergauer Passionsspiel*, 108; Winkler, *Von München nach Oberammergau*, 59; Schoeberl, *Passion-Play at Ober-Ammergau*, 7, 87; Doane, *To and from the Passion Play*, 206; Oxenham, *Recollections*, 28, 61, 78–79; Molloy, *Passion Play at Ober-Ammergau*, 34, 98; Howe, *Oberammergau in 1900*, 42; Holland, *Impressions*, 16–17; Burton, *Passion-Play at Ober-Ammergau*, 124–25.

60. Blackburn, *Art in the Mountains*, 96–99; 116, 132–34, 141–45; Molloy, *Passion Play at Ober-Ammergau*, 101, 104–105; Clarus, *Das Passionsspiel zu Ober-Ammergau*, 51; Scheffer, *Ein Besuch in Oberammergau*, 25; Schwarzmann, *Reise des Pfarrers Elias Schwartzmann*, 46–47; Greatorex, *Homes of Ober-Ammergau*, 22, 30; GAO: ZA/ Passionsspiele: article ca. April 1900; Schoeberl, *Passion-Play at Ober-Ammergau*, 85; Oxenham, *Recollections*, 73; Holland, *Impressions*, 24; Athawes, *Representation of the Passion at Ober Ammergau*, 5.

61. Patruban, *Erinnerung*, 9.

62. Greatorex, *Homes of Ober-Ammergau*, 16, 27; Jaron and Rudin, *Das Oberammergauer Passionsspiel*, 54, 80; Günzler and Zwink, *Berühmtes Dorf*, 66, 108–109; Holland, *Impressions*, 27; Cresswell, *Retrospect*, 7; Winkler, *Von München nach Oberammergau*, 35.

63. GAO: ZA/Passionsspiele: *Neues Wiener Tagblatt* (Sept. 13, 1900); article in *Avenir* (Lyon) (Sept. 30, 1900); Marianne Dale, "Impressionist Sketch," *English American Gazette* (July 1900); Browne, "Where Faith Abides," 266; Günzler and Zwink, *Berühmtes Dorf*, 109, 118; Queri, *Anton Lang*, 25–32.

64. Greatorex, *Homes of Ober-Ammergau*, 21–22, 30; Winkler, *Von München nach Oberammergau*, 40; Jaron and Rudin, *Das Oberammergauer Passionsspiel*, 106–107; Feldigl, *Oberammergau* (1900), 14–15.

65. Holland, *Impressions*, 14–15; Burton, *Passion-Play at Ober-Ammergau*, 126, 129; Schoeberl, *Passion-Play at Ober-Ammergau*, 78, 93; Steinbrecher, *Führer zum Oberammergauer Passionsspiel*, 43–44. Sellar, *Passion-Play*, 42–43, agrees with Burton that this scene was "intended to exhibit the fickleness and perversity of the Jewish people—a trait of character still commonly exhibited by Oriental and semi-Oriental nations."

66. Guido Görres, "Das Theater im Mittelalter und das Passionsspiel in Oberammergau," *Historisch-politische Blättter* (1840/6), in *Beyträge*, vol. 3, ed. von Deutinger, 261; Günzler and Zwink, *Berühmtes Dorf*, passim.

67. Wyl, *Maitage in Oberammergau*, 40; Winkler, *Von München nach Oberammergau*, 12, 20, 23, 44, 47; Scheffer, *Ein Besuch in Oberammergau*, 13–14.

68. Greatorex, *Homes of Ober-Ammergau*, 43; Winkler, *Von München nach Oberammergau*, 15, 47–48; Regnet, *Nach Oberammergau*, 1.

69. Swinglehurst, *Romantic Journey*, 150, 175; Jaron and Rudin, *Das Oberammergauer Passionsspiel*, 63; Blackburn, *Art in the Mountains*, 170; Günzler and Zwink, *Berühmtes Dorf*, 3, 91; GAO: AXV/26; AXV/90; ZA/Passionsspiele: *Neue Augsburger Zeitung* (May 18, 1934).

70. GAO: ZA/Passionsspiele: "The Ober Ammergau Passion Play, 1900," *Times* (London) (June 2, 1900): *Springfield Republican* (Sept. 16, 1900); Guido Lang, *Praktischer, Illustrierter Führer* (1900), 11–13; *Lang's Führer* (1910), 119; Huber, Klinner, and Lang, "Die Passionsaufführungen," 171.

71. GAO: ZA/Passionsspiele: *Loisach-Bote* (July 12, 1900; July 17, 1900); "Ein Besucher des Oberammergauer Passionsspieles" (no date or attribution); "Berlin" (Aug. 16, 1900); AXV/42.

72. GAO: AXV/53; Schröder, *Oberammergau* (1910), 105, 109–10.

73. Parks-Richards, *Oberammergau*, 92–93; GAO: ZA/Passionsspiele: Mrs. C. N. Williamson, "The Great Tragedy," *Daily Mail* (London) (May 16, 1900); Edith Milner, letter to the *Times* (London) (Sept. 13, 1909); Schröder, *Oberammergau* (1910), 14, 36–38, 104–105, 116; Diemer, *Oberammergau* (1900), 37; *Lang's Führer* (1910), 1, 119–20; Schumacher, *Meine Oberammergauer*, 78.

74. Jaron and Rudin, *Das Oberammergauer Passionsspiel*, 64, 75–77, 89–90, 93; Huber, Klinner, and Lang, "Die Passionsaufführungen," 172.

75. GAO: AXV/73; AXV/75; AXV/76; Feldigl, *Oberammergau* (1922), 31, 77, 86, 168, 216; Huber, Klinner, and Lang, "Die Passionsaufführungen," 172.

76. GAO: AXV/90; AXV/96; AXV/101; AXV/102; B148, 8, 23, 29–32, 54, 63; *AZ* 24/110 (Sept. 30, 1930), 1; Huber, Klinner, and Lang, "Die Passionsaufführungen," 173–74.

77. GAO: AXV/75; AXV/101; *AZ* 24/87 (Aug. 5, 1930), 1; Günzler and Zwink, *Berühmtes Dorf*, 142–67.

78. Diemer, *Oberammergau* (1922), 30–31, 34–36; Günzler and Zwink, *Berühmtes Dorf*, 123; *AZ* 24/110 (Sept. 30, 1930), 1; Browne, "Where Faith Abides," 263–72.

79. Koonz, *Nazi Conscience*, 166.

80. Harris, *People Speak!* 12, 16–17, 40, 62, 125, 130–37, 214–15, 217–18, 252–57. Harris concludes that the petitions were politically motivated and "anti-Semitic" since "Jews would always be Jews." Predominant were much smaller communities than Oberammergau. While, outside the capital, Upper Bavaria's Jewish population was miniscule in this period, granting them equality could be seen by locals as "infringing on their rural communal rights." Jewish livestock traders did deal with farmers throughout the province's countryside, but the normally despised peddlers were not Jewish. BHStA: Landtag 2656–61: Kammer der Reichs-Raethe. The piles contained in 2659 and 2660 include petitions from the general area, but none is closer than Kohlgrub. Chapters 2, 5, 6, and 7 include discussion of the relationships with Jews mentioned in this paragraph.

81. Günzler and Zwink, *Berühmtes Dorf*, 41–44: Clarus, *Das Passionsspiel zu Ober-Ammergau*, 35, 51; Blackburn, *Art in the Mountains*, 171; Patruban, *Erinnerung*, 9;

Regnet, *Nach Oberammergau*, 86ff; Fuchs, *Oberammergau und sein Passionsspiel*, 32ff, 61–62; von Schaching, *Oberammergau*, 82–86; Cresswell, *Retrospect*, 3.

82. Greatorex, *Homes of Ober-Ammergau*, 2–6, 10, 12–14, 16, 18, 21, 25–27, 29.

83. Schumacher, *Meine Oberammergauer*, 16, 22, 38; Greatorex, *Homes of Ober-Ammergau*, back cover re: Jackson; Günzler and Zwink, *Berühmtes Dorf*, 82–83.

84. Turner, *Ober-Ammergau and Its Passion Play*, 3, 5; Milner, *Oberammergau and Its Passion Play*, foreword, 45.

85. Greatorex, *Homes of Ober-Ammergau*, 25.

86. GAO: 12. 1. 5; Zull, *Ein Museum entsteht*, 52, 58, 60–64; Blackburn, *Art in the Mountains*, 41.

87. GAO AXV/42; Einwohner- u. Hausbesitzerverzeichnis 1900; *AZ* 2/32 (March 21, 1908), 1; 2/33 (March 24, 1908), 1–2.

88. GAO AXV/42; *AZ* 7/36 (April 1, 1913), 1–2; 10/39 (April 4, 1916), 2; 10/59 (May 23, 1916), 3; 10/89 (Aug. 10, 1916), 2; 18/4 (Jan. 16, 1924), 2.

89. *AZ* 2/31 (March 17, 1908), 1–2; 2/8 (Jan. 23, 1908), 2; 7/92 (Aug. 21, 1913), 3; Greatorex, *Homes of Oberammergau*, 24–28, 42; Schumacher, *Meine Oberammergauer*, 19; 102–107, 112–15, 117; *Oberammergauer Wochenprogramm* 1/5 (1938), 7, 9, 10, 13, 14, 15; 2/2 (1939), 4, 5–11; GAO: ZA/Passionsspiele: *Loisach-Bote* (June 12, 1900); Feldigl, *Oberammergau* (1900), 119, 122; MacColl, *Ober-Ammergau Passion Play*, 36; Krause-Lang, *Erinnerungen*, 98; *Festschrift* (1993).

90. Zull, *Ein Museum entsteht*, 67, reproducing "The Passion Play Oberammergau 1910: The Guido Lang House," Munich (1910); *Oberammergau damals and heute*; *AZ* 3/115 (Oct. 21, 1909), 3; 13/14 (March 1, 1919), 1; 14/32 (April 21, 1920), 1; *Lang's Führer* (1900), ad section.

91. *AZ* 12/17 (Jan. 26, 1918), 1; PAO: Pfarrchronik von Oberammergau; GAO: A II/26.

92. Alzheimer, *Einmal Oberammergau und zurück*, 53; Klinner, *Oberammergau*, 54, 87–88; GAO: ZA/Passionsspiele: *Bayerische Nachrichten* (March 13, 1890); articles dated May 1, 1890; May 13, 1890; Dec. 2, 1899; and Feb. 14, 1900; R. Schäfer, "Oberammergau" (1) and (2), *Schwäbischer Merkur* (May 1900); Feldigl, *Oberammergau* (1900), 24; Schröder, *Oberammergau* (1910), 116; Fried, *Führer nach Oberammergau*, vii; Schumacher, *Meine Oberammergauer*, 78; *Lang's Führer* (1900), 29; Parks-Richards, *Oberammergau*, ad section; Florian Lang, Ammergauer Häuser scrapbook.

93. GAO: Einwohner- u. Hausbesitzerverzeichnis 1890, 1900, 1910; *Lang's Führer* (1905), 59, Feldigl, *Oberammergau* (1900), 124, 126, and ad section; Feldigl, *Oberammergau* (1910), 18; *AZ* 1/52 (May 14, 1907), 3–4; 3/140 (Dec. 21, 1909), 3; 7/24 (March 1, 1913), 2; 13/92 (Nov. 29, 1919), 1.

94. Günzler and Zwink, *Berühmtes Dorf*, 92–93, 119–21; Feldigl, *Oberammergau* (1900), 129–30; GAO: Einwohner- u. Hausbesitzerverzeichnis 1910, 1922.

95. Zull, *Ein Museum entsteht*, 61; Alzheimer, *Einmal Oberammergau und zurück*, 53; Klinner, *Oberammergau*, 20; Feldigl, *Oberammergau* (1900), 124; GAO: Einwohner- u. Hausbesitzerverzeichnis 1890, 1900, 1910; ZA/Passionsspiele: *Loisach-Bote* (June 12, 1900); *AZ* 2/60 (May 30, 1908), 4; 3/115 (Oct. 21, 1909), 3; 7/111 (Oct. 4, 1913), 4; 21/15 (Feb. 8, 1927), 1; 23/146 (Dec. 17, 1929), 1.

96. PAO: Schublade 17: Kirchliche Statistik Deutschlands: Königreich-Bayern (1921); Chronik von Oberammergau; GAO: 12. 1. 5; Feldigl, *Oberammergau* (1900), 119; *AZ* 13/75 (Oct. 1, 1919), 1; 24/124 (Nov. 1, 1930), 1.

97. Diemer, *Oberammergau* (1900), 36–37, 115–16; von Schaching, *Oberammergau*, 50.

98. Clarus, *Das Passionsspiel zu Ober-Ammergau*, 89; Parks-Richards, *Oberammergau*, 119–21; Feldigl, *Oberammergau* (1910), 31–33; Schröder, *Oberammergau* (1910), 95, 197.

99. Huber, Klinner, and Lang, "Die Passionsaufführungen," 171–74; Schröder, *Oberammergau* (1910), 95–97; Schumacher, *Meine Oberammergauer*, 121; GAO: ZA/Passionsspiele: *Springfield Republican* (Sept. 16, 1900); Dale, "Impressionist Sketch"; Greatorex, *Homes of Oberammergau*, 26.

100. Eichbaum, *Country Parson*, 46; Bogenrieder, *Oberammergau* (1930), 5; Feldigl, *Oberammergau* (1910), 30–33; Krause-Lang, *Erinnerungen*, 106–107, 112–13; GAO: ZA/Passionsspiele: "Oberammergau Busily Preparing for 'Passion Play' Gala in 1934," *Chicago Daily Tribune* (Sept. 26, 1933).

101. GAO: AXV/90; ZA/Passionsspiele: *Springfield Republican* (Sept. 16, 1900); *Simplicissimus* 5/12 (1900), cover; Krause-Lang, *Erinnerungen*, 83; Feuchtwanger, *Success* also critiques Oberammergau's players.

102. Krause-Lang, *Erinnerungen*, 87–88; Klinner, *Oberammergau*, 80; Parks-Richards, *Oberammergau*, 200–202; *Geschichte und Geschichten*, vol. 2, 41–44; Diemer, *Oberammergau* (1922), 30; "'The Passion': An Oberammergau Chat with Hermine Diemer, née von Hillern," in *Das Passionsdorf Oberammergau*, 19; Kiefer, *Oberammergau and Its Passion Play*, 12; Holmes, *Travelogues*, 141–50; GAO: ZA/Passionsspiele: "Oberammergau: Die Stimmen der Kinder," *Der Spiegel* 29 (July 20, 1950); "Für Erwachsene Verboten," *Revue* 29 (July 22, 1950): 15; Shapiro, *Oberammergau*, 151–52, picks up on an account of one local boy caught up in practicing his part as a Jewish child in the threatening crowd.

103. Parks-Richards, *Oberammergau*, 118; GAO: ZA/Passionsspiele: Gregor Ziemer, "Chosen: Oberammergau Players in the 1934 Jubilee," *Germany and You* 3/4 (Nov. 1933), 10–11, 31.

104. Parks-Richards, *Oberammergau*, 116–23, 128–31; *Geschichte und Geschichten*, 41–44; Clarus, *Das Passionsspiel zu Ober-Ammergau*, 88–89; Diemer, *Oberammergau* (1922), 28–30; Bogenrieder, *Oberammergau* (1930), 29, 65–67, 122–28.

105. Feldigl, *Oberammergau* (1910), 30–33; Krause-Lang, *Erinnerungen*, 98, 125–26.

106. GAO: AX/58; *AZ* 9/95 (Aug. 17, 1915), 2; 9/107 (Sept. 14, 1915), 2; 10/11 (Jan. 29, 1916), 2; 10/57 (May 18, 1916), 3; 12/7 (Jan. 26, 1918), 1; 12/25 (March 30, 1918), 1–2; 12/27 (April 6, 1918), 2; 12/29 (April 13, 1918), 2; 12/31 (April 20, 1918), 1; 13/1 (Jan. 4, 1919), 1; 14/32 (April 21, 1920), 2–3.

107. *AZ* 13/1 (Jan. 4, 1919), 1; 13/2 (Jan. 18, 1919), 1; 13/12 (Feb. 22, 1919), 1–2; 13/15 (March 5, 1919), 1; 13/17 (March 12, 1919), 1; 13/66 (Aug. 30, 1919), 1; 13/78 (Oct. 11, 1919), 1; 13/87 (Nov. 12, 1919), 1; 13/93 (Dec. 6, 1919), 1; 14/15 (Feb. 21, 1920), 1; Feldigl, *Oberammergau* (1922), 184.

108. GAO: AXV/66; AXV/73; BHStA: MInn 72741; MA 102136; StAM: LRA 107021; *AZ* 16/23 (March 22, 1922), 1; 16/52 (July 1, 1922), 1; Feldigl, *Oberammergau* (1922), 31, 102.

109. GAO: AXV/76; Feldigl, *Oberammergau* (1922), 82–83; Huber, Klinner, and Lang, "Die Passionsaufführungen," 172.

110. Bogenrieder, *Oberammergau* (1930), 111; StAM: LRA 107020 and 107021; *AZ* 16/82 (Oct. 14, 1922), 1; 17/13 (Feb. 14, 1923), 3; 17/25 (March 28, 1923), 4; 17/61 (Aug. 1, 1923), 1; 17/70 (Sept. 15, 1923), 3; 17/74 (Oct. 6, 1923), 3; 17/76 (Oct. 13, 1923), 1, 4; 17/77 (Oct. 17, 1923), 1; 17/83 (Nov. 7, 1923), 2; 17/88 (Nov. 24, 1923), 4.

111. BHStA: MA 100224; MA 102136; *AZ* 17/9 (Jan. 31, 1923), 2; 17/10 (Feb. 3, 1923), 2; 17/32 (April 21, 1923), 2; 17/74 (Oct. 6, 1923), 1–2; 17/82 (Nov. 3, 1923), 1; 17/83 (Nov. 7, 1923), 1–2; 17/88 (Nov. 24, 1923), 1–2; 18/2 (Jan. 9, 1924), 1–2, quoting "Passionsspieler aus Oberammergau hier," *Newyorker Statszeitung*; 18/3 (Jan. 12, 1924), 1–2; 18/4 (Jan. 16, 1924), 1; 18/42 (May 28, 1924), 1; 18/44 (June 4, 1924), 1–2; 18/54 (July 9, 1924), 2; Swift, *Passion Play of Oberammergau*, 142–55.

112. *AZ* 18/57 (July 19, 1924), 2; 19/66 (June 13, 1925), 1; 19/73 (July 2, 1925), 1; 20/135 (Nov. 23, 1926), 1; 21/149 (Dec. 31, 1927), 1; 23/66 (June 11, 1929), 1; Bogenrieder, *Oberammergau* (1930), 24, 34.

113. Bogenrieder, *Oberammergau* (1930), 25, 53–54; Feldigl, *Oberammergau* (1922), 194; *AZ* passim from 18/4 (Jan. 16, 1924), 2, to 26/52 (May 7, 1932), 2; GAO: Einwohner- u. Hausbesitzerverzeichnis 1922, 1930; AX/73, especially Carl Bauer, *Der Fremdenverkehr in Oberammergau und die Passionsspiele 1940: Betrachtungen und Vorschläge* (Nov. 1938), 2; *Festschrift* (1993), 12, 14, 27–28.

114. *AZ* 13/57 (July 30, 1919), 1; 14/41 (May 22, 1920), 1; 18/49 (June 21, 1924), 4; 18/79 (Oct. 4, 1924), 3; 19/48 (April 30, 1925), 1; 19/64 (June 9, 1925), 1; GAO: Einwohner- u. Hausbesitzerverzeichnis 1910, 1922, 1930; Bogenrieder, *Oberammergau* (1930), 26–28.

115. *AZ* 22/20 (Feb. 18, 1928), 1–2; GAO: Einwohner- u. Hausbesitzerverzeichnis 1873, 1890, 1900, 1910, 1922, 1930; Bogenrieder, *Oberammergau* (1930), 28.

116. Feldigl, *Oberammergau* (1922), 166, 172; Bogenrieder, *Oberammergau* (1930), 34–35; *AZ* 16/35 (May 3, 1922), 1; 22/91 (Aug. 11, 1928), 1; 23/146 (Dec. 17, 1929), 1; GAO: Einwohner- u. Hausbesitzerverzeichnis, 1934, 1939.

117. *AZ* 22/90 (Aug. 9, 1928), 4; 22/91 (Aug. 11, 1928), 1; 22/127 (Nov. 6, 1928), 1; 22/148 (Dec. 25, 1928), 1; 23/57 (May 16, 1929), 1; 23/66 (June 11, 1929), 1; 23/78 (July 9, 1929), 1; 23/81 (July 16, 1929), 3; 23/118 (Oct. 12, 1929), 1; 23/124 (Oct. 26, 1929), 1; 23/147 (Dec. 19, 1929), 1; Bogenrieder, *Oberammergau* (1930), 111–13.

118. StAM: LRA61609; *AZ* 22/86 (July 31, 1928), 1; 23/101 (Sept. 3, 1929), 1; 24/110 (Sept. 30, 1930), 1; 25/13 (Jan. 31, 1931); Huber, Klinner, and Lang, "Die Passionsaufführungen," 174; GAO: AXV/101; AXV/102.

CHAPTER 2

1. Greatorex, *Homes of Ober-Ammergau*, 42–43; Daisenberger, *Geschichte* (1859), 178–79.

2. *AZ* 24/68 (June 21, 1930), 1.

3. Thränhardt, *Wahlen*, 94; Daisenberger, *Geschichte* (1859), 50, 130, 174; Spindler, *Handbuch*, vol. 4, 69–71, 79–84, 230, 318–21.

4. *AZ* 12/23 (March 23, 1918), 1–2; Rädlinger, *Zwischen Tradition und Fortschritt*, 3–4, 345; Feldigl, *Oberammergau* (1900), 125; Parks-Richards, *Oberammergau*, 79–80.

5. Huber, Klinner, and Lang, "Die Passionsaufführungen," 168–72.

6. Molloy, *Passion Play at Ober-Ammergau*, 17; Daisenberger, *Geschichte* (1859), 61, 173; Daisenberger, *Historisch-topographische Beschreibung*, 28; *AZ* 2/33 (March 24, 1908), 1–2; 2/47 (April 28, 1908), 2; 3/68 (July 1, 1909), 2; 30/140 (Nov. 24, 1936), 1; Klinner, *Oberammergau*, 46–47, 51; GAO: A111/15; Friedl Lang, *180 Jahre Musikleben in Oberammergau*.

7. PAO: Chronik von Oberammergau. It is not clear whether the use of the label "liberal" in local documents refers to representation by the National Liberal or the Progressive party in the period 1871–1914.

8. PAO: Chronik von Oberammergau.

9. *AZ* 1/29 (March 14, 1907), 2; 1/33 (March 26, 1907), 3; 2/30 (March 14, 1908), 2–3; 2/112 (Oct. 10, 1908), 2; 7/2 (Jan. 9, 1913), 2.

10. PAO: Chronik von Oberammergau; *AZ* 1/7 (Jan. 17, 1907), 2, 4; 1/8 (Jan. 19, 1907), 4; 1/9 (Jan. 22, 1907), 2; 1/10 (Jan. 24, 1907), 1; 1/11 (Jan. 26, 1907), 2; 1/13 (Jan. 31, 1907), 2; 1/18 (Feb. 16, 1907), 1; 1/21 (Feb. 23, 1907), 2; 1/34 (March 28, 1907), 1; 2/24 (Feb. 29, 1908), 1–2.

11. PAO: Chronik von Oberammergau; *AZ* 1/42 (April 18, 1907), 1; 1/57 (May 29, 1907), 4, 5, 8; 1/58 (June 1, 1907), 3; 1/141 (Dec. 19, 1907), 3; 1/143 (Dec. 24, 1907), 1–2.

12. *AZ* 1/141 (Dec. 19, 1907), 3; 1/142 (Dec. 21, 1907), 1–2; 1/143 (Dec. 24, 1907), 1–2; 2/24 (Feb. 29, 1908), 1–2; 7/79 (July 19, 1913), 3; GAO: ZA/Passionsspiele: "Die Vorbereitungen zum Oberammergauer Passionsspiel im Jahre 1910," *Münchner Neueste Nachrichten* (Nov. 8, 1907); PAO: Chronik von Oberammergau; Spindler, *Handbuch*, vol. 4, 320–21; GAO: A134/1.

13. *AZ* 13/55 (July 23, 1919), 4; GAO: AXV/42.

14. *AZ* 3/12 (Feb. 4, 1909), 2–3; 8/105 (Sept. 17, 1914), 2; 9/6 (Jan. 16, 1915), 3.

15. Edwards, *Matriarch*, 269–70.

16. *AZ* passim; Günzler and Zwink, *Berühmtes Dorf*, 125–34.

17. *AZ* 8/10 (Sept. 17, 1914), 2; 8/117 (Oct. 15, 1914), 3; 9/6 (Jan. 16, 1915), 3; 11/3 (Jan. 13, 1917), 3; 12/7 (Jan. 26, 1918), 1; 13/1 (Jan. 4, 1919), 1.

18. *AZ* passim and 10/89 (Aug. 10, 1916), 3; 11/88 (July 11, 1917), 2; 12/32 (April 24, 1918), 2; 13/1 (Jan. 4, 1919), 1; 13/7 (Feb. 5, 1919), 4; 14/14 (Feb. 17, 1920), 1; 14/15 (Feb. 21, 1920), 1; 31/151 (Dec. 18, 1937), 7; *WA* 26/85 (Oct. 23, 1918), 2.

19. *AZ* 10/89 (Aug. 10, 1916), 3; 11/88 (July 11, 1917), 2; 12/32 (April 24, 1918), 2; 13/1 (Jan. 4, 1919), 1; 13/7 (Feb. 5, 1919), 4; 14/14 (Feb. 17, 1920), 1; 14/15 (Feb. 21, 1920), 1; 31/151 (Dec. 18, 1937), 7; *WA* 26/85 (Oct. 23, 1918), 2; *Stead's Guide*, 53–54; GAO: ZA/Passionsspiele: Kees van Hoek, "Oberammergau: The World's Greatest Drama," *European Herald* 2/31 (June 1, 1934), 2.

20. Diemer, *Oberammergau* (1922), 28; GAO: ZA/Passionsspiele: *Detroit News* (Oct. 16, 1921), 9; AXV/75: especially Citizens of Oberammergau, *Origin of the Passion Plays* (1922), 1; *AZ* 13/70 (Sept. 14, 1919), 1; Friedel, *Süddeutsche Freiheit*, illustration #30, Heinrich Campendonck, *Hirte mit Verdienstkreuz* (1920).

21. *AZ* passim from 8/117 (Oct. 15, 1914), 3, to 12/24 (March 28, 1918), 2; *WA* 26/87 (Oct. 30, 1918), 2.

22. *AZ* 10/14 (Feb. 5, 1916), 2; 11/26 (April 4, 1917), 3; 11/75 (Sept. 22, 1917), 4; 12/23 (March 23, 1918), 3; 12/24 (March 28, 1918), 2.

23. *WA* 26/91 (Nov. 13, 1918), 1–2.

24. *WA* 26/91 (Nov. 13, 1918), 1–2; 26/92 (Nov. 16, 1918), 1, 6; 26/93 (Nov. 20, 1918), 1–4; 26/94 (Nov. 23, 1918), 1; 26/95 (Nov. 26, 1918), 1–2; Ostler, *Revolutionszeit 1918/19*, 40; *München*, 31, 39–40.

25. Ostler, *Revolutionszeit 1918/19*, 40–46, 51, 53, quoting StAM: LRA 131582; *WA* 26/92 (Nov. 16, 1918), 1, 6; 26/93 (Nov. 20, 1918), 1–4; 26/94 (Nov. 23, 1918), 1–2; 26/95 (Nov. 26, 1918), 1–2; 26/103 (Dec. 25, 1918), 2; 27/8 (Jan. 25, 1919), 1; 27/24 (March 22, 1919), 1–3; *AZ* 13/21 (March 26, 1919), 1; 13/44 (June 14, 1919), 1–4.

26. GAO: AII/49; Ostler, *Revolutionszeit 1918/19*, xiii, list on Dec. 8, 1918; *WA* 26/103 (Dec. 25, 1918), 2; 27/8 (Jan. 25, 1919), 1; *AZ* 13/6 (Feb. 1, 1919), 1.

27. *AZ* 13/6 (Feb. 1, 1919), 1; 13/9 (Feb. 12, 1919), 4; 13/15 (March 5, 1919), 1; 13/19 (March 19, 1919), 1; 13/20 (March 22, 1919), 1, 4.

28. *WA* 26/93 (Nov. 20, 1918), 2–3; 26/96 (Nov. 30, 1918), 8; 26/98 (Dec. 7, 1918), 3; 26/100 (Dec. 14, 1918), 2; 26/101 (Dec. 18, 1918), 2.

29. Ostler, *Revolutionszeit 1918/19*, 40–42; *WA* 26/100 (Dec. 14, 1918), 8; 26/101 (Dec. 18, 1918), 6; 26/103 (Dec. 25, 1918), 1–2; 27/5 (Jan. 15, 1919), 1–2, 6; 27/6 (Jan. 18, 1919), 8; *AZ* 13/1 (Jan. 4, 1919), 1; 13/9 (Feb. 12, 1919), 4.

30. *AZ* 13/1 (Jan. 4, 1919), 1; 13/3 (Jan. 22, 1919), 1; 13/9 (Feb. 12, 1919), 1; *WA* 27/5 (Jan. 15, 1919), 1, 6; 27/6 (Jan. 18, 1919), 8.

31. *AZ* 13/1 (Jan. 4, 1919), 1; 13/2 (Jan. 18, 1919), 1–2; 13/3 (Jan. 22, 1919), 1, 4; 13/9 (Feb. 12, 1919), 1; 13/14 (March 1, 1919), 1, 4.

32. *AZ* 13/2 (Jan. 18, 1919), 2; 13/3 (Jan. 22, 1919), 1; 13/12 (Feb. 22, 1919), 1–2; 13/13 (Feb. 26, 1919), 2; 13/14 (March 1, 1919), 1; 13/15 (March 5, 1919), 1; 13/17 (March 12, 1919), 1.

33. *München*, 34, 42–44.

34. *WA* 27/28 (April 5, 1919), 3; 27/29 (April 9, 1919), 2–3.

35. Ostler, *Revolutionszeit 1918/19*, 67–70, 82, including Mürboch letter dated April 18, 1919, in StAM: StAnw. Mü I, 2134; *WA* 27/30 (April 12, 1919), 1–2; 27/31 (April 16, 1919), 1–2.

36. *WA* 27/33 (April 23, 1919), 1–4; GAO: AIV/51.

37. *WA* 27/33 (April 23, 1919), 1–4; *WA* 27/34 (April 26, 1919), 1–4; Ostler, *Revolutionszeit 1918/19*, 72–82, including the quotation from Wilhelm Röhrl, account in Archiv Peter Adam, Garmisch-Partenkirchen, 1939.

38. *WA* 27/34 (April 26, 1919), 2; 27/35 (April 30, 1919), 1–2; 27/38 (May 10, 1919), 2–3; Ostler, *Revolutionszeit 1918/19*, 92–98.

39. *WA* 27/35 (April 30, 1919), 1–2; 27/36 (May 3, 1919), 1; 27/38 (May 10, 1919), 3; GAO: AXIV/51.

40. Ostler, *Revolutionszeit 1918/19*, 103, 123–27, 134–62; *München*, 35, 45; *WA* 27/35 (April 30, 1919), 1–3; 27/36 (May 3, 1919), 1–6; 27/37 (May 7, 1919), 1–3; 27/38

(May 10, 1919), 1–3. Evans, *Coming of the Third Reich*, illustration #7, shows the brutal handling of a "Red Guardist" by members of the Free Corps.

41. Ostler, *Revolutionszeit 1918/19*, 144, 162–63; *München*, 45; *WA* 27/36 (May 3, 1919), 1–6; 27/37 (May 7, 1919), 1–3; 27/38 (May 10, 1919), 1–2; 27/39 (May 14, 1919), 1–2; Florian Lang scrapbook.

42. *WA* 27/45 (June 4, 1919), 1; *AZ* 13/22 (March 29, 1919), 1; 13/44 (June 14, 1919), 1.

43. *AZ* 13/40 (May 31, 1919), 1; 13/44 (June 14, 1919), 1, 4; 13/46 (June 21, 1919), 1–3; *WA* 27/50 (June 21, 1919), 3; PAO: Chronik von Oberammergau.

44. GAO: AXIV/51; *WA* 27/50 (June 21, 1919), 3; *AZ* 13/63 (Aug. 20, 1919), 1; 13/70 (Sept. 14, 1919), 1; 13/73 (Sept. 24, 1919), 4; 13/76 (Oct. 4, 1919), 1; 13/77 (Oct. 8, 1919), 4; 14/71 (Sept. 8, 1920), 1.

45. Ostler, *Revolutionszeit 1918/19*, 71–72, 102, 106–109, quoting *WA* 27 (October 25, 1919); *München*, 48–49; *AZ* 13/97 (Dec. 17, 1919), 1; 14/31 (April 17, 1920), 3; 14/64 (Aug. 14, 1920), 1.

46. *AZ* passim and 13/74 (Sept. 27, 1919), 1; 13/78 (Oct. 11, 1919), 1; 13/93 (Dec. 6, 1919), 1; 13/95 (Dec. 10, 1919), 1.

47. GAO: AXIV/51; *München*, 106.

48. Ostler, *Revolutionszeit 1918/19*, 164–65; *AZ* 14/38 (May 12, 1920), 1; 14/39 (May 15, 1924), 1; 14/44 (June 2, 1920), 1.

49. *AZ* 14/45 (June 5, 1920), 2; 14/46 (June 9, 1920), 1; PAO: Schublade 17: Kirchliche Statistik Deutschlands über das Jahr 1916 through 1920.

50. *G-PT* 63/196 (Aug. 5, 1943), 3: StAM: RA 57820; SpkA K4271; LRA 198994; *München*, 58–59; *AZ* 15/25 (March 30, 1921), 1; 16/63 (Aug. 9, 1922), 1; BHStA: MA 102136.

51. *AZ* 16/15 (Feb. 22, 1922), 1; 16/19 (March 8, 1922), 1; 17/38 (May 12, 1923), 2; 17/49 (June 20, 1923), 2, 4; 17/62 (Aug. 4, 1923), 1; 17/64 (Aug. 11, 1923), 4; 17/66 (Aug. 18, 1923), 7; 17/69 (Sept. 8, 1923), 3; *G-PT* 58/217 (Sept. 17, 1938), 3; Central File.

52. StAM: LRA 105874; *AZ* 17/10 (Feb. 3, 1923), 4; 17/11 (Feb. 7, 1923), 1, 4–5; 17/12 (Feb. 10, 1923), 2; 17/13 (Feb. 14, 1923), 1, 3; 17/14 (Feb. 17, 1923), 4; 17/15 (Feb. 21, 1923), 2; 17/16 (Feb. 24, 1923), 1; 17/27 (April 4, 1923), 1; 17/30 (April 14, 1923), 2; 17/32 (April 21, 1923), 1.

53. *AZ* 17/42 (May 26, 1923), 1; 17/43 (May 30, 1923), 2; BHStA: MA 102126.

54. *WA* 31/74 (Sept. 15, 1923), 2; 31/91 (Nov. 14, 1923), 3; BHStA: MA 102126; MA 102136; *München*, 112. Hastings, "How 'Catholic' Was the Early Nazi Movement?" 11–13, discusses the Catholic ties that made Schlageter "the harmonious physical embodiment of a heroic Catholic-Nazi synthesis." Hastings stresses "the Catholic memorial mass" that accompanied a huge gathering honoring the dead martyr in June 1923.

55. *AZ* 17/84 (Nov. 10, 1923), 1–2; 17/85 (Nov. 14, 1923), 1–3; 29/21 (Feb. 19, 1935), 1.

56. *AZ* 17/82 (Nov. 3, 1923), 1; 17/83 (Nov. 7, 1923), 1–2; 17/90 (Nov. 30, 1923), 1; 18/3 (Jan. 12, 1924), 1–2; 18/45 (June 7, 1924), 1–2; 18/63 (Aug. 9, 1924), 1; *WA* 34/18 (April 30, 1924), 2; BHStA: MA 102126.

57. *AZ* 18/36 (May 7, 1924), 3; 18/98 (Dec. 10, 1924), 3; 19/47 (April 28, 1925), 1; Childers, *Nazi Voter*, 125–27, discusses this fragmentation, which set up "the spectacular rise of National Socialist fortunes."

58. *AZ* passim; 19/96 (Aug. 25, 1925), 1.

59. *AZ* 19/105 (Sept. 15, 1925), 1; 19/114 (Oct. 6, 1925), 1–2; 19/130 (Nov. 12, 1925), 4.

60. *AZ* 20/27 (March 6, 1926), 1; 20/28 (March 9, 1926), 1; 20/33 (March 20, 1926), 1; 20/66 (June 10, 1926), 1; 20/67 (June 12, 1926), 1; 20/71 (June 22, 1926), 1.

61. *AZ* 22/57 (May 19, 1928), 1, 4; 22/58 (May 22, 1928), 1; StAM: LRA 61609.

62. *AZ* 18/93 (Nov. 22, 1924), 1; 18/95 (Nov. 29, 1924), 1; 18/96 (Dec. 3, 1924), 1; 18/97 (Dec. 6, 1924), 4; 18/98 (Dec. 10, 1924), 1; 18/100 (Dec. 17, 1924), 1; 19/55 (May 16, 1925), 1; 21/130 (Nov. 15, 1927), 1; PAO: Chronik von Oberammergau.

63. *AZ* 18/96 (Dec. 3, 1924), 1; 22/30 (March 13, 1928), 1; 22/33 (March 22, 1928), 1; 22/35 (March 27, 1928), 1; 23/144 (Dec. 12, 1929), 1; GAO: A041/1.

64. *AZ* 10/49 (April 29, 1916), 2; 13/5 (Jan. 29, 1919), 1; 13/22 (March 29, 1919), 1; 13/44 (June 14, 1919), 1, 4; 13/46 (June 21, 1919), 1; 16/3 (Jan. 11, 1922), 1; 18/91 (Nov. 15, 1924), 1; 18/93 (Nov. 22, 1924), 1; 18/98 (Dec. 10, 1924), 1; 24/13 (Feb. 4, 1930), 1; GAO: AXV/87.

65. PAO: Chronik von Oberammergau; GAO: AXV/87; *AZ* 22/27 (March 6, 1928), 1; 22/33 (March 22, 1928), 1; 22/35 (March 27, 1928), 1; 24/13 (Feb. 4, 1930), 1; BHStA: MA 102137.

66. Friedrich Arnold, *Anschläge* (Ebenhausen: Langewiesche-Brandt, 1972), no. 56, in Orlow, *History of Modern Germany*, 173.

67. *AZ* 24/103 (Sept. 13, 1930), 1, 2; 24/104 (Sept. 16, 1930), 1; StAM: LRA 61610.

68. *AZ* 23/83 (July 20, 1929), 4, and passim to the end of the 1930 season in September; 24/51 (May 8, 1930), 4; Bogenrieder, *Oberammergau* (1930), 21.

69. *AZ* 23/83 (July 20, 1929), 4, and passim to the end of the 1930 season in September.

70. *AZ* 24/73 (July 3, 1930), 1; StAM: LRA 107021.

71. *AZ* 19/105 (Sept. 15, 1925), 1; 24/17 (Feb. 13, 1929), 1.

72. BHStA: MA102138; StAM: LRA 61784; LRA 107021; *AZ* 23/69 (June 18, 1929), 2; 24/49 (May 3, 1930), 4; 24/57 (May 22, 1930), 4; 24/82 (July 22, 1930), 1; Bogenrieder, *Oberammergau* (1930), 110; GAO: AXV/76.

CHAPTER 3

1. Fritzsche, *Germans into Nazis*, 1, 3–9, reproduces the photograph and comments on the significance of this "precise moment when the Third Reich became possible."

2. *München*, 157.

3. Ibid., 157–65.

4. Ibid., 162, 174–76; Kershaw, *Hitler*, vol. 1, 293, 300–303.

5. *München*, front cover and 335.

6. Ibid., 334–37.

7. *G-PT* 58/217 (Sept. 17, 1938), 3; 59/114 (May 19, 1939), insert; BHStA: MA102136; Pol Dir, München 6831.

8. BHStA: MA 102136; MA 102137; StAM: LRA 61610.

9. *AZ* 18/35 (May 3, 1924), 2; 18/36 (May 7, 1924), 3; *WA* 34/18 (April 30, 1924), 4.

10. *AZ* 18/98 (Dec. 10, 1924), 3.

11. StAM: LRA 61609; *G-PT* 59/114 (May 19, 1939), insert; *AZ* 22/58 (May 22, 1928), 1.

12. *AZ* 22/57 (May 19, 1928), 1, 4; 22/58 (May 23, 1928), 1.

13. *AZ* 22/57 (May 19, 1928), 1; 22/58 (May 23, 1928), 1.

14. *G-PT* 58/206 (Sept. 5, 1938), 3, 7; 59/114 (May 19, 1939), insert; 63/126 (June 1, 1943), 3; StAM: LRA 61609; LRA 61610; BHStA: MA 102137; MInn 81582.

15. StAM: LRA 61609; LRA 61610; *G-PT* 63/126 (June 1, 1943), 3.

16. StAM: LRA 61609; *AZ* 23/27 (March 2, 1929), 4; 23/66 (June 11, 1929), 1; 23/84 (July 23, 1929), 1; 32/30 (March 11–12, 1938), 2; Kershaw, *Hitler*, vol. 1, 310; GAO: AII/26.

17. *AZ* 19/73 (July 2, 1925), 1; 24/123 (Oct. 28, 1930), 3; 25/15 (Feb. 5, 1931), 2; 32/30 (March 11–12, 1938), 2; GAO: AII/26; AXV/102; 12. 1. 5; Einwohnermeldeamt, Oberammergau; BHStA: MInn 72741; Central File.

18. Central File; Einwohnermeldeamt, Oberammergau; *AZ* 27/42 (April 8, 1933), 3; 27/47 (April 22, 1933), 3; 29/21 (Feb. 19, 1935), 1; GAO: AII/26; AXV/147; 12. 1. 5.

19. Central File; GAO: AII/26; 12. 1. 5; Einwohner- u. Hausbesitzerverzeichnis 1910; *G-PT* 63/196 (Aug. 5, 1943), 3.

20. GAO: AII/26; AXV/102; 12. 1. 5.

21. *Festschrift* (1993), 9, 14, 15, 22, 23, 61; *AZ* 14/77 (Sept. 28, 1920), 1; 15/46 (June 11, 1921), 1; 17/59 (July 25, 1923), 1; 20/23 (Feb. 25, 1926), 1; 20/36 (March 27, 1926), 1; 20/63 (June 3, 1926), 4; 27/146 (Dec. 12, 1933), 1; Central File.

22. StAM: LRA 61609; *AZ* 23/125 (Oct. 29, 1929), 1.

23. GAO: AXV/147; AII/26; Central File; Schelle, *Chronik eines Bauernlebens*, 13; *AZ* 23/124 (Oct. 26, 1929), 1.

24. Central File; *DF* 3/27 (April 12, 1932), 7; StAM: Pol. Dir. 6805; LRA 107051.

25. Central File; GAO: AII/26; 12. 1. 5; Einwohner-u. Hausbesitzerverzeichnis 1900, 1910; *AZ* 2/24 (Feb. 29, 1908), 1–2; 20/23 (Feb. 25, 1926), 1; 20/36 (March 27, 1926), 1; Feldigl, *Oberammergau* (1910), 37, ad section; Guido Lang, *Lang's Illustrated Practical Guide*, 29.

26. *AZ* 24/24 (March 1, 1930), 4, 6.

27. Ibid., 4; 24/25 (March 4, 1930), 3; 24/28 (March 11, 1930), 1.

28. Utzschneider, *Oberammergau im Dritten Reich*, 24; *AZ* 24/38 (April 5, 1930), 1; BHStA: MInn 81583, including *Völkischer Beobachter* 91/92 (April 18/19, 1930), 3; StAM: LRA 61610.

29. BHStA: MInn 81583; Utzschneider, *Oberammergau im Dritten Reich*, 24; GAO: A134/1; *AZ* 24/104 (Sept. 16, 1930), 1; StAM: LRA 61610.

30. *AZ* 23/86 (July 27, 1929), 1; 23/105 (Sept. 12, 1929), 1; 24/47 (April 29, 1930), 1; 24/55 (May 17, 1930), 1.

31. *AZ* 22/30 (Feb. 13, 1928), 1; 23/42 (April 9, 1929), 1; 23/66 (June 11, 1929), 1; 23/73 (June 27, 1929), 1; 23/114 (Oct. 3, 1929), 1; 23/137 (Nov. 26, 1929), 1; 24/14 (Feb. 6, 1930), 1; 24/15 (Feb. 8, 1930), 1; 24/17 (Feb. 13, 1930), 1; 24/46 (April 26, 1930), 1; PAO: Pfarrchronik von Oberammergau.

32. *AZ* 24/44 (April 19, 1930), 5; 24/58 (May 24, 1930), 5; 24/59 (May 27. 1930), 4; 24/68 (June 21, 1930), 1; 24/82 (July 22, 1930), 2–3; 24/99 (Sept. 4, 1930), 1; 25/65 (June 6, 1931), 1.

33. *AZ* 24/110 (Sept. 30, 1930), 1; BHStA: MInn 81585.

34. *AZ* 24/103 (Sept. 13, 1930), 1; 24/104 (Sept. 16, 1930), 1.

35. The number of potential voters soared from 1,440 for the local election to 2,763. *AZ* 22/58 (May 22, 1928), 1; 24/13 (Feb. 4, 1930), 1; 24/104 (Sept. 16, 1930), 1.

36. *AZ* passim 1929–1930; 24/104 (Sept. 16, 1930), 1; 26/87 (Aug. 2, 1932), 3; StAM: LRA 61609.

37. *Passion-Play at Oberammergau* (1930), 7–8.

38. Allen, *Nazi Seizure of Power*, 32–33; Central File; BHStA: MInn 72741; *AZ* 19/30 (March 14, 1925), 1; 22/35 (March 27, 1928), 1; 23/123 (Oct. 24, 1929), 1; *G-PT* 59/51 (March 1, 1939), 2; 59/69 (March 22, 1939), 7; GAO: AII/26; AXV/87; 12. 1. 5.

39. *AZ* 24/113 (Oct. 7, 1930), 1; 24/123 (Oct. 28, 1930), 3; 24/127 (Nov. 8, 1930), 5; 24/128 (Nov. 11, 1930), 1; 24/129 (Nov. 13, 1930), 4; 24/143 (Dec. 18, 1930), 4; 25/5 (Jan. 13, 1931), 4; 25/6 (Jan. 15, 1931), 4; *DF* 2/3 (Feb. 1, 1931), 3.

40. *DF* 2/8 (July 18, 1931), 6; *AZ* 25/61 (May 28, 1931), 4; 25/79 (July 11, 1931), 4.

41. Central File; GAO: 12. 1. 5; *AZ* 22/61 (May 31, 1928), 4; 24/123 (Oct. 28, 1930), 3; 24/124 (Nov. 1, 1930), 5; 24/127 (Nov. 8, 1930), 4; 25/15 (Feb. 5, 1931), 2; 25/16 (Feb. 7, 1931), 1; 26/60 (May 28, 1932), 1–2; 26/61 (May 31, 1932), 1, 4; 26/62 (June 2, 1932), 3; 27/28 (March 7, 1933), 4; 27/30 (March 11, 1933), 4; 27/71 (June 20, 1933), 1; 31/96 (Aug. 12, 1937), 3.

42. Central File; StAM: SpkA K4240; LRA 107021; GAO: AII/26; 12. 1. 5; *AZ* 17/92 (Dec. 8, 1923), 4; 17/93 (Dec. 12, 1923), 2; 20/35 (March 25, 1926), 1; 24/44 (April 19, 1930), 1; 24/78 (July 15, 1930), 1; 24/118 (Oct. 18, 1930), 1; 25/98 (Aug. 25, 1931), 4; 27/28 (March 7, 1933), 4; 27/30 (March 11, 1933), 4; 27/71 (June 20, 1933), 1; 32/30 (March 11/12, 1938), 2. It is possible that a few members from surrounding communities were included in the forty-eight.

43. Central File; GAO: 12. 1. 5; AXV/147; *AZ* 25/119 (Oct. 13, 1931), 3; 25/131 (Nov. 10, 1931), 4; 25/134 (Nov. 17, 1931), 1; 25/136 (Nov. 21, 1931), 1.

44. Central File; *AZ* 10/89 (Aug. 10, 1916), 3; 25/119 (Oct. 13, 1931), 1; 25/134 (Nov. 17, 1931), 1; 25/136 (Nov. 21, 1931), 1; GAO: 12. 1. 5; AXV/102; Einwohner- u. Hausbesitzerverzeichnis 1890, 1900, 1910, 1922, 1930; *Passion-Play at Oberammergau* (1930), 7–8. More than a dozen migrants also joined from December 1931 to April 1932.

45. GAO: AXV/102; StAM: LRA 61610; *AZ* 24/118 (Oct. 18, 1930), 1; 25/2 (Jan. 6, 1931), 1; 25/94 (Aug. 15, 1931), 1; 25/98 (Aug. 25, 1931), 4; 25/105 (Sept. 10, 1931), 1; 25/107 (Sept. 15, 1931), 1.

46. *AZ* 25/27 (March 5, 1931), 1; 25/87 (July 30, 1931), 4; 25/92 (Aug. 11, 1931), 1; 25/93 (Aug. 13, 1931), 1; 25/97 (Aug. 22, 1931), 1; 25/105 (Sept. 10, 1931), 1; 25/124 (Sept. 24, 1931), 1.

47. GAO: Gem. Prot. v. Jan. 4, 1932, on, especially March 16, 1932, and Oct. 31, 1932; *AZ* 25/12 (Jan. 29, 1931), 1, 4; 25/94 (Aug. 15, 1931), 1; 25/98 (Aug. 25, 1931), 4; 25/105 (Sept. 10, 1931), 1; 25/107 (Sept. 15, 1931), 1; 25/108 (Sept. 17, 1931), 1; 25/111 (Sept. 24, 1931), 4; 25/136 (Nov. 21, 1931), 1, 4; 25/150 (Dec. 24, 1931), 1.

48. *AZ* 24/138 (Dec. 4, 1930), 3; 25/8 (Jan. 20, 1931), 1; 25/71 (June 20, 1931), 1; 25/100 (Aug. 29, 1931), 1; 25/139 (Nov. 28, 1931), 1–2; 26/85 (July 28, 1932), 1; GAO: Gem. Prot. in 1932, especially Feb. 16, 1932; March 16, 1932; and March 21, 1932.

49. *AZ* 25/42 (April 11, 1931), 1; 25/145 (Dec. 12, 1931), 1; 25/146 (Dec. 15, 1931), 1; 25/148 (Dec. 19, 1931), 1; 25/150 (Dec. 24, 1931), 1; 26/5 (Jan. 16, 1932), 2; 26/10 (Jan. 28, 1932), 3; 26/13 (Feb. 6, 1932), 3; 26/37 (April 2, 1932), 4; 26/69 (June 18, 1932), 2.

50. *AZ* 25/25 (Feb. 28, 1931), 1; 25/34 (March 21, 1931), 1; 25/71 (June 20, 1931), 1; 26/20 (Feb. 20, 1932), 3.

51. *AZ* 25/6 (Jan. 15, 1931), 1, 4; 25/43 (April 14, 1931), 1; 25/97 (Aug. 22, 1931), 1; 25/121 (Oct. 17, 1931), 3; 25/142 (Dec. 5., 1931), 3.

52. StAM: LRA 61610; LRA 107045; LRA 107046; *AZ* 25/129 (Nov. 5, 1931), 4; 25/131 (Nov. 10, 1931), 4; 25/133 (Nov. 14, 1931), 1; 25/134 (Nov. 17, 1931), 1.

53. *AZ* 25/129 (Nov. 5, 1931), 4; 25/131 (Nov. 10, 1931), 4; 25/133 (Nov. 14, 1931), 1; 25/134 (Nov. 17, 1931), 1; StAM: LRA 107045. Pamphlets seized in Garmisch County in September 1931 included one laying out the twenty-five points.

54. *DF* 2/17 (Nov. 21, 1931), 4; *AZ* 25/134 (Nov. 17, 1931), 1.

55. *DF* 2/17 (Nov. 21, 1931), 4; *AZ* 25/134 (Nov. 17, 1931), 1.

56. *AZ* 25/135 (Nov. 19, 1931), 1; 25/136 (Nov. 21, 1931), 1.

57. *AZ* 25/140 (Dec. 1, 1931), 4; 25/143 (Dec. 8, 1931), 4.

58. *AZ* 25/140 (Dec. 1, 1931), 4; 25/143 (Dec. 8, 1931), 4; 25/145 (Dec. 12, 1931), 1; 26/27 (March 8, 1932), 3; StAM: LRA 107045.

59. *AZ* 25/139 (Nov. 28, 1931), 1–2; 25/140 (Dec. 1, 1931), 1.

60. *AZ* 26/28 (March 10, 1932), 4; 26/29 (March 12, 1932), 2; StAM: LRA 107048; LRA 107050.

61. *AZ* 26/24 (March 1, 1932), 4; 26/27 (March 8, 1932), 3; StAM: LRA 107045; LRA 107046; LRA 107048; LRA 107049; LRA 107051.

62. *AZ* 26/28 (March 10, 1932), 4; 26/29 (March 12, 1932), 2; 26/30 (March 15, 1932), 1, 4.

63. *AZ* 26/29 (March 12, 1932), 3.

64. *AZ* 26/31 (March 17, 1932), 3.

65. Ibid.; 26/32 (March 19, 1932), 2; 26/34 (March 24, 1932), 3.

66. StAM: SpkA K4240; LRA 61610; *AZ* 26/30 (March 15, 1932), 1.

67. StAM: LRA 61610; LRA 107047; LRA 107050; *AZ* 26/30 (March 15, 1932), 1; 26/38 (April 5, 1932), 3–4; 26/39 (April 7, 1932), 4; 26/40 (April 9, 1932), 3–4; 26/41 (April 12, 1932), 1.

68. *AZ* 26/43 (April 16, 1932), 2; 26/44 (April 19, 1932), 2, 3; 26/46 (April 23, 1932), 1, 2, 4; 26/47 (April 26, 1932), 1; StAM: LRA 107050.

69. *AZ* 26/63 (June 4, 1932), 1; StAM: LRA 61610.

70. GAO: Gem. Prot. v. March 16, 1932; March 30, 1932; StAM: LRA 61610; *AZ* 26/49 (April 30, 1932), 3; 26/52 (May 7, 1932), 2–3; 26/84 (July 26, 1932), 3.

71. *AZ* 26/60 (May 28, 1932), 1–2; 26/70 (June 21, 1932), 1; 26/71 (June 23, 1932), 1; 26/76 (July 7, 1932), 1.

72. *AZ* 26/69 (June 18, 1932), 2; 26/94 (June 20, 1932), 1; Utzschneider, *Oberammergau im Dritten Reich*, 117, quoting Fellerer's communication with Father Bogenrieder, dated Dec. 3, 1933.

73. StAM: LRA 61610.

74. *AZ* 26/62 (June 2, 1932), 4; 26/78 (July 12, 1932), 1; StAM: LRA 107046.

75. *AZ* 26/82 (July 21, 1932), 4; 26/83 (July 23, 1932), 1; StAM: LRA 107046.

76. *AZ* 26/81 (July 19, 1932), 3–4; 26/84 (July 26, 1932), 3; 26/85 (July 28, 1932), 3; StAM: LRA 107046.

77. *AZ* 26/85 (July 28, 1932), 2–3.

78. *AZ* 26/85 (July 28, 1932), 4; StAM: LRA 107046.

79. *AZ* 32/30 (March 11–12, 1938), 2; *DF* 3/27 (July 2, 1932), 7; StAM: Pol. Dir. München 6805; Pol. Dir. München: 6831; LRA 107046.

80. *DF* 3/27 (July 2, 1932), 7; Pridham, *National Socialist Party in Southern Bavaria*, 172–73, lists Oberammergau with two or three HJ in early 1932.

81. *AZ* 26/86 (July 30, 1932), 3; 26/87 (Aug. 2, 1932), 3; StAM: LRA 61610.

82. *AZ* 26/86 (July 30, 1932), 3–4; 26/87 (Aug. 2, 1932), 3.

83. *AZ* 2/37 (March 24, 1908), 1–2; 26/85 (July 28, 1932), 4; StAM: LRA 198994; PAO: Chronik von Oberammergau; Central File.

84. Feldigl, *Oberammergau* (1922), 168; Schröder, *Oberammergau* (1910), ad section; Central File; GAO: 12. 1. 5; *AZ* passim, especially 7/35 (March 29, 1913), 3; 18/52 (July 2, 1924), 2; 20/46 (April 22, 1926), 1; 20/53 (May 8, 1926), 1; 21/40 (April 7, 1927), 1; 23/144 (Dec. 12, 1929), 1; 26/53 (May 10, 1932), 2.

85. *Passion-Play at Oberammergau* (1930), 7–8 (fifty-six listed players); Utzschneider, *Oberammergau im Dritten Reich*, 117, quoting AEM: Nachlass Fellerer 49, communication with Raimund Lang, July 25, 1932.

86. *AZ* 10/39 (April 4, 1916), 2; GAO: 12. 1. 5; Einwohner- u. Hausbesitzerverzeichnis 1890–1930; Guido Lang, *Lang's Illustrated Practical Guide*, 18, 27; *Anton Lang's 1890 Offizieller Führer*, 25, 29; Feldigl, *Oberammergau* (1900), 94–95; PAO: Pfarrchronik von Oberammergau; Günzler and Zwink, *Berühmtes Dorf*, especially 91, 101, 122, 145, 162, 164; Klinner, *Oberammergau*, 12, 76–77. Chapter 5 covers this vision in detail.

87. *AZ* 25/92 (Aug. 11, 1931), 1; 25/97 (Aug. 22, 1931), 3; 26/52 (May 7, 1932), 2; 26/53 (May 10, 1932), 2; 26/56 (May 19, 1932), 2–3; 26/57 (May 21, 1932), 1; StAM: LRA 63160.

88. *AZ* 26/118 (Oct. 15, 1932), 2; 26/120 (Oct. 20, 1932), 1; 26/122 (Oct. 25, 1932), 1; GAO: Foto-Sammlung 620/1.

89. GAO: Gem. Prot. v. Oct. 27, 1932; Dec. 9, 1932.

90. *AZ* 26/127 (Nov. 5, 1932), 5; 26/128 (Nov. 8, 1932), 3; StAM: LRA 63160, including *G-PT* 52/253 (Nov. 2, 1932), 1.

91. *AZ* 26/129 (Nov. 10, 1932), 1.

92. *AZ* 26/130 (Nov. 12, 1932), 1, which also includes one more Ackermann article on the topic.

93. GAO: Gem. Prot. v. Sept. 28, 1932; Oct. 27, 1932; Oct. 31, 1932; Nov. 8, 1932; Nov. 18, 1932; Nov. 22, 1932; Dec. 9, 1932.

94. *AZ* 26/117 (Oct. 13, 1932), 3; StAM: LRA 61610.

95. GAO: Gem. Prot. v. Aug. 1, 1932; Aug. 5, 1932; Aug. 19, 1932; Aug. 24, 1932; Sept. 23, 1932; Sept. 28, 1932; Oct. 13, 1932; Oct. 27, 1932; Oct. 31, 1932; Nov. 8, 1932; B149, 3; StAM: LRA 61610.

96. StAM: LRA 61610.

97. Ibid.; LRA 107046; RA 57944.

98. StAM: SpkA K4240.

99. *AZ* 26/121 (Oct. 22, 1932), 6; 26/123 (Oct. 27, 1932), 3; 26/124 (Oct. 29, 1932), 2, 4; StAM: LRA 107046.

100. *AZ* 26/99 (Sept. 1, 1932), 4; 26/101 (Sept. 6, 1932), 3; 26/102 (Sept. 8, 1932), 3; 26/103 (Sept. 10, 1932), 4; 26/106 (Sept. 17, 1932), 3; 26/107 (Sept. 20, 1932), 4; 26/116 (Oct. 11, 1932), 3; 26/118 (Oct. 15, 1932), 2.

101. *AZ* 26/125 (Nov. 1, 1932), 4; 26/127 (Nov. 5, 1932), 5; StAM: LRA 107046.

102. *AZ* 26/87 (Aug. 2, 1932), 3; 26/128 (Nov. 8, 1932), 3.

103. *AZ* 26/148 (Dec. 24, 1932), 8; 27/7 (Jan. 19, 1933), 3; GAO: Gem. Prot. v. Feb. 2, 1933; StAM: LRA 61610.

104. *AZ* 26/140 (Dec. 6, 1932), 3; 26/143 (Dec. 13, 1932), 3; 26/148 (Dec. 24, 1932), 8; 26/150 (Dec. 31, 1932), 7; 27/5 (Jan. 12, 1933), 3; 27/6 (Jan. 14, 1933), 4; 27/15 (Feb. 4, 1933), 3; 27/20 (Feb. 16, 1933), 4; 27/24 (Feb. 25, 1933), 4; GAO: B149, 10; Nachlass A. O. Zwink, Mappe Passions-Comitee-Wahl 1933.

105. *AZ* 27/8 (Jan. 19, 1933), 3; 27/11 (Jan. 26, 1933) through 27/15 (Feb. 4, 1933); GAO: Gem. Prot. v. Jan. 31, 1933; Feb. 2, 1933; Feb. 17, 1933; Feb. 20, 1933; March 2, 1933; March 15, 1933; March 29, 1933; March 31, 1933; April 10, 1933; April 21, 1933; B149, which shows a meeting on March 12, 1933, and another on June 28, 1933.

106. *AZ* 27/15 (Feb. 4, 1933), 1; 27/18 (Feb. 11, 1933), 3; 27/20 (Feb. 16, 1933), 3; 27/24 (Feb. 25, 1933), 3; StAM: LRA 107046.

107. *AZ* 27/24 (Feb. 25, 1933), 3; 27/26 (March 2, 1933), 1–2; StAM: LRA 107046.

108. *AZ* 27/26 (March 2, 1933), 1–2; 27/27 (March 4, 1933), 3; BHStA: OMGBY 10/48–2/6, including Josef Raab statement, 1.

109. Utzschneider, *Oberammergau im Dritten Reich*, 31–32, quoting an undated flyer in GAO: AII/26.

110. *AZ* 26/128 (Nov. 8, 1932), 3; 27/28 (March 7, 1933), 1, 4.

111. *AZ* 27/30 (March 11, 1933), 1–2; 27/33 (March 18, 1933), 1.

112. *AZ* 27/30 (March 11, 1933), 1–2.

113. Ibid., 2.

114. BHStA: OMGBY 10/48–2/6, including Josef Raab statement, 2; *AZ* 27/32 (March 16, 1933), 3; GAO: ZA/Passionsspiele: Hans Eberhard Friedrich, "Denkt Oberammergau am Umbesetzung?" *Die Neue Zeitung* (Nov. 16, 1949); StAM: LRA 199036; LRA 199041; LRA 199059; SpkA K4240; K4283.

115. *AZ* 27/34 (March 21, 1933), 3; 27/35 (March 23, 1933), 1–2.

CHAPTER 4

1. Annelies Buchwieser, Historische Fotografien, 3; *Festschrift* (1993), 22; photograph in the possession of Frau Hanna Kräh.

2. *AZ* 26/146 (Dec. 20, 1932), 4; 26/148 (Dec. 24, 1932), 8.

3. Central File. There is a substantial literature about the Nazi party's social composition both before and after January 1933, as well as its voting support. My findings reflect the now well-accepted concept of a "catch-all" party appealing to all classes, a concept put forward in Childers, *Nazi Voter*. See in particular Jürgen Falter's work, especially *Hitlers Wähler*, and the overview in Mühlberger, *Social Bases of Nazism*, especially 4, 72–77. I explore these issues later in the chapter.

4. *AZ* 27/40 (March 28, 1933), 4; 27/42 (April 8, 1933), 3.

5. *AZ* 27/47 (April 22, 1933), 3; 27/48 (April 25, 1933), 3; Central File.

6. *AZ* 27/48 (April 25, 1933), 3; 27/49 (April 27, 1933), 1; StAM: SpkA K1008; K4240.

7. Central File; *AZ* 27/50 (April 29, 1933), 1; 27/51 (May 2, 1933), 1. So many recruits had continued to flow into the Nazi party that officials decided to close the ranks as of May 1, with some exceptions.

8. Ernst Lang, *Das wars*, 40; StAM: LRA 198994; photograph in the possession of Frau Hanna Kräh.

9. StAM: LRA 198994; SpkA K1008; *AZ* 25/139 (Nov. 28, 1931), 1–2.

10. StAM: SpkA K1008; *AZ* 2/37 (March 24, 1908), 1–2; 25/38 (March 31, 1931), 1; Parks-Richards, *Oberammergau*, 122; Guido Lang, *Lang's Illustrated Practical Guide*, 24–27; PAO: Chronik von Oberammergau.

11. StAM: SpkA K1008. "Black" was the popular designation for Catholics.

12. *AZ* 23/144 (Dec. 12, 1929), 1; 27/73 (June 24, 1933), 1; PAO: Chronik von Oberammergau; GAO: A024/1.

13. BHStA: OMGBY 10/48–2/6, including Josef Raab statement, 2; StAM: SpkA K1008; Ernst Lang, *Das wars*, 40.

14. StAM: SpkA K1008.

15. *AZ* 29/48 (April 25, 1935), 4; 29/58 (May 21, 1935), 4; 29/59 (May 23, 1935), 6; 29/60 (May 25, 1935), 6; 29/99 (Aug. 24, 1935), 8; 29/135 (Nov. 16, 1935), 1–2; 30/79 (July 4, 1936), 6; GAO: AII/54; *G-PT* 58/288 (Dec. 12, 1938), 3; StAM: SpkA K1008; LRA 107045–51; Ernst Lang, *Das wars*, 40.

16. *AZ* 10/39 (April 4, 1916), 2; 21/15 (Feb. 8, 1927), 1; 31/16 (Feb. 6, 1937), 1; 31/18 (Feb. 11, 1937), 1; GAO: Foto-Sammlung 620/1; Bogenrieder, *Oberammergau* (1930), 66–67; Diemer, *Oberammergau* (1900, 1922).

17. *AZ* 8/105 (Sept. 17, 1914), 3; 21/15 (Feb. 8, 1927), 1; 23/123 (Oct. 24, 1929), 1; 24/38 (May 1, 1930), 1; *G-PT* 59/51 (March 1, 1939), 2; Diemer, *Oberammergau* (1900, 1922); "Luftkampf, 1918," in Aichner, *Der erste Weltkrieg*, front cover. Available: www.theaerodrome.com [accessed Dec. 21, 2008]; "Fluegekampf," a Diemer postcard of Franz Zeno's "double decker" in a battle. Available: www.rubylane.com [accessed Dec. 21, 2008].

18. *AZ* 21/15 (Feb. 8, 1927), 1; 26/78 (Feb. 12, 1932), 1; 31/16 (Feb. 6, 1937), 1; 31/18 (Feb. 11, 1937), 1, 4; *G-PT* 59/51 (March 1, 1939), 2; 59/53 (March 3, 1939), 3; 59/69 (March 22, 1939), 7; Central File; Caramelle, *Das Innsbrucker Riesenrundgemälde*.

19. *G-PT* 59/245 (Oct. 21, 1939), 11; Feldigl, *Oberammergau* (1922), 168; Bogen-rieder, *Oberammergau* (1930), 28; GAO: AXV/87; *AZ* 8/4 (Jan. 16, 1914), 1; 8/117 (Oct. 15, 1914), 3; 12/42 (May 29, 1918), 1; 14/77 (Sept. 28, 1920), 1; 18/52 (July 2, 1924), 2; 18/75 (Sept. 20, 1924), 2; 19/73 (July 2, 1925), 1; 21/106 (Sept. 20, 1927), 1; 23/124 (Oct. 26, 1929), 1; 24/51 (May 8, 1930), 1; 25/15 (Feb. 5, 1931), 2.

20. Central File; *Adreßbuch des Bezirksamts Garmisch, 1927–1929*, Vereinsverzeich-nis; GAO: A332; AXV/102; SpkA K4271; *AZ* 14/64 (Aug. 14, 1920), 1.

21. *München*, 231; StAM: SpkA K4271; *AZ* 30/13 (Feb. 1, 1936), 1; PAO: Schublade 31: Pfarramtliches Zeugnis, Aug. 1, 1945; Central File.

22. Central File; GAO: A150/2; Pridham, *Hitler's Rise to Power*, 146–83, makes clear the role of Catholic voters in underpinning the Nazis, resulting from a gradual desertion of their denominational party. Catholics also joined, although not many were "devout" members. He mentions that General Franz Ritter von Epp was known as the "Mother-of-God General."

23. Dickie, *Oberammergau and the Passion Play*, 27; GAO: ZA/Passionsspiele: *Detroit News* (Oct. 16, 1921), 3; Parks-Richards, *Oberammergau*, 142–44; StAM: LRA 198994; *AZ* passim before 1914; Central File.

24. *AZ* 13/89 (Nov. 19, 1919), 1; 14/2 (Jan. 7, 1920), 1; 17/59 (July 25, 1923), 1; 17/74 (Oct. 6, 1923), 2; 18/96 (Dec. 3, 1924), 1; 19/22 (Feb. 24, 1925), 1; 21/40 (April 7, 1927), 1; 22/30 (March 13, 1928), 2; 22/31 (March 15, 1928), 1; 23 /58 (May 18, 1929), 1; 24/137 (Dec. 2, 1930), 1; 25/64 (June 4, 1931), 1; 25/67 (June 11, 1931), 1; StAM: LRA 198994; SpkA K4253; GAO: AXV/Die Wahl des Passionscomitees 1934 (1932–1934).

25. StAM: SpkA K4235; K4238; LRA 198994; *AZ* 27/47 (April 22, 1933), 3; Central File; GAO: Gem. Prot. v. June 21, 1933.

26. StAM: SpkA K4238; Guido Lang, *Lang's Illustrated Practical Guide*, 24–25; *AZ* 13/19 (March 19, 1919), 1; 18/23 (March 22, 1924), 1–2; 18/96 (Dec. 3, 1924), 1; 18/98 (Dec. 10, 1924), 1; 19/43 (April 18, 1925), 1; 21/130 (Nov. 15, 1927), 1; 22/30 (March 13, 1928), 1; 23/144 (Dec. 10, 1929), 1; PAO: Schublade 31, Pfarramtliche Bestätigung, June 12, 1947.

27. StAM: SpkA K4238; BHStA: OMGBY 10/48–2/6.

28. Central File.

29. Ernst Lang, *Das wars*, 21, 40–41; Central File; *AZ* 13/7 (Feb. 5, 1919), 1; 18/96 (Dec. 3, 1924), 1; 25/122 (Oct. 20, 1931), 1.

30. Corathiel, *Oberammergau and Its Passion Play* (1950), 105; "Die evangelische Kirche in Oberammergau," 11; *AZ* 19/71 (June 25, 1925), 1; Central File; GAO: AXV/89.

31. *AZ* 13/57 (July 30, 1919), 1; 14/41 (May 22, 1920), 1; 14/91 (Nov. 17, 1920), 1; 16/85 (Oct. 25, 1922), 1; 17/59 (July 25, 1923), 1; 17/92 (Dec. 8, 1923), 4; 17/93 (Dec. 12, 1923), 2, 4; 19/122 (Oct. 24, 1925), 1; 20/35 (March 25, 1926), 1; 21/36 (March 29, 1927), 1; 22/129 (Nov. 10, 1928), 1; 23/57 (May 16, 1929), 4; 23/58 (May 18, 1929), 1; 23/65 (June 8, 1929), 1; 24/15 (Feb. 8, 1930), 1; 27/113 (Sept. 26, 1933), 1; 29/135 (Nov. 16, 1935), 1–2; 31/96 (Aug. 12, 1937), 3; BHStA: MInn 72741; *Festschrift* (1993), 27, 61; PAO: Pfarramtliches Bestätigung, July 21, 1947; Central File.

32. BHstA: MInn 72741; *AZ* 19/73 (July 2, 1925), 1; 19/122 (Oct. 24, 1925), 1.

33. *AZ* 25/124 (Oct. 24, 1931), 1; 26/60 (May 28, 1932), 1–2; 26/61 (May 31, 1932), 1; 26/62 (June 2, 1932), 3; 26/127 (Nov. 5, 1932), 5; 27/68 (June 13, 1933), 1.

34. Central File; GAO: Einwohner- u. Hausbesitzerverzeichnis 1910, 1922; AII/26; *AZ* 26/113 (Oct. 4, 1932), 3.

35. *AZ* 8/131 (Nov. 17, 1914), 3; 11/58 (July 25, 1917), 3; 12/33 (April 27, 1918), 1–2; 13/17 (March 12, 1919), 4; 18/96 (Dec. 3, 1924), 1; 22/61 (May 31, 1928), 4; 22/139 (Dec. 4, 1928), 2; 25/62 (May 30, 1931), 4; 27/117 (Oct. 5, 1933), 1; 28/59 (May 24, 1934), 4; GAO: Pk-Slg 5.

36. *AZ* 2/6 (Jan. 18, 1908), 2; 8/131 (Nov. 17, 1914), 3; 16/85 (Oct. 25, 1922), 1; 18/2 (Jan. 9, 1924), 2; 18/4 (Jan. 16, 1924), 2; 18/5 (Jan. 18, 1924), 1–2; 18/11 (Feb. 9, 1924), 2; 18/82 (Oct. 15, 1924), 2; 22/139 (Dec. 4, 1928), 2; 24/137 (Dec. 2, 1930), 1; 27/148 (Dec. 16, 1933), 1; 28/21 (Feb. 20, 1934), 4; *Festschrift* (1993), 15; GAO: A024/1.

37. Central File.

38. *AZ* 7/13 (Feb. 4, 1913), 3; 17/74 (Oct. 6, 1923), 2; 22/139 (Dec. 4, 1928), 2; Einwohnermeldeamt Oberammergau; *Festschrift* (1993), 61; Central File.

39. Central File; PAO: Pfarramtliches Bestätigung, Pfarrer Oberammergau, July 21, 1947; Pridham, *Hitler's Rise to Power*, 188–90, argues that "it was unusual to find a local branch leader with a working class background in Bavaria" and that members of the "professional middle classes" were the most common leaders.

40. Central File.

41. GAO: 12. 1. 5; StAM: SpkA K4240; *AZ* 7/109 (Sept. 30, 1913), 4; 7/111 (Oct. 4, 1913), 4; 9/107 (Sept. 14, 1915), 3; 14/12 (Feb. 11, 1920), 3; 14/17 (Feb. 28, 1920), 1; 14/62 (Aug. 7, 1920), 4; 16/6 (Jan. 21, 1922), 1; 16/41 (May 24, 1922), 1; 16/59 (July 26, 1922), 3; 18/59 (July 26, 1924), 3; BHStA: MInn 72741.

42. *AZ* 20/81 (July 17, 1926), 4; 20/82 (July 20, 1926), 4; 20/105 (Sept. 11, 1926), 4; 21/99 (Sept. 3, 1927), 2; 22/45 (April 21, 1928), 4; 22/123 (Oct. 27, 1928), 4; 24/44 (April 19, 1930), 1; 24/67 (June 19, 1930), 3; 24/69 (June 24, 1930), 4; 24/78 (July 15, 1930), 1.

43. *AZ* 7/115 (Oct. 14, 1913), 3; 9/135 (Nov. 20, 1915), 3; 13/9 (Feb. 12, 1919), 4; 13/17 (March 12, 1919), 1; 13/44 (June 14, 1919), 1; 13/73 (Sept. 24, 1919), 1; 18/96 (Dec. 3, 1924), 1; 19/114 (Oct. 6, 1925), 1–2; 19/120 (Oct. 20, 1925), 1; 19/130 (Nov. 12, 1925), 4; 21/12 (Feb. 15, 1927), 1; 24/15 (Feb. 8, 1930), 1; StAM: SpkA K4240; GAO: A024/1.

44. *AZ* 24/51 (May 8, 1930), 1; 24/108 (Sept. 25, 1930), 1; 24/116 (Oct. 14, 1930), 2; 24/118 (Oct. 18, 1930), 1; 24/131 (Nov. 18, 1930), 4; 25/15 (Feb. 5, 1931), 2; 25/38 (March 31, 1931), 4; 25/64 (June 4, 1931), 1; 25/98 (Aug. 25, 1931), 4; 25/125 (Oct. 27, 1931), 1; 25/130 (Nov. 7, 1931), 4; 26/149 (Dec. 22, 1931), 4; 26/7 (Jan. 21, 1932), 3; 26/56 (May 19, 1932), 4; Central File.

45. StAM: SpkA K4240.

46. StAM: SpkA K1008; K4240; GAO: A. O. Zwink, Album 3. Reich, numerous photographs; ZA/Passionsspiele: Hans Eberhard Friedrich, "Denkt Oberammergau am Umbesetzung?" *Die Neue Zeitung* (Nov. 16, 1949).

47. StAM: SpkA K1008; K4240.

48. StAM: SpkAK1008; K4240; H-B 3/43 (May 30, 1947), 3.

49. *AZ* 24/51 (May 8, 1930), 1; Central File.

50. *AZ* 18/52 (July 2, 1924), 2; 20/53 (May 8, 1926), 1; 21/40 (April 7, 1927), 1; 22/35 (March 27, 1928), 1; 23/144 (Dec. 12, 1929), 1; *Stead's Guide*, 52–56; Central File.

51. GAO: A332; *Stead's Guide*, 52–56; Central File.

52. *Stead's Guide*, 35, 52–56; Moses, *Passion Play of Oberammergau*, xii, xxvii; GAO: A150/2; StAM: SpkA K4238; *Detroit News* (Oct. 16, 1921), 3; *AZ* 19/122 (Oct. 24, 1925), 1; 25/51 (Jan. 13, 1931), 1; 25/67 (June 11, 1931), 1; Central File.

53. GAO: A150/2.

54. GAO: Gem. Prot. v. April 29, 1934; Jan. 29, 1935; Nov. 24, 1936; July 26, 1937; A150/2.

55. *AZ* 18/96 (Dec. 3, 1924), 1; 19/48 (April 30, 1925), 1; 20/46 (April 22, 1926), 1; 20/53 (May 8, 1926), 1; 20/132 (Nov. 16, 1926), 1; 21/43 (April 14, 1927), 1; 23/144 (Dec. 12, 1929), 1; 25/26 (March 3, 1931), 1; 26/52 (May 7, 1932), 2; 26/57 (May 21, 1932), 1; 27/88 (July 29, 1933), 1; GAO: Gem. Prot. v. Nov. 9, 1934; Central File.

56. BHStA: OMGBY 10/48 2/6, including Josef Raab statement, 1, and passim in *AZ*.

57. BHStA: OMGBY 10/48 2/6, including Josef Raab statement, 2–4.

58. Ibid.

59. Stephenson, *Hitler's Home Front*, 215, makes a similar point about restraints on Nazi leaders who were locals in their face-to-face relationships with villagers.

60. Central File. Core members include all of those on both the 1933 and the 1937 party membership lists, as well as some who appear on the 1933 list and the postwar cast list compiled in 1946. This social profile reflects the makeup of the "catchall party" revealed in the work of Brustein, *Logic of Evil*; Childers, *Nazi Voter*; Falter, *Hitlers Wähler*; Falter and Kater, "Wähler und Mitglieder der NSDAP," 155–77; Fritzsche, *Germans into Nazis*; Hamilton, *Who Voted for Hitler?*; Madden and Mühlberger, *Nazi Party*; and Mühlberger, *Hitler's Followers*. Also striking is the volatility of party membership, as much of the literature about it has already emphasized, notably Heilbronner, *Catholicism*, 59–67.

61. Central File.

62. Ibid.; *Festschrift* (1993).

63. Ibid.; StAM: LRA 198994; photograph in the possession of Frau Hanna Kräh.

64. *AZ* 18/86 (Oct. 29, 1924), 1–2; 22/89 (Aug. 7, 1928), 1; Bogenrieder, *Oberammergau* (1930), 23.

65. Central File; GAO: 000/10; 000/11; Gem. Prot. v. Feb. 7, 1934; A. O. Zwink: Album 3. Reich.

66. StAM: SpkA K4283; GAO: A. O. Zwink: Album 3. Reich; 000/10; *AZ* 27/27 (March 4, 1933), 3; 27/62 (May 27, 1933), 1; 27/109 (Sept. 16, 1933), 1; 27/110 (Sept. 19, 1933), 1.

67. *AZ* 26/84 (July 26, 1932), 3; Central File; GAO: Gem. Prot v. Jan. 4, 1932, on.

68. *AZ* 32/30 (March 11–12, 1938), 2; Central File; PAO: Schublade 31: Pfarramtliche Bestätigung, no date; GAO: 000/10; Gem. Prot. v. Oct. 31, 1932; Ernst Lang, *Das wars*, 38–39.

69. StAM: SpkA K4240; K4283; *AZ* 24/118 (Oct. 18, 1930), 1; 25/2 (Jan. 6, 1931), 1; 25/107 (Sept. 15, 1931), 1; 26/117 (Oct. 13, 1932), 3.

70. StAM: SpkA K4268; GAO: Gem. Prot. v. Oct. 13, 1932; Central File.

71. Central File; *AZ* 27/47 (April 22, 1933), 3; 27/76 (July 1, 1933), 1; GAO: Gem. Prot. v. Aug. 18, 1933.

72. GAO: Gem. Prot. passim and March 16, 1932; Oct. 13, 1932.

73. StAM: SpkA K1008; K4240; K4253.

74. Ernst Lang, *Das wars*, 38–39; StAM: SpkA K4283; LRA 61610.

75. *AZ* 25/47 (April 23, 1931), 2; 26/4 (Jan. 14, 1932), 3; 26/20 (Feb. 20, 1932), 3; 26/116 (Oct. 11, 1932), 3.

76. Diemer, *Oberammergau* (1922), 19, 30.

77. *AZ* 26/78 (July 12, 1932), 1; 26/116 (Oct. 11, 1932), 3; 27/16 (Feb. 7, 1933), 3; 27/27 (March 4, 1933), 3; Diemer, *Oberammergau* (1922), 19, 30; PAO: Chronik von Oberammergau; StAM: SpkA K1008; GAO: Gem. Prot. v. Nov. 22, 1932; StAM: LRA 61610.

78. Ernst Lang, *Das wars*, 38–39; StAM: SpkA K1008; K4240; K4268; K4311; GAO: A150/2.

79. *AZ* 27/40 (April 4, 1933), 3; GAO: AII/54; Central File.

80. *AZ* 27/42 (April 8, 1933), 3.

81. Ibid.; StAM: SpkA K1008; GAO: B149, 30–31.

82. Central File; StAM: SpkA K1008; K4253.

83. StAM K4253; K4240; GAO: A150/2; BHStA: OMGBY 10/48–2/6, including Josef Raab statement.

84. StAM: SpkA K4268; K4240; *AZ* passim and 26/69 (June 18, 1932), 1; 26/85 (July 28, 1932), 1; 27/44 (April 13, 1933), 4; 27/46 (April 20, 1933), 2; 32/30 (March 11–12, 1938), 2; Bogenrieder, *Oberammergau* (1930), 126–33; Central File.

85. GAO: Gem. Prot. v. Aug. 8, 1933; Sept. 6, 1933; Jan. 7, 1938; B149, 30–34, 39.

86. *AZ* 1/122 (Nov. 5, 1907), 1; 24/20 (Feb. 20, 1930), 1; 26/143 (Dec. 13, 1932), 3; GAO: ZA/Passionsspiele: *Münster Anzeiger* (April 15, 1934).

87. *AZ* 27/46 (April 20, 1933), 2.

88. *AZ* 27/50 (April 29, 1933), 1; 27/51 (May 2, 1933), 1; Fritzsche, *Germans into Nazis*, 215–26, discusses this first May Day extravaganza.

89. *AZ* 27/50 (April 29, 1933), 1; 27/51 (May 2, 1933), 1.

90. *AZ* 26/34 (Feb. 3, 1932), 3; 27/11 (Jan. 26, 1933), 3; 27/29 (March 9, 1933), 3; 27/31 (March 14, 1933), 3; 27/33 (March 18, 1933), 4; 27/36 (March 25, 1933), 3; 27/45 (April 15, 1933), 2, 8; 27/46 (April 20, 1933), 1; 27/47 (April 22, 1933), 3; 27/48 (April 25, 1933), 3; 27/53 (May 6, 1933), 3; 27/56 (May 13, 1933), 1; 27/59 (May 20, 1933), 1, 3, 6.

91. Central File.

92. Ibid.

93. Ibid.

94. StAM: SpkA K4240; *AZ* 27/68 (June 13, 1933), 1, 3; 27/69 (June 15, 1933), 1; 27/71 (June 20, 1933), 1; Evi Kleinöder, "Verfolgung und Widerstand der Katholische Jugendvereine: Ein Fallstudie über Eichstätt," in *Bayern in der NS-Zeit*, vol. 2, ed. Broszat and Fröhlich, 199–200, discusses the Munich events; Rauh-Kühne, *Katholisches Milieu*, 362–63, describes similar "disturbances" by young Nazis in Ettlingen.

95. StAM: SpkA K4240.

96. Ibid.

97. *AZ* 27/70 (June 17, 1933), 1; StAM: SpkA K4240.

98. StAM: SpkA K1008; K4240; Utzschneider, *Oberammergau im Dritten Reich*, 69; *AZ* 27/71 (June 20, 1933), 1; GAO: Gem. Prot. v. May 17, 1933; May 23, 1933. Lang may have been building on an earlier "movement of young Ammergau citizens for communal political interests." Late in 1932 he joined this group, which first came together to promote a slate of candidates for the 1934 season's Passion Committee. GAO: Nachlass A. O. Zwink, Mappe Passions-Comitee-Wahl 1933.

CHAPTER 5

1. Shapiro, *Oberammergau*, 37.

2. *AZ* 27/73 (June 24, 1933), 1; GAO: Gem. Prot. v. June 21, 1933; StAM: SpkA K1008; Ernst Lang, *Das wars*, 40–41.

3. GAO: B149, 5, 30–32; Gem. Prot. v. June 21, 1933; AXV/Die Wahl des Passionscomitees 1934; *AZ* 27/74 (June 27, 1933), 3; 27/76 (July 1, 1933), 1.

4. Central File; *AZ* 27/73 (June 24, 1933), 1; StAM: LRA 199042; SpkA K4240; Kershaw, *Popular Opinion*, 191–92, discusses this process.

5. *AZ* 27/73 (June 24, 1933), 1, 3; 27/77 (July 4, 1933), 1; StAM: SpkA K1008; LRA 61613.

6. GAO: Gem. Prot. v. June 21, 1933; *AZ* 27/88 (July 29, 1933), 1; 27/112 (Sept. 23, 1933), 1; Utzschneider, *Oberammergau im Dritten Reich*, 69; StAM: SpkA K4291.

7. Utzschneider, *Oberammergau im Dritten Reich*, 64; StAM: SpkA K1008; *AZ* 27/95 (Aug. 15, 1933), 1; GAO: Gem. Prot. v. Aug. 18, 1933; Sept. 6, 1933; Central File.

8. GAO: Gem. Prot. v. Jan. 7, 1938; *AZ* 27/95 (Aug. 15, 1933), 1; StAM: SpkA K4283; Rauh-Kühne, *Katholisches Milieu*, 282–83, mentions the role that Catholics played in hindering the Nazis' "destruction of parliamentary democracy." In pages 326–39 she discusses the question of carryover into the Nazi-dominated council. However, she emphasizes the "new" men who soon completely replaced any "old faces," erasing connections with the Catholic milieu. The town's mayor, however, was a holdover until 1941.

9. StAM: SpkA K1008.

10. Utzschneider, *Oberammergau im Dritten Reich*, 81–83; GAO: Gem. Prot. v. Feb. 2, 1933, on, notably, May 17, 1933; May 23, 1933; June 21, 1933; copies of stories in *AZ* 27/76 (July 1, 1933) and 27/82 (July 15, 1933); Aug. 18, 1933; April 29, 1934; *AZ* 27/121 (Oct. 14, 1933), 2; *Geschichte und Geschichten*, vol. 2, 42; Bogenrieder, *Jubiläums-Passionsspiele*, 106.

11. *AZ* 27/127 (Oct. 28, 1933), 4; 27/128 (Oct. 31, 1933), 1; 27/132 (Nov. 9, 1933), 1; 27/140 (Nov. 28, 1933), 1; GAO: Gem. Prot. v. Oct. 31, 1932; Nov. 8, 1932; Feb. 17, 1933; June 21, 1933; Oct. 30, 1933; Dec. 7, 1933; Dec. 15, 1933; B149, 30–31.

12. *AZ* 27/83 (July 18, 1933), 1, 4; 27/92 (Aug. 8, 1933), 1; 27/96 (Aug. 17, 1933), 1; 27/98 (Aug. 22, 1933), 1; 27/106 (Sept. 9, 1933), 1; 27/121 (Oct. 14, 1933), 1; 27/135 (Nov. 16, 1933), 1; 27/136 (Nov. 19, 1933), 1; 27/143 (Dec. 5, 1933), 1; 28/5 (Jan. 13, 1934), 1.

13. *AZ* 27/74 (June 27, 1933), 1; 27/115 (Sept. 30. 9, 1933), 1; 27/134 (Nov. 14, 1933), 1; 27/149 (Dec. 19, 1933), 4; 27/152 (Dec. 28, 1933), 1.

14. Ernst Lang, *Das wars*, 43–46; *AZ* 27/92 (Aug. 8, 1933), 1; 27/121 (Oct. 14, 1933), 1; 27/129 (Nov. 2, 1933), 1; 27/132 (Nov. 9, 1933), 1.

15. Kleinöder, "Verfolgung und Widerstand," 200–209, yet see GAO: A134/1 for an Eberlein letter dated Sept. 14, 1933, asking permission to hold a meeting of the journeymen; *AZ* 27/141 (Nov. 30, 1933), 1; Evans, *Coming of the Third Reich*, 363–65. He concludes that "the reconciliation of Nazism and Catholicism seemed, at least for the time being, complete."

16. PAO: Schublade 17: Seelsorgsjahresbericht 1933.

17. *AZ* 23/57 (May 16, 1929), 1; 24/8 (Jan. 23, 1930), 1; 27/142 (Dec. 2, 1933), 3; 28/49 (April 28, 1934), 3; Anton Lang, *Reminiscences*, 140; PAO: Schublade 17: Seelsorgsjahresbericht 1927, 1931, 1933; Kleinöder, "Verfolgung und Widerstand," 196–99, 201, 204–205.

18. Central File; Ernst Lang, *Das wars*, 42; *AZ* 26/22 (Feb. 25, 1932), 3; 28/5 (Jan. 13, 1934), 1; GAO: A150/2; A150/3; PAO: Schublade 17: Seelsorgsjahresbericht 1927, 1931, 1933.

19. *AZ* 27/136 (Nov. 19, 1933), 4; 27/148 (Dec. 16, 1933), 2; 28/11 (Jan. 27, 1934), 4; 28/14 (Feb. 3, 1934), 1; 28/16 (Feb. 8, 1934), 4; 28/20 (Feb. 17, 1934), 3; PAO: Seelsorgsjahresbericht 1933.

20. *AZ* 27/136 (Nov. 19, 1933), 4; 27/137 (Nov. 25, 1933), 4; 27/142 (Dec. 2, 1933), 1, 6; 27/151 (Dec. 23, 1933), 8; 27/152 (Dec. 28, 1933), 1; 28/46 (April 21, 1934), 4.

21. *AZ* 21/130 (Nov. 15, 1927), 1; 27/105 (Sept. 7, 1933), 1; 27/112 (Sept. 23, 1933), 1; 27/115 (Sept. 30, 1933), 3; 27/116 (Oct. 3, 1933), 1; 27/118 (Oct. 7, 1933), 1; 27/148 (Dec. 16, 1933), 1; 28/46 (April 21, 1934), 3; 28/52 (May 5, 1934), 3; 28/58 (May 19, 1934), 3; passim for masses and Ettal pilgrims.

22. *AZ* 28/62 (May 31, 1934), 1; 28/63 (June 2, 1934), 1.

23. GAO: B149, 3, 5, 7, 10–11, 97; *AZ* 26/143 (Dec. 13, 1932), 3.

24. GAO: B149, 13–28, 30; B163, July 31, 1933, meeting; Utzschneider, *Oberammergau im Dritten Reich*, 101–102; Bogenrieder, *Jubiläums Passonsspiele*, 8.

25. GAO: B149, 30, 34, 39.

26. GAO: B149, 30–32.

27. StAM: SpkA K1008; GAO: B149, 36–37; B163, July 31, 1933, and Sept. 28, 1933, meetings; ZA/Passionsspiele: *Kreuz-Zeitung* (Berlin) (May 13, 1934); AXV/122.

28. GAO: B149, 31; B163, July 31, 1933, and Sept. 28, 1933, meetings; AXV/102; AXV/128; *AZ* 27/125 (Oct. 24, 1933), 1.

29. GAO: B149, 41; B163, Sept. 28, 1933, meeting; BHStA: MHIG 1141.

30. GAO: AXV/121.

31. BHStA: MHIG 1141; GAO: B149, 41; B163, Sept. 28, 1933, meeting; AXV/121; ZA/Passionsspiele: *Herald Tribune* (May 20, 1934), section 6, part 2, 9; van Hoek, "Oberammergau," 3, arguing that "I have seen [the new poster] Unter den Linden, in Piccadilly and on the Boulevard de l'Opéra. It must hang somewhere on 5th Avenue, in Sydney and on Capri, as well as in the towns on the Hungarian plains, or along the Norwegian fjords."

32. GAO: B163, April 23, 1934, meeting; ZA/Passionsspiele: *Berliner Illustrierte Nachtausgabe* (Jan. 17, 1934); BHStA: MHIG 1141.

33. BHStA: MHIG 1141.

34. Bogenrieder, *Jubiläums-Passionsspiele Oberammergau*, uses the second-place image on its cover; GAO: II. 5. 1 includes a poster with the second-place image; II. 7. 2 contains prospectuses with all three images; BHStA: MHIG 1141.

35. GAO: AXV/115; B149, 47–48.

36. Utzschneider, *Oberammergau im Dritten Reich*, 17, 69, 105; *München*, 138, 145, 212, 214, 220, 230–31; Kershaw, *Hitler*, vol. 1, 178–80, 233, 270–71; GAO: B149, 48; ZA/Passionsspiele: *Südd. Corr. Büro* (Oct. 16, 1933), 27; Pridham, *Hitler's Rise to Power*, 49; Bramsted, *Goebbels and National Socialist Propaganda*, 15.

37. *München*, 138, 145, 212, 214, 220, 230–31; Ernst Lang, *Das wars*, 39; Pridham, *Hitler's Rise to Power*, 198–99.

38. Utzschneider, *Oberammergau im Dritten Reich*, 101–109; BHStA: MHIG 1141.

39. GAO: AXV/123.

40. Ibid.; *AZ* 27/100 (Aug. 26, 1933), 1.

41. GAO: ZA/Passionsspiele: Tägliches Beiblatt, *Völkischer Beobachter* 345 (Dec. 11, 1933); *Münchener Landzeitung* 83 (April 12, 1934); *Leipziger Neueste Nachrichten* 143 (May 23, 1934).

42. GAO: ZA/Passionsspiele: *Basler Volksblatt* (May 14, 1934).

43. GAO: B163: Sept. 28, 1933, meeting; ZA/Passionsspiele: H. W. Günther, *Südd. Corr. Büro* (Oct. 16, 1933), 26–27; *AZ* 27/123 (Oct. 19, 1933), 1.

44. GAO: ZA/Passionsspiele: "No Change in Passion Play: 'Reforms' Deferred for This Year to Secure Tourist Patronage," *Daily Telegraph* (April 5, 1934); Harold A. Albert, "Simplicity!" *Sunday Mercury* (April 8, 1934); "Der Beginn in Oberammergau," *Münchener Zeitung* 138 (May 18, 1934); *Scotsman* (May 23, 1934); "Das Jubiläumsspiel von Oberammergau," *Basler Nachrichten* (May 26–27, 1934), 3; "Oberammergau Passion Play: The Tercentenary Performances," *Manchester Guardian* (May 28, 1934); *AZ* 28/88 (July 31, 1934), 1.

45. GAO: ZA/Passionsspiele: "Oberammergau: The Passion Play," *Times* (May 14, 1934; May 18, 1934); Utzschneider, *Oberammergau im Dritten Reich*, 104.

46. GAO: ZA/Passionsspiele: Sophie Rützou, "Wahltage im Passionsdorf," *Deutsche Verkehrsblätter* 42 (Oct. 17, 1933), 5–7.

47. GAO: B163: Oct. 3, 1933; Sept. 22, 1934; Oct. 1, 1934, meetings.

48. GAO: B149, 74–78.

49. GAO: B149, 49–51; *Passion-Play at Oberammergau* (1930); Bogenrieder, *Jubiläums-Passionsspiele*, 56, 59.

50. GAO: B149, 49–70; *Passion-Play at Oberammergau* (1930 and 1934); Central File; Frederick T. Birchall, "Give Passion Play in Oberammergau," *New York Times* (May 18, 1934), 12.

51. *Passion-Play at Oberammergau* (1930 and 1934); Central File.

52. GAO: B179; B149, 74, 77–78, 80–83, 95; AXV/147; *AZ* 28/114 (Sept. 29, 1934), 1; Central File.

53. GAO: A000/10; A000/11; Gem. Prot. v. Dec. 15, 1933; Central File. The Stahlhelm was a group of frontline World War I veterans, although the youthful asociates were born too late to have fought in the war.

54. BHStA: MInn 72741.

55. GAO: ZA/Passionsspiele: Max Lenz, "300 Jahre Oberammergau," *Schlesische Volkszeitung* (Jan. 10, 1934); "Beim Neudichter des Passionspieles," *Schlesische Volkszeitung* (Jan. 10, 1934); B149, 78, 87; AXV/123; Shapiro, *Oberammergau*, 156–57; Gordon Mork, "Oberammergau: Interrelationships between Religious Folk-drama and the Historical Environment," in *Wesenszüge Europas*, ed. Walter Fürnrohr, 175, 179–81; Utzschneider, *Oberammergau im Dritten Reich*, 102; BHStA: MInn 72741.

56. GAO: B149, 78.

57. Ibid., 87–90; BHStA: MInn 72741.

58. BHStA: MInn 72741; Mork, "Oberammergau," 175,181–82.

59. BHStA: MInn 72741; Mork, "Oberammergau," 175, 182–83; *München*, 214; Laurentius Koch, "Die Benediktinerabtei Ettal," in *Das Erzbistum München und Freising*, vol. 2, ed. Schwaiger, 384.

60. BHStA: MInn 72741; Bogenrieder, *Jubiläums Passionsspiele*, 43–44.

61. GAO: AXV/123; ZA/Passionsspiele: Lenz, "300 Jahre Oberammergau"; "Oberammergau 1934," *Bayerischer Kurier* (Jan. 26, 1934); Alfred Mayerhofer, "Oberammergau ist bereit," *BZ am Mittag* (May 16, 1934); Peter Trumm, "Eindrücke, Erinnerungen, und Gedanken," *Münchner Telegramm Zeitung* 113 (May 18, 1934); Anton Lang, *Reminiscences*, 145.

62. Shapiro, *Oberammergau*, 158–62; *Passion-Play at Oberammergau* (1930), 21–22, and (1934), 21–22.

63. Ernst Lang, *Das wars*, 39; Central File; *Passion-Play at Oberammergau* (1934), 9–11.

64. Birchall, "Give Passion Play in Oberammergau," 12.

65. *AZ* 28/114 (Sept. 29, 1934), 1; GAO: ZA/Passionsspiele: "Die Frauen des Passionsdorf: Etwas vom Tagewerk und von den Erlebnissen Oberammergauer Hausfrauen vor und während der Spielzeit"; Gem. Prot. v. Feb. 7, 1934; March 22, 1934; April 29, 1934; Corathiel, *Oberammergau* (1934), 104–106.

66. GAO: ZA/Passionsspiele: "Warnende Worte Pius XI an Dland," *Basler Nachrichten* (April 6, 1934); Utzschneider, *Oberammergau im Dritten Reich*, 104, quoting Faulhaber's letter to Wagner, dated March 26, 1934, in *Akten deutscher Bischöfe*, ed. Stasiewski, 68.

67. StAM: SpkA K1008; SpkA K4240.

68. StAM: SpkA K1008.

69. Ibid.; K4235; Ernst Lang, *Das wars*, 45–47.

70. GAO: A000/10; StAM: SpkA K1008; *AZ* 27/78 (July 6, 1933), 1; 28/10 (Jan. 25, 1934), 4; Central File.

71. *AZ* 27/47 (April 22, 1933), 4; 27/51 (May 2, 1933), 1; 27/65 (June 3, 1933), 1; Berghahn, *Der Stahlhelm*, 263–65; StAM: SpkA K1008; K4238.

72. GAO: A000/24; StAM: SpkA K1008; LRA 61613; *AZ* 28/45 (April 19, 1934), 1; 28/144 (Dec. 8, 1934), 6; Berghahn, *Der Stahlhelm*, 267; Evans, *Coming of the Third Reich*, 373–74.

73. StAM: SpkA K1008; K4235; 4311; GAO: AIV/45; *AZ* 28/18 (Feb. 13, 1934), 1; 28/21 (Feb. 20, 1934), 1.

74. StAM: SpkA K1008; GAO: AIV/45; Kershaw, *Hitler*, vol. 1, 510–12.

75. Central File; GAO: AIV/45: StAM: SpkA K1008.

76. GAO: AIV/45: StAM: SpkA K1008; K4268; K4311.

77. *München*, 387; Pridham, *Hitler's Rise to Power*, 200; StAM: SpkA K1008.

78. Central File.

79. StAM: SpkA K1008.

80. Ibid.

81. Ibid.; K4311; Friedl Lang, *180 Jahre Musikleben in Oberammergau*, 41, 43.

82. StAM: SpkA K1008; K4235; K4341.

83. StAM: SpkA K1008; K4240; K4341.

84. StAM: SpkA K1008; K4240; K4268; LRA 61613; GAO: AIV/45; *AZ* 29/32 (March 16, 1935); 29/134 (Nov. 14, 1935), 1.

85. StAM: SpkA K1008; BHStA: MHIG 1141; Utzschneider, *Oberammergau im Dritten Reich*, 57, drawing from SpkA Arno Hesse; GAO: ZA/Passionsspiele: *Zwickauer Zeitung* (May 19, 1934); *Berlin hört und sieht* (May 18, 1934); *NS Bildbeobachter* 4/20 (May 20, 1934).

86. StAM: SpkA K1008; *München*, 228; BHStA: MHIG 1141; Kershaw, *Hitler*, vol. 1, 510–17.

87. StAM: SpkA K1008; K4240; *AZ* 28/113 (Sept. 27, 1934), 1.

88. GAO: AXV/128; B149, 126; AIV/45; *AZ* 28/76 (July 3, 1934), 1–3; 28/77 (July 5, 1934), 1–2; 28/78 (July 7, 1934), 2; 28/80 (July 12, 1934), 2.

89. GAO: AXV/123, containing Adolf Stein, "Oberammergau's deutsche Passion," *Der Tag* (May 5, 1934); AXV/128.

90. GAO: AXV/130.

91. GAO: ZA/Passionsspiele: *Neues Münchner Tagblatt* 204 (July 23, 1934); *Deutscher Verkehrsdienst* 96 (Aug. 13, 1934), 2; *Nürnberger Zeitung* 233 (Oct. 5, 1934); Peter Jens, "Oberammergau," *Jugendland* (October 1934), 14.

92. BHStA: MWi 2804; Günzler and Zwink, *Berühmtes Dorf*, 168–71.

93. GAO: ZA/Passionsspiele: *Allensteiner Volksblatt* (May 19, 1934); *Neues Münchner Tagblatt* 204 (July 23, 1934); Günzler and Zwink, *Berühmtes Dorf*, 167–68; BHStA: MWi 2804; *AZ* 28/63 (June 2, 1934), 1; 28/104 (Sept. 6, 1934), 1; 28/114 (Sept. 29, 1934), 1; 28/122 (Oct. 18, 1934), 1.

94. GAO: AXV/123.

95. GAO: AIV/45.

96. StAM: SpkA K1008.

97. *New York Times* (Aug. 14, 1934), 13; Günzler and Zwink, *Berühmtes Dorf*, 173; GAO: ZA/Passionsspiele: "Der Führer in Oberammergau," *Allgäuer Tagblatt* 184 (Aug. 14, 1934); "Der Führer beim Passionsspiel," *Völkischer Beobachter* 47/226 (Aug. 14, 1934); AXV/130; GAO Foto-Sammlung 231: Adolf Hitler Mappe.

98. Günzler and Zwink, *Berühmtes Dorf*, 171–73, GAO: A150/2; AXV/130; ZA/Passionsspiele: "Der Führer in Oberammergau," *Allgäuer Tagblatt* 184 (Aug. 14, 1934); *Der Angriff* (Aug. 16, 1934); *Bayreuther Tagblatt* 191 (Aug. 17, 1934); *Berliner Volks-Zeitung* (Aug. 16, 1934).

99. GAO: ZA/Passionsspiele: "Der Führer in Oberammergau," *Allgäuer Tagblatt* 184 (Aug. 14, 1934); *Völkischer Beobachter* 47/226 (Aug. 14, 1934); Günzler and Zwink, *Berühmtes Dorf*, 173; *AZ* 28/94 (Aug. 14, 1934), 1; Ernst Lang, *Das wars*, 45.

100. Günzler and Zwink, *Berühmtes Dorf*, 173; Utzschneider, *Oberammergau im Dritten Reich*, 109; GAO: ZA/Passionsspiele: *Bayreuther Tagblatt* 191 (Aug. 17, 1934); *Berliner Illustrierte Nachtausgabe* (Aug. 15, 1934); StAM: SpkA K1008; Ernst Lang, *Das wars*, 45–46.

101. Anton Lang, *Reminiscences*, 101; Günzler and Zwink, *Berühmtes Dorf*, 173; GAO: ZA/Passionsspiele: "Der Führer in Oberammergau," *Münchner Neueste Nachrichten* 219 (Aug. 14, 1934); Kurt Becher, " 'Neudeutschland' im Erzbistum München und Freising: Schicksale Katholischer Studierender Jugend in der NS-Zeit," in *Das Erzbistum München und Freising*, vol. 1, ed. Schwaiger, 827–28.

102. *AZ* 28/115 (Oct. 1, 34), 1; 28/153 (Dec. 31, 34), 1; GAO: B149, 155–56.

103. GAO: ZA/Passionsspiele: *Pirnauer Anzeiger* (Oct. 28, 1934).

CHAPTER 6

1. Von Hahn, *Nach Ober-Ammergau*, 81–82.

2. Münster, *Rochus Dedler*; Daisenberger, *Geschichte* (1859), 70, 111–12, 129–30, 168–70; Friedl Lang, *180 Jahre Musikleben in Oberammergau*, 16–17, 39; *AZ* 21/15 (Feb. 8, 1927), 1; Eugen Papst, "Oberammergau Passion Music," in *Oberammergau* (1950), ed. Community of Oberammergau, 46–50.

3. Bogenrieder, *Oberammergau* (1930), 65–67; Howitt, *Art Student in Munich*, 56–57; Jaron and Rudin, *Das Oberammergauer Passionsspiel*, 60–61; Burton, *Passion-Play at Ober-Ammergau*, 99–101.

4. *AZ* 21/15 (Feb. 8, 1927), 1; 31/30 (March 11, 1937), 1; *Geschichte und Geschichten*, vol. 2, 41–46; Diemer, *Oberammergau* (1922), 27, 29; Schumacher, *Meine Oberammergauer*, 22, 39; Greatorex, *Homes of Ober-Ammergau*, 12, 18, 26–28; *Passion Play at Oberammergau* (1930 and 1934), 7–8; Bogenrieder, *Oberammergau* (1930), 66–67; Klinner, *Christa*, 46.

5. Daisenberger, *Geschichte* (1859), 159; Dr. J. K., *Augsburger Postzeitung* (Aug. 2–4, 1850), Beylagen 142 and 143, in *Beyträge*, vol. 2, ed. von Deutinger, 556; *Neueste Nachrichten* 260–65 (Sept. 17–22, 1850), in *Beyträge*, vol. 3, ed. von Deutinger, 43; Devrient, *Augsburger Allgem. Zeitung* (Sept. 14–20, 1850), Beylagen, in *Beyträge*, vol. 3., ed. von Deutinger, 139; Clarus, *Das Passionsspiel zu Ober-Ammergau*, 92–93; Friedl Lang, *180 Jahre Musikleben in Oberammergau*, 18–21.

6. Friedl Lang, *180 Jahre Musikleben in Oberammergau*, 18–19; Greatorex, *Homes of Ober-Ammergau*, 4, and "Gathering of the Band," opposite 36.

7. GAO: A/III/15: Joseph Schiedermayr, *Festvortrag anlässlich des 150-jährigen Bestehens des Musikvereins Oberammergau* (Aug. 4, 1956), 1–2; Friedl Lang, *180 Jahre Musikleben in Oberammergau*, 16–41; Klinner, *Oberammergau*, 44–45.

8. Friedl Lang, *180 Jahre Musikleben in Oberammergau*, 28; Schröder, *Oberammergau* (1910), introductory material; *AZ* 3/78 (July 24, 1909), 3; GAO: 12. 1. 5.

9. Schiedermayr, *Festvortrag*, 4; *AZ* 3/78 (July 24, 1909), 3; GAO: 12. 1. 5; Friedl Lang, *180 Jahre Musikleben in Oberammergau*, 28–41.

10. GAO: AXV/128; AX/73, including C. Bauer, "Der Fremdenverkehr in Oberammergau und die Passionsspiele 1940: Betrachtungen und Vorschläge" (November 1938), 5–6; ZA/Passionsspiele: "Die Pleite in Oberammergau," *Die Stunde* (Sept. 12, 1934).

11. GAO: B149, 129, 139, 144; Gem. Prot. v. July 20, 1934.

12. GAO: B149, 155; Gem. Prot. v. Dec. 21, 1934.

13. GAO: AX/73: "Übernachtungszahlen" (1923–1938); Bauer, "Der Fremdenverkehr in Oberammergau," 27; Friedl Lang, *180 Jahre Musikleben in Oberammergau*, 28–9, 33–34, 37–39.

14. GAO: B149, 55; Gem. Prot. v. Nov. 9, 1934; Nov. 19, 1934; Friedl Lang, *180 Jahre Musikleben in Oberammergau*, 35, 44.

15. *AZ* 27/47 (April 22, 1933), 1; Schiedermayr, *Festvortrag*, 4–6; Friedl Lang, *180 Jahre Musikleben in Oberammergau*, 37; StAM: LRA 61613; LRA 61615; LRA 199059; SpkA K1008.

16. Friedl Lang, *180 Jahre Musikleben in Oberammergau*, 44; GAO: Gem. Prot. v. April 8, 1936; July 2, 1936; GAO: AII/54.

17. GAO: Gem. Prot. v. July 2, 1936.

18. GAO: Gem. Prot. v. Aug. 3, 1936; AII/54.

19. GAO: Gem. Prot. v. Aug. 3, 1936; Jan. 7, 1938; Friedl Lang, *180 Jahre Musikleben in Oberammergau*, 44–45; StAM: SpkA K1008; LRA 61615.

20. GAO: AII/54; StAM: LRA 61616; SpkA K1008.

21. Friedl Lang, *180 Jahre Musikleben in Oberammergau*, 45–46; *AZ* 30/155 (Dec. 31, 1936), 1; GAO: AII/54; Gem. Prot. v. Dec. 7, 1936; StAM: SpkA K1008; LRA 61615.

22. GAO: Gem. Prot. v. Aug. 28, 1936; Dec. 17, 1936; AII/54; StAM: LRA 61615.

23. GAO: Gem. Prot. v. March 18, 1937; AII/54; StAM: LRA 61615.

24. GAO: AII/54.

25. GAO: Gem. Prot. v. Jan. 7, 1938; AII/54; StAM: SpkA K1008; LRA 61615; Friedl Lang, *180 Jahre Musikleben in Oberammergau*, 45–46.

26. GAO: Gem. Prot. v. Jan. 7, 1938; Jan. 11, 1938.

27. Friedl Lang, *180 Jahre Musikleben in Oberammergau*, 46–47; StAM: LRA 61616; GAO: Gem. Prot. v. Nov. 20, 1938.

28. GAO: AII/54; StAM: LRA 61613; LRA 61615: LRA 199059; SpkA K1008.

29. StAM: SpkA K1008.

30. StAM: LRA 198994; SpkA K1008.

31. GAO: AII/54.

32. GAO: AIV/45; StAM: SpkA K1008; LRA 61613.

33. StAM: SpkA K1008; SpkA K4240; LRA 61613.

34. StAM: SpkA K1008; LRA 61613.

35. StAM: LRA 61613; SpkA K4240; *AZ* 29/86 (July 25, 1935), 2; Pridham, *Hitler's Rise to Power*, 316.

36. GAO: Gem. Prot. v. Aug. 17, 1937; StAM: LRA 61613; SpkA K4268; *AZ* passim from 29/26 (March 2, 1935), 1, to 32/65 (1/2 June, 1938), 3.

37. StAM: LRA 61616.

38. StAM: LRA 61613; *AZ* 29/77 (July 4, 1935), 1; 30/85 (July 18, 1936), 1–2; GAO: Gem. Prot. v. Nov. 19, 1934; Feb. 18, 1935; Nov. 24, 1936; July 26, 1937; Aug. 17, 1937; Bogenrieder, *Jubiläums-Passionsspiele Oberammergau.*

39. *AZ* 29/4 (Jan. 10, 1935), 1; 29/63 (June 1, 1935), 1; 30/78 (July 2, 1936), 3; 30/85 (July 18, 1936), 1–2; 31/53 (May 4, 1937), 1; 31/82 (July 10, 1937), 1; 31/124 (Oct. 16, 1937), 1; 32/96 (Aug. 12–13, 1938), 3; GAO: Gem. Prot. v. Jan. 29, 1935; March 15, 1935; March 27, 1935; Oct. 21, 1938; *Das Bayernland* 47/15 (Aug. 1936), 487–88, 507, 511; Utzschneider, *Oberammergau im Dritten Reich*, 90–91, 131–32.

40. *AZ* 30/85 (July 18, 1936), 1; 31/124 (Oct. 16, 1937), 1; 32/95 (Aug. 10–11, 1938), 3; StAM: LRA 61613; LRA 61614; LRA 61616; GAO: Gem. Prot. v. Dec. 14, 1934; Sept. 7, 1935; Sept 13, 1935; April 23, 1937; Sept. 29, 1937.

41. GAO: Gem. Prot. v. Nov. 19, 1934; July 5, 1935; Sept. 13, 1935; Oct. 16, 1935; Feb. 4, 1936; June 2, 1937; Feb. 12, 1939; Rädlinger, *Zwischen Tradition und Fortschritt*, 154; StAM: LRA 61615; LRA 61616; *AZ* 30/108 (Sept. 10, 1936), 1.

42. StAM: LRA 61616.

43. *AZ* 29/4 (Jan. 10, 1935), 1; GAO: Gem. Prot. v. Nov. 9, 1934; 11. 5. 4; 11. 7. 1; AX/73, "Übernachtungszahlen."

44. *AZ* 29/63 (June 1, 1935), 1; 31/50 (April 27, 1937), 1; Friedl Lang, *180 Jahre Musikleben in Oberammergau*, 45; AX/73, including Bauer, "Der Fremdenverkehr in Oberammergau," 22; Gem. Prot. v. Nov. 19, 1934; Jan. 29, 1935; July 2, 1936; July 29, 1938; Feb. 17, 1939; Florian Lang, Ammergauer Häuser; postcard collection.

45. GAO: Gem. Prot. v. Oct. 2, 1934; Nov. 9, 1934; Nov. 19, 1934; Jan. 17, 1935; Jan. 25, 1935; Feb. 28, 1935; March 29, 1935; April 17, 1935; July 1, 1935; Sept. 13, 1935; Oct. 16, 1935; Jan. 14, 1936; Feb. 26, 1936; June 3, 1936; July 26, 1936; Aug. 17, 1936; Nov. 24, 1936; June 12, 1937; July 26, 1937; Dec. 14, 1937; March 20, 1938; May 3, 1938; Nov. 29, 1938; A150/2; AX/73, "Übernachtungszahlen"; *AZ* 29/6 (Jan. 15, 1934), 1.

46. StAM: LRA 61615; SpkA: A4283; *AZ* 29/32 (March 16, 1935), 1; 30/108 (Sept. 10, 1936), 1, 4; 30/146 (Dec. 8, 1936), 3; 32/13 (Jan. 31–Feb. 1, 1938), 3.

47. *AZ* 28/16 (Feb. 8, 1934), 1; 28/129 (Nov. 3, 1934), 3–4; 28/141 (Dec. 1, 1934), 3; 29/64 (June 4, 1935), 1; 30/8 (Jan. 21, 1936), 3; 30/61 (May 23, 1936), 4; *Oberammergau Wochenprogramm* 1/10 (Aug. 7–13, 1938); 2/4 (July 9–15, 1939); 2/7 (July 30–Aug. 6, 1939); Ernst Lang, *Das wars*, 54; StAM: SpkA: K4283. See Baranowski, *Strength through Joy*, for a thorough overview of this pervasive program. She mentions on pages 119–20 that the first package tours were on Feb. 17, 1934, and included trains from northern cities to places like the Upper Bavarian mountains; some set off from southern cities, including Munich, in the next few days. They wanted to mix people from different German areas.

48. Utzschneider, *Oberammergau im Dritten Reich*, 45–46, citing *G-PT* 58/278 (Nov. 30, 1938), n.p.; StAM: LRA 61613; LRA 61615; Baranowski, *Strength through Joy*, 132–33, 165–66, mentions that complaints were common over KdF guests as the hosts were poorly paid. They worried about losing regular paying customers, so the KdF was "forced to steer its tours away from the prestigious spas and vacation spots" in the later 1930s.

49. StAM: LRA 61616; Utzschneider, *Oberammergau im Dritten Reich*, 45–46, citing *G-PT* 58/278 (Nov. 30, 1938), n.p.; *G-PT* 58/287 (Dec. 10, 1938), 3; 59/6 (Jan. 7,

1939), 10; 59/12 (Jan. 14, 1939), 10; 59/18 (Jan. 21, 1939), 10; 59/27 (Feb. 1, 1939), 12–13; 59/51 (March 1, 1939), 13; 59/72 (March 25, 1939), 10; 59/78 (April 1, 1939), 16; 59/149 (July 1, 1939), 14; *AZ* passim, 1934–1938, especially 32/15 (Feb. 4–5, 1938), 3; 32/28 (March 7–8, 1938), 4; 32/44 (April 13–14, 1938), 5; 32/64 (May 30–31, 1938), 5; 32/67 (June 7–8, 1938), 3; 32/75 (June 24–25, 1938), 5; 32/81 (July 8–9, 1938), 3.

50. PAO: Schublade 17: Seelsorgsjahresbericht 1936; *AZ* 29/61 (May 28, 1935), 1; 29/149 (Dec. 19, 1935), 4.

51. *AZ* 27/96 (Aug. 17, 1933), 1; 27/106 (Sept. 9, 1933), 1; 27/143 (Dec. 5, 1933), 1; 28/4 (Jan. 11, 1934), 4; 28/129 (Nov. 3, 1934), 3–4; 28/130 (Nov. 6, 1934), 1; 28/133 (Nov. 13, 1934), 1; 28/135 (Nov. 17, 1934), 3; 28/136 (Nov. 20, 1934), 1; 28/141 (Dec. 1, 1934), 3.

52. *AZ* 29/12 (Jan. 29, 1935), 1; 29/39 (April 2, 1935), 1; 29/136 (Nov. 19, 1935), 1, 4; 30/24 (Feb. 27, 1936), 1; 30/90 (July 30, 1936), 1.

53. PAO: Schublade 31: Pfarramtliche Bestätigung, June 12, 1947; GAO: Gem. Prot. v. Jan. 17, 1935; *AZ* passim from 27/116 (Oct. 3, 1933), 4, to 32/13 (Jan. 31–Feb. 1, 1938), 5; Evans, *Third Reich in Power*, 484–90.

54. *AZ* 28/148 (Dec. 18, 1934), 3; 30/34 (March 21, 1936), 1; GAO: Gem. Prot. v. Nov. 22, 1934.

55. *AZ* passim from 27/115 (Sept. 30, 1933), 1, to 32/36 (March 2–3, 1938), 3; *G-PT* 61/82 (April 7, 1941), 9; GAO: A150/2.

56. *AZ* passim from 29/25 (Feb. 28, 1935), 1, to 32/34 (March 21–22, 1938), 4.

57. *AZ* 27/113 (Sept. 26, 1933), 1; 27/132 (Nov. 9, 1933), 1. Work evenings continued every week to 27/147 (Dec. 14, 1933), 1, then again from 28/6 (Jan. 16, 1934), 1, to 28/27 (March 6, 1934), 1; passim from 28/36 (March 27, 1934), 1, to 32/95 (Aug. 10–11, 1938), 3; *G-PT* 58/223 (Sept. 24, 1938), 4; 59/51 (March 1, 1939), 3; 59/99 (April 29, 1939), 20.

58. *AZ* 28/36 (March 27, 1934), 1; 28/48 (April 26, 1934), 4; 28/49 (April 28, 1934), 1; 29/30 (March 12, 1935), 1; 29/34 (March 21, 1935), 4; 29/44 (April 13, 1935), 1; 31/46 (April 17, 1937), 1; 31/148 (Dec. 11, 1937), 5; 32/12 (Jan. 28–29, 1938), 1.

59. *AZ* 29/48 (April 25, 1935), 1; 30/48 (April 23, 1936), 3; 31/46 (April 17, 1937), 1; 31/48 (April 22, 1937), 1, 4; 32/47 (April 21, 1938), 3; *G-PT* 59/91 (April 19, 1939), 4; 61/128 (June 4, 1941), 5.

60. *AZ* 27/132 (Nov. 9, 1933), 4; 28/152 (Dec. 29, 1934), 1; 29/14 (Feb. 2, 1935), 1, 4; 29/15 (Feb. 5, 1935), 1; *G-PT* 59/27 (Feb. 1, 1939), 12.

61. *AZ* passim from 28/21 (Feb. 20, 1934), 1, to 31/67 (June 5, 1937), 5; *G-PT* 63/104 (May 6, 1943), 3; GAO: Gem. Prot. v. March 25, 1937; GAO: A000/12.

62. Central File; *AZ* passim from 28/48 (April 26, 1934), 1, to 32/42 (April 8–9, 1938), 8; *G-PT* 58/287 (Dec. 10, 1938), 3; 59/91 (April 19, 1939), 4; 59/99 (April 29, 1939), 20; 60/171 (July 24, 1940), 6; 61/1 (Jan. 2, 1941), 4.

63. StAM: LRA 61616; GAO: Gem. Prot. v. Oct. 16, 1935; Evans, *Third Reich in Power*, 484–90, mentions that in July 1936 the HJ controlled facilities and activities for youths under fourteen years of age and soon for older ones as well. By early 1939 almost all of the young people were in the HJ, and on March 25, 1939, it was "legally binding from the age of ten," with the threat of fines for parents, who were "even imprisoned if they actively tried to stop them [from] joining." *AZ* 27/52 (Dec. 28,

1933), 1; 28/5 (Jan. 13, 1934), 1; 28/51 (May 3, 1934), 1; Pössinger, *Lebensbilder eines Gebirgsjägers*, 14; *G-PT* 63/157 (July 8, 1943), 3; Schellenberger, *Katholische Jugend und Drittes Reich*, 158; Kleinöder, "Verfolgung und Widerstand," 212–18.

64. Ernst Lang, *Das wars*, 42–46; *AZ* 32/68 (June 9–10, 1938), 3; Central File.

65. GAO: Gem. Prot. v. Nov. 19, 1934; *AZ* passim from 28/49 (April 28, 1934), 1, to 32/41 (April 6–7, 1938), 5; *G-PT* 60/171 (July 24, 1940), 6; 63/157 (July 8, 1943), 3.

66. Ernst Lang, *Das wars*, 42–46; *AZ* 31/66 (June 3, 1937), 4; *G-PT* 58/287 (Dec. 10, 1938), 3; GAO: A000/12; Gem. Prot. v. Feb. 11, 1938.

67. *AZ* 28/74 (June 28, 1934), 1; 29/90 (Aug. 3, 1935), 1; 31/67 (June 5, 1937), 6.

68. *AZ* passim from 27/149 (Dec. 19, 1933), 4, to 32/52 (May 2/3, 1938), 3; StAM: LRA 61615.

69. *AZ* 32/28 (March 7–8, 1938), 3; 32/29 (March 9–10, 1938), 3; 32/30 (March 11–12, 1938), 2.

70. StAM: SpkA K1008.

71. GAO: Gem. Prot. v. Feb. 8, 1935; May 18, 1935; June 1, 1935; June 4, 1935; June 5, 1935; Utzschneider, *Oberammergau im Dritten Reich*, 84; StAM: SpkA K1008.

72. StAM: SpkA K1008; SpkA K4283; LRA 199059.

73. StAM: LRA 61613; LRA 61614; LRA 199036; LRA 199041; *AZ* 29/135 (Nov. 16, 1935), 1–2; Alte Friedhof.

74. GAO: A150/2; BHStA: OMGBY 10/48–2/6, including Josef Raab statement; Central File.

75. StAM: SpkA K1008; SpkA K4253; SpkA K4283; *AZ* 29/7 (Jan. 17, 1935), 1; 29/103 (Sept. 3, 1935), 1; 29/135 (Nov. 16, 1935), 1–2; Bergerson, *Ordinary Germans in Extraordinary Times*, especially 146–69, stresses the role of changed practices like greetings in Nazifying everyday life, as well as the challenge that such required signs of support for the regime posed to the nonbeliever. Johnson, *Nazi Terror*, especially 485–86, stresses the leeway for ordinary citizens left by the Gestapo if they avoided unnecessary provocation and, of course, denunciations.

76. StAM: SpkA K1008; *AZ* 32/6 (Jan. 14–15, 1938), 1; GAO: Gem. Prot. v. June 2, 1937; Jan. 7, 1938; PAO: Schublade 17: Seelsorgsjahresbericht 1936.

77. StAM: SpkA K1008.

78. Central File; StAM: SpkA K4253; PAO: Schublade 31: Pfarramtliche Bestätigung, n.d.; Evans, *Third Reich in Power*, 241–46.

79. StAM: SpkA K4235; LRA 198994; Evans, *Third Reich in Power*, 246–47.

80. StAM: LRA 61613.

81. Ibid. 61615; Kershaw, *Popular Opinion*, 196–98.

82. StAM: LRA 61615.

83. Ibid.; LRA 61616.

84. PAO Schublade 17: Seelsorgsjahresbericht 1933, 1935, 1936, 1937, 1938; StAM: LRA 61614.

85. StAM: LRA 61613; LRA 61614.

86. *AZ* 29/96 (Aug. 17, 1935), 1; StAM: LRA 61614; LRA 61615; LRA 61616; Fröhlich, "Der Pfarrer von Mombris," in *Bayern in der NS-Zeit*, vol. 6, 54–55, reveals a similar bent toward martyrdom.

87. StAM: LRA 61613; LRA 61615; LRA 63089; AEM: Fragebogen vom July 1, 1946: Fragebogen A: Nationalsozialistische Verfolgung Kath. Geistlicher, Bogenrieder. Kershaw, *Popular Opinion*, 194–201, stresses the leadership of the priests and curates.

88. PAO: Schublade 17: Seelsorgsjahresbericht, 1936; Gottfried Lang, "Hitler's Visit in 1934," 2–4.

89. PAO: Schublade 17: Seelsorgsjahresbericht, 1936, 1937; StAM: LRA 61614.

90. PAO: Schublade 17, Seelsorgsjahresbericht 1935, 1936, 1937, 1938.

91. PAO: Schublade 17: Seelsorgsjahresbericht 1933–1939; Central File; StAM: LRA 61613; LRA 61616; AZ 28/144 (Dec. 8, 1934), 1; 29/29 (March 9, 1935), 6; 29/49 (April 27, 1935), 8.

92. PAO: Schublade 17: Seelsorgsjahresbericht 1933–1939; Central File; AZ 28/77 (July 5, 1934), 1; 28/144 (Dec. 8, 1934), 4; 29/5 (Jan. 12, 1935), 3; 29/14 (Feb. 2. 1935), 3; 29/144 (Dec. 7, 1935), 5; 30/22 (Feb. 22, 1936), 4; 30/46 (April 18, 1936), 4; 30/109 (Sept. 12, 1936), 5; 31/31 (March 13, 1937), 4; 31/41 (April 6, 1937), 1; 31/61 (May 22, 1937), 4.

93. Central File; PAO: Schublade 17: Seelsorgsjahresbericht 1933–1939; StAM: LRA 61614; AZ 7/115 (Oct. 14, 1913), 3; 13/19 (March 19, 1919), 1; 14/35 (May 1, 1920), 1; 20/32 (March 18, 1926), 1; 21/38 (April 1, 1927), 1; 22/30 (March 13, 1928), 1; 22/31 (March 15, 1928), 1; 28/129 (Nov. 3, 1934), 5; 28/138 (Nov. 24, 1934), 5; 28/141 (Dec. 1, 1934), 6; 29/32 (March 16, 1935), 5; 29/38 (March 30, 1935), 6; 29/54 (May 11, 1935), 4; 30/31 (March 14, 1936), 4; 30/90 (July 30, 1936), 1.

94. Gottfried Lang, "Hitler's Visit in 1934," 2.

95. Central File; Gottfried Lang, "Hitler's Visit in 1934," 2–4; Anton Lang, *Reminiscences*, 146–47; Kleinöder, "Verfolgung und Widerstand," 219, discusses the participation in pilgrimages that allowed youths to continue congregating.

96. PAO: Schublade 17: Seelsorgsjahresbericht 1937–1939; StAM: LRA 61615; LRA 61616.

97. StAM: LRA 61615; PAO: Schublade 17: Seelsorgsjahresbericht 1937.

98. Koch, "Die Benediktinerabtei Ettal," in *Das Erzbistum München und Freising*, vol. 2, ed. Schwaiger, 384; AZ passim from 28/25 (March 1, 1934), 1, to 32/96 (Aug. 12–13, 1938), 4; StAM: LRA 61615; PAO: Schublade 17: Meldebogen, March 14, 1944.

99. GAO: Gem. Prot. v. June 2, 1937; StAM: LRA 61613; LRA: 61614; AZ 28/62 (May 31, 1934), 1; 28/63 (June 2, 1934), 1; 30/76 (June 27, 1936), 5; 31/61 (May 22, 1937), 4; 31/63 (May 27, 1937), 1; 31/64 (May 29, 1937), 1.

100. StAM: LRA 61615.

101. Ibid., 61614; LRA 61616; SpkA K1008; Koch, "Die Benediktinerabtei Ettal," in *Das Erzbistum München und Freising*, vol. 2, ed. Schwaiger, 384; AZ 32/60 (May 20–21, 1938), 5.

102. PAO: Schublade 17: letter dated May 30, 1938; AZ 32/48 (April 23, 1938), 3; 32/60 (May 20/21, 1938), 3; PAO: Seelsorgsjahresbericht 1938; StAM: LRA 61616.

103. PAO: Schublade 17: letters dated June 6, 1938, and June 14, 1938.

104. AZ 32/71 (June 15–16, 1938), 3; PAO: Schublade 17: letter dated June 12, 1939.

105. StAM: LRA 61614; LRA 61615; PAO: Schublade 17: Seelsorgsjahresbericht 1936; Rädlinger, *Zwischen Tradition und Fortschritt*, 183.

106. GAO: A150/2; StAM, SpkA K4240; Kaplan, *Between Dignity and Despair*, 15, discusses such "mixed signals" that kept "a glimmer of hope" alive for Jews in the mid-1930s.

107. GAO: A150/2; StAM: LRA 61615.

108. *AZ* 29/65 (June 6, 1935), 1; 29/83 (July 18, 1935), 4; 29/84 (July 20, 1935), 1, 6; 29/85 (July 22, 1935), 1; 29/87 (July 27, 1935), 1; GAO: ZA/Passionsspiele: Clipping, no provenance but possibly 1935, about a report in Czech newspapers, including "Lidove Listy," saying that the play was to be forbidden and so on. Friedman, *Oberammergau Passion Play*, 123, makes a mistake by identifying Anton Lang rather than Alois as playing the lead in *Ernte*.

109. *AZ* 29/44 (April 13, 1935), 1; 29/48 (April 25, 1935), 4; 29/60 (May 25, 1935), 1, 6; 29/99 (Aug. 24, 1935), 8; 29/111 (Sept. 21, 1935), 1; 29/114 (Sept. 28, 1935), 1; 29/122 (Oct. 17, 1935), 2.

110. *AZ* 29/133 (Nov. 12, 1935), 1; 29/135 (Nov. 16, 1935), 1–2.

111. *AZ* 29/144 (Dec. 7, 1935), 1; 29/147 (Dec. 14, 1935), 1; 30/121 (Oct. 10, 1936), 1; 31/116 (Sept. 28, 1937), 4; StAM: LRA 198994.

112. *AZ* 30/93 (Aug. 6, 1936), 1; 31/148 (Dec. 11, 1937), 5; GAO: AII/54.

113. StAM: SpkA K1008; K4283; K4252; GAO: A150/2; *AZ* 31/157 (Dec. 31, 1937), 2; 32/10 (Jan. 24–25, 1938), 3; Fröhlich, "Der Pfarrer von Mombris," 52–75, discusses the negative reaction of a local priest and his congregation to these efforts to display Streicher's *Der Stürmer*.

114. *AZ* 29/135 (Nov. 16, 1935), 1–2.

115. StAM: LRA 61615; SpkA: K4252.

116. Ernst Lang, *Das wars*, 39; GAO: A150/2; Rädlinger, *Zwischen Tradition und Fortschritt*, 182; Central File; LRA 61613.

117. StAM: LRA 61615; LRA 61616; Central File; GAO: A150/2.

118. Ernst Lang, *Das wars*, 39; Central File.

119. GAO: A150/2; StAM: SpkA K1008; K4240; K4252; K4253; K4268; K4271; K4311.

120. GAO: A150/2; Kaplan, *Between Dignity and Despair*, 40–46, discusses the escalating pressures on friendships and the gradual turning of Jews into "pariahs."

121. StAM: LRA 61616; SpkA K4240; Utzschneider, *Oberammergau im Dritten Reich*, 127, including the county leader's "summons."

122. StAM: SpkA K4240; Utzschneider, *Oberammergau im Dritten Reich*, 127, citing GAO: A070/6.

123. Rädlinger, *Zwischen Tradition und Fortschritt*, 184; Utzschneider, *Oberammergau im Dritten Reich*, 127, citing GAO:A 070/6; StAM: LRA 61616; LRA 61668; SpkA K4252; *H-B* 3/43 (March 7, 1947), 3; Kaplan, *Between Dignity and Despair*, 122–23.

CHAPTER 7

1. Ernst Lang, *Das wars*, 80, 134–235.

2. Kaltenegger, *Die Stammdivision der deutschen Gebirgstruppe*, 365–67; de Bernières, *Captain Corelli's Mandolin*, and the 2001 movie with the same title, directed by John Madden.

3. *Oberammergau* (1950), ed. Community of Oberammergau, 52; StAM: LRA 61619.

4. StAM: LRA 61616; Kershaw, *"Hitler Myth,"* 122–47.

5. StAM: SpkA K1008; Ernst Lang, *Das wars*, 128.

6. StAM: LRA 61616.

7. GAO: AXV/145.

8. Ibid.; StAM: LRA 61616; LRA 61617.

9. StAM: LRA 61617.

10. StAM: LRA 61616; LRA 61617.

11. StAM: LRA 61617; LRA 61618.

12. StAM: LRA 61618.

13. Ibid.

14. Ibid.; LRA 61619.

15. StAM: LRA 61619.

16. Ibid.

17. Ibid.

18. Ibid.

19. Ernst Lang, *Das wars*, 80, 111–13; Central File; Kaltenegger, *Die Stammdivision der deutschen Gebirgstruppe*, 365; GAO: Foto-Sammlung, 251; Pössinger, *Lebensbilder eines Gebirgsjägers*, 20–23; *AZ* 32/33 (March 18–19, 1938), 7–8.

20. *Alte Friedhof, Oberammergau*; van Hoek, "Oberammergau," 2; Lanz, *Gebirgsjäger*; Kaltenegger, *Die Stammdivision der deutschen Gebirgstruppe*, 1–49; Central File; *AZ* 32/10 (Jan. 24–25, 1938), 3; *G-PT* 59/160 (July 14, 1939), 8; 60/163 (July 15, 1940), 6; 60/191 (Aug. 16, 1940), 5; 61/203 (Aug. 29, 1941), 3; 61/237 (Oct. 8, 1941), 4; 61/249 (Oct. 22, 1941), 3; 61/260 (Nov. 4, 1941), 4; 61/301 (Dec. 22, 1941), 3; 62/142 (June 20, 1942), 8; 62/157 (July 8, 1942), 3; 62/190 (Aug. 15, 1942), 1; 62/204 (Sept. 1, 1942), 4; 62/208 (Sept. 5, 1942), 3, 8; 62/211 (Sept. 9, 1942), 3; 62/262 (Nov. 7, 1942), 3, 8; 62/267 (Nov. 13, 1942), 3; 63/71 (March 25, 1943), 3; 63/296 (Dec. 17, 1943), 4; GAO: A150/2; A060/12; Gem. Prot. v. Jan. 15, 1943; A0931; Ernst Lang, *Das wars*, 133.

21. Ernst Lang, *Das wars*, 128; StAM: LRA 61616; LRA 61617; LRA 198994; GAO: Gem. Prot. v. Dec. 21, 1939; Bartov, *Hitler's Army*, 45, 56.

22. Lanz, *Gebirgsjäger*, 49–56, 59, 63, 68; Ernst Lang, *Das wars*, 132–44; Pössinger, *Lebensbilder eines Gebirgsjägers*, 22–25; Meyer, *Blutiges Edelweiß*, 27–30, 58–65; Stephan Stracke, "Mörder unter dem Edelweiss: Kriegsverbrechen der Gebirgsjäger," in *Mörder unterm Edelweiss*, ed. Klein, Mentner, and Stracke, 37–67; *G-PT* 63/28 (Feb. 3, 1942), 3; Evans, *Third Reich at War*, 222–23.

23. Lanz, *Gebirgsjäger*, 75–76, 79–93, 112, 116–24, 127, 131–33; Central File; Pössinger, *Lebensbilder eines Gebirgsjäger*, 26–37.

24. Ernst Lang, *Das wars*, 148–77.

25. Kaltenegger, *Die Stammdivision der deutschen Gebirgstruppe*, 157, 268–302, 365–66; Lanz, *Gebirgsjäger*, 134–67; Pössinger, *Lebensbilder eines Gebirgsjäger*, 48–68.

26. Lanz, *Gebirgsjäger*, 136–46; Pössinger, *Lebensbilder eines Gebirgsjäger*, 48–55.

27. Lanz, *Gebirgsjäger*, 146–53, 197; Bartov, *Hitler's Army*, 12–28; Pössinger, *Lebensbilder eines Gebirgsjäger*, 55.

28. Lanz, *Gebirgsjäger*, 136–46, 153–57, 192, 233–41; Pössinger, *Lebensbilder eines Gebirgsjäger*, 84–85; Evans, *Third Reich at War*, 406, quoting Speer, *Inside the Third Reich*, 332.

29. Lanz, *Gebirgsjäger*, 157–61, 218–19, 224–33; Pössinger, *Lebensbilder eines Gebirgsjäger*, 74–88.

30. Tieke, *Caucasus and the Oil*, 99–117, 191–219, 301–28; Lanz, *Gebirgsjäger*, 161–67; Pössinger, *Lebensbilder eines Gebirgsjäger*, 88; Bartov, *Germany's War and the Holocaust*, 3–32.

31. Mazower, *Inside Hitler's Greece*, 159; G-PT 63/28 (Feb. 3, 1943), 3; Meyer, *Blutiges Edelweiss*, 60–63, reproduces his similar characterizations when exploiting the Lvov slaughters in 1941 to indoctrinate his troops against their Communist foes. A member of the Signal Corps also recorded his observations of the brief but bloody presence of the 1st Mountain troops in Lvov.

32. Lanz, *Gebirgsjäger*, 150, 199; Pössinger, *Lebensbilder eines Gebirgsjäger*, 74; Meyer, *Blutiges Edelweiss*, 75–76. Ernst Lang, *Das wars*, 191–95, suggests that both accounts could be true since he stayed with the locals for a time, but the villagers were later removed from the area.

33. Pössinger, *Lebensbilder eines Gebirgsjäger*, 70; Lanz, *Gebirgsjäger*, 139–241; Kaltenegger, *Die Stammdivision der deutschen Gebirgstruppe*, 272–73; Meyer, *Blutiges Edelweiss*, 84.

34. Lanz, *Gebirgsjäger*, 182; Kaltenegger, *Die Stammdivision der deutschen Gebirgstruppe*, 272–73; Pössinger, *Lebensbilder eines Gebirgsjäger*, 72, 118; Meyer, *Blutiges Edelweiss*, 43–46.

35. StAM: SpkA K4240.

36. Bartov, *Hitler's Army*, 89–105. See also Shepherd, *War in the Wild East*, 76, 81, 126–27, 190, which explores the role of the Wehrmacht's security divisions in following "brutalizing" occupation practices, particularly in Belarus. However, he points out that the occupation was not always negative; "fraternization on a daily, personal level between occupier and occupied did take place." Meyer, *Blutiges Edelweiß*, 84, 108; Mazower, *Inside Hitler's Greece*, 176, and his *Hitler's Empire*.

37. Meyer, *Blütiges Edelweiss*, 272–80, 289–453; Kaltenegger, *Die Stammdivision der deutschen Gebirgstruppe*, 302–24; Mazower, *Inside Hitler's Greece*, 149–50, 176–215; Lanz, *Gebirgsjäger*, 243–79; Burdick, *Hubert Lanz*, 1–5, 172–77, 180–95; Mazower, "Military Violence and National Socialist Values," 129–58; Pössinger, *Lebensbilder eines Gebirgsjäger*, 114–18; Stracke, "Mörder unter dem Edelweiss," 41–44; Evans, *Third Reich at War*, 471.

38. Kaltenegger, *Die Stammdivision der deutschen Gebirgstruppe*, 302–24; Mazower, *Inside Hitler's Greece*, 149–50, 176–215; Lanz, *Gebirgsjäger*, 243–79; National Archive, *Europa unterm Hakenkreuz*, vol. 6; Meyer, *Blutiges Edelweiss*; Klein, Mentner, and Stracke, *Mörder unterm Edelweiß*.

39. Kaltenegger, *German Mountain Troops in World War II*, 217; Mazower, *Inside Hitler's Greece*, 157–98; Kaltenegger, *Die Stammdivision der deutschen Gebirgstruppe*, 302–24. Kaltenegger describes the brutal antipartisan actions against Greece and the Balkans as acting "as a 'fire brigade,' taking part in difficult and psychologically

demanding operations against the numerous partisan bands active in Greece, Albania, and Yugoslavia." He does mention "incidents that severely tarnished the Edelweiss and the reputation of the German mountain troops," especially the Cephalonian massacre. Mazower, "Military Violence and National Socialist Values," 155; Lanz, *Gebirgsjäger*, 245–46, 250, 258; Stracke, "Mörder unter dem Edelweiss," 44–53; Meyer, *Blutiges Edelweiss*, 142–238, 463–646.

40. Lanz, *Gebirgsjäger*, 245–46, 258; Kaltenegger, *Die Stammdivision der deutschen Gebirgstruppe*, 310; Mazower, "Military Violence and National Socialist Values," 158, mentions "widely accepted notions of racial inferiority" in the mix; Deakin, *Embattled Mountain*, 10–24, 29–32.

41. Mazower, *Inside Hitler's Greece*, 157–98; Lanz, *Gebirgsjäger*, 245–46, 250, 258, 272; Deakin, *Embattled Mountain*, 34, 95–106; Kaltenegger, *Die Stammdivision der deutschen Gebirgstruppe*, 310.

42. Pössinger, *Lebensbilder eines Gebirgsjäger*, 105–11.

43. Mazower, *Inside Hitler's Greece*, 198–211.

44. Ibid., 198–211; Mazower, "Military Violence and National Socialist Values," 131; Pössinger, *Lebensbilder eines Gebirgsjäger*, 105.

45. Mazower, *Inside Hitler's Greece*, 219–56; Lanz, *Gebirgsjäger*, 255–58; Meyer, *Blütiges Edelweiss*, 583–609; Stracke, "Mörder unter dem Edelweiss," 57–61; Pössinger, *Lebensbilder eines Gebirgsjäger*, 113, 122–26; Wiesel, *Night*, 1, 6–20.

46. Lanz, *Gebirgsjäger*, 96, 140, 263, 318; Kaltenegger, *Die Stammdivision der deutschen Gebirgstruppe*, 48.

47. A list of World War II war dead hung on tablets from Oberammergau's Catholic church; Kaltenegger, *Die Stammdivision der deutschen Gebirgstruppe*, 360; Lanz, *Gebirgsjäger*, 278–99; Ernst Lang, *Das wars*, 145; Stingley, "Woodcarver Draws Crowds"; graves in Oberammergau's two cemeteries; Mazower, *Inside Hitler's Greece*, 210; *G-PT* passim for war years; GAO: A060/12.

48. Central File; StAM: SpkA K4311; GAO: A150/2; *AZ* 61/256 (Oct. 30, 1941), 8.

49. Central File; Ernst Lang, *Das wars*, 182, 196–98; StAM: LRA 61619; *G-PT* 59/251 (Oct. 28, 1939), 4; 62/20 (Jan. 24, 1942), 6.

50. A list of World War II war dead hung on tablets from Oberammergau's Catholic church; StAM: LRA 61618; LRA 61619; *G-PT* 62/4 (Jan. 6, 1942), 3; 62/20 (Jan. 24, 1942), 6; GAO: Foto-Sammlung, 251, includes a cutting from the *Münchner Illustrierte Presse* (March 7, 1940) that covers the three "apostles" on leave in Oberammergau.

51. StAM: SpkA K4235; LRA 61616; LRA 61617; LRA 61618; LRA 61619; GAO: AXV/145.

52. *Oberammergauer Wochenprogramm* (1938–1939); GAO: AX/73, containing Bauer, *Der Fremdenverkehr in Oberammergau*; StAM: LRA 61617.

53. GAO: Gem. Prot. v. Sept. 18, 1941; A092/1; A092/3; A092/5; PAO: Schublade 17: Seelsorgsjahresbericht 1943; Rädlinger, *Zwischen Tradition und Fortschritt*, 195; Utzschneider, *Oberammergau im Dritten Reich*, 139; StAM: LRA 61616; LRA 61617; LRA 61618; LRA 61619.

54. Utzschneider, *Oberammergau im Dritten Reich*, 139; PAO: Schublade 17: Seelsorgsjahresbericht 1943; StAM: LRA 61617; GAO: A092/3.

55. StAM: LRA 61616; LRA 61617; LRA 61618.

56. Rädlinger, *Zwischen Tradition und Fortschritt*, 194; PAO: Schublade 17: Seelsorgsjahresbericht 1940; StAM: LRA 61617; Gellately, *Backing Hitler*, 155, while illustration 24 shows the "P"; Stephenson, *Hitler's Home Front*, 271–72.

57. StAM: LRA 61618; LRA 61619; SpkA K4268; SpkA K4235; GAO: A060/9; A092/3; Rädlinger, *Zwischen Tradition und Fortschritt*, 194–95.

58. The "Aryan" refugees and the Tyroleans occupied rooms normally available to tourists. Bergerson, *Ordinary Germans in Extraordinary Times*, 220–22, makes this point about the "undesirable degrees of contact with those who were officially their racial inferiors" and mentions badges marking Eastern forced workers; Stephenson, *Hitler's Home Front*, 271–86, also makes this point and discusses the positive integration enjoyed by some of the foreign workers. See also Delaney, "Racial Values vs. Religious Values."

59. PAO: Schublade 17: Seelsorgsjahresbericht 1943; Utzschneider, *Oberammergau im Dritten Reich*, 139, quoting Ruth Schmitt-Grüntgens, "Alle Erinnerung ist Gegenwart," in *Ein Rucksack voll Geschichten*, ed. Kratz and Kummer, 20; StAM: LRA 61618; Rädlinger, *Zwischen Tradition und Fortschritt*, 195–97.

60. StAM: LRA 61617; GAO: A0931.

61. PAO: Schublade 17: Seelsorgsjahresbericht 1940; GAO: A0931; Central File; StAM: LRA 61617.

62. GAO: A060/9; A0931; Rädlinger, *Zwischen Tradition und Fortschritt*, 194–95; StAM: LRA 61619; SpkA K4235; K4268.

63. *G-PT* 59/202 (Sept. 1, 1939), 7; 59/203 (Sept. 2, 1939), 7; Rädlinger, *Zwischen Tradition und Fortschritt*, 189, 191–92; StAM: LRA 61618.

64. StAM: LRA 61618; LRA 61619; LRA 61670; GAO: A092/5.

65. Utzschneider, *Oberammergau im Dritten Reich*, 58–60; *G-PT* 59/251 (Oct. 28, 1939), 3; 59/283 (Dec. 5, 1939), 3–4; 59/286 (Dec. 8, 1939), 3–4; StAM: LRA 61617; LRA 61618; Central File; GAO: Gem. Prot. v. Dec. 21, 1939; July 9, 1940; July 11, 1941; March 31, 1943.

66. *G-PT* 61/64 (March 17, 1941), 4; 61/82 (April 7, 1941), 9; 61/128 (June 4, 1941), 5; 61/153 (July 3, 1941), 4; 61/155 (July 5, 1941), 3; 61/200 (Aug. 26, 1941), 5; 61/301 (Dec. 22, 1941), 3; 62/64 (March 17, 1942), 3; 62/262 (Nov. 7, 1942), 8; 62/267 (Nov. 13, 1942), 3; 63/28 (Feb. 3, 1943), 3; 63/94 (April 21, 1943), 1; 64/8 (Jan. 11, 1944), 4; 64/9 (Jan. 12, 1944), 4; 64/18 (Jan. 22, 1944), 4; 64/27 (Feb. 2, 1944), 4; 64/38 (Feb. 15, 1944), 4; 64/54 (March 4, 1944), 4; 64/60 (March 11, 1944), 1–3; 64/66 (March 18, 1944), 4; 64/91 (April 19, 1944), 4; 64/101 (May 2, 1944), 3; 64/102 (May 3, 1944), 3; 64/106 (May 8, 1944), 4; 64/109 (May 11, 1944), 4; 64/117 (May 20, 1944), 3; 64/120 (May 24, 1944), 3; 64/150 (June 29, 1944), 4; 64/185 (Aug. 9, 1944), 4; 64/204 (Aug. 31, 1944), 4; 64/207 (Sept. 4, 1944), 4; 64/244 (Oct. 17, 1944), 4; 64/252 (Oct. 26, 1944), 4; 64/258 (Nov. 2, 1944), 4; 64/269 (Nov. 15, 1944), 4; 64/291 (Dec. 11, 1944), 4; Lanz, *Gebirgsjäger*, 220, 235; Pössinger, *Lebensbilder eines Gebirgsjägers*, 68–70, 84–85; GAO: Foto-Sammlung, 251; PAO: Schublade 17: Seelsorgsjahresbericht 1943; StAM: LRA 61616; LRA 61617; LRA 61618; LRA 61619.

67. Central File; GAO: 000/13; A092/1; A092/3; A092/5; A150/1; *G-PT* 60/125 (May 31, 1940), 3; 60/192 (Aug. 17, 1940), 4; 60/240 (Oct. 12, 1940), 6; 61/23 (Jan. 28,

1941), 4; 61/56 (March 7, 1941), 4; 61/121 (May 26, 1941), 4; 61/257 (Oct. 31, 1941), 3; 62/4 (Jan. 6, 1942), 3; 62/25 (Jan. 30, 1942), 4; 62/267 (Nov. 13, 1942), 3; 62/282 (Dec. 1, 1942), 3.

68. GAO: A092/1; Gem. Prot. v. July 9, 1940; StAM: LRA 61617; Rädlinger, *Zwischen Tradition und Fortschritt*, 190–91; G-PT 60/228 (Sept. 28, 1940), 5; 60/230 (Oct. 1, 1940), 6; 61/53 (March 4, 1941), 4; 61/169 (July 22, 1941), 5; 62/296 (Dec. 17, 1942), 3.

69. GAO: 000/12; Gem. Prot. v. Sept. 18, 1941; Sept. 14, 1943; *G-PT* 62/70 (March 24, 1942), 3.

70. Rädlinger, *Zwischen Tradition und Fortschritt*, 193; GAO: 000/12; A092/5; PAO: Schublade 17: Seelsorgsjahresbericht 1939; Utzschneider, *Oberammergau im Dritten Reich*, 59; G-PT 60/171 (July 24, 1940), 6; 61/1 (Jan. 2, 1941), 4; 61/2 (Jan. 3, 1941), 5; 61/8 (Jan. 10, 1941), 4; 61/20 (Jan. 31, 1941), 7; 1/114 (May 17, 1941), 8–11; 61/128 (June 4, 1941), 5; 61/276 (Nov. 22, 1941), 4; 62/221 (Sept. 21, 1942), 3; 62/296 (Dec. 17, 1942), 3; 63/104 (May 6, 1943), 3; 64/27 (Feb. 2, 1944), 4; 64/91 (April 19, 1944), 4; 64/101 (May 2, 1944), 3; 64/120 (May 24, 1944), 3; StAM: LRA 61618.

71. Kershaw, "*Hitler Myth*," 83–104, 169–99, 216–17; StAM: LRA 61616; LRA 61617; LRA 61618; LRA 61619.

72. Central File; StAM: LRA 61616; LRA 61619; Johnson, *Nazi Terror*, 258–59, 310–11, 322–33, 554, 567, discusses this willingness even by the Gestapo to tolerate such defiant listening habits and similar miscreancies.

73. StAM: LRA 61616; LRA 61617; LRA 61618; LRA 61619; PAO: Schublade 17: Seelsorgsjahresbericht, 1939.

74. PAO: Schublade 31: Pfarramtliche Bestätigung, Oct. 1, 1946; Schublade 17: Seelsorgsjahresbericht, 1941, 1943; StAM: LRA 61618; LRA 61619; LRA 63089.

75. StAM: LRA 61617; LRA 61618; LRA 61619.

76. PAO: Schublade 31: Pfarramtliche Bestätigung, Sept. 16, 1945, Oct. 1, 1946; BHStA: OMGBY: 0/48–2/6; StAM: LRA 61618.

77. PAO: Schublade 17.

78. Ibid.; StAM: LRA 61619.

79. PAO: Schublade 31: Pfarramtliche Bestätigung, n.d.; Schublade 17: Seelsorgsjahresbericht, 1939, 1940, 1941, 1943.

80. BHStA: OMBGY: 10/48–2/6; StAM: SpkA K4253; PAO: Schublade 17; Schublade 31: Pfarramtliche Bestätigung, n.d.; May 23, 1947; July 21, 1947.

81. PAO: Schublade 17: Seelsorgsjahresbericht, 1939, 1940, 1941, 1943; Schublade 31: Pfarramtliche Bestätigung, Oct. 1, 1946.

82. PAO: Schublade 17: Seelsorgsjahresbericht, 1939, 1940, 1941, 1943.

83. BHStA: OMGBY: 10/48–2/6, including Josef Raab statement, 10.

84. StAM: LRA 61617; LRA 61618; Kershaw, *Popular Opinion*, 340–57; PAO: Schublade 17.

85. StAM: LRA 61618.

86. StAM: LRA 61618; PAO: Schublade 17: Seelsorgsjahresbericht 1941; Schublade 31; Kershaw, *Political Opinion*, 349–52, mentions the mothers' key role in the revolt, while their husbands were fighting the "crusade" against Bolshevism.

87. PAO: Schublade 31: Pfarramtliche Bestätigung, July 21, 1947; StAM: SpkA K4235; GAO: A150/1; Kershaw, *Political Opinion*, 342, 345–57.

88. StAM: LRA 61618; PAO: Schublade 17: Seelsorgsjahresbericht 1941.

89. Central File; StAM: LRA 61617; SpkA K4235; GAO: Einwohner- u. Hausbes-itzerverzeichnis 1922; Rädlinger, *Zwischen Tradition und Fortschritt*, 185; Kaplan, *Between Dignity and Despair*, 207, discusses the vital role of passable official documents.

90. StAM: LRA 61617; SpkA K4235; SpkA K4271; SpkA K4283; GAO: A150/1; A070/6; Kaplan, *Between Dignity and Despair*, 205–206, 225–27, gives details about other families of wanderers.

91. Pössinger, *Lebensbilder eines Gebirgsjäger*, 102; Rigg, *Hitler's Jewish Soldiers*, especially 61–65, 231–35.

92. StAM: LRA 61618; Central File; Utzschneider, *Oberammergau im Dritten Reich*, 128; GAO: A150/1.

93. Central File; Johnson, *Nazi Terror*, 484, concludes that "many ordinary Germans even provided Jews with understanding and support," according to various survivors. Kaplan, *Between Dignity and Despair*, 201–28, discusses the efforts of German Jews to evade the Nazis during World War II.

94. Wood, *Survey of Messerschmitt Factory*, 64, 72; Günzler and Zwink, *Berühmtes Dorf*, 173–74, VIII; GAO: A092/5; A0931.

95. Heigl, "Die Messerschmitt AG in Oberammergau," 234–35, 245; Wood, *Survey of Messerschmitt Factory*, 64–65, 72, 120.

96. Heigl, "Die Messerschmitt AG in Oberammergau," 234–35; Wood, *Survey of Messerschmitt Factory*, 64–65, 120, 525.

97. Heigl, "Die Messerschmitt AG in Oberammergau," 236, 238–42; Wood, *Survey of Messerschmitt Factory*, 31, 35, 44–45, 365.

98. Heigl, "Die Messerschmitt AG in Oberammergau," 238, 240–41; Wood, *Survey of Messerschmitt Factory*, 113, 195–97, 201–204.

99. StAM: LRA 61619; LRA 61620; PAO: Schublade 17: Seelsorgsjahresbericht 1943, 1944–1945; Heigl, "Die Messerschmitt AG in Oberammergau," 247–53; Wood, *Survey of Messerschmitt Factory*, 502–503; Rädlinger, *Zwischen Tradition und Fortschritt*, 199–200.

100. Wood, *Survey of Messerschmitt Factory*, 502–503; StAM: LRA 61619.

101. StAM: LRA 61619; SpkA K4235; Heigl, "Die Messerschmitt AG in Oberammergau," 254–55; GAO: A092/6; Wood, *Survey of Messerschmitt Factory*, 504–506, 535–36; Utzschneider, *Oberammergau im Dritten Reich*, 144–45.

102. StAM: LRA 61619.

103. Heigl, "Die Messerschmitt AG in Oberammergau," 256–58, StAM: LRA 61619; LRA 61620; GAO: A092/7.

104. GAO: A092/7; Heigl, "Die Messerschmitt AG in Oberammergau," 252, 258; StAM: LRA 61619; LRA 61620.

105. Heigl, "Die Messerschmitt AG in Oberammergau," 243–44; StAM: LRA 61619; LRA 131441.

106. StAM: LRA 61619; Gem. Prot. v. Sept. 18, 1941; Dec. 10, 1943; GAO: A092/3; A092/7; Zull, *Georg Lang sel. Erben*, 242, includes details about a special prosthesis that served as a working hand.

107. GAO: Gem. Prot. v. Sept. 15, 1944; StAM: SpkA K4311; LRA 61619; LRA 61620.

108. Günzler and Zwink, *Berühmtes Dorf*, 173–74, VIII; GAO: A092/1; A092/5; A092/6; A092/7.

109. Heigl, "Die Messerschmitt AG in Oberammergau," 235; StAM: LRA 61619; GAO: A/070; *Das Ende des Zweiten Weltkriegs*, part 2, ed. Pfister, 973, mentions orders from the county leader to this effect.

110. Utzschneider, *Oberammergau im Dritten Reich*, 136–38; GAO: Gem. Prot. v. May 15, 1944; StAM: LRA 61618; LRA 61619.

111. GAO: A/070; StAM: SpkA K4235; *Das Ende des Zweiten Weltkriegs*, part 2, ed. Pfister, 973.

112. GAO: A/070; StAM: SpkA K4235.

113. GAO: A/070; StAM: SpkA K4235; SpkA K4238; SpkA K4252; LRA 61619.

114. Central File.

CHAPTER 8

1. Central File.

2. StAM: SpkA K4253; Stephenson, *Hitler's Home Front*, 326–27.

3. StAM: SpkA K4253; GAO: A094/9; Treml, *Geschichte des modernen Bayern*, 345.

4. StAM: SpkA K4253.

5. Ibid.; Pössinger, *Lebensbilder eines Gebirgsjäger*, 146, downplays any danger from the county leader.

6. StAM: SpkA K4253; Utzschneider, *Oberammergau im Dritten Reich*, 148.

7. Eisenhower, *Crusade in Europe*, 397–98, 414–19; Agoston, *Blunder!* 20–26; Minott, *Fortress That Never Was*, 23–61; Pössinger, *Lebensbilder eines Gebirgsjäger*, 165.

8. Minott, *Fortress That Never Was*, 37–41, 135; StAM: SpkA K4253; Utzschneider, *Oberammergau im Dritten Reich*, 148; Agoston, *Blunder!* 16–26, 54–56, 134; Cadbury, *Space Race*, 23, 29. Pössinger, *Lebensbilder eines Gebirgsjäger*, 142, describes being sent to defend the redoubt, which suggests that his commander and other higher-ups believed in it.

9. StAM: SpkA K4253; *AZ* 27/55 (May 11, 1933), 4; 27/84 (July 20, 1933), 2; 28/113 (Sept. 27, 1934), 4; 29/66 (June 8, 1935), 8; 30/61 (May 23, 1936), 5; 31/66 (June 3, 1937), 4; 32/73 (June 19–20, 1938), 4; Schlosspark Linderhof, Bayerische Verwaltung der staatl. Schlösser, Garten, und Seen, information posted at the recreated Hundingshütte on the castle grounds. Local wisdom suggests that because the Hundingshütte had become a café, Hacker may have wanted to destroy it on behalf of local hunting interests.

10. StAM: SpkA K4253; Günzler and Zwink, *Berühmtes Dorf*, 174; *Das Ende des Zweiten Weltkriegs*, vol. 2, ed. Pfister, 966, 973.

11. StAM: LRA 61619; GAO: A070.

12. StAM: LRA 61620; GAO: Gem. Prot. v. Nov. 1, 1944; A070.

13. GAO: A000/12; A0931; A094/9; StAM: LRA 61619.

14. StAM: LRA 61619; LRA 61620; GAO: A070; Rädlinger, *Zwischen Tradition und Fortschritt*, 202.

15. Agoston, *Blunder!* 3–13, 16–18, 27–28, 45, 52, 107, 126; Eisenhower, *Crusade in Europe*, 258–60; Piszkiewicz, *Nazi Rocketeers*, 198–99; Wood, *Survey of Messerschmitt Factory*, 202; GAO: A092/7; Sereny, *Albert Speer*, 404, 489.

16. Kammler was never highlighted in the postwar trials, so he became what Tom Agoston calls a "no-person" to history. Braun's V-2 rockets were the precursors of both the Cruise and Pershing/Soviet SS missiles. Cadbury, *Space Race*, 29; Minott, *Fortress That Never Was*, 135–36; Piszkiewicz, *Nazi Rocketeers*, 198–211; Wood, *Survey of Messerschmitt Factory*, 65; Agoston, *Blunder!* 17, 128; von Braun and Ordway, *History of Rocketry and Space Travel*, 115–18; Agoston, *Teufel oder Technokrat?* 50, 65, 67.

17. Günzler and Zwink, *Berühmtes Dorf*, 174, ix; PAO: Chronik von Oberammergau; Utzschneider, *Oberammergau im Dritten Reich*, 148–49; Minott, *Fortress That Never Was*, 85–86, 122, 153; Wood, *Survey of Messerschmitt Factory*, 2–3, 99, 107, 195, 201, 204; GAO: A070/3; *Das Ende des Zweiten Weltkriegs*, vol. 2, ed. Pfister, 959, 966, 973; StAM: SpkA K4244; K4253; SpkA K4283; Pössinger, *Lebensbilder eines Gebirgsjäger*, 149–50.

18. GAO: A070; 094/9; StAM: SpkA K1008; K4253; K4268; K4283; *G-PT* 64/265 (Nov. 10, 1944), 3; 64/266 (Nov. 11, 1944), 3; 64/267 (Nov. 13, 1944), 1.

19. StAM: SpkA K4235; K4253; K4268; BHStA: OMGBY 10/48–2/6; GAO: A094/9.

20. Utzschneider, *Oberammergau im Dritten Reich*, 146–47, quoting *G-PT* 65/68 (March 21, 1945); GAO: A070; StAM: SpkA K4235; SpkA K4271.

21. GAO: A070; StAM: SpkA K4253; SpkA K4283.

22. GAO: A070; StAM: SpkA K4235; K4244.

23. GAO: A070; StAM: SpkA K4235; K4244; K4283.

24. GAO: A070; StAM: SpkA K4235; K4244.

25. StAM: SpkA K4253.

26. Minott, *Fortress That Never Was*, 112; Günzler and Zwink, *Berühmtes Dorf*, 174, ix; GAO: A070; StAM: SpkA K4253; Central File.

27. GAO: A070; StAM: SpkA K4235; 4244; K4253; Central File; BHStA: OMGBY 10/48–2/6.

28. BHStA: OMGBY 10/77–3/2; PAO: Chronik von Oberammergau; GAO: A070; StAM: SpkA K4253; Günzler and Zwink, *Berühmtes Dorf*, 175–76; Pössinger, *Lebensbilder eines Gebirgsjäger*, 153–55.

29. PAO: Chronik von Oberammergau; GAO: A070.

30. PAO: Chronik von Oberammergau; GAO: A070; Günzler and Zwink, *Berühmtes Dorf*, 175–76; Central File.

31. GAO: A070; A070/4; A070/13; A464/2; BHStA: OMGBY 10/48 2/6; StAM: LRA 61620; Rädlinger, *Zwischen Tradition und Fortschritt*, 206; PAO: Chronik von Oberammergau; Schublade 17: Seelsorgsjahresbericht 1944/45, 1946; Central File; Wood, *Survey of Messerschmitt Factory*, 1–3, 5–8, 312.

32. StAM: LRA 61620; PAO: Schublade 17: Seelsorgsjahresbericht 1946; GAO: A060/12; Pössinger, *Lebensbilder eines Gebirgsjäger*, 127, 136; Bartov, *Hitler's Army*,

29–58. Ernst Lang, *Das wars*, 178–79, 201–204, 229–30, describes his time with a new and mixed-up unit, but it was not unpleasant. His loyalty to comrades in his unit had led Lang to leave Burgundy for the eastern front in 1942.

33. Lanz, *Gebirgsjäger*, 278–98.

34. Central File.

35. Ernst Lang, *Das wars*, 233–42.

36. Central File.

37. GAO: A070; A070/4; Ernst Lang, *Das wars*, 242–45; BHStA: OMGUS CO 450/3.

38. PAO: Chronik von Oberammergau; Central File.

39. Central File; Utzschneider, *Oberammergau im Dritten Reich*, 150; PAO: Einmarschbericht Pfarrei Oberammergau, 1945; GAO: A070; A070/3; A070/10; StAM: LRA 61620.

40. Central File; GAO: A070/3.

41. Ernst Lang, *Das wars*, 243; GAO: Gem. Prot. v. May 11, 1946; A070; BHStA: OMGBY10/48–2/6, including Josef Raab statement, 6; StAM: SpkA K1008; K4229; K4240; K4268; K4271; K4311; Peter Jakob Koch, "Bayern nach dem Zweiten Weltkrieg," in Treml, *Geschichte des modernen Bayern*, 387.

42. BHStA: OMGBY 10/77–3/2; StAM: LRA 61620; Central File; GAO: A070; A070/6; A070/8; A070/9; A070/12; Niethammer, *Entnazifizierung in Bayern*, 147–259.

43. PAO: Chronik von Oberammergau; StAM: SpkA K1008; GAO: A070; A070/3; A070/7.

44. PAO: Chronik von Oberammergau; GAO: A070; A070/3.

45. Central File; PAO: Chronik von Oberammergau; GAO: A070; StAM: SpkA K1008.

46. PAO: Chronik von Oberammergau; Schublade 17: Seelsorgsjahresbericht 1944–1945; StAM: LRA 61620; LRA 61621; GAO: A070; A070/4.

47. GAO: A070; A070/4; A070/6; A092/1; A464/2.

48. GAO: A070/4.

49. BHStA: OMGBY 10/77–3/2; StAM: SpkA K1008; GAO: A070; A070/5.

50. StAM: LRA 61620; SpkA K1008; GAO: A070; A070/5.

51. Ernst Lang, *Das wars*, 243; Central File; GAO: A070/5.

52. BHStA: OMGBY 10/77–3/2; GAO: A070; Richard Lang article in *New Orleans* (Sept. 1964); Ackermann-Pasegg, *Amerika in Oberammergau*; Zull, *Georg Lang sel. Erben*, 240–41, 302.

53. GAO: A070; A070/6; A070/12; A150/4; Gem. Prot. v. Aug. 7, 1945; BHStA: OMGBY 10/48–2/6, including Josef Raab statement, 7.

54. GAO: A070/12; StAM: LRA 61620.

55. GAO: A070/12; Ackermann-Pasegg, *Amerika in Oberammergau*; BHStA: OMGBY 10/77–3/2; Tent, *Mission on the Rhine*, discusses the entire process of "reeducation" in postwar Germany.

56. GAO: A070/6; A070/12.

57. BHStA: OMGBY 10/77–3/2; Utzschneider, *Oberammergau im Dritten Reich*, 150; PAO: Schublade 17: Seelsorgsjahresbericht 1944–1945; Chronik von Oberammergau; GAO: A331/3.

58. Richard Lang, *New Orleans*; GAO: A070; A070/11.

59. GAO: A070/13.

60. GAO: Gem. Prot. v. July 27, 1945; AXV/147; BHStA: OMGBY 10/48–2/6.

61. BHStA: OMGUS CO 450/3; OMGBY 10/48–2/6; GAO: Gem. Prot. v. Dec. 15, 1945; StAM: LRA 61620.

62. StAM: LRA 61620; GAO: Gem. Prot. v. Dec. 15, 1945, Dec. 31, 1945.

63. GAO: A070; Gem. Prot. v. May 28, 1945; BHStA: OMGBY 10/48–2/6, including Josef Raab statement, 6.

64. GAO: Gem. Prot. v. May 28, 1945.

65. GAO: Gem. Prot. v. July 27, 1945; Aug. 7, 1945; Aug. 20, 1945; Sept. 12, 1945; Nov. 25, 1945; Dec. 15, 1945; Dec. 31, 1945; BHStA: OMGBY 10/48–2/6, including Josef Raab statement, 6.

66. GAO: A070; StAM: LRA 61620.

67. StAM: LRA 61620; BHStA: OMGBY 10/48–2/6, including Josef Raab statement, 6; GAO: A070; *H-B* 2/11 (Feb. 5, 1946), 1.

68. StAM: LRA 661620.

69. BHStA: OMGBY 10/77–3/2; StAM: LRA 61620; LRA 61621; *H-B* 4/7 (Jan. 27, 1948), 1–4; PAO: Schublade 17: Seelsorgsjahresbericht 1946; Lanzinner, *Zwischen Sternenbanner und Bundesadler*, 106–11.

70. StAM: LRA 61620; LRA 61621.

71. GAO: A070; A464/2; StAM: LRA 61621.

72. Central File; GAO: A070; A150/4; A460/3; Gem. Prot. v. June 7, 1946.

73. GAO: A070/13.

74. Central File; PAO: Schublade 17: Seelsorgsjahresbericht 1948; StAM: SpkA K4235; K4240; LRA 61620; LRA 61621; GAO: A150/2; A150/3; Gem. Prot. v. May 28, 1945-Jan. 16, 1947; A070; A070/9; BHStA: OMGBY 10/77–3/2; *H-B* 3/43 (May 30, 1947), 3.

75. GAO: Gem. Prot. v. March 8, 1946; BHStA: OMGBY 10/77–3/2; *H-B* 4/13 (Feb. 17, 1948), 4.

76. GAO: A464/2; *H-B* 4/13 (Feb. 17, 1948), 4; StAM: LRA 61620.

77. PAO: Chronik von Oberammergau; GAO: A331/3.

78. GAO: A331/3.

79. *H-B* 4/67 (Aug. 17, 1948), 3; 4/83 (Sept. 25, 1948), 8; 4/87 (Oct. 7, 1948), 8; 4/89 (Oct. 12, 1948), 7–8.

80. Central File; PAO: Schublade 17: Seelsorgsjahresbericht, 1946, 1947, 1948, 1949.

81. PAO: Schublade 17: Kirchliche Statistik Deutschlands von das Jahr 1946–1950; Seelsorgsjahresbericht 1944–1945, 1946, 1947, 1948; Chronik von Oberammergau, including a loose sheet dated Nov. 20, 1950; Kossert, *Kalte Heimat*, 229–69, discusses the mix of religions created by the massive relocations.

82. PAO: Schublade 17: Seelsorgesjahresbericht 1946, 1947, 1948, 1949; *H-B* 4/89 (Oct. 12, 1948), 8; GAO: Gem. Prot. v. 26. 7. 1946.

83. GAO: A464; Central File; PAO: Schublade 17: Seelsorgsjahresbericht 1946, 1947, 1948, 1949; Schublade 31.

84. GAO: A070; A070/4; A070/12; A460/3; A464/2; Gem. Prot. v. Feb. 8, 1946; March 8, 1946; May 11, 1946; July 6, 1946; June 27, 1946; PAO: Chronik von Oberammergau, including a loose sheet dated Nov. 20, 1950.

85. GAO: A464; PAO: Chronik von Oberammergau, including a loose sheet dated Nov. 20, 1950.

86. GAO: Gem. Prot. v. Dec. 15, 1945; A070; A070/6; A070/8.

87. GAO: A070/6; B151, 23–25.

88. GAO: A070.

89. GAO: A070/6; PAO: Chronik von Oberammergau, including a loose sheet dated Nov. 20, 1950.

90. Central File; Kossert, *Kalte Heimat*, 27–42, 57; de Zayas, *Terrible Revenge*, 88–94, 115; StAM: LRA 61621.

91. PAO: Chronik von Oberammergau, including a loose sheet dated Nov. 20, 1950; Schublade 17: Seelsorgsjahresbericht 1946; Central File; Kossert, *Kalte Heimat*, 22–23, 27–42; de Zayas, *Terrible Revenge*, xxxviii, 94–115; GAO: A070/4; A150/2; A464. The wide variety of birthplaces recorded for these exotic newcomers reveals the extraordinary impact they had on what had been a relatively homogeneous population.

92. Corathiel, *Oberammergau and Its Passion Play* (1950), 134; de Zayas, *Terrible Revenge*, xxxix, xlii, 127–28; Kossert, *Kalte Heimat*, 58, 62–63, 67–71; GAO: A460; A464.

93. GAO: A460; A464; Gem. Prot. v. July 26, 1946; Central File.

94. GAO: 070/9; A150/3; Niethammer, *Entnazifizierung in Bayern*, 343–44; StAM: LRA 61620.

95. GAO: A150/1; A150/3; BHStA: OMGBY 10/77–3/2.

96. *H-B* 2/70 (Aug. 30, 1946), 3; 2/80 (Oct. 4, 1946), 7; StAM: SpkA K1008; K4240; GAO: A150/2; BHStA: OMGBY 10/77–3/2; Niethammer, *Die Mitläuferfabrik.* Johnson, *Nazi Terror*, 463–81, discusses the many "Persilscheine" written on behalf of ex-Nazis coming up for hearings.

97. StAM: SpkA K4235; K4253.

98. StAM: SpkA K4238; K4283; GAO: A150/2; *H-B*, especially 3/43 (May 30, 1947), 3; 3/45 (June 7, 1947), 3.

99. StAM: SpkA K4240; *H-B* 3/43 (May 30, 1947), 3.

100. StAM: SpkA K4240. Each community set up this type of committee to feed information about defendants to the tribunals.

101. Central File; *H–B*, especially 3/80 (Oct. 7, 1947), 4.

102. Koch, *Bayerns Weg*, 162, 215, 226; GAO: Gem. Prot. v. Aug. 29, 1946; Jan. 16, 1947; PAO: Chronik von Oberammergau.

103. Koch, *Bayerns Weg*, 162, 215, 226; Treml, *Geschichte des modernen Bayern*, 397; *H-B* 2/11 (Feb. 5, 1946), 1; 2/35 (April 30, 1946), 1; 2/53 (July 2, 1946), 1; 2/78 (Sept. 27, 1946), 5; 2/97 (Dec. 3, 1946), 1; PAO: Chronik von Oberammergau, newspaper cutting of *H-B* 2/9 (Jan. 29, 1946).

104. PAO: Chronik von Oberammergau; GAO: 11. 3. 1; A024/5; StAM: SpkA K1008.

105. GAO: 11. 3. 1; Florian Lang private collection.

106. StAM: SpkA K1008.

107. Ibid.

108. GAO: 11. 3. 1; StAM: SpkA K1008.

109. *H-B* 4/27 (April 6, 1948), 1–2; Joseph Maria Lutz, "The 1950 Play and Its Performers," in *Oberammergau* (1950), ed. Community of Oberammergau, 53.

110. Joseph Maria Lutz, "Oberammergau and Its Highland Landscape," in *Oberammergau* (1950), ed. Community of Oberammergau, 110; Lutz, "1950 Play," 54; StAM: LRA 61621; PAO: Chronik von Oberammergau, including a loose sheet dated Nov. 20, 1950; Schublade 17: Kirchliche Statistik Deutschlands über das Jahr 1948–1950; GAO: B151, 215.

111. Lutz, "1950 Play," 54; Corathiel, *Oberammergau and Its Passion Play* (1950), 134; PAO: Chronik von Oberammergau; Ackermann-Pasegg, *Amerika in Oberammergau*; Rädlinger, *Zwischen Tradition und Fortschritt*, 219–20, 227–28; GAO: A070/13.

112. Lutz, "1950 Play," 54; Corathiel, *Oberammergau and Its Passion Play* (1950), 137–38; GAO: ZA/Passionsspiele: Fritz Ihrt, "In 8 Wochen beginnen die Passionsspiele in Oberammergau," *Rheinische Illustrierte* (March 16, 1950); GAO: B151, 46.

113. *Oberammergau* (1950), ed. Community of Oberammergau, 1, 4–5, 7, and front cover.

114. Ibid., 1–8, 20, 113–28, inserts and covers.

115. Ibid., front cover; Rädlinger, *Zwischen Tradition und Fortschritt*, 220; Barthel, *Lovely Place, Ammergau*, etching opposite 6, 8.

116. *Oberammergau* (1950), ed. Community of Oberammergau, 13.

117. Ibid., 13 and passim.

118. GAO: A060/12; ZA/Passionsspiele: passim, including Hans Eberhard Friedrich, "Denkt Oberammergau am Umbesetzung?" *Die Neue Zeitung* (Nov. 16, 1949); "Haben die Nazis gesiegt?" *Quick: Die Aktuelle Illustrierte* 2/48 (Nov. 27, 1949); A. Schwenger, "War Oberammergau ein 'braunes Nest?'" *Schwäbisches Tagblatt* (Dec. 30, 1947), 4; B151, 151–59, 165–74, 187–220, 304–305; Central File; *Oberammergau* (1950), ed. Community of Oberammergau, 58–69; Lutz, "1950 Play," 55; Rädlinger, *Zwischen Tradition und Fortschritt*, 223.

119. GAO: B180: Pressestelle der Passionsspiele Oberammergau 1950: information number 14, 15, 18, 20, 22, 23; ZA/Passionsspiele: Otto Nocker, "Ein Dorf, das in Jahrzehnten denkt," *Süddeutsche Sonntagspost* 49 (Dec. 24, 1949), 15–17; Alfred Mayerhofer, "Die Passionsspiele haben begonnen: Oberammergau's Botschaft an die Welt," *General-Anzeiger* (May 19, 1950); "Grosser Tag in Oberammergau: Passionsspiel-Eröffnung in Anwesenheit hoher Gäste," *Westfalenpost* 115 (May 19, 1950); Rädlinger, *Zwischen Tradition und Fortschritt*, 219–26; GAO: B151, 78, letter from Cardinal Faulhaber, Aug. 20, 1949.

120. Rädlinger, *Zwischen Tradition und Fortschritt*, 227–28; *Oberammergau* (1950), ed. Community of Oberammergau, 17, 21, 26; GAO: B151, 352–356; Z/A Passionsspiele: "Cook and Co. in Oberammergau," *Illus* 30 (July 30, 1950), 18–19; Ludwig Hillenbrandt, "Ein Dorf erlebt eine friedliche Invasion," *Wochenend* 60 (May 11, 1950); "Oberammergau: Welt im Dorf," *Der Spiegel* (May 18, 1950), 35–36; Mayerhofer, "Die Passionsspiele haben begonnen"; Anneliese Schuller, "Lobet den Herrn—alle Völker,"

Süddeutsche Zeitung (May 19, 1950); Corathiel, *Oberammergau and Its Passion Play* (1950), 137–43; PAO: Schublade 17: Seelsorgsjahresbericht 1950.

121. *Passion-Play at Oberammergau* (1934) and (1950), frontispiece and 9–11; PAO: Schublade 17: Seelsorgsjahresbericht 1950; GAO: B151, 451; B180: Pressestelle der Passionsspiele Oberammergau 1950: information number 21.

122. *Passion-Play at Oberammergau* (1934) and (1950), 9–11; Hans Heinrich Borcherdt, "The Style of the Oberammergau Passion Play and Its Historical Background," in *Oberammergau* (1950), ed. Community of Oberammergau, 78; Rädlinger, *Zwischen Tradition und Fortschritt*, 220–21, 228, 327; GAO: B151, 246.

CONCLUSION

1. GAO: A150/2.

2. Central File.

3. *Das schreckliche Mädchen*, directed by Michael Verhoeven, first appeared in 1990.

4. Goldhagen, *Hitler's Willing Executioners*; Atina Grossmann, "The 'Goldhagen Effect': Memory, Repetition, and Responsibility in the New Germany," in Eley, *"Goldhagen Effect,"* 96, 110–29. Victor Klemperer describes his personal experience of this varied set of responses to helpless Jews during the entire twelve years of the Third Reich in his *Diary of the Nazi Years*.

5. Némirovsky, *Suite française*, 363.

6. Koonz, *Nazi Conscience*, 272.

7. Ibid., 74–75, 272–73; Gellately, *Backing Hitler*, explores the concept of "consent" but primarily from the point of view of denunciations rather than a willingness to go along with the regime's expectations.

8. Owings, *Frauen*, 247; Peukert, *Inside Nazi Germany*, 14–15.

9. Owings, *Frauen*, 257–58.

Appendix: Central File

FREQUENTLY CITED SOURCES

Ammergauer Zeitung 1906–1938.
Garmisch-Partenkirchener Tagblatt 1938–1945.
Hochland-Bote 1945–1950.
Werdenfelser Anzeiger 1918–1930.
Ostler, *Revolutionszeit, 1918–1919.*

BHStA

MInn 72741

GAO

Gem. Prot. v. 1932–1947.
000/10; 000/11.
A060/12; A070; A070/4; A070/9; A070/12; A150/1; A150/2; A150/3; A150/4;
    A464; AII/26; AXV/147.
B151.
12. I. 5.
Einwohner- u. Hausbesitzerverzeichnis, 1890–1949.
Nachlass A. O. Zwink: NSDAP Ortsgruppe Oberammergau: Präzenz-Liste;
    Mitgliederverzeichnis der Ortsgruppe Oberammergau (July 1, 1933);
    Mitgliederliste nach dem Stand vom Jan. 15, 1937.

Interviews

Melchior Breitsamter, Aug. 20, 1993; July 29, 1996.
Franz Haertle, Dec. 6, 1993; July 27, 1996.
Hannah Kräh, Aug. 19, 1993; Aug. 20, 1993; June 28, 1997.
Martha Krause, Nelly Lang, and Tidda Raab, July 25, 1996.
Edeltraud Porkert, Sept. 23, 2001.
Tidda Raab, July 26, 1996; July 11, 1997; July 23, 2001; Sept. 18, 2001; June 25, 2003.
Antonie Zwink, Aug. 16, 1993; Aug. 18, 1993; Aug. 27, 1993; July 31, 1996.

National Archives: Berlin Document Center Microfilm

1. NSDAP Ortsgruppenkartei, Microfilm Publication A3340 (MFOK):
   A003; A004; A014; A018; A022; A032; A038; A054; A063; A0078; A0090; A0097;
   A099; B007; B014; B0019; B0033; B0037; B039; B066; B069; C001; C003; C018;
   C020; C024; C026; C0049; C0051; C0059; C0062; C0063; D0002; D0007;
   D0010; D0020; D0029; D0033; D0048; D0049; D0054; D0064; D0068; D071;
   E0021; E027; E0028; E0030; E041; E049; E054; F0004; F016; F020; F023; F024;
   F0033; F056; F057; F087; G007; G042; G050; G055; G069; G070; G071; G081;
   G083; H043; H072; I029; I031; I033; I034; I042; I043; I047; J018; J036; K005;
   K043; K048; K060; K061; K069; K075; K078; L003; L007; L014; L019; L023; L025;
   L032; L038; L041; L065; L076; M017; M018; M021; M033; M064; M073; M074;
   M075; M076; N004; N008; N041; N044; N054; N058; O009; O0010; O015; O017;
   O020; O021; O022; O025; O028; O034; O040; O049; O075; P027; P033; P044;
   P053; P055; P065; P085; Q012; Q013; Q021; Q034; Q062; R022; R040; R057;
   R082; R084; R090; S046; S054; S073; S086; T017; T021; T023; T031; T038; T040;
   T041; T044; U001; U025; U060; V014; V042; V058; V068; W003; W004; W005;
   W017; W024; W031; W042; W048; W050; W059; W061; W071; W092; X027;
   X046; X049; X076; X085; Y010; Y047; Y066; Z028; Z031; Z041; Z055; Z061;
   Z072; Z081; Z096; Z098.
2. NSDAP Zentralkartei, Microfilm Publication A3340 (MFKL):
   A020; A078; A123; A130; B029; B067; B039; B132; B134; C076; C0118; C147;
   D0012; D045; D0087; E031; E091; E107; E115; F002; F0024; F0062; F0070; F118;
   F158; G006; G019; G067; G157; G158; G167; H067; H072; H094; I018; I021; I095;
   I112; I129; I143; J025; J093; J095; J099; K055; L006; L091; L141; M011; M079;
   N045; N147; N158; O007; O021; O063; O081; P003; P031; P054; P055; P136; R026;
   R029; R038; R138; S041; S134; T007; T016; T020; T032; T097; T105; T107.
3. NSDAP: SA Personal and Process Akten, Microfilm Publication A3341 (SA):
   003; 046; 139.
4. NSDAP: RuSHA: Microfilm Publication A3343 (RS):
   B5013; G5541.
   A3343 (SM):
   B0051; F035.

5. NSDAP Frauenschaft: Microfilm Publication A3344 (FS):
A003; A004; A014; A031; A130; A134; A144; A177; A212; A219; A239; A246; A262;
A348; B150; B164; B249; B266; B275; B315; B334; C005; C029; C080; C243; C262;
C273; C305; C336; C339; C0354; D002; D002; D003; D024; D101; D150; D152;
D368; E079; E121; E165; E174; E217; E220; E230; F030; F039; F084; F104;
F175; F396.

StAM

LRA 61609–61621; 61670; 107021.
SpkA K1008; K4229; K4235; K4238; K4240; K4244; K4252; K4253; K4268; K4270;
    K4271; K4283; K4288; K4290; K4291; K4304; K4311; files for OA, JA, ES, and JS.

Tablets listing the war dead for World War Two on the south wall of the parish church.

Bibliography of Cited Works

Ackermann-Passeg, Otto. *Amerika in Oberammergau*. Diessen: Huber, 1945.

Adreßbuch des Bezirksamts Garmisch, 1927–1929. Partenkirchen: Tiefenbacher, 1929 (Vereinsverzeichnis).

Agoston, Tom. *Blunder! How the U.S. Gave Away Nazi Supersecrets to Russia*. New York: Dodd, Mead, 1985.

———. *Teufel oder Technokrat? Hitlers graue Eminenz*. Hamburg: Nikol, 1993.

Aichner, Ernst. *Der erste Weltkrieg: Zeitgenössische Gemälde und Graphik*. Ingolstadt: Bayerisches Armeemuseum, 1980.

Allen, William S. *The Nazi Seizure of Power: The Experience of a Single German Town, 1922–1945*, 2nd ed. New York: Watts, 1984.

Alzheimer, Heidrun. *Einmal Oberammergau und zurück: Reisetagebuch des Bauern Matthäus Storath aus Stockheim/Rhön im Passionsjahr 1890*. Würzburg: Historischer Verein Oberammergau, 2001.

Anderson, Margaret Lavinia. *Practicing Democracy: Elections and Political Culture in Imperial Germany*. Princeton: Princeton University Press, 2000.

Athawes, John. *The Representation of the Passion at Ober-Ammergau, in the Bavarian Highlands*. London: Parker, 1871.

Baranowski, Shelley. *Strength through Joy: Consumerism and Mass Tourism in the Third Reich*. New York: Cambridge University Press, 2004.

Barthel, Gustav. *Lovely Place, Ammergau: A Little Guide round about the Passion-Play*. Trans. Elisabeth Martini. Ebenhausen: Langewiesche-Brandt, 1950.

Bartov, Omer. *Germany's War and the Holocaust: Disputed Histories*. Ithaca: Cornell University Press, 2003.

———. *Hitler's Army: Soldiers, Nazis, and War in the Third Reich*. New York: Oxford University Press, 1992.

Bergerson, Andrew Stuart. *Ordinary Germans in Extraordinary Times: The Nazi Revolution in Hildesheim.* Bloomington: Indiana University Press, 2004.

Berghahn, Volker R. *Der Stahlhelm: Bund der Frontsoldaten, 1918–1935.* Düsseldorf: Droste, 1966.

Birchall, Frederick T. "Give Passion Play in Oberammergau." *New York Times* (May 18, 1934).

Blackbourn, David. *Marpingen: Apparitions of the Virgin Mary in Nineteenth-century Germany.* New York: Knopf, 1993.

Blackburn, Henry. *Art in the Mountains: The Story of the Passion Play.* London: Sampson Low, Marston, Searle, and Rivington, 1880.

Bogenrieder, Franz X. *Jubiläums-Passionsspiele Oberammergau 1634–1934: Offizieller Führer der Gemeinde.* Munich: Müller und Sohn, 1934.

———. *Oberammergau: Das Passionsdorf.* Munich: Schnell and Steiner, 1950.

———. *Oberammergau und sein Passionsspiel: Offizieller Führer der Gemeinde.* Oberammergau: Knorr and Hirth, 1930.

Bramsted, Ernest K. *Goebbels and National Socialist Propaganda 1925–1945.* East Lansing: Michigan State University Press, 1965.

Brauneck, Manuel. *Religiöse Volkskunst: Votivgabe—Andachtsbilder—Hinterglas—Rosenkranz—Amulette.* Cologne: DuMont, 1978.

Broszat, Martin, and Elke Fröhlich, eds. *Bayern in der NS-Zeit.* 6 vols. Munich: Oldenbourg, 1977–1983.

Browne, P. W. "Where Faith Abides." *Magnificat* (1923): 263–72.

Browning, Christopher. *Ordinary Men: Reserve Police Battalion 101 and the Final Solution in Poland,* rev. ed. New York: Harper Perennial, 1998.

Brunner, Sebastian. *Das Passionsspiel zu Oberammergau in den Jahren 1860 und 1870.* Vienna: Braumüller, 1870.

Brustein, William. *The Logic of Evil: The Social Origins of the Nazi Party, 1925–1933.* New Haven: Yale University Press, 1996.

Burdick, Charles B. *Hubert Lanz: General der Gebirgstruppe, 1896–1982.* Osnabrück: Biblio, 1988.

Burton, Isabel. *The Passion-Play at Ober-Ammergau.* London: Hutchinson, 1900.

Cadbury, Deborah. *Space Race: The Epic Battle between American and the Soviet Union for Dominion of Space.* New York: HarperCollins, 2006.

Caramelle, Franz. *Das Innsbrucker Riesenrundgemälde: The 1809 Tyrolean Struggles for Liberation Depicted on 1,000 Sq. Metres of Canvas.* Innsbruck: Athesia-Tyrolia, ca. 1984.

Childers, Thomas. *The Nazi Voter: The Social Foundations of Fascism in Germany, 1919–1933.* Chapel Hill: University of North Carolina Press, 1983.

Christian, William. *Person and God in a Spanish Valley,* rev. ed. Princeton: Princeton University Press, 1989.

Citizens of Oberammergau. *The Origin of the Passion Plays.* Oberammergau: Gemeinde Oberammergau, 1922.

Clarus, Ludwig. *Das Passionsspiel zu Ober-Ammergau,* 2nd ed. Munich: Lentner, 1860.

Community of Oberammergau, ed. *Oberammergau and Its Passion Play 1950: Official Guide.* Munich: Süddeutscher, 1950.

Conway, John. *The Nazi Persecution of the Churches, 1933–1945.* New York: Basic Books, 1968.

Corathiel, Elisabethe. *Oberammergau and Its Passion Play.* London: Burns, Oates, and Washbourne, 1950.

———. *Oberammergau: Its Story and Its Passion Play.* London: Burns, Oates, and Washbourne, 1934.

Cresswell, Beatrix. *A Retrospect: Life at Oberammergau in 1890.* London: Simpkin, Marshall, Hamilton, Kent, 1890.

Daisenberger, Joseph Alois. *Geschichte des Dorfes Oberammergau.* (originally in *Oberbayerische Archiv für vaterländische Geschichte* (1859–1861): 53–244. Reprint, Oberammergau: Selbstverlag der Gemeinde Oberammergau, 1988.

———. *Historisch-topographische Beschreibung der Pfarrei Oberammergau.* Oberammergau: Gastl and Lang, jun., 1880.

Das Passionsdorf Oberammergau: Das Land, das Volk, und sein Spiel. Munich: Verlag der Alpen-freund, 1922.

De Bernières, Louis. *Captain Corelli's Mandolin.* London: Minerva, 1995.

de Zayas, Alfred-Maurice. *A Terrible Revenge: The Ethnic Cleansing of the East European Germans, 1944–1950.* New York: St. Martin's, 1994.

Deakin, F. W. D. *The Embattled Mountain.* New York: Oxford University Press, 1971.

Delaney, John. "Racial Values vs. Religious Values: Clerical Opposition to Nazi Anti-Polish Racial Policy." *Church History* 70(2) (June 2001): 271–94.

Deutinger, Martin. *Wallfahrt nach Oberammergau.* Reissued by Johannes Fellerer. Munich: Hueber, 1934.

Dickie, J. F. *Oberammergau and the Passion Play.* Berlin: Strenitz and Lang sel. Erben, 1910.

Die evangelische Kirche in Oberammergau, 2nd ed. 1936/1937. In Annelies Buchwieser, Historische Fotografien 1.

Diemer, Hermine. *Oberammergau and Its Passion Play,* 3rd ed. Trans. Walter S. Manning. Munich: Seyfried, 1922.

———. *Oberammergau und sein Passionsspiele.* Munich: Seyfried, 1900.

Dietrich, Donald. *Catholic Citizens in the Third Reich: Psycho-social Principles and Moral Reasoning.* New Brunswick: Transaction Books, 1988.

Doane, G. H. *To and from the Passion Play, in the Summer of 1871.* Boston: Donahoe, 1872.

Edwards, Anne. *Matriarch: Queen Mary and the House of Windsor.* New York: Morrow, 1984.

Eichbaum, F. A. G. *The country Parson at the Passion Play at Ober Ammergau, on Trinity Sunday, 1890, and how he got there.* London: Church Extension Association, 1890.

Eisenhower, Dwight D. *Crusade in Europe.* Garden City, N.Y.: Doubleday, 1948.

Eley, Geoff, ed. *The "Goldhagen Effect": History, Memory, Nazism—Facing the German Past.* Ann Arbor: University of Michigan Press, 2000.

Evans, Richard. *The Coming of the Third Reich.* New York: Penguin, 2003.

———. *The Third Reich at War.* New York: Penguin, 2009.

———. *The Third Reich in Power, 1933–1939.* New York: Penguin, 2005.

Falter, Jürgen. *Hitlers Wähler: Der Austieg der NSDAP im Spiegel der Wahlen.* Munich: Beck, 1991.

———, and Michael Kater. "Wähler und Mitglieder der NSDAP." *Geschichte und Gesellschaft* 19(2) (1993): 155–77.

Farrar, F. W. *The Passion Play at Oberammergau.* London: Heinemann, 1890.

Feldigl, Ferdinand. *Oberammergau und sein Passionsspiel in Vergangenheit und Gegenwart.* Partenkirchen: Wenzel, 1900.

———. *Oberammergau und sein Passionsspiel 1910: Reich illustrierter Führer.* Oberammergau: Rutz, 1910.

———. *Oberammergau und sein Passionsspiel 1922: Offiziell genehmigter Reich illustrierter Führer.* Oberammergau: Rutz, 1922.

Festschrift zum 100 jährigen Gründungsfest des Volkstrachtenvereins "D'Ammertaler" Oberammergau. Oberammergau, July 18, 1993.

Feuchtwanger, Lion. *Success: A Novel.* Trans. Willa Muir and Erwin Muir. New York: Literary Guild, 1930.

Finkenstaedt, Thomas. *Wies: Wallfahrt-Kirche-Museum.* Freilassing: Pannonia, 1993.

———, and Helene Finkenstaedt. *Die Wieswallfahrt: Ursprung und Ausstrahlung der Wallfahrt zum Gegeißelten Heiland.* Regensburg: Pustet, 1981.

Fischer, Humilis, and Hugo Schnell. *Die votiv- und Wallfahrtskirche St. Anton in Partenkirchen: Erzdiözese München-Freising,* 3rd ed. Munich: Schnell and Steiner, 1950.

Foreman, Thomas Beck. *A Pilgrimage to Oberammergau with the London Polytechnic with some account of the Passion Play of 1900.* London: Era Press, n.d.

Frick, Otto. *Das Passions-Spiel in Ober-Ammergau: Ein Vortrag.* Berlin: Rauh, 1871.

Fried, Rudolf. *Führer nach Oberammergau zum Passionsspiele 1880.* Munich: Finsterlin, 1880.

Friedel, Helmut. *Süddeutsche Freiheit: Kunst der Revolution in München 1919.* Exhibition catalog. Munich: Städtische Galerie im Lenbachhaus, November 1993–January 1994.

Friedman, Saul. *The Oberammergau Passion Play: A Lance against Civilization.* Carbondale: Southern Illinois University Press, 1984.

Fritzsche, Peter. *Germans into Nazis.* Cambridge: Harvard University Press, 1998.

Fuchs, Max. *Oberammergau und sein Passionsspiel: Vollständiger Führer zu demselben.* Munich: Fuchs, 1880.

Fuller, Raymond Tifft. *The World's Stage: Oberammergau: The History, Meaning, and People of the Passion Play.* London: Cobden-Sanderson, 1934.

Fünfundzwanzig Jahre Katholischer Deutscher Frauenbund. Cologne: Bachemdr., 1928.

Fürnrohr, Walter, ed. *Wesenszüge Europas: Historische Genese und weltweite Ausstrahlung unter geschichtsdidaktischem Aspekt.* Flensburg: Institut für Forschung und Information im Deutschen Grenzverein, 1989.

Gellately, Robert. *Backing Hitler: Consent and Coercion in Nazi Germany.* New York: Oxford University Press, 2001.

Geschichte und Geschichten von Werdenfels, vol. 2. Garmisch-Partenkirchen: Adam, n.d.

Glasthaner, Placidus. *Abtei Ettal in Oberbayern.* Düsseldorf: Verlag für Architektur-, Industrie-, und Stadt-werke, 1927.

———. *Wirtschaftliche, rechtliche, und soziale Verhältnisse der bäuerlichen Untertanen der Grund- und Gerichtsherrschaft Ettal in den Ämtern des Oberlandes im ausgehenden Mittelalter und zur Zeit des Bauernkrieges.* PhD diss., University of Munich, 1920.

Goldhagen, Daniel Jonah. *Hitler's Willing Executioners: Ordinary Germans and the Holocaust.* New York: Knopf, 1996.

Greatorex, Eliza. *The Homes of Ober-Ammergau.* Munich: Albert, 1872.

Günzler, Otto, and Alfred Zwink. *Berühmtes Dorf, berühmte Gaste: Drei Jahrhunderte Passionsspiel im Spiegel seiner Besucher.* Munich: Münchener Dom-Verlag, 1950.

Hahn, Cynthia. "'Joseph Will Perfect, Mary Enlighten, and Jesus Save Thee': The Holy Family as Marriage Model in the Mérode Triptych." *Art Bulletin* 68(1) (March 1986): 54–65.

Hamilton, Richard. *Who Voted for Hitler?* Princeton: Princeton University Press, 1982.

Harris, James. *The People Speak! Anti-Semitism and Emancipation in Nineteenth-century Bavaria.* Ann Arbor: University of Michigan Press, 1994.

Harvolk, Edgar. *Votivtafeln aus Bayern und Österreich aus dem Museum für Deutsche Volkskunde.* Berlin: Mann, 1977.

Hastings, Derek. "How 'Catholic' Was the Early Nazi Movement? Religion, Race, and Culture in Munich, 1919–1924." *Central European History* 36(3) (2003): 383–433.

Heigl, Richard. "Die Messerschmitt AG in Oberammergau (1943–1945): Auslagerung, Projekte, Fremdarbeitereinsatz." *Mohr, Löwe, Raute* 3 (1995): 233–62.

Heilbronner, Oded. *Catholicism, Political Culture, and the Countryside: A Social History of the Nazi Party in South Germany.* Ann Arbor: University of Michigan Press, 1998.

Henker, Michael, Eberhard Dünninger, and Evamaria Brockhoff, eds. *Hört, sehet, weint, und liebt: Passionsspiele im alpenländischen Raum.* Katalogbuch zur Ausstellung im Ammergauer Haus, Oberammergau, May 28–September 30, 1990.

Hoedl, Franz Xaver. *Bruder Konrad: Ein Pilgerbüchlein,* 6th ed. Altötting: Franziskusverlag, 1984.

Höhl, Leopold. *Führer zum Ammergauer Passionsspiel im Jahre 1880.* Würzburg: Woehl, 1880.

Holland, Henry Scott. *Impressions of the Ammergau Passion-Play.* London: Hayes, 1870.

Holmes, Burton. *Travelogues with Illustrations from Photographs by the Author.* New York: McClure, 1910.

Howe, Sarah Willard. *Oberammergau in 1900: The Village, the People, the Passion Play.* New York: Abbey, 1902.

Howitt, Anna Mary. *An Art Student in Munich.* London: De La Rue, 1853 (reissued 1880).

Jablonka, Alfred. *Freiwillige Feuerwehr Oberammergau.* Exhibition Catalog: August 9–10, 1969.

Jaron, Norbert, and Bärbel Rudin, *Das Oberammergauer Passionsspiel: Eine Chronik in Bildern.* Dortmund: Harenberg, 1984.

Jerome, Jerome K. *A Diary of a Pilgrimage.* Leipzig: Tauchnitz, 1891.

Johnson, Eric. *Nazi Terror: The Gestapo, Jews, and Ordinary Germans.* New York: Basic Books, 1999.

Kaltenegger, Roland. *Die Stammdivision der deutschen Gebirgstruppe: Weg und Kampf der 1. Gebirgs-Division, 1935–1945.* Graz: Stocker, 1981.

———. *German Mountain Troops in World War II: A Photographic Chronicle of the Elite Gebirgsjäger.* Atglen, Penn.: Schiffer Military History, 2005.

Kaplan, Marion. *Between Dignity and Despair: Jewish Life in Nazi Germany.* New York: Oxford University Press, 1998.

Kershaw, Ian. *The "Hitler Myth": Image and Reality in the Third Reich.* New York: Oxford University Press, 1987.

———. *Hitler, 1889–1936: Hubris.* New York: Norton, 1999.

———. *Popular Opinion and Political Dissent in the Third Reich, Bavaria, 1933–1945.* New York: Oxford University Press, 1983.

Kiefer, Joseph P. *Oberammergau and Its Passion Play.* London: Catholic Truth Society, 1934.

Klein, Ralph, Regina Mentner, and Stephan Stracke, eds. *Mörder unterm Edelweiss: Dokumentation des Hearings zu den Kriegsverbrechen der Gebirgsjäger.* Cologne: Papyrossa, 2004.

Kleiner, Karl. *Bruder Konrad und Altötting.* Würzburg: Echter, 1984.

Kleinschmidt, P. Beda. *Antonius von Padua in Leben und Kunst, Kult, und Volkstum.* Düsseldorf: Schwann, 1931.

Klemperer, Victor. *I Will Bear Witness: A Diary of the Nazi Years 1933–1941.* Trans. Martin Chalmers. New York: Random House, 1998.

———. *I Will Bear Witness: A Diary of the Nazi Years 1942–1945.* Trans. Martin Chalmers. New York: Random House, 1999.

Klinner, Helmut, ed. *Joseph Alois Daisenberger: Das Urbild eines gütigen Priesters.* Katalog zur Ausstellung im Pilatushaus Oberammergau, July 1–11, 1999.

———. *Oberammergau in Aufnahmen seines ersten Fotografen: Korbinian Christa (1854–1916).* Horb am. N.: Geiger, 1997.

Koch, Peter Jakob. *Bayerns Weg in die Bundesrepublik,* 2nd ed. Munich: Oldenbourg, 1988.

Koch von Berneck, M. *Oberammergau: Ein Führer zu den Passionsspielen 1890.* Munich: Weihrauch, 1890.

Koonz, Claudia. *The Nazi Conscience.* Cambridge: Harvard University Press, 2003.

Kossert, Andreas. *Kalte Heimat: Die Geschichte der deutschen Vertriebenen nach 1945.* Munich: Siedler, 2008.

Kratz, Matthias, and Bernd Kummer, eds. *Ein Rucksack voll Geschichten: Lebensgeschichten aus dem Landkreis Garmisch-Partenkirchen.* Garmisch-Partenkirchen, 1997.

Krause-Lang, Martha. *Erinnerungen an Christus Anton Lang aus Oberammergau.* Eggenfelden: Aventinus, 1980.

Kriß, Rudolf. *Die Volkskunde der Altbayrischen Gnadenstätten.* 3 vols. Munich: Fisher, 1953–1956.

Lampert, Friedrich. *Das Passionsspiel in Oberammergau: Zür Führung und Orientirung.* Würzburg: Studer, 1870.

Lang, Anton. *Offizieller Führer zum Oberammergauer Passionsspiel im Jahre 1890.* Munich: Literar. Instituts Dr. M. Huttler, Konrad Fischer, 1890.

————. *Reminiscences*, 3rd ed. Munich: Knorr and Hirth, 1938.

Lang, Ernst. *Das wars, wars das: Erinnerungen*. Munich: Piper, 2000.

Lang, Friedl. *180 Jahre Musikleben in Oberammergau, 80 Jahre Musikverein Oberammergau: Eine Chronik*. Oberammergau: Musikverein Oberammergau, 1986.

Lang, Gottfried. "Hitler's Visit in 1934 to the Oberammergau Passion Play: An Eye-witness Account," *Association of Contemporary Church Historians*. Newsletter 24(12) (December 1996).

Lang, Guido. *Lang's Illustrated Practical Guide to the Passion Play at Oberammergau*. Trans. Hugo Lang and Rose Bogart. Oberammergau: Lang sel. Erben, 1900.

————. *Praktischer, Illustrierter Führer zum Besuche der Passions-Spiele in Oberammergau*. Munich: Seyfried, 1900.

Lang, Richard. Article in *New Orleans* (September 1964).

Lang's Führer: Die Kreuzschule Oberammergau 1905. Munich: Seyfried, 1905.

Lang's Führer: Oberammergau und sein Passionsspiel. Oberammergau: Lang sel. Erben, 1910.

Lanz, Hubert. *Gebirgsjäger: Die 1. Gebirgsdivision, 1935–1945*. Bad Nauheim: Hans-Henning Podzun, 1954.

Lanzinner, Maximilian. *Zwischen Sternenbanner und Bundesadler: Bayern im Wiederaufbau, 1945–1958*. Regensburg: Pustet, 1996.

MacColl, Malcolm. *The Ober-Ammergau Passion Play*. London: Rivingtons, 1880.

Madden, Paul, and Detlef Mühlberger. *The Nazi Party: The Anatomy of a People's Party, 1919–1933*. New York: Lang, 2007.

Mann, Thomas. *Joseph and His Brothers*. Trans. H. T. Lowe-Porter. New York: Knopf, 1948.

Mazower, Mark. *Hitler's Empire: Nazi Rule in Occupied Europe*. London: Lane, 2008.

————. *Inside Hitler's Greece: The Experience of Occupation, 1941–44*. New Haven: Yale University Press, 1993.

————. "Military Violence and National Socialist Values: The Wehrmacht in Greece 1941–1944." *Past and Present* 134 (February 1992): 129–58.

Meyer, Hermann Frank. *Blutiges Edelweiß, Die 1. Gebirgsdivision im Zweiten Weltkrieg*. Berlin: Links, 2007.

Minott, Rodney G. *The Fortress That Never Was: The Myth of Hitler's Bavarian Stronghold*. New York: Holt, Rinehart, and Winston, 1964.

Möller, Horst, Andreas Wirsching, and Walter Ziegler, eds. *Nationalsozialismus in der Region*. Munich: Oldenbourg, 1996.

Molloy, Gerald. *The Passion Play at Ober-Ammergau, in the summer of 1871*. London: Burns, Oates, 1872.

Moses, Montrose. *The Passion Play of Oberammergau*. New York: Duffield, 1930.

Mühlberger, Detlef. *Hitler's Followers: Studies in the Sociology of the Nazi Movement*. New York: Routledge, 1991.

————. *The Social Bases of Nazism, 1919–1933*. New York: Cambridge University Press, 2003.

Mühlstrasser, Bernd. *Murnau-Oberammergau und die E69: Bayerische Eisenbahn-Geschichte*. Munich: GeraMond, 1998.

München: "Hauptstadt der Bewegung." Katalog zur Ausstellung im Münchner Stadtmuseum, October 22, 1993–March 27, 1994.

Münster, Robert. *Rochus Dedler (1779–1822): Ein Lebensbild des Komponisten der Oberammergauer Passionsmusik.* Munich: Musica Bavarica, 1970.

National Archive. *Europa unterm Hakenkreuz, die Okkupationspolitik des deutschen Faschismus in Jugoslawien, Griechenland, Albanien, Italien, und Ungarn (1941–1945),* vol. 6. Berlin: Hüthig Verlagsgemeinschaft, 1992.

Némirovsky, Irène. *Suite française.* Trans. Sandra Smith. New York: Vintage, 2006.

Niethammer, Lutz. *Entnazifizierung in Bayern: Säuberung und Rehabilitierung unter amerikanischer Besatzung.* Frankfurt am Main: Fischer, 1972.

———. *Die Mitläuferfabrik: Die Entnazifierung am Beispiel Bayerns.* Berlin: Dietz, 1982.

Oberammergau and the Passion Play 1950. Oberammergau: Ammerverlag, 1950.

Oberammergau damals and heute: Ein Dorfrundgang mit der Kamera, 2nd ed. Oberammergau: Freundeskreis Pilatushaus e. V., 1989.

Orlow, Dietrich. *A History of Modern Germany: 1871 to the Present,* 2nd ed. Englewood Cliffs, N.J.: Prentice Hall, 1991.

Orsi, Robert. *Thank You, St. Jude: Women's Devotion to the Patron Saint of Hopeless Causes.* New Haven: Yale University Press, 1996.

Ostler, Josef. *Revolutionszeit 1918/19 im Bezirk Garmisch.* Garmisch-Partenkirchen: Verein für Kunst- und Kulturgeschichte im Landkreis Garmisch-Partenkirchen, 1996.

Owings, Alison. *Frauen: German Women Recall the Third Reich.* New Brunswick: Rutgers University Press, 1995.

Oxenham, Henry Nutcombe. *Recollections of the Passion Play at Ober-Ammergau.* London: Rivingtons, 1880.

Parks-Richards, Louise. *Oberammergau: Its Passion Play and Players: A 20th-century Pilgrimage to a Modern Jerusalem and a New Gethsemane.* Munich: Piloty and Loehle, 1910.

Passion-Play at Oberammergau, The. Diessen: Huber, 1930, 1934.

Patruban, Hermine. *Erinnerung an Oberammergau vom Jahre 1870.* Vienna: Kirsch, 1871.

Peukert, Detlev. *Inside Nazi Germany: Conformity, Opposition, and Racism in Everyday Life.* Trans. Richard Deveson. New Haven: Yale University Press, 1982.

Pfister, Peter, ed. *Das Ende des Zweiten Weltkriegs im Erzbistum München und Freising,* part 2. Munich: Schnell and Steiner, 2005.

Phayer, Michael. *Protestant and Catholic Women in Nazi Germany.* Detroit: Wayne State University Press, 1990.

Piszkiewicz, Dennis. *The Nazi Rocketeers: Dreams of Space and Crimes of War.* Westport. Ct.: Praeger, 1995.

Pössinger, Michl. *Lebensbilder eines Gebirgsjägers,* 2nd ed. Grainau: Bader, 1998.

Pridham, Geoffrey. *Hitler's Rise to Power: The Nazi Movement in Bavaria, 1923–1933.* New York: Harper and Row, 1973.

———. The National Socialist Party in Southern Bavaria, 1925–1933: A Study of Its Development in a Predominantly Roman Catholic Area. PhD diss.: University of London, 1969.

Queri, Georg. *Anton Lang: Christ*. Trans. A. Albert Noelte. Munich: Sutter, 1910.

Rädlinger, Christine. *Zwischen Tradition und Fortschritt: Oberammergau, 1869–2000*. Oberammergau: Gemeinde Oberammergau, 2002.

Rauh-Kühne, Cornelia. *Katholisches Milieu und Kleingesellschaft: Ettlingen, 1918–1939*. Sigmaringen: Thorbecke, 1991.

Regnet, Carl Albert. *Nach Oberammergau: Wohlunterrichteter Begleiter zum Passionsspiel im Jahre 1880 auf der Hin- und Heimnreise sowie im Gebirge*. Munich: Ackermann, 1880.

Rigg, Bryan Mark. *Hitler's Jewish Soldiers: The Untold Story of Nazi Racial Laws and Men of Jewish Descent in the German Military*. Lawrence: University Press of Kansas, 2002.

Rinderle, Walter, and Bernard Norling. *The Nazi Impact on a German Village*. Lexington: Kentucky University Press, 1993.

Salberg, Adalbert. *Geschichte des Wallfahrtsortes Ettal im bayerischen Hochgebirge*, 3rd ed. Ettal: Selbstverlag des Klosters, 1927.

Scheffer, R. *Ein Besuch in Oberammergau*. Essen: Bädeker, 1880.

Schelle, Heinz. *Chronik eines Bauernlebens vor Zweihundert Jahren*. Rosenheim: Rosenheimer, 1988.

Schellenberger, Barbara. *Katholische Jugend und Drittes Reich: Eine Geschichte des Katholischen Jungmännerverbandes 1933–1939 under besonderer Berücksichtigung der Rheinprovinz*. Mainz: Grünewald, 1975.

Schlosspark Linderhof, Bayerische Verwaltung der staatl. Schlösser, Garten, und Seen, information posted at the recreated Hundingshütte on the castle grounds.

Schoeberl, Franz. *The Passion-Play at Ober-Ammergau*. Trans. Catherine Thompson. Munich: Kruell, 1880.

Schreiber, Georg. *Wallfahrt und Volkstum in Geschichte und Leben*. Düsseldorf: Schwann, 1934.

Schröder, Joseph. *Oberammergau und sein Passionsspiel*, 2nd ed. Munich: Lama, 1910.

Schumacher, Tony. *Meine Oberammergauer von einst und jetzt*. Stuttgart: Levy and Müller, 1910.

Schwaiger, Georg, ed. *Das Erzbistum München und Freising in der Zeit der national-sozialistischen Herrschaft*, vol. 2. Munich: Schnell and Steiner, 1984.

Schwarzmann, Elias. *Reise des Pfarrers Elias Schwarzmann, eines geborenen Hirschauers, zum Passionsspiel in Oberammergau im Juli 1860*. Landshut: Wölfle, 1862.

Sellar, Alexander Craig. *The Passion-Play in the Highlands of Bavaria*. Edinburgh: Blackwood, 1871.

Sereny, Gitta. *Albert Speer: His Battle with Truth*. New York: Vintage, 1996.

Shapiro, James. *Oberammergau: The Troubling Story of the World's Most Famous Passion Play*. New York: Pantheon, 2000.

Shepherd, Ben. *War in the Wild East: The German Army and Soviet Partisans*. Cambridge: Harvard University Press, 2004.

Speer, Albert. *Inside the Third Reich: Memoirs*. Trans. Richard Winston and Clara Winston. London: Cardinal, 1975.

Spindler, Max, ed. *Handbuch der bayerischen Geschichte: Das neue Bayern, 1800–1970*, vol. 4. Munich: Beck, 1974.

Stasiewski, Bernhard, ed. *Akten deutscher Bischöfe über die Lage der Kirche 1933–1945.* Vol. 1, 1933–1934. Mainz: Kommission für Zeitgeschichte, 1968.

Stead's Guide: The Passion Play at Oberammergau 1930. London: Benn, 1930.

Steinbrecher, Oscar. *Führer zum Oberammergauer Passionsspiel.* Munich: Kellerer, 1880.

Stephenson, Jill. *Hitler's Home Front: Württemberg under the Nazis.* New York: Hammbledon Continuum, 2006.

Stingley, J. "Woodcarver Draws Crowds." *Southern Cross* (May 2, 1969).

Swift, Janet. *The Passion Play of Oberammergau: Its History and Significance.* New York: Revell, 1930.

Swinglehurst, Edward. *The Romantic Journey: The Story of Thomas Cook and Victorian Travel.* London: Pica, 1974.

Tent, James. *Mission on the Rhine: Reeducation and Denazification in American-occupied Germany.* Chicago: University of Chicago Press, 1982.

Theopold, Wilhelm. *Votivmalerei und Medizin: Kulturgeschichte und Heilkunst im Spiegel der Votivmalerei.* Munich: Thiemig, 1978.

Thränhardt, Dietrich. *Wahlen und politische Strukturen in Bayern, 1848–1953.* Düsseldorf: Droste, 1973.

Tieke, Wilhelm. *The Caucasus and the Oil: The German-Soviet War in the Caucasus, 1943/4.* Trans. Joseph G. Welsh. Winnipeg: Fedorowicz, 1995.

Treml, Manfred. *Geschichte des modernen Bayern: Königreich und Freistaat.* Munich: Bayerische Landeszentrale für Politische Bildungsarbeit, 1994.

Tweedie, Ethel. *The Oberammergau Passion Play.* London: Kegan Paul, Trench, Trübner, 1890.

Utzschneider, Ludwig. *Oberammergau im Dritten Reich, 1933–1945.* Oberammergau: Der Historische Verein Oberammergau, 1999.

von Braun, Wernher, and Frederick I. Ordway. *History of Rocketry and Space Travel.* New York: Crowell, 1966.

von Deutinger, Martin. *Beyträge zur Geschichte, Topographie, und Statistik des Erzbisthums München und Freysing.* 3 vols. Munich: Lindauer, 1851.

von Hahn, Alban. *Nach Ober-Ammergau, Wanderung zum Passionsspiel.* Leipzig: Spamer, 1890.

von Oettingen, Alexander. *Der Passion: Erinnerungen eines Pilgers nach Oberammergau.* Leipzig: Duncker and Humblot, 1880.

von Schaching, Otto. *Oberammergau im Jahre 1900: Führer zum Passionsspiel.* Oberammergau: Korbinian Rutz und Sohn, 1900.

Waddy, Helena. "St. Anthony's Bread: The Modernized Religious Culture of German Catholics in the Early Twentieth Century." *Journal of Social History* 31(2) (Winter 1997): 347–70.

Wiesel, Elie. *Night.* Trans. Stella Rodway. New York: Bantam, 1960.

Winkler, Leonhard. *Von München nach Oberammergau und zurück.* Augsburg: Schmid, 1880.

Wood, Robert J. *Survey of Messerschmitt Factory and Functions, Oberammergau, Germany.* Air Technical Intelligence Review, Report no. F-IR-6-RE (August 1, 1946).

Wyl, Wilhelm. *Maitage in Oberammergau: Eine artistische Pilgerfahrt*. Zürich: Schmidt, 1880.

Zainer, Werner. "Kult und Kampf—Räter und Römer in Oberammergau." *Mohr—Löwe—Raute: Beiträge zur Geschichte des Landkreises Garmisch-Partenkirchen* 3 (1995): 5–25.

Zull, Gertraud. *Ein Museum entsteht: Das Verleger Lang'sche Kunst- und Kulturgeschichtliche Oberammergauer Museum und die Entdeckung der Volkskunst um 1900*. Munich: Kommission für Bayerische Landesgeschichte, 1998.

———. *Georg Lang sel. Erben: 230 Jahre Produktion und Vertrieb von Oberammergauer Holzschnitzwaren: Eine Familien-, Häuser-, und Firmengeschichte*. Munich: Kommission für bayerische Landesgeschichte, 2005.

Illustration Credits

Figure 1.1. GAO: 3.107/1. Passionsspiele Oberammergau 1910: #105: Einzug in Jerusalem. Photograph by H. Traut, Munich, and F. Bruckmann, Munich.

Figure 1.2. GAO: 9.1.1, #91. Das Passionsspiel in Oberammergau. After a sketch by G. Sunblad in *Leipziger Illustrierte Zeitung* 1467 (August 12, 1871), 121.

Figure 1.3. GAO: 11.1. Aus Oberammergau. Cartoon by Th. Th. Heine in *Simplicissimus* 15 (1910).

Figure 1.4. GAO: 9.4/3: Oberammergau vom Bahnhof aus gesehen. Artistic postcard #2502 by Ottmar Zieher, Munich, 1900. After a painting by Michael Zeno Diemer.

Figure 2.1. Private collection, Florian Lang. "Oberammergau 1929: Fronleichnamsprozess." Postcard by W. Pfingstl, Oberammergau.

Figure 2.2. Private collection, Florian Lang. Die große Bildhauerwerkstatt im ersten Stock des Verlegerhauses. Photograph by H. Traut, Munich, 1905/1910.

Figure 3.1. GAO: 3.107/1. Passionsspiele Oberammergau 1910: #52: Herodes (Hans Mayr). Photograph by H. Traut, Munich, and F. Bruckmann, Munich.

Figure 3.2. GAO: 3/212/1. Mayor Raimund Lang. Photograph by W. Pfingstl, Oberammergau.

Figure 4.1. GAO: 9.4/5. Oberammergau. Bahnhofstraße mit Laber. Postcard by Heinrich Uhlschmid, Oberammergau (ca. 1930), #39.

Figure 4.2. GAO: Bibliothek. Der Verwaltungsinspektor Josef Raab. Photograph by Hermann Rex, Oberammergau. Reproduced in Franz X. Bogenrieder, *Oberammergau: Bilder aus seinem Leben und Wirken* (Diessen: Huber, 1930), 71.

Figure 4.3. GAO: 10.2 (Nachlass A. O. Zwink). Der Fahneneid. Album 3. Reich, 7/4. Photo: No attribution.

Figure 5.1. (a) GAO: 11.11. Blutende Hand am Kreuz, von einem Nagel durchbohrt. Design by Hermann Keimel, Munich. Advertising sticker printed by Herm. Sonntag and Co., Munich, 1934. (b) GAO: 11.11. Germany Invites You! Design by Jupp Wiertz, Berlin. Advertising sticker by the Reichsbahnzentrale für Deutsche Verkehrswerbung, 1934.

Figure 5.2. GAO: 10.2 (Nachlass A. O. Zwink). Appell. Album 3. Reich, 4/2. Photograph: No attribution.

Figure 5.3. GAO: 3.231. Adolf Hitler im Auto vor Hotel Wittelsbach am 13. 8. 1934. Photograph with no attribution. (Possibly by Heinrich Hoffmann, Hitler's official photographer.)

Figure 5.4. GAO: 3.231. Adolf Hitler bei den Oberammergauer Passionsspielen hinter der Bühne. Photograph by Hans Kronburger. Reproduced in *Das 12 Uhr Blatt* (August 16, 1934.)

Figure 6.1. GAO: 11.7.1. Oberammergau 850 m. Mit seinem Alpenbad. Title page of the 1937 summer prospectus by Eugen Max Cordier, Munich.

Figure 6.2. GAO: 3.241. Musikzug der Oberammergauer HJ. Photograph by Hans Holdt, Munich.

Figure 7.1. GAO: 3.251. Heldengedenktag, 21. März 1943 in Oberammergau. Photograph by Hans Kronburger, Oberammergau.

Figure 8.1. (a) GAO: Bibliothek. Haus des Christus Darstellers Alois Lang. Sketch by Otto Ackermann-Pasegg in *Amerika in Oberammergau*. (b) GAO: Bibliothek. Translation an der Rottenbucherstr. Sketch by Otto Ackermann-Pasegg in *Amerika in Oberammergau*.

Figure 8.2. GAO: 11.3.1. Schluss mit der CSU Gesellschaft! Wählt KPD. KPD poster for the April 25, 1948, elections.

Index